D1299136

The Ends of Science

About the Book and Author

In this path-breaking and controversial book, Harry Redner provides a systematic study of how the epistemologically interesting features of contemporary science are to be understood. Taking "science" to include knowledge from the social sciences and humanities as well as the physical sciences, Redner shows how the history of science, philosophical theory, and current scientific research reveal connections between scientific developments and features of the social organization of science.

Redner argues that the shift from Classical science to a more complex and less orderly World science after World War II has changed the way scientific research is done and how its knowledge is organized. His aim, however, "is not merely to interpret science, but to change it." Thus, this examination is more than a survey and critique—it is a positive program for the development of future science.

Remarkable for its breadth and insight, the book is especially valuable for its discussions of authority and social organization (with the accompanying themes of academic politics, competition, power, and corruption) and for its catalog of the various contemporary critiques of science. Some of these are European in origin and will be new to many U.S. readers.

A tour de force on several levels, this book is essential reading for scientists, philosophers, sociologists of science, historians of ideas, critics of contemporary culture and, indeed, for anyone who takes a serious interest in scientific research and higher learning.

Harry Redner is senior lecturer in the Faculty of Economics and Politics at Monash University, Melbourne, Australia. In 1987 he is a senior Fulbright Fellow at both the Institute for Social and Policy Studies, Yale University, and the University of California, Berkeley. He is the author of *In the Beginning Was the Deed: Reflections on the Passage of Faust* (1982), *The Ends of Philosophy: An Essay in the Sociology of Philosophy and Rationality* (1986), and (with Jill Redner) *Anatomy of the World* (1983).

The Ends of Science

An Essay in
Scientific Authority

Harry Redner

WESTVIEW PRESS
BOULDER AND LONDON

Q158.5
R43
1987

All rights reserved. No part of this publication may be reproduced or transmitted in any form or by any means, electronic or mechanical, including photocopy, recording, or any information storage and retrieval system, without permission in writing from the publisher.

Copyright © 1987 by Westview Press, Inc.

Published in 1987 in the United States of America by Westview Press, Inc.; Frederick A. Praeger, Publisher; 5500 Central Avenue, Boulder, Colorado 80301

Library of Congress Cataloging-in-Publication Data
Redner, Harry.
  The ends of science.
  Bibliography: p.
  Includes index.
  1. Science. 2. Science—Philosophy. 3. Science—
Social aspects. 4. Knowledge, Sociology of.
I. Title.
Q158.5.R43 1987   501   87-8248
ISBN 0-8133-0452-0

Composition for this book originated with conversion of the author's word-processor disks.

Printed and bound in the United States of America

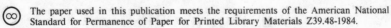 The paper used in this publication meets the requirements of the American National Standard for Permanence of Paper for Printed Library Materials Z39.48-1984.

10   9   8   7   6   5   4   3   2

To
Ed Lindblom

MAY 15 1992

Contents

PART 3
A SCIENTIFIC REFORMATION

Preface

A book can be misread from the start if its title is misunderstood. This work is entitled *The Ends of Science*, not *The End of Science*. There is no suggestion that science has or is about to come to an end in the obvious sense; in fact, the opposite seems to be the case. Science is expanding at such a rate that it threatens to take over everything else. However, science has changed its ends. It is no longer the old science of the last few centuries. That old science is coming to an end in the sense of approaching the limit of its potential scope. It has been apparent for some time that it had to give way sooner or later to a new science because of its own internal dynamic. The change has come sooner rather than later because of the unparalleled external circumstances through which European science has passed during the course of this turbulent century. The internal and external factors came together to speed up the pace of transition. Now it is almost complete, despite the numerous functioning survivals of the old science still dedicated to the old ends. The title *The Ends of Science* is designed to focus attention on these multiple senses of 'ends'.

The subtitle, too, should be understood correctly: this work is not only a study *of* scientific authority; it is also a study *in* scientific authority. It aims to be authoritative about authority, through a continual appeal to authority. For this reason the authoritative pronouncements of scientists of notable achievement or high standing are continually quoted. The art of quotation assumes a particularly crucial role in studies of authority in contemporary science. Today no-one can have a close knowledge of all the sciences—I certainly make no such claims. But only those who are intimately acquainted with a science—frequently only those who have contributed to it at a high level—have the necessary understanding and standing to pronounce upon it. They are the authorities in their field. Hence they have to be listened to with particular attention when they speak ex cathedra. Fortunately, however, since authorities frequently contradict each other, scientific laypersons to some extent can pick and choose which dictates they will follow and select those which best fit their approaches. And they invariably will have to select some, for without such authoritative backing no approach will itself have any authoritative standing.

This necessary appeal to authority must not, however, be misconstrued to imply that there is no more to any approach to the sciences than the pronouncements of scientists which can be mustered on its behalf. An approach is a theory about science in general that does not belong to the sciences which it is covering but to a science of science—a history, sociology, politics of science—or to some other discourse on science, such as a philosophy of science. Only the 'data' necessary to sustain any such theory will in fact be contributed by the first-hand intuitions and asseverations of scientists. Any theory of science that goes counter to the sense that major scientists have of the nature of their work—no matter how logically persuasive otherwise—must be found faulty. For this reason the best approaches to the sciences have tended to come from thinkers who have been at one time working scientists and who consequently can act as theorists and practitioners at the same time.

Science is in this respect different from art. The critic can, and often does, have a better understanding of a work of art than the artist. But no-one has a better understanding of a scientific discovery at the time it is made than its discoverer, especially if it is a highly original finding. Later, when the discovery has become generally accepted and incorporated into the body of science—frequently in ways which its originator might not have anticipated—then it becomes possible for others to understand it differently and possibly better. But, of course, through this process the original idea would have changed, so it would no longer be the same discovery. Thus students of the recent findings of science, that is, of those disciplines at the frontiers of knowledge, are particularly bound to listen to the opinions of the scientists working at those isolated reaches where no-one except a fellow practitioner in the field can follow. Others literally cannot follow what these scientists are doing unless the latter interpret it in a more generally intelligible manner, most frequently by way of scientific popularizations. But at this point, because of the need to 'translate' the original ideas, these scientists themselves become prone to misconceptions. They are authoritative but not infallible. They are frequently unable to evaluate the status or importance of their findings and tend to exaggerate their achievements—hence the many published claims to break-throughs and even scientific revolutions. This is where the critics of science come into their own.

Thus the relation of scientists and critics of science—philosophers, sociologists, historians of science—in the understanding of science is ultimately mutually dependent and reveals itself in the use of quotations echoing the views of the one side by the other. Without that echo and response, like the 'cooee' exchanged by two exploring parties in the Australian wilderness, both would be lost: the former not seeing the wood for the trees, the latter seeing only wood and no trees. The scientists are, as it were, the advance party reaching into terra incognita; the critics are the backup party bringing logistic support from the rear bases of already established territory.

As a study of contemporary science, this work relies heavily on authorities to bring back reports of how the advance is proceeding. But in one respect it is taking the lead, namely, in establishing a science of authority, a political science of science. The politics of science is an unexplored and particularly dangerous field, full of pitfalls and swamps where the unwary investigator can so easily be sucked under, and it is already inhabited by ferocious natives, some suspected of cannibalistic tastes, eager to slay any interlopers. Many of these prefer to keep the political jungle of science dark and resent the intrusion of theoretical light. Others denigrate what such illumination might reveal by boasting that it is only what they have been seeing all along. Still others will say nothing but will feel their bad conscience eased, believing themselves justified in continuing to do what they have been doing all along. This work would defeat its intended purpose if it helped the cynics thrive. It does not presume to offer Machiavellian practical advice to the princes of academia. Not that they need any and not that the author would be capable of doing so even if he wanted to, for he is himself but a poor player in the power play of the academic stage. The same might be said of this work as was supposedly said by Marx's mother on receiving a copy of *Das Kapital*: 'Ach, mein armer Karl, he only writes Kapital; he never makes any'. Symbolic capital can no more be gained by theoretical effort than the real stuff.

Nevertheless, it is gratifying to report that despite my poverty, I have not been altogether bereft of friends and supporters without whom this work would not have seen the light of printed day even if I had managed to compose it by my own unaided efforts. Such support was motivated by sheer generosity, without expectation or hope of recompense. I am all the more grateful because it was so freely given.

First, thanks are owing to those associated with Westview Press for welcoming such a project: to Kellie Masterson who asked for the book before it was even complete, to Spencer Carr who supported it once it was. Steve Fuller read and commented on it with intimate understanding and generosity of spirit. Next, I thank those whose support was in one way or another influential in shaping the book during the process of its composition. I am grateful to Kenneth Boulding who showed real friendship in taking the trouble to subject my early efforts to stringent criticism. I thank Erwin Chargaff for helpful conversations and invariably cordial reception on my visits to New York. I am thankful to Pierre Bourdieu, Gunther Stent, and Atuhiro Sibatani for making their published and un-published papers available to me, some of which I have been ungrateful enough to criticise—but they will understand this as an act of appreciation. To the late F. R. Leavis I owe a debt of remembrance that extends back nearly fifteen years, the last time I saw him, when he both terrified and inspired me with his uncompromising honesty and naked sensitivity, which at the time mattered to me more than his views or values, many of which I did not share. This book is dedicated to Ed Lindblom as an expression of my deepest gratitude for the moral support and encouragement he extended to me over the years during the long process of composition, for comments on the work in progress and for his friendship in general.

Since I have striven to write a book for general readers interested in science, not just for scientific specialists or specialists on science, I have tried to make it as readable as the subject permits, avoiding technical jargon. In this quest I have been immensely aided by the literary and stylistic talents of Jill Redner, a non-scientist, who is also my touchstone of what should be comprehensible to the kind of reader I want to address.

I take this opportunity to express my deep appreciation for the work she has done on this as on all my other books. I also thank Pat Peterson of Westview Press for ably furthering this unending chore of making books more readable and free of solecisms. Anything in this book that might still be incomprehensible or ill-expressed is due solely to my own stubbornness and confusion. Pauline Bakker, Carol Clark and Nina McLean have patiently attended to the typing of the manuscript from the original version through numerous corrections to its present state. Finally, I take this opportunity to acknowledge that this book was published with the assistance of the Monash University Publication Committee.

Harry Redner

The Ends of Science

Part One

From Classical Science
to World Science

1
The Great Transformation

Intuitions of Change

As Heisenberg reflected over the climax of physical science in his lifetime, he agreed with his colleague, Weizsäcker, that the great age of natural science was nearing its end. In finishing his own Unified Field theory, he felt that an era was over. When he was a young musician Heisenberg had felt that the great era of European music had reached its consummation and that the mind of Europe could be better raised to new heights in physics. His intuition had always been good, and now he intuitively felt our culture was reaching its limit. . . . There was no sadness in Heisenberg's sense of the passing of the great age of natural science. . . . He saw the limit and accepted it with humility. . . . Heisenberg felt that human culture could now reorient itself by making the limit part of its new bearing (Thompson 1973, 89).

Heisenberg's sense of the passing of an era in science is an intuitive awareness of a deep transformation in the nature of the sciences, the full scope and dimension of which is as yet hidden from us. It is perhaps too rash and precipitate to speak of an end to the progress of science, but questions as to the changed meaning of what now constitutes progress in science must certainly be asked. According to Heisenberg, the progress of European science, and with it the very idea of progress, has reached its limit: 'the ecological limit on the growth of civilization, he maintained, only expressed the outward sign of the limits to the growth of the human spirit in the material dimension it had been exploring since the Renaissance' (ibid.). Heisenberg invites us to explore these limits and insists on this exploration as a prerequisite for further thought, even for science itself: 'human culture could now reorient itself by making the limit part of its new bearing' (ibid. 90). Thus, according to Heisenberg, raising the question of the end of European science is a necessary step in the further development of science. The limit is not to be surpassed or overcome, but accepted and incorporated in the very attempt to continue within the bounds set by it. The limit is not a full stop marking a final finish; rather it is a kind of caesura indicating the break or discontinuity of an historical threshold. It is an end that science must acknowledge before it can seek new ends.

Heisenberg places the limit of European science within the context of the limits of European culture in general. He is aware that 'European music had reached its consummation' even as the golden age of European physics was under way. First music and perhaps the European arts in general, next physics and perhaps the European sciences as well—the mind of Europe was reaching the end of its tether; the human spirit could go no further in the direction it had been exploring since the Renaissance. In linking science to music Heisenberg is unconsciously echoing the earlier verdict of Spengler on the fate of Europe. Spengler, too, had foreseen the completion of music—that Faustian art par excellence—and on that completion had premised the doom of European culture, the decline of the West. Spengler had expressly advised the young minds of Europe to abandon cultural pursuits and give themselves to science and technology. Those who either knowingly or unwittingly acted on this advise, as did Heisenberg, are now facing an even more difficult predicament as science, too, seems to be nearing some kind of culmination.

Heisenberg is not advising young people to give up physics or science as a whole for some other endeavour in which the future achievements of humanity will be made. He is not advocating the substitution of technology for science, despite the unparalleled technical accomplishments now being made in so many fields. He obviously does not believe that this approach will be very productive for science or that it will lead to the completion of the grand architectonics of science in the way envisaged throughout the course of this century. On the contrary, such specialized achievements often have the effect of narrowing the scope of science and of blinding scientists to a vision of the whole. Scientists are no longer architects who can plan a grand design, but piece-meal builders who extend a ramshackle structure: 'scientists now work as stonemasons did once on cathedrals. They put the stones next to one another with great attention to detail and the work of the fellow next to them, but they have no sense of the architectonics of the whole. And sometimes they do not even have a sense of the purpose of a cathedral' (Thompson 1973, 89).

It would be easy but glib to dismiss what Heisenberg is saying as the gloomy ranting of an elderly physicist whose style of work is no longer in fashion, or worse still, as a German who served on the wrong side during the last great war. It is true that Heisenberg was the leader of the losing team of physicists against which the Manhattan Project was so successful. Yet it would be naive to believe that science, like history, must be on the side of the victors. The kind of science that the Manhattan Project inaugurated—first, in physics, then throughout the sciences—is precisely what Heisenberg questions. And he is not alone. Even physicists who were on the winning side are raising similar doubts. Thus Gamow declares:

> After the thirty fat years in the beginning of the present century, we are now dragging through the lean and infertile years, and looking for better luck in the years to come. In spite of all the efforts of the old-timers like

Pauli, Heisenberg and others, and those of the younger generation like Feynman, Schwinger, Gell-Mann and others, theoretical physics has made little progress during the last three decades as compared to the previous decades (Gamow 1972, 161).

One might wonder with Heisenberg whether this is really a matter of sheer luck or of cycles of fat and lean years; perhaps something deeper is at stake, more serious even than a decline in the rate of achievement. From still another side—from what is now the opposing team—comes the voice of Kapitsa, speaking in an accent of nostalgia charged with equal pessimism: 'the year that Rutherford died (1938) there disappeared forever the happy days of free scientific work which gave us such delight in our youth. Science has lost her freedom. Science has become a productive force. She has become rich but she has become enslaved and part of her is veiled in secrecy. I do not know whether Rutherford would continue nowadays to joke and laugh as he used to do' (McEltey 1966, 25).

If physics, the premier science of this century, is now in some uncertainty, it is little wonder that doubts are also being expressed about other sciences. Not even molecular biology, perhaps the outstanding scientific triumph of the post-war period, has escaped similar questioning. One of its original founders, the biochemist Chargaff, has grown disenchanted with the seemingly spectacular progress of the field: 'the phenomenal growth of biology and biochemistry . . . disheartened and frightened me' (Chargaff 1978, 139). He goes on to express his sense of the failing of science in general:

> I gain the impression that, in the last fifteen years the world of science, or at any rate that part that I can overlook, has undergone a deformation whose dimensions I find it difficult to fathom. . . . Whereas before, every practitioner of a science, i.e. everybody doing original scientific research, was never far from the core of his particular discipline, from what one could call its specific character and code of conduct, at present, one is confined to the outskirts, which are ever more distant from the centre (ibid. 138).

Perhaps even more dauntingly than anyone else, Chargaff foresees the likely end of science itself: 'in the last fifteen or twenty years the sciences have grown in a direction that makes their extinction very probable: they have, one could say, painted themselves into a corner' (ibid. 139). Like a latter-day scientific Cato—'I am an inveterate Catonist'—he is a stern critic of the current ways of practising science:

> To be a pioneer in science has lost much of its attraction: significant scientific facts and, even more, fruitful scientific concepts pale into oblivion long before their potential value has been utilized. New facts, new concepts keep crowding in and are in turn, within a year or two, displaced by even newer ones. . . . Now in our miserable scientific mass society, nearly all discoveries are born dead; papers are tokens in a power game, evanescent reflections on the screen of a spectator sport, news items that do not outlive the day on which they appeared (ibid. 78–81).

An avowed opponent of Chargaff, the outstanding molecular biologist Stent has reached analogous conclusions concerning the impasse of science, though he started from premises diametrically opposed to those of Chargaff. Instead of proceeding from a sense of European cultural pessimism, Stent is embued with American optimism. In effect, he argues that because contemporary science has already achieved too much of what there is to be done, rather than too little, any further effort inevitably runs into the law of steeply diminishing returns. The end of progress in science is at hand because science has already advanced so far and so fast at an ever-accelerating rate that it is reaching the limits of possible advance, given that its progress is not limitless: 'though progress has occurred in the past, its accelerating kinetics preclude it from being an everlasting feature of human history. Indeed, the dizzy rate at which progress is now proceeding makes it seem very likely that progress must come to a stop soon, perhaps in our lifetime, perhaps in a generation or two' (Stent 1978, 31). Stent buttresses this general end of progress thesis with numerous other arguments—some utilizing econometric information theory involving mathematical extrapolations of present tendencies towards a limit, which are purely formalistic and historically dubious. But like Heisenberg, he invokes the idea of an end to the Faustian era of culture and the exhaustion of the potentialities of music—basing it not on Spenglerian notions of the role of music as the expression of a European Faustian spirit, but on information theory speculations concerning the diminishing amount of information conveyed by current musical styles. According to Stent, the Faustian spirit is also declining because of a biological drop in the necessary 'will to power' required for cultural and scientific achievements. The 'golden age' of least effort and easy satisfaction is upon us (ibid.). Such a view might have seemed more plausible before the economic recession; now it appears somewhat dated.

In contrast to both the optimism of Stent and the pessimism of Heisenberg and Chargaff is the measured attitude of Prigogine, which is oriented more to future possibilities than to past accomplishments. Prigogine makes it clear that the present impasse of science is not a crisis of knowledge as such but only of what he calls Classical science, the main tradition of modern European science lasting from before Newton till after Einstein. In a work with his collaborator Stengers, he writes that 'it is classical science, considered for a certain period of time as the very symbol of cultural unity, and not science as such that led to the cultural crisis we have described' (Prigogine and Stengers 1984, 54). Thus, whereas for Heisenberg natural science as such has reached its limit and for Stent the progress of knowledge as such has been exhausted, for Prigogine only 'classical science has now reached its limit' (ibid.). This scientific mode has now come to an end: 'classical science, the mythical science of a simple passive world, belongs to the past, killed not by philosophical criticism or empiricist resignation but by the internal development of science itself' (ibid. 55). Prigogine's and Stengers' account shows, however, that not only the internal development of science itself—which Prigogine's work as a scientist is designed to further—but equally as much the external changes in culture, society, and even demography are responsible for this momentous transformation. Stengers' contribution to the joint work serves to emphasise the rootedness of science within general culture and reinforces their claim that

> the changes that science is undergoing today lead to a radically new situation. This recent evolution of science gives us a unique opportunity to reconsider its position in culture in general. Modern science originated in the specific context of the European seventeenth century. We are now approaching the end of the twentieth century, and it seems that some more universal message is carried by science, a message that concerns the interaction of man and nature as well as that of man with man (ibid. 7).

Thus the demise of Classical science is at one with the fate of European civilization, for science has outgrown the cradle of its birth and has entered a stage of world development that is coextensive with humanity as a whole. Science is radically transforming itself because

> the human race is in a period of transition. Science is likely to play an important role at this moment of demographic explosion. It is therefore more important than ever to keep open channels of communication between science and society. The present development of Western science has taken it outside the cultural environment of the seventeenth century, in which it was born. We believe that science today carries a universal message that is more acceptable to different cultural traditions (ibid. p. XXVIII).

This science of today is actually a science of tomorrow—a promised future World science. For strictly speaking science as practised today, present World science, rarely carries any 'universal message', not to speak of one 'acceptable to different cultural traditions'. Prigogine and Stengers indulge somewhat in an utopian vision of a possible future science which hardly yet exists. They have little to say about the grim realities of today's science, though doubtless they are aware of them. These realities are what prompts the more pessimistic assessments.

Although the scientists so far quoted all differ in their sense of what is taking place, they do agree that something problematic has arisen in the sciences during recent developments, and those who have lived through most of this century know that things are not as they were before, even in their own life times. We could quote many more outstanding scientists, for example, Wigner, Feynman, and McFarlane Burnet (Rescher 1978) and some sociologists of science to this effect. They all feel that in recent years—in the period beginning not much before the Second World War— science has begun to change and continues to change in a drastic manner. Although few are able to describe it with any exactitude, most insist that this transformation is somehow bound up with the question of the progress of science and with the belief in progress altogether. Some, such as Heisenberg and Chargaff, look back and refer the changed state of science to the catastrophic decline of European culture and the whole of Western civilization. In one way or another they link the fate of Faustian culture to that of Faustian science. Others, such as Prigogine, look forward and more optimistically relate the transformation of science to a new epoch of world civilization which ought to bring forth a new kind of science.

Perhaps an initial indication of what is happening to the sciences is provided by those down-to-earth practitioners and managers of science who are most engrossed in everyday scientific activity and least given to any historical speculations about the future of science. These people have begun to speak of science in a way that would have been incomprehensible before the Second World War. They speak now of Big Science—a term coined by Alvin Weinberg, a scientific administrator (itself a new role not encountered before in science). They refer to science as 'mission-oriented', a term as well as a practice not found before the large-scale funding of scientific research after the war. Some sociologists of science have taken their cue from such partial insights and have developed conceptions of a science different from that hitherto recognized. Thus Ravetz has propounded a theory of 'industrialized science', and a group of German sociologists of science headed by Boehme and van den Daele have put forward the concept of 'finalized science'—both of these approaches we shall eventually discuss. In pursuing this line of thought I will begin by exploring the changes wrought in science by the Second World War and its aftermath and then relate these back to our earlier questions concerning the present state of science.

Science and War

No single event can be responsible for decisive transformations in the history of science. Nevertheless, with hindsight it is now apparent that the Second World War—sometimes referred to as the physicists' war—had a drastic impact on the course of science, even more so than did the First World War, the so-called chemists' war. All in all, the mobilization of science for the purposes of war from 1914 till now, well into the Cold War, transformed all sciences, even those devoted solely to 'peaceful' or pure research. It reinforced tendencies in science which were a long time in the making but which had been marginal till these war preparations expanded and institutionalized them. Although the beginnings of a large-scale organization of research and the linkage of science to high technology go back well into the nineteenth century, the enormous financial and human resources made available by governments for war were necessary to amplify these trends and make them paramount throughout the sciences. We can take the Second World War as an arbitrary but nevertheless historically convenient cut-off point for the transformation of science, provided it is understood that such dating depends on very rough approximations.

During the war itself, almost everywhere the usual course of research and publication ceased as in all combatant nations scientists were mobilized to work on projects devoted to the war effort, usually of an applied technical nature. This redirection of science for war ends continued after the war with the almost uninterrupted onset of the Cold War. Most sciences changed their fundamental character and mode of research as a result of these war-time activities even when the scientists returned to peaceful pursuits. Thus one commentator notes that in physics 'the massive development of particle physics originated in the period after the Second World War; as a result of this it cannot historically be separated from the military applications of nuclear physics proper' (Rose and Rose 1976, 282). In addition to the reorientation of the existing sciences, many new sciences were founded on the basis of war-time research. The massive technological developments inaugurated during the war have had a far-reaching effect on science; one need only mention such well-known developments as radar, rocketry, jet propulsion, computers and automata, the mass production of penicillin and other pharmaceuticals, as well as such new technical procedures in the social sciences as operations research, econometrics, mass psychological testing, and the information sciences of the communications media. Thus out of radar research came radio astronomy and the new astro-physical sciences; out of rocketry came all the space sciences; out of jet propulsion came the aero industry and its applied sciences; out of automata and computers—both largely war-time developments based on neglected earlier beginnings—have emerged the myriads of cybernetic and computer sciences ranging from robotics to information theory. Indirectly even such post-war discoveries as transistors would not have been made except for war-time work, as Gibbons and Johnson note, 'without these improvements in the doping and purity of crystals the transistor effect could not have been observed. The spur to the development of these techniques came from the massive research and development effort in search of more efficient detectors for the radar equipment needed by the armed forces' (Barnes and Edge 1982, 183). The medical sciences were revolutionized by war-induced researches. Operations research emerged as 'an attempt to apply the methodology of the natural sciences to the improvement of the efficiency of war and, later, to industrial activities' (Rose and Rose 1969, 62). Econometrics—including such theoretical extensions as input-output analysis—developed out of the needs of planning a war economy. Many other social sciences—including such seemingly impractical ones as Transformational Grammar, according to Chomsky's own testimony—developed in the post-war scientific climate dominated by the new sciences (Chomsky 1977, 128). But no war researches had as much impact as those of physics after its atomic triumph; as a result the degree of scientificity of any form of knowledge was thereafter measured by its proximity to this science.

Directly or indirectly the Manhattan Project had a profound effect on most sciences; it tended to push them in the direction of the formalism and arithmeticism characteristic of physics as well as the organizational structures typical of Big Science. As Whitley notes in passing:

> As an ideal, arithmeticism offers considerable scope for the "rational" administration of research and it is not surprising that after the success of organizing one of the most recondite fields of science to make the atomic bomb, similar structures have been established to solve numerous "problems" and "pure" science has become extensively subsidised by the State and industry. Even if in practice organizational procedure and bureaucratic structure do not mean much in many laboratories—especially those working on more "configurational" phenomena—they indicate the spread and influence of administrative rituals and rhetoric (Whitley 1977a, 162).

The effect of the Manhattan Project has been historically decisive not only for science; Stimson, the U.S. Secretary of War at the time, put it in prescient terms: 'the atom bomb is not just a weapon but a mode of transforming man's relation to the universe.' He has been proved right in ways he could not have imagined and to an extent he very likely under-estimated. Humanity's relation to the universe has been transformed not only by the weapons produced but also by the mode of production itself.

Big Science had finally reached maturity. Starting with small beginnings, such as the low-temperature physics laboratory of H. Kammerlingh-Onnes in Leyden early in the century and then going a stage higher and bigger with the cyclotron construction in E. O. Lawrence's Radiation Laboratory in Berkeley in the 1930s, the culmination of this approach to science only came with the gigantic scaling up required by the Manhattan Project, involving, for example, the plutonium reactors at Hanford and the isotope separation plant at Oak Ridge. The triumph of the project itself and the new prestige attained by nuclear physics made this kind of approach and its accompanying mentality irresistible in all the sciences. 'After the Man-hattan Project, big, very expensive government-funded laboratories became the order of the day' (Tame and Robotham 1982, 43), and such large-scale scientific undertakings became national goals of all the major powers. Science policy became an adjunct of national policy as everywhere the State intervened in the production process of science.

Since the war, thanks largely to the power of the model of scientific organization provided by the Manhattan Project, no science has been able to escape completely the trammels of control exercised by the State through its funding policies. Some of these State-initiated programs have assumed a scope as large as that of the nuclear project (for example, the space program and the cancer campaign). Most of these are militarily funded programs, designed to provide militarily usable knowledge. However, at present, given the variety of ways of waging war and the diversification of possible weapons, most knowledge is militarily usable, as Leitenberg (1971) shows. Apart from the bulk of knowledge procured by the military, the rest of State-funded research is usually intended to serve a national purpose to ensure the health, education and economic welfare of the population.

The transition in science—which I have here presented only in the greatest sociological generality—can be illustrated in detail through the experiences and lives of a whole generation of scientists, especially those physicists who were caught up in the Manhattan Project. Hardly one outstanding physicist resident in the United States was not involved, with the possible exception of Einstein, after he had himself helped to initiate the project. Their work and thought before and after the war reveal clearly the transformation of the nature of science. The autobiography of the physicist Freeman Dyson (1979)—who was not at Los Alamos, but whose scientific development was moulded by those who were—shows how the younger generation of scientists were drawn into the new way of doing science. Dyson, like so many other physicists, came from a highly cultured musical family; his father was the composer of that name. He began his studies as a pure mathematician at Oxford just prior to the outbreak of the war. He spent the war years in British Bomber Command doing operations research. After the war, as a student of physics, he was drawn to Bethe at Cornell where he met Feynman, then fresh from Los Alamos. He made some outstanding mathematical contributions in relating the work of Feynman and Schwinger on quantum electrodynamics. This work brought him to the attention and patronage of Oppenheimer, who appointed him to a professorship at Princeton on the implied understanding that in this ivory tower of research he would devote himself to pure physics. But this did not prove to be the case; in a scene reminiscent of Mann's *Doktor Faustus,* Dyson was 'seduced' by Teller, Oppenheimer's enemy, into undertaking technological nuclear research first for apparently peaceful purposes but essentially on weapons production (Dyson 1979, 92). From that position Dyson graduated to becoming an influential scientific politician in Washington with the Arms Control and Disarmament Agency. His brilliant career was not unlike that of many other equally brilliant physicists, with the exception of very few, such as Feynman, who refused to have anything further to do with the military after Los Alamos.

Dyson's life story, as well as that of most of the leading European participants in the Manhattan Project, exemplified a change in science that had less to do with the purposes of war in general than with the effect of the Second World War in transferring the main centre and cultural milieu of science from Europe to America (Fleming and Bailyn 1969). As a result of the war and the enforced migration of so many, science ceased to a significant degree to be an almost exclusively European enterprize and became American. The European cultural setting in which science had been nurtured since its inception was largely destroyed in the thirty year war period from 1914 till 1945. And along with the culture many national scientific traditions were devastated or seriously weakened, above all the German scientific establishment, which until the early 1930s had been the strongest and most productive in Europe. Europe's loss became a partial gain for America as the refugee scientists from Germany and other parts of war-torn Europe transformed what had been till then a provincial scientific backwater into the scientific centre of the world.

However, in crossing the Atlantic science underwent a sea change, becoming something quite different from what it had been. For in re-establishing science in America the expatriate scientists had to adapt to working in a different cultural environment and had to come to terms with native American ways of proceeding with much more technologically, technically and organizationally oriented research than anything in Europe. This change made a great difference to the nature and quality of the science produced and has not yet received sufficient attention from sociologists of science. However, Ravetz does note in general terms how important the cultural milieu in which a form of scientific knowledge develops is for its traditions of research practice and for the reception and use of the resultant knowledge. Even the same knowledge transferred from one cultural locale to another might change its meaning and its utility:

> In a new environment it may be adopted as a tool for the accomplishment
> of practical tasks or even for the solution of scientific problems; but in that

case the objects of knowledge will soon be recast so as to make the tool meaningful and effective to its users. Moreover, only some parts of what seemed a coherent body of knowledge will survive the transfer; and it may be that those which are considered as the essential components will be rejected as false or meaningless by the borrowers (Ravetz 1971a, 317).

Something of this kind has come about as a result of the transfer of Classical science from Europe to America.

We might examine this process of the Americanization of science by once more turning to its formative crucible, the Manhattan Project. Though the project was first thought of and initiated by the refugees, above all by Szilard and Wigner on the basis of European work, once it was under way it assumed a much more American character. The theories and ideas required were almost without exception of European origin; Americans contributed almost nothing to this aspect of the work; in fact the American physics establishment had been comparatively backward. Yet it was in America, rather than in Europe, despite the efforts of Heisenberg and his team of outstanding German physicists, that the break-through to nuclear energy was achieved, as Grabner and Reiter explain:

> This is all the more interesting as the emergence of an internationally competitive academic establishment in the U.S. was, at the time, still very recent— it took place no more than about 15 years before the Manhattan Project started. Up to that point, American science had largely to orient itself on the intellectually superior European model. In contrast, the U.S. had a strong and successful tradition of technological invention based on cultural values such as individualism, pioneer spirit, success and economic competition. As American science ascended after 1920, this tradition immediately took root in the experimental sciences. Physicists such as E. O. Lawrence served as links between the popular world of the Edisons and Bells and the world of scientific research still alien to the American tradition. It is significant that the invention and perfection of the cyclotron was the most important genuinely American contribution to nuclear physics before 1940; a contribution that was fully honored by the American public who saw in Lawrence a worthy representative of that line of Edison-like wizards to whom the glory of American inventiveness was due (Grabner and Reiter 1984, 245).

Lawrence continued his work at the Radiation Laboratory at Berkeley on his program of building ever larger cyclotrons of higher energy output to accelerate sub-atomic particles, and this work became the most important technical determinant of the future course of physics and a model for all subsequent scientific development. The program, however, did suffer from notable failings; at first few important scientific discoveries emerged from Lawrence's work. 'The Radiation Laboratory is thus said to have missed out on a number of important discoveries, such as induced radioactivity, which could easily have been made with the available equipment' (ibid. 248); furthermore 'the idea of an utilization of nuclear energy was not taken seriously by Lawrence or any of his American colleagues' (ibid. 249). In fact, though Lawrence did take an important part in the Manhattan Project once it was started, his 'work did not finally contribute to the success of the Manhattan Project' (ibid.). Nevertheless the style of research he inaugurated, such as the construction of giant accelerators, 'would, to a considerable extent, shape the form and direction of nuclear physics research directed to military ends' (ibid.). This procedure introduced what Grabner and Reiter call the principle of 'technological extrapolation for the sake of the production of new physical phenomena (which) became the most spectacular frontier of physical research' (ibid.). The success of the Manhattan Project owed much to this principle and to Lawrence's 'influence and example [which] seemed to prove that the strategy of scaling up existing (or even barely outlined) technologies would work . . . almost every part of the Project . . . involved such a scaling up' (ibid.).

This unique merger of American technological vision and organization with European theories and ideas produced the new post-war science. It proved to be unbeatable and irresistible for the rest of the world. The European national scientific establishments had to transform themselves with greater or lesser reluctance along American lines in order to compete effectively. The process proved to be easiest in West Germany where as a result of war devastation the scientific institutions had to be rebuilt almost from scratch with American help (Wilson 1972). The German scientific establishment, once the strongest in Europe, was already in decline after the First World War and was even more seriously depleted as a result of the Nazi purge of academia, so there was little to resist its reconstruction along new lines after the war (Haberer 1969). Of the other two major scientific centres, France and Britain, France had been stagnant since before the First World War—despite some very creditable individual achievements, such as those of the Curie dynasty—for reasons which have much to do with the antiquated character of French academia, unchanged since Napoleonic times (Ben-David 1964). Contributing to this stagnation were the meagre resources devoted to research by successive French governments, at least until de Gaulle attempted to establish an independent science policy as part of a program for military and industrial independence. Even then, some of the outstanding French achievements, such as those of Lwoff and his team at the Pasteur institute, were accomplished with American help and collaboration. Britain, the remaining major scientific centre, has fared much better than its neighbours and has continued to maintain its traditional high standards of pure research which have always placed it second in the national Nobel prize stakes. However, the British scientific establishment has always been narrow and elitist, and for that reason, and because of its very limited economic resources, Britain has been unable to establish a broad scientific or industrial base. Thus neither Germany, France nor Britain could continue successfully the European traditions of scientific research.

Inevitably Europe was forced to compete with the United States on terms set by the latter, which meant it could not do so effectively because the United States spends about three times as much on science as all of Western Europe combined. To compete more effectively the European countries have set up joint projects, such as CERN (Commission Européenne pour la Recherche Nucléaire), but to succeed to any extent they have had to engage in American-style Big Science research and, as in the case of CERN, use models partly devised by Americans. For 'it is of

interest that American scientists figured prominently in the early negotiations for the establishment of CERN, notably Rabi and Oppenheimer,
two of the U.S. scientists who had been closely involved with the bomb
project' (Rose and Rose 1969, 191). In other such undertakings, notably
in their space program, the Europeans have been less successful.

The non-Western scientific powers, notably the USSR and Japan, have
also had to move in the American direction, sometimes even preceding
the Americans in some developments. Almost since the Revolution the
Soviet Union has practised a State-planned science policy which is organizationally different from the State directed free-enterprize science policy
system of the United States. However, it has also emphasised technology
and Big Science in research for reasons to do with the needs of rapid
industrialization and its status as a major military power, as well as with
the materialist tenets of Marxist ideology which emphasise technology or
the so-called forces of production (Joravsky 1961). Its slender labor and
finance resources for science have had to be devoted largely to keeping
up with the Americans in military technology, so its achievements outside
the nuclear and space fields have been minor.

Japan has made very few contributions to 'pure' science, though it has
developed an extensive industrial and technological base. Its science research program has been closely geared to that of the United States ever
since the war when its scientific institutions were reconstructed by the
occupation authorities. However, the Japanese have made great strides in
restricted fields of science, such as computers, and are now in a position
to equal their mentors. In time this parity could develop into a general
challenge for scientific supremacy. But Japan still has major problems to
overcome before any such transplantation of science proves capable of
producing outstanding original research. Sibatani, a Japanese scientist,
points to at least two such difficulties: 'first, there is an incompatibility
between the traditional code of values and the principles of science originally introduced from the West. Second, there is a significant disparity
between domestic science and technology, the latter of which has so far
been seeking quick beneficial effects' (Sibatani 1972). Thus far Japanese
university-based scientists have mainly undertaken 'meticulous refinements,
viable for rather short periods, of developments that were probably 'selected' because they were more easily grasped by those who tried to
transplant science from abroad' (ibid.). The cultural problem is the most
difficult to overcome, for any long-term project for an original Japanese
science 'would have to be based on the indigenous culture of the society'
(ibid.). The implication is that if the project were to succeed and Japan
were to emerge as a leading scientific power, this development would
culturally affect the nature of science itself, as did the move from Europe
to America. But it is doubtful whether the difference would be as great
as this example suggests because the science of any large scale technologically advanced society is likely to be much the same as that of any other:
'the similarity of the planning apparatus that exists in Europe, Britain,
Russia and America, and the resemblance of the goals perceived for this
policy bear witness to this' (Rose and Rose 1969, 248). Hence what we
have called American science is really only the first example of a science

which for historical reasons emerged in America in the period during and after the Second World War, and from there it has spread to all other technological societies to become in effect a World science.

Contemporary World science is worldly in every sense of the word and quite different in its essential character from the European science of the recent past which, following Prigogine, we have called Classical science. As we shall show, these differences are apparent in all dimensions of scientific research—intellectual, instrumental and organizational. They also are revealed in the changed relations of science, technology and production. Prior to the Second World War, within the dispensation of Classical science, pure science was kept apart from technology, the realm of mere applied science, and technology was only gradually applied to economically productive purposes useful to society. But in the context of World science, technology and science are no longer distinct; the old separation of pure and applied science has broken down. Furthermore, technology is no longer applied haphazardly to production, as and when it happens to be found useful; rather the needs of production have become a motive force for research and development planned and organized on this basis. Thus science itself has become merely another productive force, part of the total system of production and destruction embracing all activities from the practical to the intellectual.

World science is a techno-science that was inextricably linked to war from its inception, thus making the Manhattan Project its most potent symbol. Man's transformed relation to the universe, in Secretary of War Stimson's words, is revealed in a new relation of knowledge and power. Bacon's formula that knowledge is power has been fulfilled in a new way because power has taken on such an enormously expanded scope in so many new dimensions. To explore this new confluence of knowledge and power we must turn to another military man, President Eisenhower, who was among the very first to see some of the implications of the new science.

> Today the solitary inventor, tinkering in his shop, has been overshadowed by task forces of scientists in laboratories and testing fields. In the same fashion, the free university, historically the fountainhead of free ideas and scientific discovery, has experienced a revolution in the conduct of research. Partly because of the huge costs involved, a government contract becomes virtually a substitute for intellectual curiosity (Eisenhower 1961, 1038).

These words, drawn from President Eisenhower's valedictory address, sum up the essential difference between the nature of contemporary World science and that of the Classical epoch of science preceding it. The difference is metaphorically as well as materially encapsulated in the remark: 'for every old blackboard there are now hundreds of electronic computers'. Eisenhower states expressly that there 'has been a technological revolution during recent decades', and he goes on to embrace science in general, saying that 'in this revolution research has become central; it also becomes more formalized, complex and costly'. Thus President Eisenhower (or Malcolm Moos who probably drafted this part of the speech) was among the first to draw attention to the changed state of science since (approximately) the Second World War, insofar as dates can be assigned to such eventualities. Few philosophers or sociologists of science were yet aware of this new revolution; most assumed that science continued to be much the same kind of enterprize as that which Galileo and Descartes had inaugurated with the Scientific Revolution in the seventeenth century. The intrinsically very different, but in their effects equally 'revolutionary', changes that brought about the contemporary epoch of science escaped their notice.

Eisenhower's main point in his speech was not so much to describe the new scientific establishment as to warn of its close collusion with the military-industrial complex. The 'scientific-technological elite', as he calls it, is exercising an undue influence on public policy, even to the point of holding it captive for its own ends. This scientific establishment has become a political power on par with the other main agencies of State. But at the same time, the State has decisively entered into the very process of scientific research: 'the prospect of domination of the nation's scholars by Federal employment, project allocations, and the power of money is ever present'. Thus Eisenhower points to a new symbiotic relation between politics and science—specifically between the State acting through the military-industrial complex and the scientific-technological elite—which is unprecedented in history and which has decisively transformed the whole character and inner constitution of both science and politics. This development represents a new stage in the relation between knowledge and power.

Even though Eisenhower was not primarily interested in describing the character of the new science, he presciently focussed on the key organizational and institutional aspects of scientific work that had undergone a drastic alteration. Science is no longer a matter of individual inventors—or of single individuals, whether they be brilliant theorists or experimentalists or great innovators or projectors—for the individual is powerless to achieve anything alone in most fields of science. It has mostly become an enterprise of teams and organizations, task forces of many kinds of experts, hierarchically ordered and usually set to work on useful pre-planned assignments. Generally these assignments are chosen on grounds other than purely scientific ones. Unlike the inventors who tinkered in their own shops with their own instruments, frequently designed and made by themselves, the members of these task forces no longer own the means of scientific production, nor are any of them in a position to produce them for themselves. The means of production now far surpass the few craft tools and string-and-sealing-wax devices of earlier days; they have become at times gigantic technological complexes utilizing quasi-industrial plant, consuming huge resources in power and money that frequently only a large State can afford.

Though they rely almost exclusively on outside contracts for their work, most scientists still consider themselves academics for they are formally attached to universities. But these present-day universities, as Eisenhower realized, are no longer the free universities of old. The university as the 'fountainhead of free ideas and scientific discovery' is now a mere historical relic, whose core is more or less artificially preserved in a few antiquarian localities and traditional establishments but whose outer form has almost completely decayed. It has been displaced by another institution known as the multiversity (a term first coined by Clark Kerr just a few years after Eisenhower's speech) which was formed when the university broke its mural boundaries, expanded and proliferated into a huge academic conglomerate of autonomous schools, institutes, laboratories, hospitals, think tanks, and whatever other institutions now fall under its legal aegis (Redner 1987). This development was more or less inevitable—beginning in the United States and spreading all over the world—because of the appropriation of scientific research by the State through its funding policies of hiring scientific brain power to serve its own projects and needs. The resultant direction of research changed the conduct of traditional scientific practice and gradually destroyed the freedom of the old university.

As the universities ceased to be free in any but a purely legal sense, the ideas produced in them also ceased to be free (Coser 1965, 290).[1] The free theorising that was known as 'pure' science and stringently separated from 'applied' science, began to lose its point when most research was carried out by contract on pre-determined projects to solve problems that involved at once pure and applied research. Free intellectual curiosity, pursuing basic research into problems inherently arising from the intrinsic development of scientific theories, gave way to mission-oriented research, determined by extrinsic ends and useful goals prescribed by outside authorities. The contract displaced the free idea, as Eisenhower puts it.

Thus in a few brief sentences President Eisenhower conveyed the gist of the momentous changes that science had undergone and is continuing to undergo, since the Second World War. His statement holds true in gross and general terms and provides a good beginning for a more adequate account. All the necessary qualifications, the details, the exceptions, the explanations of how and why some things changed and others did not, and above all the theoretical underpinning for a proper sociological account—all these and more have to be filled in.

Eisenhower implicitly focusses on the three basic aspects of all scientific work: the organizational, instrumental and cognitive—in short, people, machines and ideas. These can be ranked in this order of importance because the changes that brought about the contemporary epoch of science can be graded with this weighting scale. The most crucial changes took place in the organization of science, that is, in the socio-political system and institutional arrangements under which science is produced. Next in importance were the changes in instrumentation, in the new technological machinery and the new techniques of research made available in all the sciences. Of least importance were the cognitive changes, the new theories, ideas and hypotheses, which, although altered, were largely developments of previous ones. This kind of weighting is more or less in historical conformity with other major changes in contemporary, so-called advanced society where the ideological or cultural dimension is least altered and least developed whereas the technological and organizational dimensions are most pronounced.[2]

The relatively lesser importance of changes in the cognitive content of science, compared with the other factors, is attested to by comments from scientists and from sociologists of science. Thus in reference to particle physics, an area of great achievement since the war, Panofsky remarks that 'with all respects to the theorists and the experimentalists, the real rate of progress by which we are able to understand things at such small dimensions is governed by technology' (Panofsky 1984). Symes notes that in chemistry 'a revolution took place in the aftermath of the Second World War [which] involved no great conceptual leap [but merely] involved the introduction of two particular spectroscopic techniques, infrared spectroscopy and nuclear magnetic resonance', and he stresses that 'the key point is that it was the instruments not the theory that was lacking before the war' (Symes 1976, 341). Progress in molecular biology, a new postwar science, was more a combination of 'hypotheses and techniques', as Crick claims, but his stress is more on the latter than the former: 'molecular biology made progress for several reasons. The experimental techniques have been very powerful: radioactive tracers, electron microscopy, antibodies as tools to dissect the process' (Judson 1979, 207). This development is echoed by his colleague Brenner in the context of a catalogue of the new technical devices: 'without these labelling methods nothing would have been possible. That can't be overemphasized' (ibid.). A similar view is maintained by Heilbroner for post–Second World War economics: 'econometrics is the child of this era. So is the application of mathematics to economic theory. So is vectoral analysis, linear programming, input-output theory and description' (Heilbroner 1979, 193). The basic ideas in economics show little advance on Keynes. Thus in the social sciences as in the natural sciences, indeed in the whole field of knowledge (Wissenschaft), the tendency has been for changes in technique and social organization to exceed those in pure cognition.

Perhaps the clearest single statement summing up the nature of the multiple changes in post-war science is one from Harvey Brooks:

> The growth of science in the post-war era has been characterized by the spectacular expansion of hybrid disciplines such as geophysics, geochemistry, biochemistry, chemical physics, computer science and systems analysis. Techniques such as radiocarbon dating, the use of radioactive tracers, paper and gas chromatography, microwave and nuclear resonance spectroscopy, and X-ray diffraction have spread rapidly. Interdisciplinary subjects such as oceanography, atmospheric sciences, and space science draw on all the more classical disciplines, and it is difficult to tell at what point they do or should be considered disciplines in their own right. Whole areas of research often move from one discipline to another. For example, atomic spectroscopy, which used to be a major branch of physics, has now moved almost entirely into astronomy. Similarly, molecular spectroscopy has largely moved from physics into chemistry. The study of cosmic rays has largely moved from physics into a branch of space science, the theory of low energy nuclear reactions has become an important aspect of astrophysics. It becomes increasingly difficult to define a discipline except by the organizational framework within which it is pursued—for example, physics is what is done currently in academic physics departments (Brooks 1968, 57).

Noteworthy in this account is the clear distinction between the classical disciplines, or the idea of a discipline in Classical science, and disciplines in contemporary science defined largely by their 'organizational framework'. The extract clearly indicates that in post-war science a reorganization has taken place: specialties have moved from one discipline to another or specialties from different disciplines have fused to form a new hybrid. The spread of instrumental techniques and the development of new machines and their shift from one specialty to another have also been crucial for this reorganization. The prime importance of organization is emphasised further when Brooks proposes criteria for the classification of research 'in terms of the primary purpose of the institution in which it is conducted or of the institution's organizational subdivisions' (ibid. 59).

The Limits of Classical Science

As shown in the foregoing, science has undergone a historically unique and peculiar transition from what we have called a Classical science to a World science stage. It is part of the same historical process as the general transformation from an European civilization into a world civilization the character of which, like that of the new science, is not as yet fully apparent because it is still in the making. However, it is apparent that the new science, separated from its European cultural context, has become one of the major forces of world civilization and is shared by all nations to a lesser or greater degree, depending on their so-called level of modernization. This science is at one with such other features of world civilization as the industrial-technological economy, State bureaucracy and the diffusion of the communications media. In other respects, of course, nations still differ in their approach to science depending on parochial and traditional peculiarities, as shown with respect to Japan. But science is one of the most important unifying factors of world civilization, allowing for only minor local variants.

If the transformation of European into world civilization is an unprecedented step in history, it follows that the transition from Classical science to World science is also without previous parallel. Science has already undergone a number of fundamental changes in its long history, but none of these is anything like what we are now witnessing. To show this I will briefly outline some of the past stages of science, focusing primarily on its developments in the West and momentarily overlooking its very different history in China, India and other places where scientific cultures arose more or less autonomously. In the West there have already been two major scientific epochs: the ancient-medieval and the post-Renaissance. The first might be called Aristotelian-Ptolemaic science in honour of its outstanding theorists; along similar lines the second might be referred to as Newtonian-Einsteinian science, and I have called it Classical science for short. Each of these long-lasting epochs had its own relatively distinct internal phases and divisions, which might be listed in the following stages. Aristotelian-Ptolemaic science began with a Greek phase which culminated in the achievements of the Museum of Alexandria, followed by a more pedestrian Roman phase; subsequent to the fall of the ancient classical world, it went through at least three successive revivals and transformations, which might be called Arab medieval, Christian medieval and Renaissance, but basically it remained the same kind of speculative science throughout. The first epochal transition took place only with the Scientific Revolution of the seventeenth century, which established Newtonian science in total opposition to the previous Aristotelian-Ptolemaic science. This epoch might in turn be divided into two major phases: the first from the formation of the scientific academies or Royal Society till the French Revolution and the second from the new French Grandes Ecoles and the German universities till the onset of the Second World War. (See Chapter 4 for an exposition of these institutional changes and their importance for science.) Although it is hardly necessary to describe in any detail these epochs and their phases, a few words to specify their defining features are called for to show how the character of science expounded and practised by each differed from that of present science and thereby also to show how varied have been the enterprizes going under the name of science.

The knowledge sought in ancient science was 'essentialist', that is, largely conceptual. From the start it was metaphysically ordered and guided; first in Aristotle, then in the Stoics and later still in the Aristotelian scholastics it could be expressed as part of a philosophical system. The cosmological correlate of such a system was the Ptolemaic picture of a closed and hierarchically ordered world with 'the earth at the centre, surrounded by the concentric shells of the hierarchy of spheres, and the hierarchy of values associated with the Scale of Being' (Koestler 1959, 218). By this world view every piece of knowledge had its assigned place in the overall scheme, and anything that could not be fitted in was not considered true or was not even counted as knowledge (*theoria*) as distinct from mere opinion (*doxa*). Knowledge was essential, necessary, certain, perfect, eternal and divine; opinion was accidental, contingent, corrupt, historical and worldly.

The Scientific Revolution which inaugurated Classical science destroyed this metaphysical epistemology and broke open the closed world to reveal an 'unbounded universe without centre or circumference; no region or sphere ranked "higher" or "lower" than another either in space or on the scale of values' (ibid.). The universe was everywhere the same and governed by universal laws. Knowledge was no longer of the 'whatness' of things (*essentia*), merely of their 'howness' (*regulae*)—how they related and with what laws they were bound. Substance gave way to function when Newton declared 'hypothesis non fingo'. The functions had to be mathematical laws, arrived at through rational deduction from first principles, followed by empirical experimental confirmation. And just as the universe was infinite, so the quest for knowledge was in principle unending; no limit could be set for either thought or experience since there was none for Nature itself. This conceptualization made possible the idea of an endless progress of science—an idea that is itself historically relative, as shall be shown in Chapter 2.

However, by the close of the Classical era of science, in the twentieth century, the Newtonian picture of the universe and the scientific epistemology correlated with it had been drastically revised. On the scale of the whole universe, or the macrocosm, Einstein's general relativity theory had made possible a cosmology based on the conception of a curved and bounded space that was endless but finite. Newtonian gravity or action at a distance could be interpreted as a function of the geometry of this space. On the scale of the microcosm, or the smallest particles of the atom, quantum theory introduced quantum jumps and other discontinuities in physical processes. This approach culminated in Bohr's complementarity and Heisenberg's indeterminacy principles which overthrew the determinism of cause and effect; these were radical conceptions which Einstein himself was not willing to accept because he still clung to the older Rationalist epistemology. But this epistemology had become discredited both because of developments within the sciences themselves and also because of changes in the philosophical conceptions of science, mainly of a Positivist nature. In retrospect we can now see that all these new theoretical departures were culminating in Classical science, as Prigogine now recognizes, rather than, as was thought at the time, opening up another epoch of scientific progress to rival the Classical one. Newton and Einstein are thus the opening and concluding figures of the one scientific epoch.

This Classical era was punctuated by a partial intermediate break that roughly divided it into two phases (Redner 1987). The first, which might be called the period of natural philosophy, lasted till approximately the close of the eighteenth century, and this was also the period of what Foucault (1970) calls 'classical' science in a narrower sense, characterizing it through his account of natural history, analysis of wealth and general grammar, the precursors of biology, economics and philology which arose in the next phase. This second phase also saw a transition in the natural sciences towards more abstract, mathematical techniques—non-Euclidean geometry, for instance—which together with the empirical exploration of new physical phenomena gradually being uncovered, such as electromagnetism and radioactivity, led eventually to the theoretical reconceptualizations of relativity theory and quantum theory. During this phase, too, statistical methods applied to familiar phenomena such as heat led to the foundation of the thermodynamic sciences of irreversible processes, beginning with Fourier and Carnot and culminating with Boltzmann and Gibbs. Time and development became key preoccupations in most sciences. Evolutionary theory was established in many natural sciences and Historicism became widespread in the social and cultural ones. As compared with the first phase of Classical science, the second phase made science much more of an abstract intellectual enterprize far removed from the traditional and still partly common-sense notions that prevailed in the first phase. These changes resulted to a considerable extent from the institutional innovations which transformed the pursuit of science into a professional enterprize and established the career role of scientist. The renovated German university system was extremely influential in this respect, for it institutionally separated pure science from applied science and technology, locating them in separate schools, and thereby promoting this tendency towards purely abstract theorizing in the sciences.

Having thus briefly reviewed the major transitions in the history of Western science, I will once again consider how the current change that science is undergoing compares with those of the past. Clearly from what

I have already shown, it is utterly different from anything that had occurred previously. It is not another Scientific Revolution for there is no great intellectual innovation—in fact, there are relatively few radical changes in theorizing taking place; the changes are much more on the instrumental and organization levels. Science is merging with technology in a large-scale organized pursuit of knowledge that is part of and serves a crucial role in social production. Thus World science has many of the worldly features—mass process, anonymity—of world civilization as a whole. Few crucial scientific discoveries can now be associated with single famous names; no Aristotle, Copernicus, Newton or Einstein is now capable of totally revising our picture of the universe. Science is produced by large organized teams as a matter of gradual construction rather than by any single vision. As William Broad notes:

> Born out of the complexity of modern science, an era of vast, lavishly financed research teams appears to be replacing the days when individuals dominated science. The trend reached new heights last year when platoons of scientists tested a vaccine against cancer, found planets circling distant stars, created dozens of new kinds of computers, uncovered a 1500-year-old Mayan tomb, discovered the probable cause of AIDS and located an ancient drainage system under the Sahara. Scientific teams also added the 108th element to the periodic table and shared a Nobel Prize for the creation of a giant atom smasher that stretches 6 1/2 kilometres beneath the French-Swiss border. Impressive by any standard, such triumphs nonetheless raise questions about the direction of 20th century science. Is research now totally dominated by impersonal teams and astronomic budgets? (Broad 1985).

If the role of the individual in science has become so marginal, then there are bound to be many problems. Most important developments in World science cannot be ascribed to individuals, and some—for instance, fusion research or computers—do not even have identifiable originators. As a result many of the individualist epithets applied to changes in science—the introduction of world views, altered perceptions of things, new 'pictures' of Man or the universe—are hardly relevant, and by implication neither are terms such as epistemological breaks or paradigm revolutions. Instead slow and subtle shifts in the way science is practised take place, the extent and nature of which depend largely on technical achievements and organizational readjustments. These changes hardly constitute a Scientific Revolution, though their effects might be as far reaching as any of the revolutions of the past.

Given all these differences in scientific approach, it follows that the kind of knowledge produced by contemporary World science is very different from that produced by Classical science, ultimately perhaps even as different as the latter was from Aristotelian science. It does not follow however that these different forms of knowledge are incommensurable; clearly they cannot be since each builds on the previous ones, though not cumulatively, along the one line of progressive development. World science is based on Classical science and would not have been possible without it. Yet the knowledge to which it gives rise has a different character, as I shall seek to show.

The overall intellectual quest of Classical science can be characterized as a search for fundamental simplicity, universality and total determinism. This direction is well brought out in Einstein's programatic declaration:

> In regard to his subject matter . . . the physicist has to limit himself very severely: he must content himself with describing the most simple events which can be brought within the domain of our experience; all events of a more complex order are beyond the power of the human intellect to reconstruct with the subtle accuracy and logical perfection which the theoretical physicist demands. Supreme purity, clarity, and certainty at the cost of completeness. But what can be the attraction of getting to know such a tiny section of nature thoroughly, while one leaves everything subtler and more complex shyly and timidly alone? Does the product of such a modest effort deserve to be called by the proud name of a theory of the universe? In my belief the name is justified; for the general laws on which the structure of theoretical physics is based claim to be valid for any natural phenomenon whatsoever. With them, it ought to be possible to arrive at the description, that is to say, the theory, of every natural process, including life, by means of pure deduction, if that process of deduction were not far beyond the capacity of the human intellect. The physicist's renunciation of completeness for his cosmos is therefore not a matter of fundamental principle (Einstein 1954, 225).

Einstein's own work best exemplifies the scope of this program at the culmination of Classical science in its search for fundamental laws and unifying theories. Such a search had been implicit in the course of Classical science from the start, and the great systems of physics, chemistry and biology were its final fruits. And so, too, were the allied comprehensive evolutionary schemas of development in the sciences of time, the earth and life sciences and the progressivist patterns in the anthropological and historical sciences.

The search for fundamental laws and unifying schemas meant that the Classical sciences were inherently reductive in tendency. Classical scientific method expounded a program to reduce complexities to the simplest 'objects' and the simplest models. Usually these were theoretical constructs devised by means of analytic restriction through the elimination of all parameters except the ones that could be subject to law-like regularity. These simplified, restricted objects of one science were to be further reduced theoretically to those of a still more basic science dealing with yet simpler and more restricted objects (Pantin 1968).[3] In this way through a general program of successive reduction the theoretically unified system of the sciences could be built up. This scientific method was first adumbrated as Galileo's *metodo resolutivo* and the second maxim of Descartes' *Discourses on Method*. Eventually it seemed as if the whole scientific project would be completed when all the separate sciences, each reducible to those still more fundamental, would be embraced in a few basic laws to constitute a complete structure of unified science. The Logical Positivists of the Vienna Circle tried to carry through this project in theory.

In theory it seemed as if this reduction could be achieved, but in practice it proved impossible because it was based on an inherent simplification of reality and of how scientific explanations of real objects could be attained. Both Galileo and Descartes assumed that once the resolving analysis was carried through and reduction accomplished, it could easily be followed by the inverse process of synthesis whereby the complex object would be reconstituted out of the simple elements into which it had been dissolved. In a similar spirit the Logical Positivists assumed that if one kind of object (X) could be scientifically reduced to another more basic kind of object (Y), then in theory, at least, X could be derived from Y. Given the basic laws of Y it should be possible in principle to deduce from these the laws of X. This procedure is what Einstein means when he speaks of arriving at a description of life 'by means of pure deduction'.

However, in practice this approach was not successful. Analysis and synthesis, reduction and deduction were not mutually reversible because of the insurmountable problem of complexity. Most interactions of the kind that are required to constitute a real object are too complex to be reconstructed from their basic terms and relations. Even where it is possible to express this complexity mathematically, say in the form of numerous simultaneous equations, such equations are frequently not solvable with present methods, even allowing for the largest computers. Heisenberg states that 'in the great majority of cases, the complete mathematical calculation of a set problem will technically not be possible for all too great complications can no longer be mastered in mathematical terms' (Elias 1982a, 65). In elementary physics even such a simple constellation as the three-body problem cannot be solved except through approximations. Or to take a more substantive example, it is possible theoretically to reduce water to atoms of hydrogen and oxygen, but from this it does not follow that the ordinary physical properties of water can be deduced from the fundamental properties of hydrogen and oxygen atoms. In principle it is possible to imagine such a derivation taking the form of innumerable 'Schrödinger equations' of the energy states of atoms; in practice even if all the equations necessary had been arrived at—itself an unwarranted assumption—they would be unsolvable. As the biologist Waddington remarked apropos the chemical derivation of life, such equations are 'a trifle on the inscrutable side if they contain everything necessary to understand protein molecules, no-one can get it out of them' (Woodcock and Davis 1978, 77).

Thus the most serious shortcoming of the Classical sciences was their inability to deal with organized complexity—and the capacity to handle complexity in objects and systems is the key to the application of science to most practical problems in the real world. Hence the application of Classical science to reality was mostly in the nature of an open promissory note guaranteeing that the problems which had been solved in principle, usually only in relation to artificially simplified objects and situations, could also be solved in practice in the context of the full complexity of real objects and situations. Although this promise could seldom be kept, this inadequacy was not taken as any kind of defeat for science itself but merely as a temporary difficulty. Thus the uselessness of Classical science to problems of technology throughout most of its history did not worry the pure scientists. They were unconcerned with complexity as such and did not see it as presenting an inherently insuperable difficulty. The Laplacean boast was emblematic of the indifference to the issue of complexity evinced by Classical science in general. Laplace wrote that an intelligence that knew at any one moment of time 'all the forces by which nature is animated and the respective positions of all the entities which compose it would embrace in the same formula the movements of the largest bodies in the universe and those of the lightest atom: nothing would be uncertain for it, and the future like the past, would be present to its eyes' (Polanyi 1958, 140). The idea of a world formula which could embrace every single atom is the illusion generated by the belief that complexity is in principle no barrier to knowledge once the simple is known. The complex is taken to be the simple multiplied by as many times as required, even though the number might be astronomical.

In fact the Classical sciences could not reduce complex objects to simple laws. Even such a simple complexity as the three-body problem proved too difficult. Unorganized complexities or mass phenomena could sometimes be dealt with by means of statistical laws: thermodynamics was the outstanding classical example of how to cope with mass atomic interactions; and some of the social sciences tried similarly to find a statistical basis for human masses. But the organized complexities of systemic forms and configurations both in nature and in humans were usually beyond the reach of the Classical sciences.

Contemporary World sciences, by contrast, have tended to be applied to precisely such complexities. Complexity is a feature of the objects they deal with, the methods with which they work and the way they are organized to utilize such methods. Thus cognitively, instrumentally and organizationally the World sciences are complex and deal with complexity. This aspect is broadly understood for these sciences are commonly referred to as practising Big Science—though this formulation is not very accurate because not all contemporary sciences are Big Science in any obvious sense. The term 'Big Science' is meant to reflect their organizational complexity; it tells us less about their other dimensions. These might be indicated colloquially by saying that these sciences deal with Big Objects.

Another way of approaching the specificity of the contemporary developments in the sciences is to treat them as sciences of organized complexity dealing with systems. Systems are Big Objects—namely, multiple organized wholes of any kind occurring in any field of scientific investigation, in nature or society, human or machine, group or individual. This is how systems theorists, such as von Bertalanffy, Boulding and Laszlo, as well as some Structuralists, such as Piaget, approached the matter (Buckley 1968). They went on to try to develop a General System Theory as an overarching meta-science dealing with all systems regardless of their specific content or constituents, or in what specific scientific field they are found. Unfortunately such a general undertaking has proved relatively empty, providing only generalized conceptual tools which are not very informative when applied to actual systems. Systems seem to be too specific and variable to be encompassed in one general theory; they can only be dealt with individually through detailed unravelling in separate sciences. Nevertheless, the attempt to define the contemporary sciences as systems theories dealing with organized complexity is in essence correct; it merely needs to be qualified because systems are too complex for any generalized systems approach.

Many of the fundamental features of the World sciences follow from this basic orientation towards organized complexity. Thus on the instrumental level the need to cope with complex objects has demanded a very high degree of technification in both machines and procedures. Without computers, for example, most of the calculations required to solve complex problems simply could not be done in anything like the permissible time. Without the high resolution instruments of detection and analysis most complex processes could not be tracked or recorded and work in many sciences would be next to impossible. Without the techniques for handling very large numbers of individuals no survey work could be undertaken. The ready availability of such high-powered technologically sophisticated machines and large-scale techniques requiring organized human resources has in turn prompted and encouraged the investigation of the kinds of complex processes, systems and situations which Classical science simply could not handle, even when it already possessed all the basic laws that in principle could afford an explanation.

Since they have to deal with complex objects, the World sciences are frequently no longer concerned with basic laws or fundamental explanations in the way that the Classical sciences were. They are often engaged in what Lettvin calls 'patching', a procedure made possible by the high technification afforded by the use of computers:

> Computers have vastly increased our ability to work with data points. It is possible, for example, to patch together weather prediction, or the location of oil deposits, or putting a man on the moon, because the dogwork of patching data can be done easily and rapidly by machine. Where a clearly determined human goal can inform a human judge to reorganize computation, patching becomes a fine art, the blending of apparently irrelevant procedures to produce wanted results. *However the patchwork is not usually a theory in any classical sense.* It is prescriptive like a good recipe. But when the same algorithms and programs, so successful in directed engineering, are used in cases where there is neither a theory to be checked nor a goal to be approached, the system turns bizzare, a thing out of Jonathan Swift. Then the output of the machine, whatever it is, can become the goal, the program become the theory, as you can actually see occurring in certain branches of biophysics. What first occasions the work disappears and the real objects of discourse are revealed as the workings of the machine (Lettvin 1971, 144).

In Chapter 3 I shall examine in detail the effect of high technification on those procedures of the World sciences which distinguish them from the Classical sciences. In Chapter 6 I shall investigate the pathologies of science to which such technification can give rise—among them the problem that, as Lettvin discerned, arises when programs take the place of theories. These are problems which I shall discuss further in Chapter 8, where I shall show how in some sciences when dealing with very complex objects— for example, ecological systems—explanation and prediction no longer coincide as the joint goals of scientific understanding. Patching reveals that prediction can often be achieved without any corresponding increase in the degree of explanation attained. Science becomes more a matter of recipes.

Many of the previously mentioned features of World science can be illustrated by a simple example: the attempt to find a description and an explanation for the forms of snow crystals. At one level this explanation is already known and is 'elementary textbook stuff', according to a review article on the subject by John Maddox:

> Qualitatively and crudely, an ice crystal growing from a saturated vapour will grow most quickly at those points on its surface where the latent heat escapes most quickly, which will be the places where the radius of curvature is smallest. But for a growing snowflake, the radius of curvature is least, or the curvature is greatest, precisely where rapid growth has already taken place, at dendritic tips. So positive feedback or the Matthew principle . . . applies, and dendritic growth as in a snowflake is a manifestation of instability (Maddox 1983, 13).

At this so-called textbook level, Classical science provides a general explanation in principle. But to explain the actual shape that emerges from an interplay of these forces requires dealing with immense complexities since 'it is a problem with nearly as many degrees of freedom as there are atoms or molecules on the growing surface' (ibid.). For this reason no crystallographer can predict the shape of a snow crystal from first principles alone. However, computer simulation can now provide a rough approximation which shows that 'the essence of the problem may be understood—and that there is still a long way to go' (ibid.). Numerous researchers are working on it; some such as F. C. Franck have devoted the whole of their lives to it. The problem is not discovering the formula or law to cover a given general case but modeling the possibility of an indefinite set of individual variations, each of which is unique yet immediately recognizable as a form belonging to a certain species of crystals, those of snow flakes. Unstable relations, non-linear causalities, feedback mechanisms and other such non-Classical principles are involved. To unravel their intricate operation one needs the most up-to-date techniques of the World sciences: laser-based instruments for detecting and measuring particles, computer simulation, powerful mathematical techniques deriving from statistics and topology.

Scientists agree that 'the importance and ubiquity of the problem is not in doubt' (ibid). And yet it is only a simple instance of a huge range of problems belonging to what might be called integrative or configurational sciences, those which deal with forms and systems. In Chapter 8, I shall explore a number of such sciences, those which are particularly important for they seem to be opening up new possibilities which point to future developments. They seem to represent a departure from the more technical and mundane activities of present 'normal' World science. A key instance of such a new science is the work of Prigogine on so-called dissipative structures in chemistry, work on the emergence of ordered structures out of near chaotic complexity.

Prigogine distinguishes the new sciences that he seeks to develop from the Classical sciences on three basic grounds: they are sciences of complexity as against simplicity, they are sciences of irreversible processes as against reversible dynamic paths, and finally they are sciences that allow for the free play of chance as against strict and total determinism. Taken together these differences represent a fundamental departure from the Classical paradigm: whereas the Classical sciences are ultimately atemporal, those which Prigogine is developing are sciences of time. As Prigogine and Stengers assert: 'what are the assumptions of Classical science from which we believe science has freed itself today? Generally those centering around the basic conviction that at some level the world is simple and is governed by time-reversible fundamental laws. . . . The denial of time and complexity was central to the cultural issues raised by the scientific enterprize in the classical definition' (Prigogine and Stengers 1984, 7–8). Once again as before the Scientific Revolution, time is of the essence. Prigogine and Stengers deliberately revert to pre-Classical conceptions of science. This archaism is designed to re-establish a new alliance or relationship between humankind and Nature so as to locate the subject as observer within the objective order being investigaged. 'The ambition of Newtonian science was to present a vision of nature that would be universal, deterministic, and objective inasmuch as it contains no reference to the observer, complete inasmuch as it attains a level of description that escapes the clutches of time' (ibid. 213). The new Prigogian science aims to show that the observer is a product of the natural order which as pure consciousness he or she thinks to be surveying from the outside.

Taking one by one the key characteristics of Classical science—simplicity, reversibility and determinism—Prigogine shows that far from being universal principles of nature, each is no more than a qualified presupposition which only applies within strict limits in artificially bounded situations. The striving for simplicity in nature, or the unity of science based on a few fundamental laws, is an expression of the Rationalism of Classical science which no longer holds in the context of the contemporary World sciences and the altered vision of nature these are elaborating. This striving for simplicity achieved its fullest realization in Einstein:

> Einstein, like many physicists of his generation, was guided by a deep conviction that there was a fundamental, simple level in nature. Yet today this level is becoming less and less accessible to experiment. The only objects whose behaviour is truly "simple" exist in our own world, at the macroscopic level. Classical science carefully chose its objects from this intermediate range. The first objects singled out by Newton—falling bodies, the pendulum, planetary motion—were simple. We know now, however, that this simplicity is not the hallmark of the fundamental: it cannot be attributed to the rest of the world (ibid. 216).

An analogous argument can also be applied to determinism and reversibility, the other key characteristics of Classical science:

> [In Classical science] the basic processes are considered as deterministic and reversible. Processes involving randomness or irreversibility are considered to be exceptions. Today we see everywhere the role of irreversible processes, of fluctuations. The models considered by Classical physics seem to us to

occur only in limiting situations such as we can create artificially by putting matter into a box and then waiting till it reaches equilibrium (ibid. 9).

Thus reversibility applies only in Classical basic physics; it is not found even in thermodynamics, also a Classical science developed in the nineteenth century, but which for the first time introduced a time orientation into physics. Prigogine tries to show that this non-reversibility is not the result of any shortcoming; it is not—as the usual Classical interpretation would have it—that thermodynamic irreversibility arises out of its being a mere statistical approximation on a macroscopic level to a fully deterministic dynamic system on the microscopic level. 'The world of dynamics, be it classical or quantum is a reversible world . . . no evolution can be ascribed to this world; the "information" expressed in terms of dynamic units remains constant. It is therefore of great importance that the existence of an evolutionary paradigm can now be established in physics—not only on the level of macroscopic description but also on all levels' (ibid. 297). He insists that 'on all levels, from elementary particles to cosmology, randomness and irreversibility play an ever-increasing role', including above all 'the level of so-called macroscopic physics, which comprises the physics and chemistry of atoms and molecules either taken individually or considered globally as, for example, in the study of liquids or gases' (ibid. p. XXVIII).

The biggest abomination for Classical science to countenance is the abandonment of total determinism and the acceptance of a degree of randomness. This approach is something that few scientists even now would be prepared to allow. We must therefore consider it a feature of a potential Prigogian science of the future (which we shall consider in Chapter 8) rather than an acknowledged property of present World science. Yet Prigogine and Stengers insist that it is the basis for other characteristics which many scientists would accept, for they argue that 'only when a system behaves in a sufficiently random way may the difference between past and future, and therefore irreversibility, enter its description' (ibid. p. XX). They have in mind the systems which arise out of nonequilibrium processes, and these 'may lead to situations that would appear impossible from the classical point of view' (ibid. 150). It must remain a moot point whether such situations cannot be accounted for in some other way short of having to allow randomness to enter. Only future developments in science can resolve this issue.

Prigogine and Stengers thus conclude in agreement with Heisenberg that 'classical science has now reached its limit' (ibid. 54), both for internalist and externalist reasons. Purely autonomous internal developments of the sciences have led to the point where 'randomness, complexity, and irreversibility enter into physics as objects of positive knowledge' (ibid.). But at the same time external historical pressures on the sciences, such as already examined, tend inexorably to a redirection of scientific effort and refocus and transform the character of scientific work and organization. The new interest in time and chance that Prigogine and his co-workers pursue is also the outcome of such a double motivation: 'discoveries such as those of unstable elementary particles or of the expanding universe clearly belong to the internal history of science, but the general interest in nonequilibrium situations, in evolving systems, may reflect our feeling that humanity as a whole is in a transition period' (ibid. 19). The transformation of science and the transition in the history of humanity are thus closely correlated. And this brings us back once more to the original questions concerning science and progress and the shift from a European to a world phase of civilization.

2
Science and Progress

The Idea of Progress

In the context of the previous discussion in Chapter 1 it should now be possible to understand what Heisenberg means by 'the passing of the great age of natural science' and why he states that 'our culture is reaching its limit' but might 'now reorient itself by making the limit part of its new bearing'. Prigogine's work in particular might be taken as a cardinal instance of this claim, though not in a way foreseen by Heisenberg. However, it is still not altogether clear why Chargaff speaks of science having 'painted itself into a corner' or what Stent has in mind when he asks if 'the arena of Faustian strife against the mysterious unknown is mainly gone'. To explain these statements we need to explore the historical relation between science and progress stressing the separation between Classical science and World science.

The idea of progress outside science—in historical, social, and cultural dimensions of thought—has already been historically relativized and so reduced to insignificance. Apart from the obvious ideological contexts where undiminished faith in capitalism or socialism is still de rigueur, few now seriously believe in the evolutionary or revolutionary improvement of humankind or of human society in all the respects anticipated by nineteenth-century thinkers. Even where social conditions have unquestionably improved, this development is no longer seen as part of an inherent progress in history itself. Such improvements result from multiple historical causes and bring with them as much evil as good. History now appears in a morally ambiguous light—if not altogether bereft of any value or meaning. If nothing else, the two world wars have taught even scientists this lesson; yet many are not prepared to give up their belief in scientific progress. As Ravetz (1971a, 409) states, 'the idea of progress with which the rise of modern science was intimately associated received its mortal blow in the First World War and its aftermath; but in science itself the assumption survived for nearly another half-century'. Has science been too good or simply too slow to catch up with the rest of history?

Ravetz believes that inevitably history has finally caught up with science; he maintains that 'the long "golden age" of science is now definitely ended' (ibid.). Yet to say that progress has ended and, therefore, that science no longer progresses can be very misleading, especially for older scientists nurtured on this belief. Such an assertion suggests a cessation of scientific discovery, and that is simply not true. Science does go on, and, as I shall show, ever newer kinds of knowledge are continually being produced. But is this alone sufficient to permit one to speak of progress in science? Or is the idea of progress any longer relevant to the scientific discoveries and the way of doing science at present?

The scientists we have previously quoted believe that the idea of progress is no longer relevant in science in the way it was in the past. Invariably they link this belief to the end of the progressive age of history in general. Heisenberg maintains that European science has followed the fate of European civilization in this respect. In a totally different vein, Stent believes that the Faustian era of history is over and with it the Faustian stage of progressive science. In my book *In the Beginning Was the Deed* (1982) I develop an analogous argument with implications somewhat closer to those of Heisenberg than to those of Stent. The gist of my argument is that the idea of progress must now be taken as no more than an historically received conception which we cannot easily abandon for it shapes our current modes of thought—like a ghost from the past that haunts us still. But we are now aware of the duplicity of this idea that holds us in thrall: that progress is inextricably coupled with Nihilism. All those tendencies in history which under the aspect of progress were seen as creative and developing, we now also see as nihilistic and reductive. In my next work, *The Ends of Philosophy* (1986), I show how science, taken to have been the main source of progress and enlightenment, was also the instigator of nihilistic reductive tendencies in culture and society—reduction being the fundamental principle of the 'method' of Classical science. This unanticipated nihilistic outcome of Classical science has now come to the fore most obviously in the application of science to war in a way which has potentially annihilating consequences. But annihilation through reduction is as much a cultural effect as a simple physical one, as I show in *In the Beginning Was the Deed*.

If the idea of progress is still held to be relevant to the further development of science, it cannot have the same sense that it had for Classical science, from the Scientific Revolution down to its close around the Second World War. From an historical point of view this difference should not be surprising, for science cannot be said to have progressed in this way prior to the Scientific Revolution either. This change is implicitly acknowledged in histories of science, such as those by Bachelard and Kuhn, which distinguish the development of science prior to the so-called epistemological break and after it, or between pre-paradigm science and paradigm science. However, most histories assume with Bachelard and Kuhn that once the epistemological break has occurred or once paradigm science has been introduced, further progress is assured and will continue forever after, with one paradigm succeeding another in a constant revolutionizing process that constitutes the onward march of science. The possibility that another kind of scientific development altogether might ensue, which might no longer progress in this way, is not seriously countenanced.

The idea of progress in this sense originated from tenets held by the very same thinkers who inaugurated the methods and assumptions of Classical science, primarily Bacon and Descartes. The advancement of learning and the methodical pursuit of certain knowledge are both early versions of what later came to be called progress. This idea fulfilled the function of a supporting ideology of Classical science. From science it was generalized to all of history. Those who invoked the idea of progress invariably referred in the first place to science: the philosophes of the *Encyclopédie* culminating in Condorcet's paean to progress, the Positivists from St. Simon and Comte to the Vienna Circle, Evolutionists, Hegelians and Marxists—all invoked science to back up their belief in progress. The historian of science, George Sarton, asserted emphatically as late as 1936: 'the history of science is the only history which can illustrate the progress of mankind. In fact, progress has no definite and unquestionable meaning in other fields than the field of science' (Nisbet 1980, 346). Thus if the idea of progress is rendered questionable in science itself, it will be all the more difficult to invoke it outside science.

But what is the idea of progress? What does it really mean in the context of Classical science where it does properly apply? The idea of progress in science carries with it at least three interlocking themes: the dissolution of mysteries by piercing the obscurities of Nature with the light of the intellect and so producing enlightenment; the construction of the one unified and coherent system of knowledge through the reduction of all complex entities to simple and basic ones governed by a few universal laws; and, finally, the application of the rational approach of science to all areas of thought and thereby the extension of the realm of universal rationality. Enlightenment, reduction, and Rationalism were the hallmarks of the progress of Classical science. We shall examine these one by one and test what relevance they still have, if any, to World science. If indeed they are no longer applicable to the latter, this fact will provide further grounds for distinguishing World from Classical science.

Progress as Enlightenment

Classical science was assumed to bring about enlightenment because it broke through the mysteries of Nature and disclosed the unknown. Without the mystery, the numinous darkness of Nature, there could have been no enlightenment. The sense of sacred obscurity had been religiously sanctioned and sustained for millennia. Hence a residual shudder of transgression was always felt by the early scientists in their delving into the unknown, as, for example, the horror of the anatomist's violation of the sanctity of the corpse to reveal the secrets of the body. The other arcane mysteries of the universe were also guarded and had to be no less sacreligiously breached. Science was enlightening precisely because its light pierced this sanctified obscurity. And for most early scientists the light of reason never reached very far. The one who cast more than perhaps any other, the great Newton himself—whom Pope's famous couplet ironically apostrophized as the bringer of universal light—was himself aware of just how little he had illuminated and how much remained hidden: 'I do not know what I may appear to the world, but to myself I seem to have been only like a boy playing on the seashore and diverting myself in now and then finding a smoother pebble or a prettier shell than ordinary, whilst the great ocean of truth lay all undiscovered before me' (Lerner 1973, 9). Even now a conservative-minded scientist like Chargaff is conscious of the need for a sense of darkness; in his view, without it science cannot bring enlightenment.

> It would seem to me that man cannot live without mysteries. One could say, the great biologists worked in the very light of darkness. We have been deprived of this fertile night. The moon, to which as a child I used to look up on a clear night, really is no more; never again will it fill grove and glen with its soft and misty gleam. What will have to go next? I am afraid I shall be misunderstood when I say that through each of these great scientific-technological exploits the points of contact between humanity and reality are diminished irreversibly (Chargaff 1978, 109).

Science, according to Chargaff, is no longer productive of light because it is unaware of darkness. It is solely preoccupied with 'scientific-technological exploits' and 'surrounded by a surfeit of solved riddles' (ibid. 110); in other words, it has become technically exploitative and problem-solving. The nexus between science and enlightenment has been broken. And if science can no longer be enlightening, it cannot be said to bring progress in the old sense either—for technical exploits and puzzle solving are not conducive to enlightenment within the circumambient mystery of Nature.

The molecular geneticists against whom Chargaff's strictures are directed were a new breed of scientists in biology who believed they could solve the mystery of life and did not see the need to respect any other mystery of Nature. They were usually physicists by training who, on launching themselves into biology, campaigned against the established biologists precisely on the ground that these were still enamoured of mystery and darkness. They carried over from the recent successes of physics a new confidence in the inherent solvability of all problems. Leo Szilard said that the physicists brought to biology

> not any skills acquired in physics, but rather an attitude: the conviction which few biologists had at the time, that mysteries can be solved. If secrets exist they must be explainable. You see, this is something which modern biologists [i.e., post-1940] brought into biology, something which classical biologists did not have. They often were astonished, but they never felt it was their duty to explain. They lacked the faith that things are explainable—and it is this faith which leads to major advances in biology. An example is the Watson-Crick model for D.N.A. (Fleming and Bailyn, 1969, 161).

Stent, who belongs to this generation of molecular biologists, maintains that the mystery of Nature has been finally broken and that this spells an end to progress in science, but for reasons quite opposite to those put forward by Chargaff. Whereas Chargaff believes that mystery is inherent in Nature and must be respected by scientists, Stent holds that all mysteries are forever gone. All is known in principle or could be known if we only had the mind and means to do so. Faustian striving to reach ever further into the unknown is over, just as Faustian moral transgression is a thing of the past. Even the highly secularized sense of Faustian striving as a march forward towards an endless horizon is also about to disappear (Stent 1978, 8). The open frontier of science has been closed off as have all of America's other frontiers. Stent tries to show for one after another of the major areas of scientific activity that a limit is soon to be reached.

Stent begins with his own science, molecular biology. This science, according to Monod, has dissolved the mystery of life: 'the secret of life? But this is in large part known—in principle if not all details' (Judson 1977, 216). The mere spelling out of the details does not have all that much further to go; according to Stent, 'genetics is not only bounded, but its goal of understanding the mechanism of transmission of hereditary information has, in fact, been all but reached' (Stent 1978, 49). No mysteries are left, and even though 'as a subject matter for future research, molecular genetics is far from exhausted, its appeal as an arena of Faustian strife against the mysterious unknown is mainly gone' (ibid. 80). Stent believes that a few major problems are left in biology, but 'the insights offered by the Central Dogma of molecular genetics will presently provide the key for solving also these last problems' (ibid. 49). Biology and chemistry are like geography, which 'is bounded because its goal of describing the features of the earth is clearly limited. Even if the totality of the vast number of extant topographic and demographic details can never be described, it seems evident nevertheless that only a limited number of significant relations can ultimately be abstracted from these details' (ibid.). Hence, it seems that in the molecular sciences 'though the total number of possible chemical molecules is very great and the variety of reactions they can undergo vast, the goal of chemistry of understanding the principles governing the behaviour of such molecules is like the goal of geography, clearly limited' (ibid.). Further efforts in researching such disciplines only bring ever diminishing returns.

At this level Stent's argument is purely formalistic and in principle mathematical. He seems to have underestimated the problem of complexity and what it entails. Certainly the total number of chemical molecules is in principle finite and so limited, but only a Laplacean intelligence could ever survey this number for it could well be higher than the number of neurons in a human brain or greater than the information it can store. Hence, this purported limitation in principle of chemistry and biology does not in practice need to be significant for science. Even the seeming limitations of geography are of little practical relevance, as anyone engaged in oceanography, meteorology, or any other earth science which falls under the ambit of geography will be well aware. It is possible that there is nothing mysterious or still to be discovered about the weather (as opposed to climatic changes), for example, but the complexities are so great and the causal relations so non-linear that long-range weather forecasting with any exactitude may be forever impossible. Thus in some branches of meteorology as in many other sciences where nothing is any longer mysterious or unknown, a problem of systemic complexity nevertheless must be dealt with; this is in fact the real task of the science, and it is more than just the tidying up of details where the fundamentals are already known. It is like the problem of predicting the configuration of a snow crystal, though on a still higher level of difficulty. Such problems call for a very different scientific approach from that which has proved successful in molecular genetics during its classical phase.

Stent's argument for the boundedness of molecular genetics and biology in general becomes less formalistic and more substantive when he claims that the past triumphs of the subject exhaust it insofar as anything of significance for progress is concerned. And even though 'the domain of investigation of a bounded scientific discipline may well present a vast and practically inexhaustible number of events to study', yet 'there is imminent in the evolution of a bounded scientific discipline a point of diminishing returns; after the great insights have been made and brought the discipline close to its goal, further efforts are necessarily of ever-decreasing significance' (ibid.). Stent believes that there are only three such problems of detail to be worked out in biology: the origin of life, the mechanism of cellular differentiation, and the functional basis of the higher nervous system.

> In my view, the insights offered by the central dogma of molecular genetics will presently provide the keys for solving also these last problems. And, considering the host of biologists now standing ready to do battle and the vast armory of experimental hardware at its disposal, origin of life, differentiation, and the nervous system cannot help but soon suffer the fate that was accorded heredity in these last twenty years (ibid.).

As it happens, biology has not turned out to be quite as simple or as easy to unravel as Stent imagined. To begin with, the Central Dogma has been all but abrogated as, foreseen all along by its critics, such as Chargaff and Commoner, and as finally demonstrated by the work of McClintock. Gould comments as follows:

> A substance called "reverse transcriptase" can read RNA into DNA and insert new material into genetic programs by running backward along the supposedly one-way street of the central dogma. A class of objects, called retroviruses, uses this backward path, placing new material into chromosonal DNA from the outside. In short, a set of new themes—mobility, rearrangement, regulation and interaction—has transformed our view of genomes from stable and linear arrays, altered piece by piece and shielded from any interaction with their products, to fluid systems with potential for rapid reorganisation and extensive feedback from their own products and other sources of RNA. The implications for embryology and evolution are profound, and largely unexplored (Gould 1984, 3).

This new understanding has largely been made possible by the recently rediscovered and newly acknowledged work of Barbara McClintock on jumping genes, work dating from the 1950s which was long shunned and dismissed by the main dogmatic exponents of molecular biology. But now, even the very doyens of this movement, such as Crick and Brenner, are coming to realise that the problem of the mechanism of cellular differentiation—namely, the whole subject of embryology, the biology of growth and organic repair—is more difficult than genetics itself. The problems of the origin of life and the higher nervous system are likely to be even more difficult, especially the latter which is really the problem of explaining the functioning of the brain. These problems have proved to be far more than mere matters of detail once the principles of molecular genetics had been confirmed. They call for a new scientific approach very different from the classical reductive procedures still involved in the success of molecular genetics. Crick maintains that those procedures proved successful because the problem was simple and because the necessary techniques were available—the standard preconditions for Classical science:

> The other reason for the rapid progress was that at a certain stage a set of hypotheses emerged that were very simple, a well-defined theoretical framework with which we could guide experimentation and from which we could predict, to some extent, what was likely to be discovered. . . . The main reason it was possible was the nature of the nucleic-acid molecules, because the functions of these are rather limited (Judson 1979, 208).

Compared to this 'simple problem' the other problems of biology, such as cellular differentiation, are staggeringly difficult. As Crick put it, 'if you look at the problem in its full horror, it's like Rutherford surveying the atom at the beginning of subatomic physics' (ibid.).

Does it follow that in fact the opposite view from that of Stent is the truth—that progress, only in its infancy with molecular genetics, is likely to advance much further once these outstanding problems of biology are solved? This is hardly the conclusion to draw from Stent's error. Brenner, Crick's colleague, makes clear that future advances in biology will not involve the kind of progress which was provided by classical molecular genetics. He doubts 'whether the problems of developmental biology could be solved by one insight like the double helix' (ibid. 209). And he implies that the issue is not 'whether higher organisms have some unique piece of molecular biology that's unknown to us' (ibid.). In other words, there are no mysteries left in biology of the kind that existed before life was understood in molecular terms. There are no vitalist assumptions to be made such as Driesch or the earlier organicist biologists had propounded. The secret of life has been revealed, so progress in the sense of further enlightenment is no longer in question.

The future of biology does encourage the belief in further advances but not the kind that were called progress in Classical science. Thus Brenner proposes a very different approach from that which was previously so successful in molecular genetics. I shall outline this new tack in biology in Chapter 8 where I shall try to show that it relates closely to other new departures which proceed from the opposite end, such as McClintock's procedure starting with the whole organism and moving to the chemistry of its genes as contrasted with Brenner's proposal to start with the gene chemistry and try to reconstruct the organism. But both these procedures can be considered part of a new Integrative approach in biology and in science in general, an approach which is the very opposite to the reductionism of the Classical sciences still inherent to an extent in molecular genetics. Integrative science belongs with the post-classical developments of World science, and in that respect it is no longer progressive; nevertheless it must be separated and distinguished from the normal, routine manifestations of World science for it contains the seeds of future developments. Standard and worldly forms of World science, such as genetic engineering, have clearly failed to address the more difficult complexities of multi-celled organisms. The hopes entertained even as recently as a decade ago by most researchers in the field—that all problems would be solved in a routine fashion—have clearly been dashed. Genetics and biology are now in a very confused state because such earlier easy assumptions have been proved wrong. To clarify the situation it is necessary to outline the stages of development of these sciences and to distinguish the various forms they have taken.

In brief outline one might set out the stages of development of molecular biology as follows. The early pioneering period, to the 1960s, was still a progressive phase, or in Kuhnian terms, a phase of revolutionary paradigm articulation. This stage was followed by a phase of 'normal science' during which molecular biology assumed most of the characteristic features of World science and soon became genetic engineering. This development was accompanied by unwarranted optimistic beliefs that the fundamental problems of biology had been solved. Stent clearly shared these attitudes; and basing his stand on the new developments and the hopes they generated, he put forward his view that progress in this science was over. He was partly right insofar as he focused on these developments which were indeed routine and, therefore, non-progressive; but he was wrong insofar as he overlooked other developments which constitute an alternative possibility within molecular biology pointing to a future Integrative science. However, because it is doubtful whether even this line of development can be considered progressive in the same sense as Classical science, he was right despite himself but in a way he did not anticipate.

The first period of molecular biology, the stage immediately leading up to and following the epochal decoding of DNA by Crick and Watson, can still be considered part of the Classical science tradition because it is inherently reductive in narrowing down the basic problem of genetics— the 'problem of life'—to one kind of molecule and in proposing successfully a simple structural model, the double helix, for explaining this molecule. In other respects, however, even at this stage molecular genetics went beyond Classical science in that it no longer depended on simple law-like relations but on the new ideas of information storage and decoding and it made use of the highly technified x-ray methods of crystallography. Eventually the extraordinary success of molecular genetics brought the Classical science phase of biology to an end; it removed all mystery from life and transformed it into a solvable problem. At the same time it isolated and excluded the other practitioners of biology who still held that not everything had been explained, as Fox Keller notes with respect to Barbara McClintock:

The early twentieth century saw the transformation of biology into an experimental science. But for many researchers, commitment to the integrity of the organism and reverence for the opulent variety of nature, remained. Not until the advent of molecular biology did the final break with earlier tradition occur. The long-standing tension between the organism as a whole and its constituent physico-chemical parts appeared at last to be relieved. Biology could now be seen as a science of molecular mechanics, rather than of living organisms, or even of "living machines". Old-timers like McClintock who were still committed to the inherent complexity and mystery of life were expected to step aside (Fox Keller 1983, 181).

Eventually, once the basic discoveries of molecular biology were made, it began to be transformed into a mechanistic and routine undertaking, one which even some of the early pioneers now refer to as the 'vulgarization of molecular biology' and which Stent with some irony calls the Academic Period (Sibatani 1981a). It steadily developed most of the features which are characteristic of normal World sciences. It ceased being a pioneering endeavour and became an established disciplinary speciality with an accredited authority structure, textbooks and a fixed training procedure. These developments have made it less interesting to some of its own pioneers, such as Seymour Benzer who remarked that 'a field to work in, to me personally, when it becomes a discipline, becomes less attractive', and he adds, 'there's no question there are many surprises left' (Judson 1979, 271). As it became disciplined, it also became highly technified: advanced technologies were employed, and new standard techniques were developed, the most crucial among these being DNA splicing which permitted genetic engineering. This technology in turn opened up what had been a pure academic science to innumerable practical applications, some of great commercial and military value, so that the usual competition for priority and authority in science became intensified by the prospects of high material rewards. At the same time, the field proliferated in numerous directions, giving rise to what Sibatani calls a 'plethora of advancing frontiers in biochemistry and cell biology' (Sibatani 1981a). But most of this work is purely routine, carried out according to a 'methodology', as Sibatani puts it. 'In DNA sequencing, as performed today, there seems to be very little of the personal touch that existed in the original thought-collective of molecular biology' (Sibatani 1981b).

These 'normal' World science developments in molecular biology, especially the new techniques of DNA sequencing, made it seem as if all problems in biology were solvable. Sibatani records that at a conference in 1980, 'a European colleague of mine, a Drosophila developmental biologist, observed that the main group attending believed that all the problems in developmental biology could be solved by sequencing DNA' (Sibatani 1981a). Sibatani himself is extremely sceptical of this approach, but it typifies to this day the attitude of most scientists in the field. As Judson notes; 'many molecular biologists were confident—certainly most of those who had taken part in building that outline were confident—that the outline could be stretched to take care of higher organisms without great difficulty. They spoke of filling in classical molecular biology' (Judson 1979, 613). Stent evinces this attitude in his book *Paradoxes of Progress,* and it is the mistaken basis for his belief that progress is at an end in the biological sciences. His formal-mathematical argument—that biology is bounded, just as geography is, because its object is inherently circumscribed in that there is only a limited range of chemical molecules—can be diagnosed as merely a rationalization of this unwarranted feeling of confidence that the game is up in biology.

As I have tried to show, Stent was not altogether mistaken in believing that progress was over in science, but if he was right it was not for the reasons he gave or in the way that he meant it. It is true that when molecular biology moved beyond its Classical science phase, it could no longer be taken to progress in the way it had previously done. But the main reason for this new type of development is not that all molecular possibilities are in principle exhaustible but rather that molecular biology followed along the typical lines of the other World sciences and adopted methods and techniques which restricted it to tackling routinely solvable problems. As Sibatani notes in regard to this tendency:

> In 1950, one was well aware that classical biology was incapable of solving the problem of life. So it was natural to turn to molecular biology. But today it is difficult to feel the same way with DNA studies for instance. There are many things to be done on DNA, and undoubtedly many new findings are being obtained. But they are all "solvables", rather than the "unsolvables" such as were tackled in the emerging days of molecular biology (Sibatani 1981a).

Thus, the whole organized apparatus of this facet of molecular biology is directed to answering questions which Sibatani claims belong to 'enumerative biology': 'now what we are seeing is the enumerative biology of DNA, which will not end until all the varieties of DNA sequences on earth have been exhaustively recorded' (ibid.). He even proposes, ironically, that an international collection be made of all these varieties of DNA sequences and that they be stored in a kind of natural museum or 'genothec'.

We note here a tendency characteristic of many World sciences to move towards what the finalization theorists Boehme, van den Daele and Krohn call 'theoretical maturity' in science, following Heisenberg's idea of closed theories (Schäfer 1983, 133). 'Contrary to the assumptions of fallibilism (Popper, Feyerabend), the history of science exhibits the surprising phenomenon that theoretical developments arrive at a completion. Scientific theories may gain not only provisional acceptance but may also acquire classical status. Heisenberg has apostrophised such theories as "closed theories"' (Boehme et al. 1976, 316). Roughly speaking their characteristic feature is that 'they no longer can be improved by minor modifications' (ibid.). Such 'closed theories' are fundamental theories which 'already contain the basic structure of their subject matter' such that any 'further development of the discipline which deals with this research field will, therefore, be more phenomenon-oriented, more strongly determined by a practical interest in the subject matter' (ibid. 317). In Kuhnian terms, such fundamental theories are fully worked out and are complete paradigms which only leave room for further developments in application rather than in theory. Further developments in application take the form of specialised branching theories going off in various directions, usually to satisfy social or technical requirements, but all of which are mere differentiations of the fundamental theory. In Chapter 3 I shall discuss finalization as an essential characteristic of World science and examine other sciences where it is to be found.

Though some branches of molecular biology have attained theoretical maturity in this specified sense and are now closed disciplines, it is equally apparent that others are not mature and therefore are theoretically still open. These are the sub-fields where we have located tendencies towards Integrative science. They are those where 'anomalies' in the fundamental paradigm have arisen; that is, surprising discoveries have been made which show that the fundamental theory is incomplete. Sibatani lists these as follows:

> repair of DNA; fundamental differences between prokaryotes and eukaryotes in molecular machinery; fragmentary synthesis of DNA and its priming with RNA; repeated sequences of DNA; reverse transcription; jumping genes; multiple reading frames of a single DNA sequence; split genes; RNA splicing; somatic DNA switching for immunoglobulin-producing cells; and variation of the genetic code (Sibatani 1981a).

Sibatani maintains that these discoveries 'should have been regarded, at least at the outset, as meaningless' in relation to the accepted fundamental theory and he claims that they 'still elude our understanding'. He thinks that essentially what is theoretically complete is only 'a special theory for prokaryotes' and that a general theory for eukaryotes is still far from being attained (Sibatani 1981b). The early hopes of molecular biology have proved a delusion, and 'the methodology followed during the initial phase of molecular biology has collapsed' (ibid.). So he concludes in effect that 'life might still be a mystery'.

If this is so, does it follow that progress in the old sense is still possible in these areas of molecular biology? To answer this question we have simply to compare the style of work in these new fields with the old style in the Classical sciences. Progress in the pioneering days of genetics and molecular biology was possible because, as Crick claims, the problem was simple as the function of the nucleic acids was 'rather limited', or as Brenner points out, 'it could be solved by one insight like the double helix' (Judson 1979, 208–9). In other words, at this stage the science still had some of the hallmarks of old-style Classical science. Though even here there were already fundamental differences; since proteins and nucleic acids are uniquely specific to the species, 'with that vanished the possibility of a general law, or physical or chemical rule, for their assembly'; instead what was required was a code, as Judson notes (ibid. 611). However, even this procedure is no longer adequate to the problems of biology which are still unsolved, such as the ones that Sibatani lists. These problems call for a new stage of Integrative science which is no longer a matter of discovering unique simple laws or even one code or model of very wide generality but instead involves a reconstructive effort aimed at the intensive unravelling and decoding of extremely complex biological processes such as take place in embryology or growth and renovation. This kind of unknotting of detailed mechanisms requires a new style of work which, according to Brenner, involves 'algorithms, recipes, procedures': as he states, 'I believe that in biology, programmatic explanations will be algorithmic explanations' (ibid. 221). He likens this approach more to the building of computer programs than to law-like explanation in the old Classical science style.

In conclusion, it has become apparent that the issue of progress in science appears to be very different in the main dominant tendency of molecular biology, which leads to the 'mature' science of genetic engineering, than it appears in the exploratory field of biology where an Integrative science approach is arising. But in neither field is progress in the old sense to be expected. Sibatani, who examines both these tendencies, implicitly confirms this conclusion. He distinguishes the two approaches in Kuhnian terms as the pursuit of 'normal' science, following what he calls the scientific revolution in molecular genetics during Stent's so-called Dogmatic Period (1953–63), and as the attempt by the original founders of this revolution, such as Crick, Stent, Brenner, Benzer, Watson and others including himself, to carry through a second scientific revolution, so far without success. He sees the original revolutionary founders as having left voluntarily or been pushed out of the 'normal' science developments, for, as he states, 'in an era of "high-speed" science the initial revolutionaries/founders of the paradigm may become superfluous to the field' (Sibatani 1981c, 283). He puts the issue in obvious academic political terms as a clash between two elite groups:

> The founders of molecular biology were revolutionaries, and might be variously described as young Turks or guerilla forces; as open-frank-non-competitive or playful-and-rebellious. Their minority status made them a close-knit community. By contrast, the second-generation molecular biologists were and are workers for a Kuhnian normal science, the character of which may often be exactly the opposite to revolutionary. We find them steadily working within the new paradigm and legitimizing its orthodoxy (ibid. 283).

(I shall examine such legitimations of authority in Part Two of this book.) The original founders then turned to investigating problems in biology dealing with greater complexities and more developed organisms under the mistaken impression that these would yield to the kind of treatment that had been so successful at the start of molecular genetics. But a second scientific revolution did not ensue. These problems of complexity require methods of integration which have so far resisted formulation: 'The remaining perennial problems in biology all represent very complex phenomena, for which the choice of simple systems may not be the right answer. We may have to devise wholly new methods for solving these complex problems' (ibid. 284).

In their search for new methods, many biologists now are returning to some of the old formulations. Thus, Sibatani points out that 'in a certain school of developmental biologists there is now sympathy towards reviving Hans Driesch (1891)—the notorious protagonist of neovitalism whose preaching has been almost totally banned in science' (ibid. 285). Nevertheless, this is not some kind of regression to Classical science; as Sibatani makes clear, Driesch is being invoked 'not for the answer he devised but for the problem he raised: the size-independent regulation of the morphogenetic field with flexible epigenetics' (ibid.). Modern biologists are dealing with these problems in a spirit that follows the great reductive achievements of molecular biology, even though many of the assumptions of the early days of that science, such as the search for molecular specificity, no longer hold. Hence, there is no place in the new science for any mysterious vital forces.

Life still has surprises in store for science, even if it no longer contains any of the old mysteries. The biological phenomena of living organisms have been finally reduced to biochemical processes and molecular structures. Thus, the basic reductive program of the Classical sciences has been vindicated. The work that now proceeds, though integrative and no longer reductive, is also characterized by an absence of mystery. In other words the Enlightenment stage of science is over and progress in that sense is at an end.

Progress as Reduction

The idea of progress, with its connotations of the breaking of mysteries, was also intimately linked to the reductive and unifying program of Classical science. Progress was measured in terms of the basic reductive moves that had been accomplished, and with every such move a greater degree of unity was attained in science. The more basic the entities to which everything could be reduced, the more coherent became the overall structure of the sciences. Thus in biology, as we have seen, every reductive step unified further the diverse areas of organic being and broke another seal of the secrets of life. Mysteries were unveiled when the growth of organisms was shown to be reducible to the division of cells, when the life of cells was reduced to bio-chemical processes, when the bio-chemical process of the cell nucleus was reduced to a function of the chemical arrangement of DNA, and finally when DNA was decoded as a structure of simple atoms. With the last the reduction of life was complete and the unity of all biological phenomena established as variants of DNA, so Watson in his Nobel prize speech could justifiably declare: 'at that time we knew that a new world had been opened up and that an old world which seemed mystical was gone' (Judson 1977, 581).

Something like this program of progress through reduction and unification was operative throughout the history of Classical science. The reduction of the basic entities of one science to those of a more fundamental one always marked a step in progress. Thus, for example, the reduction of the chemistry of elements to the physics of atomic structure was a crucial development in the progress of science completed by quantum mechanics. The more such reductions were accomplished the more it seemed as if all the sciences could finally be unified by being reduced to the one basic theory, which obviously would have to be some version of physics. With the final reduction the task of science would be complete and its progress at an end.

Heisenberg voices such a view when he claims that the progress of science is well nigh over because he has finally succeeded in unifying all of physics with his Unified Field theory. His colleague Weizsäcker insists 'that physics is characterized by a greater real conceptual unity today than at any time in its history' and 'that completing the conceptual unity of physics is a finite task, and that this task will be solved someday in history—a day that might even be close—if mankind does not ruin itself physically or spiritually before then' (Weizsäcker 1980, 168). Both Heisenberg and Weizsäcker see the history of physics, and by implication the whole of science, as a sequence of ever more unified, all embracing theories, each a 'closed theory' in that it cannot be corrected or 'improved by small changes', but each in turn taken up into the framework of a larger theory as a special case: 'A development of this sort occurred repeatedly in the history of physics: think of classical mechanics, electrodynamics, special relativity, quantum mechanics; we hope for the same development in the physics of elementary particles. In this process the earlier theories are modified by the later ones' (ibid. 169). At the present stage of the development of physics Weizsäcker believes that there are only five fundamental theories: 'a theory of space-time structure (special or perhaps general relativity), a general mechanics (quantum theory), a theory of possible species of objects (elementary particle theory), a theory of irreversibility (statistical thermodynamics), and a theory of the totality of physical objects (cosmology)' (ibid. 189). The project for a total unity of science would thus require the unification of these fundamental theories of physics. Weizsäcker holds that it is 'both necessary and possible to combine these three disciplines—quantum mechanics, elementary particle theory, cosmology—in a unified argument' (ibid. 179). This process requires that 'one ought to try to deduce elementary particle physics and cosmology from quantum mechanics' (ibid. 180). Like Heisenberg, Weizsäcker 'conjectures that elementary particle theory and cosmology are already logical consequences of a quantum mechanics in which one requires the forces themselves to be described as objects, i.e. in the end as fields' (ibid. 180), so that a Unified Field theory would complete physics.

Such a total unification of physics is still far from being accomplished, but work toward it is proceeding apace. The four fundamental forces—gravity, electromagnetism, the strong force and the weak force—seem to be coming together. The unity of electromagnetism and the weak force, or the so-called electroweak field postulated by Weinberg and Salam, has been confirmed by the recent discovery of W and Z particles. Already a Grand Unified Theory is being mooted to embrace the strong force and gravity as well. At the same time a basic constitution of matter as made up of six kinds of quarks and six leptons is emerging with new evidence for the sixth or 'top' quark. In the light of these recent successes, are we to say with Weizsäcker and Heisenberg that physics will soon be unified and that therefore the progress of science will come to an end?

But it is not as simple as that because physics seems to have entered a highly paradoxical state; while many are foreseeing the completion of the grand project begun centuries ago in the one unified theory, others see the whole structure collapsing in confusion. Where some already speak of one 'superforce' and a 'perfect symmetry' of total unity, others are equally convinced that the very bases of these theories are flawed, that even quantum theory is riddled with paradoxes, or, metaphorically, that Heisenberg's cathedral is built on shifting sands. As Briggs and Peat put it:

> Bohr had said in his Copenhagen interpretation that the quantum paradigm was paradoxical. At what point does paradox become confusion? Some scientists are beginning to feel that point has been reached. Are the laws of nature eternal and contradictory? Some commentators, including Kuhn, feel that contemporary physics, now dominated by quantum theory, relativity and the pursuit of grand unification, is in a paradigm crisis (Briggs and Peat 1985, 94–5).

Before examining the sources of confusion and limitation in physics and the possible break-down of its seemingly unimpeded progress towards completion, let us first consider Stent's formal arguments against its perpetual progress. He begins with purely formal limits, following some ideas of Pierre Auger, such as that 'there are purely physical limits to physics because of man's own boundaries of time and energy' (Stent 1978, 50). An example of such limits is the impossibility of observing events in the universe more than 10–15 billion light years distant. He then goes on to expound a heuristic and a semantic limit as well. The first arises from the formal impossibility of ever arriving at an end term either in the dimension of the very small or the very large:

> Insofar as I am able to judge, the frontier disciplines at the two open ends of physics, cosmology and high-energy physics, seem to be moving rapidly toward a state in which it is becoming progressively less clear what it actually is that one is trying to find out. What, actually, would it mean if one understood the origin of the universe? And what would it mean if one finally found the most fundamental of the fundamental particles? Thus the pursuit of an open-ended science also seems to embody a point of diminishing intellectual return. That point is reached with the realization that its goal turns out to be hidden in an endless, and ultimately tiresome succession of Chinese boxes (ibid. 51).

And finally, Stent puts forward what he calls the semantic limit to the effect that the concepts of physics have lost any contact with ordinary language and intuitive conceptions and that as a result they have become 'semantically meaningless symbols' (Stent 1979, 9).

Stent's arguments do not seem very convincing as they stand for similar reasons to those we directed against his argument for the exhaustion of possibilities by which he tried to show the boundedness of biology and chemistry. The purely physical limits of physics are so distant that they may have no effect in the time span of the likely history of science. The so-called heuristic limit hardly seems a limit at all since it points out that there does not need to be an end or final goal to the pursuit of initial states or fundamental entities in physics. But it does not follow from this that the further into fundamentals physics proceeds the less is gained for knowledge; the law of diminishing returns need not apply; new discoveries at the frontiers of physics may force a total revision of the whole science, as happened at the time of the young Einstein when it was also thought that everything was basically known and all that was left to do was to put in the decimal points. And finally, the semantic limit is not so much a limit to the development of physics as a science as to its relevance for culture in general, as I shall show in Chapter 6.

Stent's arguments for the limits of physics seem mistaken as they stand, but they nevertheless point to problems which might amount to at least historical limitations, though not absolute limits, about which it would be pointless to speculate. Thus the so-called physical limits of physics might have more immediate relevance if restated as socio-economic constraints. The size and energy requirements of instruments such as cyclotrons and space probes are already coming up against the limits of what can feasibly be built. Thus, a machine ten times bigger than the planned CERN collider called LEP (large electron-positron) would call for a ring 100 times larger than its 27 kilometres, in other words, a 2,700-kilometre tunnel, which is not practically feasible. Some proposals even now being mooted would absorb sizeable proportions of national budgets. Hence if the progress of physics depended solely on the continual expansion of such large-scale instruments then there must be a deceleration in the rate of such progress for socio-economic reasons alone, if not for technological ones as well (Rescher 1978). And in any case, even if these limits were to be overcome for some time still, it is doubtful whether all that much would be gained for the progress of knowledge, for it is already becoming apparent that the knowledge gained through sheer increase in the level of technification is not all that significant. As Dyson states concerning such developments, 'the long-range prospects of going on with accelerator physics in this style are not good . . . we are running into a law of steeply diminishing returns' (Dyson 1970). And Ravetz is even more pessimistic, according to him 'nuclear physics now finds itself at a dinosaur state: unable to evolve further, it awaits extinction unless some happy accident rescues it' (Ravetz 1971, 61). Thus it is not so much that there must be absolute limits to knowledge in physics as such—which is what Rescher seeks to counter— but rather that limitations to significant knowledge have arisen in physics as it is currently being pursued, that is, as a highly technified World science proceeding in the style it has assumed since the Manhattan Project. As the Roses put it:

What is finite is not the total of scientific knowledge, but the total of meaningful scientific knowledge—that is, knowledge which significantly extends man's understanding of himself and his world. The first synthesis of an unnatural element was an intellectual and technical achievement. Elements 100, 101, 102 may be worth working for. Elements 120, 130, 140, 150? . . . . And a precisely similar argument may well apply to the investigations by the particle physicists which demand the 300 machine—a vastly more expensive enterprise (Rose and Rose 1976, 252).

And in all, something like this situation seems to have already arisen in particle physics, as one reporter comments:

> The field has been dominated for two generations by the glittering abstractions of high-energy particles and quantum mechanics. The achievements have changed the 20th-century landscape. But to some—especially younger physicists—progress year to year is beginning to seem cluttered. There has long been a feeling, not always expressed openly, that theoretical physics has strayed far from human intuition about the world (Gleick 1985, 58).

Physics proceeding in its current style seems also to have reached something approximating a heuristic limit, though not in Stent's sense. The experimental findings generated by the huge technological instruments at the level of the very small and very large, in particle physics and astro-physics, seem to be more and more out of step with theory elaborations. Monstrous anomalies have arisen, and purely ad hoc theorizing is being utilized to try to account for them. Already the word 'confusion' is being invoked in this context.

> Experiments with new and more powerful research tools . . . have thrown into turmoil science's efforts to comprehend nature on its most basic level. In the words of Dr. Wolfgang K.H. Panofsky, who is the director of the Stanford Linear Accelerator in California, the new findings there and elsewhere have led to a "state of maximum confusion" in the world of physics. . . . Dr. Panofsky, commenting on the turmoil consequent to the new surprising experimental findings said that physicists were being forced to consider such "crackpot" ideas as the possibility that the electron has internal structure of some sort (*Science in the Twentieth Century* 1976, 78–9).

Along with such 'crackpot ideas', new theories are being put forward which no longer make sense in terms of the Classical scientific tradition, but which seem to be reinvoking metaphysical conceptions, such as Steven Weinberg's suggestion which harks back to the Platonic conception that Nature is somehow illusory and not to be completely trusted: 'Dr. Weinberg . . . suspects that the really fundamental laws of nature are not, in all cases, directly manifest. They may instead be only imperfectly demonstrated by observed phenomena . . . and that nature, as we observe it, is but an imperfect representation of its own underlying laws' (ibid.). Reports on current developments in astro-physics tell a similar story of confusion and barely intelligible proposals which go counter to the whole conception of science. 'Recent astronomical observations have so shaken the foundations of current theory that some physicists are proposing that laws governing events here and now may not be valid in other regions of space and time' (ibid. 117). And not only is the universality of the laws of Nature denied, but other monstrous ideas abound: 'virtual particles' that can never in principle be perceived are postulated; barely meaningful speculations abound as to what goes on at the other end of black holes; analogous speculations are entertained as to what happened in the first ten-thousandth of a second after the start of the universe; the spontaneous generation of matter out of nothing is believed possible; it is thought that 'the entire universe, including the time in which it exists, may have been created by a spontaneous quantum fluctuation—a "twitch" in the nothingness that preceded it' (Browne 1980); and some cosmologists, such as Alan Guth and Sheldon Glashow, believe that alternative universes might in principle be created at will and that, once generated, such a new universe could no longer be perceived or reached from this one. On the other hand, sceptics deny that the Doppler effect should be interpreted as the recession of the galaxies, which is the foundation of all current cosmologies. The situation in astrophysics and cosmology reminds one of the problem that Wittgenstein diagnosed in psychology: 'there are experimental methods and conceptual confusion. . . . The existence of experimental methods makes us think we have the means of solving the problems which trouble us; though problem and method pass one another by' (Wittgenstein 1956, 232).

Clear symptoms suggest that the sciences of the outer frontiers of knowledge are reaching some kind of heuristic limit of intelligibility, at least in their present form. It is possible, therefore, that these frontiers will steadily collapse into the anarchy of experimental anomalies and theoretical confusions and in that sense they may be temporarily closed off. Thus whatever one may speculate about the limits of the physical sciences in any absolute sense, they undeniably have reached historical limitations. The sense that classical physics purveyed of continually progressing into the unknown and uncovering the mysteries of space, time, matter and energy can no longer be sustained. If the physical sciences can still be said to progress then they do so in a very different sense. Although their courses are unpredictable, it is becoming increasingly doubtful whether they lead towards some ultimate revelation of the basic nature of things.

However, one frontier of knowledge is still to be considered—the inner frontier of humankind, or the human body and mind. This study is the concern of both the natural sciences such as medicine and neurology and the social sciences such as psychology and sociology. Stent argues that in both these areas a limit to knowledge has been reached and that this frontier is also now closed. The progress of science is coming to an end even in those fields which have usually been considered so undeveloped and therefore so full of potential for the advancement of knowledge. Once again, I shall try to show that his reasoning is mistaken, although there is a valid point to his claim.

Neurology, the science of the brain, is perhaps the most important of the natural sciences dealing with humans. It has recently attracted many of the molecular biologists, such as Crick and Stent, who at one time believed that most problems in biology had in principle been solved. It has also attracted scientists from many other disciplines, such as cybernetics and Artificial Intelligence, for they, too, look on the brain as in some ways the last frontier. Thus from every direction of the medical and the other natural sciences a concerted assault is being mounted on the brain, one of the last unexplored regions of science. The stakes are very high because in this area, perhaps more than in any other, knowledge brings control, and control spells power. All the researchers into the functioning of the brain believe that this approach is the only way of gaining objective scientific knowledge of the behaviour of human beings, the kind of knowledge already obtained for the rest of the human body.

Stent, however, maintains that a limit to the possibility of objective knowledge is fast approaching in neurology. He holds that at least in those more interesting fields which involve 'system-analytical studies of the structure and function of large and very complicated networks', where 'neural networks approach the psyche in their complexity', 'neurology takes on some of the characteristics of hermeneutics' (Stent 1979, 17). In a lengthy paper focussing on the work of David Marr on the computer modeling of pattern vision in Artificial Intelligence, Stent argues that 'the student of a complex neural network must bring considerable pre-understanding to the system as a whole before attempting to interpret the function of any of its parts' (Stent 1981, 123). Because numerous such pre-understanding standpoints are possible and because, therefore, a number of alternative interpretations or models can be offered for any one brain function, Stent concludes that 'the explorations that are advanced about complex neural systems may remain beyond the reach of objective validation' (ibid.). This he calls a cognitive limit to science.

I shall return to this argument in Chapter 8 and try to show that the question of objective validation is not at issue. Any model of the brain can be tested as against alternative models, and that condition is sufficient for the possibility of objective validation. However, Stent's interpretation of what is involved in the construction of models of brain functions does make it apparent that the science of neurology and associated sciences such as Artificial Intelligence no longer proceed in the same way as the Classical sciences do, or as neurology still does where it is solely concerned with electrophysiological, anatomical and biochemical studies of single nerve cells. Current work in neurology will not produce a theory of the brain in the Classical science sense of a single unified law or description covering the innumerable performances, functions and modes of behaviour of the one complex system. Even the most optimistic exponents of Artificial Intelligence are being forced to acknowledge this kind of conclusion, as Jeremy Bernstein notes in a conversation with Marvin Minsky:

> What would it mean to understand the mind? It is difficult to imagine that it will consist of an enumeration of the component parts. . . . People, like Minsky and others working in the field, believe that in time the functional parts of the brain will be identified and their function described in some language we can understand. They admit that at least in principle it is possible that no such description exists, or not in any single form of language that would enable us to understand the entire picture in a unified sense. Of one thing the present workers in the field seem sure: that the description, whatever it is, will not be like the great unifying descriptions in physics in which a single equation or a few equations can be derived from what appears to be almost self-evident principles, and which describe and predict vast realms of phenomena. If the artificial intelligence programmes are a clue, the more lifelike they become, the more they resist simple description in mathematical terms (Bernstein 1982, 122).

Thus, regardless of the validity of Stent's absolute cognitive limit, the kind of progress which was expected from the Classical sciences will no longer be forthcoming in this latest round of scientific attacks on the inner frontier. The sciences of the brain will not proceed through a series of simplifying reductions and unifications to produce finally the one grand neural theory. Advances will certainly continue to be made, but they will have a totally different character from those regarded as progress in the Classical sciences. Thus, progress is not at an end in any unequivocal sense, but rather the nature and meaning of what is called progress are changing in the context of the new scientific epoch. And once again no mysteries in the old sense are to be plumbed; the secrets of the mind and its relationship to matter are no longer the questions at issue; all that is involved is the staggering complexity of neural networks. In one sense there is nothing mysterious about that complexity, but at the same time this fact does not make the task any easier because the complexity is so great that it defies complete description.

Something similar also holds for the other sciences of the mind, the social and cultural sciences. For these, too, Stent tries to devise a cognitive limit in order to show that further progress towards objective knowledge is impossible beyond a certain point. Stent refers to Mandelbrot's mathematical researches in econometric statistics, such as fluctuations of the price of cotton which follow a Pareto distribution (Stent 1978, 57). Mandelbrot argues on this basis that no law can be established for such seemingly random phenomena, among which fall many social activities. Mandelbrot calls this the second stage of indeterminism, the first stage being that of the indeterministic sciences such as the kinetic law of gases and quantum mechanics. At the second stage of indeterminism even statistical laws are not possible. Hence, Stent concludes that the degree of scientific objectivity possible in the social sciences is limited. 'For that reason it may be a vain hope to expect an imminent flowering of the social sciences'; they are in principle precluded from progressing very much further and certainly can never attain the proper scientific status of the natural sciences (Stent 1979, 14).

It may, indeed, be a vain hope to expect an imminent flowering of the social sciences, but not for that reason. It is futile to expect the social sciences to have the law-like exactitude of the natural sciences. And at best this is all that Mandelbrot's argument shows. The general fluctuations in the price of cotton or any other such social sequential process cannot be covered by any one single statistical formula. But from this irreducibility to a single generalization it does not follow that no objective scientific explanation is possible for any one instance of the rise or fall in the price of cotton on any one historical occasion. Such an explanation can be as objective as necessary in the social sciences, taking into consideration all the factors that can be recognized as affecting the prices of commodities on the market. This kind of specific historical explanation has its own norms of objectivity which are very different from those appropriate to the natural sciences, as Max Weber has shown in his methodological studies (Weber 1949). Objectivity in the social sciences does not depend on law-like generalizations but on historically specific causal imputation. Although no laws of history exist in a strict sense, causal connections in terms of which general hypotheses can be framed are objectively ascertainable. Weber's work is full of such hypotheses and their objective validation.

An imminent flowering of the social sciences cannot be expected partly because the norms of objectivity appropriate to the natural sciences have been imposed on them, and as a result, they have become reified and stunted. Mandelbrot's statistical study in econometrics is but one example of this trend, so prominent in the World sciences of the post-war era. Econometrics, a science typical of the new dispensation, is an attempt to quantify economic data and subject them to strict mathematical analysis. It is an objectifying technique very different from economic theorizing. In an analogous manner, recent developments in the other social sciences have brought to an end the previous attempts at large-scale theories of society and history. And perhaps this fact, rather than any inherent limits, gives the impression of a lack of progress in these sciences.

I conclude this whole dispute with Stent by re-affirming that no absolute limits for scientific knowledge such as he tries to draw can be ascertained but that there are limitations that the sciences will encounter at given periods in their historical and social development. There were such limitations to the development of the sciences in the ancient world for which extensive explanations can be given in terms of both the external socio-logical factors governing those sciences and their inner cognitive content. From the contemporary vantage point the Classical sciences of the recent European past also appear to have encountered similar historically deter-mined limitations to their further progress. What eventuated was a new kind of science I have called World science. In this new guise science does not cease to discover new knowledge or to develop and in that way to advance, but this development is of a very different nature from that of Classical progress when science was the source of enlightenment and when a unified corpus of laws of Nature was first determined. The present transition of the sciences is perhaps as historically momentous as that of ancient science; it too will need to be explained both externally in terms of the outside social forces influencing science (such as the two world wars) and internally in terms of the content of scientific theorizing itself (such as the conclusion of the reductive program).

Progress as Rationality

One final argument for the continuity of progress in science is that based on its inherent rationality. It can be contended that as long as science proceeds, knowledge must become more rational since the less rational forms of knowledge are discarded. But progress simply means the growth of rational knowledge. Hence, it follows that as science proceeds and knowledge becomes more rational it ipso facto must progress. Thus rational progress is made to appear as a kind of evolutionary law of science.

In the Enlightenment tradition of science, rationality and progress were so inextricably linked as to be almost mutually definable. Beginning with Bacon and Descartes, scientific method was identified with rational thought.

It was considered a new logic (Novum Organum) which was to take over from the older Aristotelian logic (Organon). But whereas the old logic was final and fixed and, so it was thought, could not advance further, the new logic was thought to be inherently progressive, continually productive of newer and better knowledge. This knowledge was taken as the motive force for all other progressive developments in history. Thus the ésprit du raison, as embodied mainly in science, became for the French philosophes the principle of progressive enlightenment for all civilization.

The enlightenment thinkers of the eighteenth century assumed that reason was constitutive of progress, that history progressed because humankind was becoming more rational. However, in the subsequent Historicist phase of the nineteenth century, this relation was reversed and progress was held to be constitutive of reason. At its most explicit, for example among the Marxists, it was maintained that rationality is simply that which is more progressive. No method, approach or science was taken as rational in itself; it was only rational insofar as and for as long as it contributed to historical progress. Thus, every science is only rational so long as it has not been superseded by a superior science.

The inevitable dialectical tension between Enlightenment rationalist progressivism and Historicist progressivist rationalism has been re-enacted within contemporary approaches to science. The present-day exponents of scientific method in the Enlightenment tradition consider progress to be the outcome of rationality. Thus, Popper argues in his numerous works that scientific thought, because it is rational and subject to the self-critical and self-correcting norms of falsificationist method, must lead to the progress of knowledge and to all the other forms of progressive enlightenment and libertarianism, above all as tolerance of criticism, leading ultimately to the freedoms of an open society. On the other hand, the Historicist sociologists of science such as Lakatos, Kuhn, Toulmin and Laudan maintain that the progressiveness of scientific thought determines and defines its rationality. Thus according to Kuhn a new scientific paradigm is more rational than its predecessor in the same science because it is a revolutionary way of coping with anomalies and because it constitutes a new historical stage in the development of the science (Kuhn 1964). A scientific revolution is rational not because it conforms to some pre-established universal norm of rationality, such as a scientific method, but only because it is a further step in the historical progress of science. Toulmin has put forward a more gradualist evolutionary version of a similar Historicism based on a neo-Darwinist conception of a survival of the fittest among concepts and theories in science (Toulmin 1972). Laudan has sought to provide a scholarly compromise—what he calls 'a healthy middle ground'—between the divergent views of Lakatos, Kuhn and Toulmin. He defines rationality in science in terms of the relative rates of progress of research traditions, maintaining that 'it is always rational to pursue any research tradition which has a higher rate of progress than its rivals (even if the former has a lower problem-solving effectiveness)' (Laudan 1978, 111). Hence, according to this view, 'the chief way of being scientifically reasonable or rational is to do whatever we can to maximize the progress of scientific research traditions' (ibid. 124). Laudan expressly states that he wishes to turn the usual Enlightenment view on its head: instead of 'progress [being] seen as a successive attainment of the truth by a process of approximation and self-correction' to 'make rationality parasitic upon progressiveness: to make rational choices is, on this view, to make choices which are progressive' (ibid. 125).

On either of these approaches to progress and rationality in science, whether Enlightenment or Historicist, the current state of World science must be taken to be both more rational and more progressive than the previous stage of Classical science. Either that or—what is on these views hardly admissable and even unthinkable—science must be judged to have entered a regressive phase in which it has become less progressive and so by definition less rational than before. And, based on these views, to speak of science as regressing and becoming less rational is to speak of it as in effect becoming less scientific. Hence, any denial of the continuing progress of science is always interpreted as a denial of science itself. Thus criticism of current science is usually taken by its conservative exponents as an irrationalist attack on science, and any attempt to secure recognition of the changed nature of contemporary science is treated as a threat to science. The position maintained in this work—that current World science is intrinsically different from Classical science—continually runs up against this problem of the equation of progress with rationality. To avoid being treated as some kind of an irrationalist critique of science, it must seek to preclude any possible misunderstanding on this score.

The resolution of this problem requires an even more radical step than the idea already expounded that there are historically distinct stages of science; that is the further idea that there are also different modes of rationality. Within the Western history of science we can distinguish at least three basic forms of rationality: Reason, Rationalism, and Rationalization (Redner 1986). Each of these is an inherently distinct form of rationality, and though comparison between the three forms is possible, for they are not incommensurable, yet such comparisons are not carried out in terms of some superordinating universal principle that underlies these historical ones. Rationality cannot be unitary and universal, for it has numerous historically developing forms which cannot be ordered linearly according to the one dimension of rational progress. Nor are they necessarily successive, for in the history of Western science approaches which exemplify aspects of Reason or Rationalism or Rationalization can occur at all times. Formalized geometry, which is an instance of Rationalization, is already fully developed within ancient science; critical scientific method and even experimentation, which exemplify Rationalism, can also be found in ancient and medieval science; and the kind of system building characteristic of metaphysical Reason is also present in the Idealist episodes of nineteenth-century Naturphilosophie and in twentieth century speculative science such as General Systems Theory. Nevertheless, despite the historical ubiquity of all three forms of rationality, in a given scientific epoch usually only one tends to be dominant. Reason was dominant as Aristotelian science during the ancient and medieval periods; Rationalism was dominant as Newtonian science during the period of Classical science in general; and now Rationalization has become dominant in World science.

To say that a form of rationality is dominant in a given epoch of science is not necessarily to imply that it was consciously expounded and adhered to by all scientific practitioners. Rather, this assertion is based on a sociological reconstruction of a selection of cases of rational ideas, beliefs and practices, specific to and characteristic of the discourse in which they inhere, to be found at a given time and culture. Hence, each of these forms of rationality is an ideal-type construct in Weber's sense. I define Reason, Rationalism and Rationalization as ideal types abstracted from the innumerable rational discourses and practices to be found in different scientific cultures in the West. And like all such ideal-typical definitions, these call for selection, abstraction, simplification and to some degree distortion of the actual ideas and beliefs current in specific historical discourses and practices. Such ideal types are not meant to be historically accurate portrayals—in a sense they are historical 'utopias' which nowhere exist exactly as set down—only analytically useful constructions created for purposes of comparison on account of their clarity and comprehensibility (ibid. 367–398).

I begin with an ideal-type definition of Reason which historically first arises as the *logos* of Greek philosophy; subsequently it becomes translated—and so inevitably transformed—into the Latin *ratio* of scholasticism and finally close to the current time into the *Vernunft* of classical German philosophy. Each of these fundamental philosophical concepts underlies a very different approach to science, but nevertheless each is related to the others as historical phases of the one tradition of philosophical Reason. Thus, Greek science was metaphysically based in accordance with the norms of the Logos as most decisively and influentially formulated by Aristotle. Aristotle's *Metaphysics* together with his *Organon* constitute an attempt at a unification of the extant sciences on the basis of a metaphysical conception of Reason. The basic concepts of this conception are the well-known Aristotelian terms: 'morphos', 'hyle', 'energeia', 'dynamis', 'entelecheia' and the formal, material, efficient and final causes. These figured from then on as the basic concepts of Aristotelian science, even when, as in medieval impetus theory, they went against the views of Aristotle himself. The rational mode of procedure typical of this science is a preoccupation with (1) definitions of concepts (discovering the essence of things); (2) categorization (the distinction and subsumtion of things under genus proximum and differentia specifica); (3) derivation of lower categories from higher ones; and (4) the unification of them all into a hierarchical system, leading ultimately to a generalized architectonic of Being as the apparent starting point or first principle. The Stoic philosophy dominant during Hellenistic and Roman times developed somewhat different theories as compared to the strictly Peripatetic, especially in logic and physics, and pursued the idea of a world system (systema) more rigorously than Aristotle, but in essentials it did not depart from this approach. Medieval science, too, following a more numerically proportional conception of Ratio, revised the Aristotelian corpus, developing new theories of optics and mechanics (impetus theory), without ultimately departing from the basic norms of Reason. Even the German philosophy of Vernunft, especially as expounded scientifically in the Idealist program of a Naturphilosophie, though a departure from Aristotelian science, nevertheless remained within the ambit of the tradition of Reason. It sought to ground science on a conception of dialectical Reason and to build up an encyclopaedic system of all rational knowledge. Perhaps a last surviving representative of an approach to science based on Reason is to be found in certain aspects of General System Theory. Thus, even now this form of rationality has not been completely eliminated from science, though obviously it has been much reduced, largely as a result of the general onslaught on metaphysics in modern times.

The attack on Reason in science first began as a rejection of Aristotelian science and medieval scholasticism during the course of the Scientific Revolution. With the emergence of the new sciences and philosophies another form of rationality, Rationalism, became dominant. But Rationalism did not begin at that time from scratch; in key respects it, too, went back to some of the ancient Greek philosophers, above all to the Atomists, Sophists and Sceptics who deployed rationalist modes of critical thought against the so-called Dogmatics. But this critical spirit fell into abeyance during the intervening Christian period of the imposition of the dogmas of metaphysics and theology, and it had to be reconstituted anew in the context of the Scientific Revolution. Rationalism—variously translated and understood as the ésprit de raison, as Verstand, as empirical or positive reason and as subjective rationality—once in force remained dominant from Newton till Einstein, who was one of its last great exponents in science. Einstein's refusal to accept the indeterminism of the Copenhagen interpretation of quantum mechanics—as he said, 'God does not play dice with the world'—was the expression of his refusal to surrender a Rationalist approach to science. Bohr recounts that his debates with Einstein took the quasi-whimsical form of trying to decide what Spinoza, the Rationalist philosopher par excellence, would have made of the new developments, Einstein being intent on arguing that these would still have to be in keeping with basic Rationalist principles such as that of causality (Bohr 1963, 56).

Such principles of modern Rationalism were philosophically defined by the Empiricist and Rationalist philosophers in the context of scientific method. This so-called method—which had in fact little reference to the actual practices of the sciences—might now retrospectively be seen as simply the philosophical attempt to establish Rationalist underpinnings for the new scientific culture. The main principle of this Rationalism was in fact reduction, first presented by these philosophers as follows: to be known an object has to be analysed or anatomized and so reduced to its elementary terms, then reconstituted through an act of synthesis; and finally apprehended only when it had been thus rationally reconstructed. Thus, knowledge involves understanding an object through its perspicuous representation carried out either in mathematical terms, as in so-called natural philosophy, or in the form of a classificatory table on the basis of characteristics, signs and symptoms, as in natural history and the other sciences (Foucault 1970). Representation, the main aim of science, permits the attainment of certainty and clarity—key values of Rationalism from which the idea of Enlightenment derives. The main outcome of this approach and of scientific method in general was the constantation of the so-called laws of nature such as those of Newtonian mechanics. In the second phase of Classical science, during the nineteenth century, laws of nature were also conceived of as evolutionary sequences or laws of progress and referred to all temporal and historical phenomena. Thus the idea of progress was itself a function of Rationalism to whose thought context it inherently belongs.

The changed character of science in the post–Second World War period entailed a gradual departure from Rationalism and the emergence of a scientific approach characterized by another form of rationality: Rationalization, also called instrumental reason, formal rationality, and Zweckrationalität. This is not to say that Rationalism completely disappeared or that Rationalization emerged suddenly without preparation out of nowhere. On the contrary, most of the tenets of Rationalism were still consciously adhered to by most scientists even when they had long departed in their scientific practices from the procedures of Classical science that made these meaningful. Hence Rationalism might be said to serve a somewhat ideological function in the present situation of transition in maintaining the persistence of an ideal view of science that serves partly to disguise the actual changes taking place. Behind the backs of scientists themselves and only dimly apparent to them, the actual practice of science is becoming steadily more rationalized. This process might be said to have begun in the last century with the establishment of Liebig's laboratory, even more so with Edison's factory for inventions, and as gradually in all areas science began to become systematic, routinized and planned. But not till after the Second World War did Rationalization become the dominant principle in nearly all branches of scientific enquiry (Redner 1986, 81–2). At present rationalized research involves teams practicing an intricate division of labour, utilizing high-precision technological equipment and proceeding according to planned routines of work. Not only the work procedure but also the very method and intellectual content of science have become rationalized. As I shall show in Chapter 3, the main features of the new approach in science involving technification, formalization, abstraction, problem-solving and finalization are in fact characteristics of Rationalization.

This rationalization of the work methods of science was a slow process which has only been partially completed in the present stage of what Ravetz calls 'industrial science' (Ravetz 1971). It first began as early as the foundation of Liebig's chemical laboratory at Giessen, for, as Whitley shows, Liebig's practice of employing students during their training to do research required rationalizing procedures, such as the standardization of equipment, 'fairly simple and reliable technical procedures', 'a rational division of labour', more refined or 'purer' raw materials, and in general a reduction in what he calls 'task uncertainty' (Whitley 1982, 320–5). The reduction of task uncertainty has continued to be one of the main driving forces calling for ever greater rationalization, which has meant ensuring exact replicability in all aspects of scientific work. As Whitley observes: 'the more control scientists can exert over their cognitive environment so that task outcomes are predictable and visible—i.e., reliably replicable— the lower is task uncertainty in that field' (ibid. 335). Rationalization has as its basic defining principles standardization and exact repetition for it is a computating and calculating form of rationality.

The rationalization of the cognitive content of science is closely bound up with techniques of computation and calculation, above all those involving mathematics. This process takes the form of what Whitley, following Georgescu-Roegen has called arithmomorphism: the tendency towards mathematical formulation of all relations in a science and finally its formalization as a closed theory (Georgescu-Roegen 1971). This tendency reaches its most concentrated and logically highest expression in computer programming whereby some of the formal sciences are completely formalized and subjected to automatic processes, such as the programming of proof procedures in branches of mathematics. The attempt to program intelligent thought processes in the Artificial Intelligence project constitutes the final realization of Rationalization. Weizenbaum, a critic of this project, has clearly perceived that it involves a form of rationality quite different from the rational modes which had prevailed in science, and according to him it is less humane than the others (Weizenbaum 1976). But there is no need to make any such invidious comparisons to realize that Rationalization is fundamentally different from Reason or Rationalism.

Not only are these forms of rationality different in principle, but in practice they often stand in a contradictory relation to each other, as revealed in historical tensions and dialectical conflicts. The opposition to Reason waged by Rationalism, which was historically manifest in the battle against Aristotelianism by the new sciences of the Scientific Revolution, continued in the ever growing hostility to allowing Reason any place in science and culminated in the Positivist rejection of anything that was supposedly metaphysical. But at the same time there were during this period occasional episodes of the reassertion of Reason, as in the Idealist elevation of Vernunft as against mere Verstand. In our time we are also witnessing an analogous historical tension between Rationalism and Rationalization as the Classical sciences are displaced by the new World science. Historical precedence seems to indicate that this transition does not mean that Rationalism will completely vanish, anymore than Reason disappeared previously; it will almost surely survive in subordinate areas of science or in counter-movements. To suppose otherwise would be to assume that inevitably science will enter a Marcusian one-dimensional state of technological domination, which is unlikely.

Already there are some counter-currents to Rationalization in our time. The work of Prigogine exemplifies an attempt to show both the limitations of Rationalism and the failings of Rationalization. Prigogine and Stengers quote a characteristic Rationalist view of science asserted by Lévy-Bruhl: 'nature around us is order and reason exactly as is the human mind. Our everyday activity implies a perfect confidence in the universality of the laws of nature' (Prigogine and Stengers 1984, 292). And they comment on it as follows:

> This feeling of confidence in the "reason" of nature has been shattered, partly
> as the result of the tumultuous growth of science in our time . . . our vision
> of nature is undergoing a radical change toward the multiple, the temporal,

and the complex. . . . We were seeking general, all-embracing schemes that could be expressed in terms of eternal laws, but we have found time, events, evolving particles. We were also searching for symmetry, and here also we were surprized, since we discovered symmetry-breaking processes on all levels, from elementary particles up to biology and ecology (ibid.).

Prigogine and Stengers go so far as to reinvoke Aristotelian ideas of a time and space of biological tenses and protensions as well as Lucretian atomism, so in these respects they are returning to a form of Reason. It is not yet clear how seriously all this is to be taken. Nevertheless, they do demonstrate that there are attempts to break out of the simple opposition of Rationalism to Rationalization. Where these might eventually lead and what future forms of rationality they foreshadow are not as yet evident.

Having thus expounded and explored the diverse forms of rationality, we can answer briefly our original question and show why science, merely because it is rational knowledge, need not continue to advance in the way previously called progress. The original conception of the progress of science was closely bound up with Rationalism and applicable to the development of Classical science, especially in its second phase during the nineteenth century. Hence once the Rationalization of science was under way, the character of scientific advance changed and it could no longer be said to progress in the same way or in the same sense. One must not assume any linear, cumulative movement from one stage of science to another or from one form of rationality to another. The Enlightenment idea that knowledge and reasonableness are continually advancing in one direction is based on the premise of a universal rationality which can no longer be maintained. Instead we must recognize basic discontinuities in history, no less so in the history of rationality than of science in general. However, this must not be taken to mean that the different forms of science and rationality are incommensurable. On the contrary, the existence of historical conflicts and tensions, which take the form of intellectual disputes and dialectical confrontations between scientists, show that such comparisons must continually be made. And furthermore, the historical fact that one kind of science or rationality can win out over another indicates that at critical points in history there are good grounds for choosing one over another. Science, which by definition produces true and rational knowledge, does not become historically relativized when it is recognized that it can proceed in different ways and in different directions. It has long been granted that the relation between its past superseded stages and present ones is not that past science was an erroneous or immature way of expressing the truths of present science. The real relationship is much more complex historically than the simple picture of progress as an advance towards the truth. Hence it must also be granted that if some of the past advances are called progress, those of the present when science has taken a different course can no longer be so regarded.

The argument we have deployed against progress in science is specifically an argument about the meaning of progress and the continued applicability of this concept to the present stage of scientific development. It is a matter of definition, not an argument against scientific advance as such nor is it designed to touch on speculations as to whether scientific knowledge is in principle limited or unlimited or whether science is approaching any such absolute limit faster or more slowly. Such questions—entertained by Rescher (1978) and many others as far back as C. S. Peirce and Henry Adams— are no more than idle speculations since it is impossible for us to foresee future stages of science beyond World science. Whether the concept of progress will have any relevance to the next stage is doubtful since it is a concept tied to the Enlightenment culture of Classical science which is unlikely to be soon repeated—though historical renaissances are always possible.

Rescher's arguments for continued progress, albeit at a decelerating pace, are mainly econometric in character, involving an attempted measurement of the rate of scientific advance at different times in the history of science. Like all such calculations of the rate of scientific achievement, this attempt entails comparing the products of different stages of science according to the one measuring scale. This comparison can be made in a superficial way for the circumstantial factors of science, such as the rate of investment, publication, human resources or any of the other economic and technical factors, even for technological success, but it is meaningless to do so for the quality of scientific discovery since the achievements of different scientific epochs are in this respect incomparable. Does Newton's discovery of the laws of planetary motion merit more or less marks than the first NASA planetary probe? How many genetic engineers equal one Mendel? How does Wiener compare with Babbage? Clearly, evaluating scientific achievements across scientific epochs does not make much sense since only the same kinds of discoveries can be compared. To argue, as Rescher does, that 'the progress of science will be taken to rest on its pragmatic aspect— the increasing success of its applications in problem solving and control, in cognitive and physical mastery over nature' (Rescher 1978, 190) is both to take technological advance as synonomous with progress in science and to overlook the fact that every science only solves its own problems and that there is no way of ranking all solutions. Pace Rescher and others, it might make sense to rank the solutions of problems within Classical science and work out some rough rate of progress, but it does not make sense to compare these to those for the problems of World science or to ascribe the same concept of progress to their solution.

The question of progress in science has thus opened up three new grounds on which to distinguish Classical science from World science. The Classical sciences were progressive in that they were concerned to pierce the primal mystery of Nature, to reduce everything to a few basic entities, and to further the one rational mode of knowledge. As I have shown, these three fundamental aspects of enlightenment, reduction and Rationalism no longer apply to the World sciences. These are not concerned with the mysteries of Nature, since everything is in principle explicable; nor are they reductive, but tending to integration; and finally, they are governed by procedures of Rationalization, rather than the 'method' of Rationalism. In Chapter 3 I shall explore these very general differentiations in detail and show how they result in very different scientific practices.

3

The Characteristics
of World Science

Problems of Periodization

The contemporary transformation from the Classical to the World sciences is taking place in key groupings of sciences, though by no means in all. Nor is it proceeding with equal rapidity in all these groups, for some are clearly giving the lead to others. According to Prigogine and Stengers (1984, 10) one transformation in the sciences is at present leading towards new sciences of time and irreversible processes. They also maintain that this tendency is evident throughout many other sciences at key levels, though doubtless they would agree that it is not occuring everywhere or at the same rate or in the same way; yet they insist that 'the evolution of science proceeds on somewhat parallel lines at every level'. These variations raise the issue of how a general transformation of science is to be assessed or what marks a period break.

The solution to the periodization problem is that of steering a course between the Scylla of neo-Positivism, which takes the sciences singly, allowing each its own life cycle (as entailed by the theories of paradigm stages of Kuhn, Ravetz and the finalizationists); and the Charybdis of neo-Idealism, which treats the sciences as totalities collectively manifesting the one spirit or episteme (as asserted by Hegel and implied by the early theory of Foucault). In this chapter, the historical assumption is adopted that individual sciences do not have a completely separate history or autonomous paradigms and that, consequently, they cannot go through stages totally out of phase with one another. Rather, it is assumed that the sciences develop as a more or less differentiated whole—not a totality—in close correlation with other historical processes. Thus, at any one period close links tie every single science then present to at least some of its neighbouring sciences, but not to all. Such ties and relations are established by common intellectual and practical predispositions and even sometimes by superordinating theories which cover groups of sciences. The sciences can also be related hierarchically when a group of sciences establishes an intellectual dominance so effectively that the others are obliged to follow its models and procedures—for example, the preponderance of the mechanical model of physics during the early Classical scientific era. In this sense one can speak of some sciences as being ahead of others and giving a lead for others to follow. Hence, unless a science is for some reason retarded, due to neglect or censorship or unusual internal theoretical or practical difficulties, it is usually as developed as the scientific complex in which it finds itself permits it to be. At present some social sciences are more or less as developed as the natural sciences.

Hence, to propound the thesis of a general transformation from the Classical to the World sciences in this way is not to follow Hegel in maintaining that the one Zeitgeist determines all ideas at a given time, that there is a total unity in the development of the sciences. Nor is it necessarily to invoke, as Foucault (1970) does in his early work, the unity of an underlying determining structure, or episteme, governing all the sciences at a given time, or even most groups of sciences. A proper historical approach to the sciences will have to steer a middle course between the two extremes of the individuated autonomy of each science, as postulated by those who invoke paradigm development stages (van den Daele et al. 1977) and the total unity of all the sciences as the one field subject to the same rate of progress, as postulated by those who speak of uniform stages of scientific development. Rejecting both approaches, we must search for unifying terms for varying groupings of sciences and explore what Whitley (1984, 269) calls the 'strategic dependence between fields'.

To characterize adequately the contemporary situation of the sciences requires a set of concepts which will describe the changes that have taken place in large groups of sciences. Such a set of terms must constitute a syndrome of mutually inter-penetrating and interweaving characterizations which will not act as exclusive categories, for each term will serve as a typification marking out a group of sciences whose members also belong to other groups typified by other terms in the syndrome. Like overlapping circles of varying sizes, the terms will cover the whole field of contemporary science without any one term applying to every single science but only to a shifting constellation of sciences, for there is no such thing as one definitive criterion or essence of all the contemporary sciences. Science is what Wittgenstein calls a family concept. It is not possible to categorize the sciences according to *genus proximum* and *differentia specifica*. All kinds of groupings and divisions are possible depending on what factors are taken as most significant. The traditional groupings into pure and applied sciences, or natural and social sciences, or empirical and logical sciences are based on past institutional arrangements or outdated philosophical distinctions. Nor is there any rigorous way of demarcating the boundary between science and non-science, in the way Popper tried to stipulate through the falsification principle, for at every point scientific disciplines merge into those which might be considered non-scientific, there being no such foolproof principle to separate all possible cases.

The approach we have adopted has much in common with Weber's ideal-type methodology, which, as Adorno (1973, 164) points out, also deals with constellations or syndromes of terms. Each major ideal type is a concept constructed out of a constellation of constituent concepts, themselves made up in the same way; the whole typology is thus one of a conceptual universe comprizing constellations of constellations. Approaching the sciences in terms of constellations of ideal types permits what Adorno considers to be 'a third possibility beyond the alternatives of Positivism and Idealism' (ibid. 166) in characterization and periodization. Instead of the Positivist habit of dealing with single sciences and the Idealist tendency to take the sciences as a whole, this third approach will treat groups of sciences which can form and reform over given periods. Major historical divisions need not be taken as complete ruptures or epistemological breaks in which all sciences are transformed together; they can be taken as conjunctures at which a number of partial transformations coincide, but not necessarily all at once. Thus the transition from the Classical to the World sciences which we outlined previously is not one single unified break but a series of overlapping divisions between many sciences changing in different ways and at different rates.

How this period break is taking place in shifting constellations of sciences can be described and explained by utilizing a syndrome of ideal-type concepts. For this purpose I shall present the following key terms: technification, formalization, abstraction, problem-solving and finalization. The first term is the most important for it marks a new kind of relationship between science and technology, one which justifies referring to many sciences as techno-sciences. But clearly, not all sciences are technified in this sense, nor are all necessarily formalized, abstract, problem-solving, or even finalized; these terms only apply to changing constellations of sciences. If there is to be one general comprehensive concept to cover all these conjoined transformations, it is Rationalization, which we have already expounded in Chapter 2. As I argue elsewhere (Redner 1986), the transition to the present state of the sciences exemplifies a process of Rationalization parallel to the rationalizing trends in most other spheres of society.

Such a major break as I am about to outline changes not only the sciences themselves but the whole disposition of knowledge, discourse and practice in which the sciences inhere. The kind of knowledge produced in any given scientific era is the outcome not only of the specific interaction of the sciences but also of the relation of science to technology, philosophy, art and other intellectual and practical concerns. Thus, for example, the relation between science and technology was very different during the nineteenth century compared to now and was different again during the seventeenth century as compared with medieval times. So, too, the relations between the sciences alter with each change in the overall character of the formation of knowledge. In every period new constellations of the sciences arise, only to be dispersed when knowledge changes again.

The official conception of the present disposition of the sciences is largely anachronistic, though still influential, for the university system is even now formally administered according to it. Historically it derives from the latter phase of the Classical scientific era of the nineteenth and early twentieth centuries. The earlier phase of this era (1600–1800) saw rather different constellations; during this period the sciences were only gradually differentiated from other discourses as well as from each other. Beginning with the so-called Scientific Revolution, there began the process of dissociating natural philosophy from metaphysical philosophy, that is, the process of constituting the separate sphere of science. In this early state, science was still closely linked to the arts and crafts, and the earliest philosophy of science advocated the practical utility of scientific knowledge, as is evident in both Bacon and Descartes. However, in the second phase, during which science was first incorporated into the university system in Germany, the idea of pure science totally divorced from technology and practical concerns became the dominant ideology of research. (And this idea has persisted against all the evidence of actual practice till now.) In contradistinction to pure science, applied science was developed in technical and other practical engineering institutions closely linked to the technological changes taking place elsewhere, mainly in industry. In the universities a further internal separation was instituted between the natural sciences (*Naturwissenschaften*) and the social and humanistic sciences (*Geisteswissenschaften*). One by one each of the now well-known divisions was set up, and each of the sciences was separated into its own compartmentalized section in the university and developed itself in an increasingly pure and abstract form—every now and then hiving off a practical discipline to take care of the more mundane problems arising from the outside world. Thus the whole scientific university department system, as it still formally operates, was constituted.

For some time, however, the departmental system has ceased to have any real cognitive relevance to the actual research activities going on within university confines or outside in the research institutions. For in the contemporary era of science this now Classic scientific disposition has lost its meaning. Pure science divorced from applied technology hardly exists because the very instrumentation required for most research assumes a highly technological character. The research teams required in the fields of finalized science are made up of assorted 'experts' who originate from diverse disciplines but are no longer bound to them; for such teams the departmental boundaries are mere administrative fictions. In such cross-disciplinary team work the research problem is primary, not the furtherance of pure theory in a specialized science. 'The objects of problem-research are frequently non-disciplinary. They belong to several disciplines or lie outside the "internal" program of the disciplines concerned' (van den Daele et al. 1977, 241). At the same time, common techniques are being utilized in different sciences; whole fields are growing around techniques which no longer belong to any of the old disciplines, for example, computer science, genetic engineering, operations research, astro-physics. Also in some cases over-arching theories and methods are appearing which span the old divisions of the formal, natural and social sciences, for example, game theory, cybernetics, information and systems theory, mathematical set theory, diverse forms of structuralism and functionalism.

Each of the elements of the contemporary disposition of the sciences has been a long time in the making. Only the constellations are relatively new, that is, the conjunction of all these elements as a dominant system of sciences. We can trace each of the main characteristics of contemporary World science back into the nineteenth century; forms of technification, formalization, abstraction, problem-solving and finalization have always been there to some degree. They are not associated with any single new philosophy or theory, or even with any famous names—which is another reason why the present transition is not to be compared to the Scientific Revolution. Nevertheless, once these slow changes in the way things are done in science came together and began amplifying each other, they transformed the whole procedure of scientific work and consequently the relation of science to the other discourses and practices. It is almost as if these characteristics seeped—by a kind of institutional osmosis—through the disciplinary walls of the sciences.

We shall trace this process beginning with the technification of science, then going on to the other features: formalization, abstraction, problem-solving and finalization. It is necessary to stress again that these developments in science do not necessarily entail each other. Thus, the tendency towards a high level of technification in such so-called 'frontiers of knowledge' sciences as elementary particle physics and astro-physics in no way causes any commensurate intrusion of external values to direct research inquiry; in this respect such sciences still constitute relatively 'pure' research. And conversely, highly finalized sciences—certain kinds of policy studies for instance—can evolve with a bare minimum of technification, if any at all. There is no necessary reciprocity between these categories, though there are elective affinities between them with the result that the introduction of any one will tend to promote some of the others as well.

Technification

The term 'technification of the sciences' designates a process whereby techniques—frequently, though not always, involving technology—become preponderant over earlier, more traditional methods of the practice of research. Thus, as a result of technification, theory construction has to some extent been rendered redundant through the systematic application of techniques and technical procedures to the given materials of research; these might be collections of data to be analyzed, or problems to be solved, or given practical results to be produced, or proof constructions to be formed, or whatever else might be the set task to be achieved by technical elaboration. Thus, as the physicist Ziman (1976, 234) puts it, 'research itself—the tussle with a problem of natural philosophy—has given way to professional expertise in a variety of techniques.' Of course, techniques have also played a partial role in most sciences in the past, and almost no science has been without its technical features. Under the general heading of tools, Ravetz establishes techniques as an inherent feature of the methods of science. But, as I shall show, there is an enormous disparity between the tools or techniques utilized in the traditional sciences during the Classical era, the days of string-and-sealing-wax devices, and those now employed. Most obviously, the nature and role of technological tools in contemporary science are very different from those of the craft tools that were available to many sciences even late in the era of Classical science during the early years of this century. The computer, for example, is no longer on the same level as any of the craft tools. The ready availability of computers brings about far-reaching changes in the practice of science, for utilizing these tools in a science restructures the whole process of research and alters the very meaning of data and knowledge. Computerized knowledge is technified knowledge.

In some contemporary sciences the computer is much more than an indispensable research tool or instrument, as it still is in space research; it is the very raison d'être of these sciences—for without it they would be inconceivable. The new science of chaos theory is one example; it owes its existence solely to the availability of computers. As James Gleick reports:

> Scaling was an intimate feature of the peculiar world Feigenbaum was beginning to explore. It is a world that depends on the existence of computers as no discipline ever has before. For Feigenbaum, to begin with, the computer was a way to bridge a professional gap between theory and experimentation. For particle physicists, any experiment is costly in time, money and technical sophistication. But to explore the realm of partial differential equations, Feigenbaum and others have made the computer their own accelerator, cloud chamber and camera all in one (Gleick 1985, 60–1).

In such a science the relation between the research carried out and the instrument used has altered as compared with that in previous sciences. The instrument no longer functions to test and explore the objects that have been designated by theories or other requirements formulated independently of it. Rather the relationship becomes reversed: the instrument itself is being explored and theories devised and objects found to satisfy the results of that exploration. Thus in such a science technification assumes prominence over all the other factors of science. In many other sciences technification is almost of equal importance in that the phenomena being studied would not exist or at least would not be available for purposes of investigation without highly technified means. This is particularly the case in sciences dealing with extreme conditions not usually encountered in terrestial nature, as Pierre Auger observes:

> science is pushing its investigations into all the newly conquered areas of extreme conditions, which are deviating increasingly from the normal. These are the areas of high and low temperatures, high and low pressures, extreme electric and magnetic fields, very high and very low energies, ultra-long and ultra-short intervals of time. In each case, these areas have been reached and the necessary measurements made as a result of the discovery and development of new techniques (Auger 1961, 20).

Ellul was among the first to have realized the full impact and import of technification for science. Utilizing this very term, he puts it rather bluntly and not altogether accurately: 'scientific activity has been superseded by technical activity to such a degree that we can no longer conceive of science without its technical outcome. . . . The very fact that techniques advance with great rapidity demands a corresponding scientific advance, and sets off a general acceleration' (Ellul 1973, 9). Furthermore he states that 'science has become an instrument of technique' to such an extent that 'where the technical means do not exist science does not advance' (ibid. 8). Sometimes Ellul uses the word 'science' in the sense of traditional science, not in order to distinguish contemporary science from technique but in order to show that such a separation cannot be made. Thus he states: 'the relation between science and technique becomes ever less clear when we consider the newer fields, which have no boundaries. Where does biological technique begin and where does it end? In modern psychology and sociology what can we call technique, since in the application of these sciences everything is technique . . . it is economic technique which forms the very substance of economic thought' (ibid. 9).

Ellul is extremely pessimistic about the effect of technification on society and also about the technification of science: 'our omnivorous technique (and this represents in part Einstein's thought) may in the end make science sterile' (ibid. 10). He also quotes Wiener to the effect that 'the younger generation of research workers in the United States consists primarily of technicians who are unable to do research at all without the help of machines, large teams of men, and enormous amounts of money' (ibid. 9). Ellul's critique of science is of a piece with his diagnosis of the whole of our technological society which transforms all activities into technical accomplishments. The technification of science is the very same general process as the technification of work or organization or law. Science is subject to the same processes as society in general, and this, as we shall see, also holds for the other developments, such as finalization and formalization, which constitute contemporary Rationalization.

Historically speaking, the technification of science is the final outcome of the gradual approach and mutual incorporation of science and technology, resulting in what I have called techno-science. This outcome is the convergence and unification of two quite separate historical developments. The first, 'the scientification of technology' (Boehme 1978, 233), is the gradual application of scientific theory to technological practice, which only began on a significant scale around the middle of the nineteenth century. The second—at first quite separate but parallel process—can be called 'the technification of science', and it begins when technological instrumentation and techniques assume crucial importance in science. When these two processes meet and merge 'the differentiation between science and technology becomes blurred, if not altogether suspended' (Weingart 1978, 279). Weingart goes on to insist that it is not a question

> of an influence in only one direction. Rather, the new pattern emerges because two conditions are mutually supporting each other: the development of scientific knowledge has reached a point where its explanatory and predictive power can be extended to a rapidly increasing variety of phenomena; technical problems have reached such a complexity that their solution requires the use of scientific methods, notably theory construction based on mathematical description of systematic experiments (ibid.).

Thus, as Boehme puts it, 'natural knowledge and technology now tend to unification at the level of theory' (Boehme 1978, 239).

The scientification of technology was a late development because as long as technology arose out of—and was still based on—craft practices it had little to learn from scientific knowledge. That knowledge was for a long time too general and abstruse to find any ready purchase on early technological developments, with their very practical requirements that only craftsmen and technicians could devise. Although the early scientific philosophers—for instance, Bacon and Descartes—had aspirations for the application of science to human welfare through technological improvements, these were for several centuries no more than pious hopes. Scientific knowledge led to a few useful inventions mainly in instrumentation—the thermometer, for example—and navigational aids. During this period and well into the nineteenth century the technological inventions of the industrial revolution came mainly from self-taught inventors and engineers, often with no formal scientific education. Proper scientification of technology began when the industrial processes themselves, at a certain advanced stage of their development, demanded scientific knowledge, and, simultaneously, when scientific knowledge became the source of new industrial processes and technical developments, as in the electrical and chemical industries. Technology could come to be based on scientific knowledge also because the sciences were at a stage where they could assume an 'applied' form, in contra-distinction to a 'pure' or theoretical form, when their theories were mature enough to be applied in practice. Consequently, a two-tier education system arose: universities for the pure scientists and technical institutes for the applied scientists or scientific engineers.

Parallel with this process the inverse process of the technification of science began very gradually, as the sciences came increasingly to depend on technical developments and new technological apparatus. Perhaps the earliest of the new machines were the electrical devices introduced towards the end of the nineteenth century, such as radio and x-ray apparatus; and older devices, such as the microscope and telescope, were perfected. From that time on new machines and instruments arrived with ever greater rapidity: x-ray crystallography, radar, television, the Geiger counter, and eventually, just before and during the Second World War, the cyclotron, electron microscope and, most ominous, the nuclear reactor.

The Second World War had an extraordinary effect on the production and perfection of both old and newly invented apparatus; without the war it is unlikely that most of the machines now utilized would have reached their present size and quality. From that point on many of the sciences were firmly attached to military developments, which have now assumed the forefront in providing these sciences with their technical means as, for example, in astronomy where most of the recent discoveries were made through the use of equipment originally devised for the military; the same holds for laser research. In chemistry, as Symes (1976, 341) notes, a 'revolution took place in the aftermath of the Second World War which involved no great conceptual leap', but merely 'involved the introduction of two particular spectroscopic techniques, infrared spectroscopy and nuclear magnetic resonance; these, together with mass spectrometry and gas chromotography, are the indispensable tools of every modern chemistry laboratory'. He points out with regard to the new devices; 'the key point is that it was the instruments not the theory that were lacking before the war', and success in developing them 'was due to the technical developments associated with radar' (ibid. 344), a wartime research speciality. A similar story might be told for many sciences, including the bio-medical ones, which owe so much to radio-active isotopes deriving from nuclear research.

For reasons that Symes makes clear, technification in such sciences has become of crucial importance to their further individual disciplinary development and also for the technical development of groups of sciences as a whole, since 'instruments and techniques provide the vehicle for ideas and men to flow from one discipline to another (for example, from physics to chemistry and biology)' (ibid. 341). The instruments determine the type of knowledge produced in such sciences: they make available a certain kind of data, they suggest the problems to be solved through their use, and 'not only are the problems closely defined, the type of solution is pre-determined as well'; finally, they compel their own utilization 'just because they are there' and are too expensive to be allowed to lie idle (ibid. 345). Ineluctably, therefore, machines determine the nature of the research undertaken and the knowledge resulting from it; so as Ziman (1976, 225) put it, 'Big machines lead inevitably to Big Science—that is, to large-scale research organizations with planned programmes'.

In a technified science the relationship between knowledge and instrumentation is, therefore, theoretically different from that in a science that is not technified. This difference should lead to a radical revision of the whole idea of experiment and experience as propounded in the philosophy of science. It might have been appropriate to think of such simple instruments used in earlier science, as telescopes and microscopes, as mere tools to facilitate measurement and observation, that is, almost as extensions of people's natural faculties. And it was possible to theorize that what was being observed with the aid of such instruments was 'out there' in the world as an 'object' quite independent of the process of observation. By contrast, however, the instruments employed in a technified science can no longer be conceived of as mere aids to observation for, in a certain sense, they themselves generate the data which are being observed. The 'object' observed is, therefore, no longer independent of the machine either in practice or in theory. A cyclotron is not a device permitting us to 'see' sub-atomic particles in any simple sense; rather it is a machine which in a very straightforward way generates sub-atomic particles, most of which only come into being through the operation of the machine. The workings of the machine are an integral part of the theory of what is being produced and 'observed' by means of the machine, for without such a theory the data are meaningless. And such 'observation' becomes subject to limiting principles, such as Heisenberg's uncertainty principle, which express the interaction between observer and 'object'. With such machines we act on Nature in our experiments rather than merely passively observing it, as the old philosophy would have it. Hence, new philosophical conceptions of how we technically engage with Nature in science have had to be developed, notably by Bachelard and others.

The total transformation in the technical mode of production of science only took place when this process of the inner technification of science through instrumentation converged with the previously described parallel process of the scientification of technology. Only then did a full technification of science take place permitting a unification of science and technology. Science increasingly came to be concerned with large-scale technological projects, for these constitute a new source of scientific problems and constantly produce new findings demanding scientific explanation. Most scientific 'progress' is now expected to take place in such areas.

The technification of the sciences is even evident in the social sciences since the end of the Second World War. The utilization of such sciences for 'social engineering' ends brought into being a whole range of applied social sciences or policy studies whose goals of research are determined by social requirements and political directives, stimulated in the first place by the war itself and the need to manage a post-war warfare and welfare state. What eventuated was a whole host of sciences dedicated to producing what Lindblom and Cohen (1979) call 'usable knowledge'. Each of these sciences is invariably based on techniques of systematic working procedures which in most cases do not require any technology or even extensive instrumentation. Thus, we encounter in this sphere the phenomenon of technification without technology, and this peculiarity can also occur in some of the natural sciences, especially those devoted to what used to be called natural history studies. Such techniques invariably go back to processes first developed in academic experimental, analytic or scholarly work, frequently with a highly theoretical or even speculative rationale. Divorced from its originating theoretical context and applied to a practical task, such a technique can give rise to a special science of its own which often simply goes by the name of its constituent technique: for example, operations research and systems analysis, input-output analysis, mathematical programming and cost-effectiveness analysis (ibid. 9). Statistical and data gathering techniques are applied in numerous specialized social studies in many disciplines, ranging from psychology (intelligence and aptitude tests) to cultural anthropology (market research on preferences and choices). Mathematical modelling techniques operate in such formally inclined social studies as economics or in that strategic analysis which is based on game theory; non-mathematical modelling techniques feature in most other areas. For those techniques involving calculation, the computer is used as the indispensable labour- and time-saving device, but invariably it imposes its own technified requirements on the kind of data it will allow. Quantification in the social sciences in general is always relative to an available technique for without it there is no determining in what respects and to what degree something can be measured.

Many techniques are available that require some degree of quantification, but there are also some that do not, such as field study techniques, interviewing techniques and policy analysis techniques. The humanities, which are now also being technified, are introducing many other non-quantified techniques, such as those for language analysis, textual interpretation and historical research. But unfortunately there are also quantified techniques entering the humanities, and these are frequently no more than a parody of those in the other sciences, for example, word frequency counts used to establish meaning in literature, or general information theory accounts of meaning such as those propounded by Zipf and MacKay (Lilienfeld 1978, 83). Indeed, the attempt by the humanities to deck themselves out in the trappings of organized science, its methods as well as its academic structure and procedures of publication, is something of a charade. Technification has, clearly, limited purpose or value in the humanities; though some techniques are no doubt useful, pervasive technification is not suited to these subjects; nevertheless, it is forced on them despite the resistance of the subject matter itself. Le Roy Ladurie has declared that 'in history the scholar of the future will have to be a computer programmer' (Lepenies 1981, 259). Presumably he imagines that all historical work will have become technified as a culmination of the increasing technification practised by the Annales school.

The benefits of technification are beginning to be questioned even in the social sciences. Undeniably, many techniques and numerical procedures were developed in the social sciences, useful both for scholarly pursuits, as in history and anthropology, as well as for practical purposes. Modern society, given its level of organization and planning, is not conceivable without such social scientific knowledge. Nevertheless, the over-utilization of such techniques has inevitably exposed their limits. Sheldon Wolin (1969, 1070) has criticized technification in political science under the name of 'methodism': 'the knowledge which the methodist seeks is fairly characterized in his own terms as composing a "kit of tools" or a "bag of tricks"'. More recently Lindblom and Cohen have sought to reveal the limits of technification in policy studies. What they call 'professional social inquiry' yields knowledge for policy decisions that is frequently no better and often worse than what they call 'ordinary knowledge':

> Already, earlier enthusiasm for highly scientific policy analysis and systems analysis looks naive, an indication that we have only begun to think carefully about the competing attractions of formal completeness of analysis, on the one hand, and selective contribution, on the other—and about the competing attractions of science and art in problem solving. . . . Waste, noise, and an excess of "policy analysis" all reflect, we suggest, a kind of hyper-rationalism among practitioners of professional social inquiry. . . . A realistic view of social problem solving stands in contrast to the rationalistic view implied among the most enthusiastic advocates of professional social inquiry (Lindblom and Cohen 1979, 91).

The hyper-rationalism referred to is what I have called Rationalization. However, 'ordinary knowledge' is perhaps not quite as ordinary as Lindblom and Cohen suppose. An analysis of ordinary knowledge in a manner that harks back to Aristotle's 'practical wisdom' has been attempted by Ravetz (1971, 239), who at the same time stresses the non-technified craft aspects of scientific work itself, that which is the ineradicable residue of 'personal knowledge' in Polanyi's sense. But more thought needs to be given to the nature of ordinary knowledge, that is, knowledge based on personal experience and judgement, and also to 'the competing attractions of science and art' in such knowledge.

Technification in the natural sciences—despite its undoubted achievements—is causing serious problems even in standard scientific work. Ravetz has explored at length the problems of what he calls 'industrialized' science, which is very largely technified science. The loss of skill and craft competence among the general run of research workers as a result of the over-utilization of big machines, methodical techniques and routines of organized research procedure is gradually revealing all the symptoms of work in bureaucratized organizations. There is a diminution of inventiveness, a lapse of personal responsibility, over-authoritativeness, and, eventually, an absence of purpose. Such science cannot even serve practical ends adequately, for as Ravetz points out, there is a 'tendency for immediate technical problems to displace the initiating practical problem in the execution of a project [which] becomes very marked as soon as a stable organization has been formed, and "welfare invention" has given way to "welfare engineering"' (Ravetz 1971a, 342). I shall eventually consider further these problems of problem-solving science in Chapter 6.

Formalization

Technification in the sciences has frequently, though not always, been accompanied by formalization, abstraction and problem-solving. But it is always possible for an independent development in the latter to occur on its own without any reference to technification. These thematic categories are usually linked by a more general tendency towards what Whitley (1977a), following Georgescu-Roegen, has called 'arithmomorphism' or the 'arithmetic ideal'. The introduction of mathematical techniques into a science can take place for many reasons. These can be technical and practical—to facilitate calculation, for example, and to make certain kinds of problems solvable; or formal—to place the science on a more rigorous and so scientistic footing, for example, by introducing quantification and exactitude in definitions, relations and 'laws'; or institutional—to establish criteria of professional expertise and technical competence, for instance; or philosophical—to permit a theoretical reduction of the objects of the science to those of a more general science, and eventually of all sciences to physics. But no matter why such techniques are included, their introduction will almost inevitably set up a tendency towards formalization, abstraction and problem solving. Formalization occurs because once mathematical techniques operate to quantify relations and 'laws' there will be an irresistible intellectual pull to bring them together as a systematic and fully formal theory, which in extreme cases will be 'closed' and even axiomatized. Abstraction occurs because a mathematical description governing a few exact parameters constitutes an abstraction from reality; it is only applied to an ideal or abstract object selected from the multiplicity of actual objects and their properties. And finally, a science operating with mathematical formulae will invariably couch all questions in the form of exact problems for which there are presumed to be specific, if not unique, solutions, like those for a set of solvable equations. A mathematical, 'closed' and axiomatic science operating on highly abstract objects to solve intellectually constructed problems will almost always need to be finalized as well, since there will no longer be any 'internal' direction for further research, the guidance of which will have to come from outside ends.

According to Whitley, formalization is an implicit constitutive feature of physics: 'because the ideal of the discipline is that all physical phenomena will eventually be expressed as derivatives of a basic axiomatic structure, work on that structure and on associated formalisms in principle affects all work in physics and therefore has more impact, at any rate potentially, than most experiments' (Whitley 1977a, 154). This ideal of formalization relates closely to the authority structure of the discipline:

> The greater authority of theoretical work in restricted, arithmetised sciences is not only due to the use of mathematical formalism per se, but also arises from the emphasis on completeness and coherence in such a science. Because the ideal is the reduction of all the special fields of research to a coherent formalism, work directly focussing on this goal is more central to the discipline as a whole than research in any derivative field (ibid.).

As we shall see, the cognitive forms of a discipline, an emphasis on formalization, for example, and its authority structure are mutually legitimating. Formalization, as Whitley shows, plays an extremely important legitimizing function in such disciplines at all stages of research; it serves as a selection device for young researchers, as a criterion of acceptable theory and proof and as a mode of exposition. Usually, as in physics, it tends to be accompanied by a high degree of technification, abstraction and problem-solving.

Such a complex compound of technification, formalization, abstraction and problem-solving obtains also to an almost grotesque degree in certain branches of economics. The econometric pursuit of a total all-embracing mathematical model of the whole economy to be operated by computers, and so to give instantaneous solutions to any problems posed to it, is the kind of totally rationalized dream of science entertained by some exponents in this field. In an interview Lawrence Klein explains his grand economic design as follows: 'you see, my view is that the economy is really definable in fine detail as a grand equation system . . . it has billions of equations each with many parameters. So we here, with the model, are making an enormous simplification—but for the human mind it's still a complicated thing to deal with a thousand-equation system' (Judson 1980, 125). Such a model has become its own goal and is no longer to be judged in relation to economic theory or economic policy goals: 'originally the first models built were to test theories in economics . . . but now, really, the role of theories is to give us hunches about the way the economic system is put together, so we can try to improve the model' (ibid. 127). Eventually, the model is to assume global proportions and embrace the whole world, as one country and institution after another join the model building super-project. Klein is keen to proselytize his approach even to his ideological enemies, the Soviets, 'we want them to think along engineering and modeling lines, so that there will be more rational ways of interpreting each others actions' (ibid. 129). We already know what ideal of rationality this approach is invoking, and what projects it has for a rational world. His ultimate aim is 'to internationalize the world—and to automate it' (ibid.).

This is by no means the most extreme example of the Rationalization of contemporary science run riot. Many scientists share at least some features of this kind of thinking. Its absurdities are all too evident: it seeks to build a rational model or map of the world on the scale of one to one so that the map will literally cover the ground—an inexhaustible undertaking doomed to failure. The whole point of a model or map is that its utility depends on how and on what it selects from the world to incorporate within itself; one that tries to include everything would be of no use since we could not read it, even if some deus ex machina were to give it to us. Today the computer often figures as a deus machina, and is worshipped as such. But even if computers, like the gods, could operate econometric models that performed perfectly ex post facto and could retrospectively account for everything that happened in the past—and this is one aim of the modelling programme—then even this accomplishment might be useless in predicting anything in the future. With every minute of historical time some unforeseeable changes are taking place, as people act out new decisions, and this is true even in economics; thus it would be impossible for a computer to keep up with or predict such novel features even on the simplest level, not to speak of major historical revolutions, which are themselves always sudden and unpredictable.

Many other cases of model building and computer programming in principle exhibit this kind of technified, formalized and abstracted mentality. Even where no computers are involved, the arithmetic ideal and formalization alone can give rise to complementary propensities towards an abstract rationalization. Whitley (1977a, 157) remarks that in General Equilibrium theory 'the fetishization of formalism and concomitant disregard of what Coddington terms "sematic properties" or substantive issues seems to be almost parodied by this part of economics'. Whitley accounts for this tendency towards the arithmetic ideal and the consequent formalization, both of the content of science and its outer organizational forms, by the institutional imperative of professionalization; all this 'has had major consequences for the organization of all the sciences by establishing, on the one hand, an organizationally reified image of scientificity which has had a considerable impact on struggling sciences trying to acquire respectability and, on the other hand, by serving as a model of how work should be organized and disciplines structured' (Whitley 1977a, 163). As a result, we have had axiomatic schemes in the social sciences, and 'the full panoply of Ph.D. training, journals, referees, and conferences, throughout the sciences' (ibid.).

The tendency towards formalization on its own without reference to technification or finalization is particularly evident in those disciplines being maintained in the 'pure' form of academic research, untouched by worldly considerations. In these disciplines there arose 'an emphasis on formalism at the expense of physical interpretation' (ibid. 157). Examples of this emphasis abound and are to be found in nearly all academic sciences, especially as these developed after the Second World War. Quantum physics, symbolic logic, finite-group mathematics, statistical and probability theory, generative grammar in linguistics, learning theory in S-R psychology, functionalist sociology, information and systems theory, and, as we have seen, branches of economics—these and many more exemplify extreme formalization. The historical reasons for this development are numerous and complex; obviously it had much to do with professionalization and arithmomorphism, and there was also the newly achieved prestige of mathematical physics; but apart from these intellectual factors there were also cultural, psychological and philosophical determinants. The Second World War and the ideological battles fought out in the name of science, both before and after, prompted many scientists to withdraw into the hermetic purity of formal disciplines where everything would be non-contentious, value-free, purely rational and logical—but often also empty. Formalization promised the removal of all ambiguities and the attainment of pure concepts and systems untainted by the grime of values, metaphysics and, even more dangerous, ideologies.

As a formal scientific procedure, the quest for formalization originated in the earlier period of Classical science—and even earlier if we count Euclid's geometry—though it only became particularly important in mathematics and logic towards the end of the nineteenth century. At that time it was intended to realize the purely intellectual design of placing at least the formal disciplines on sound logical foundations, that is, to elicit their fundamental terms by showing how from these as axioms all other notions could be derived as theorems. Russell and Whitehead's *Principia Mathematica,* based on Frege's and Peano's work, was a milestone in this quest. However, Goedel's incompleteness proof showed the impossibility in principle of a complete formalization of mathematics. Wittgenstein's mistitled *Foundations of Mathematics* also worked to erode the search for foundations and made all foundational studies questionable in certain circles of philosophy. Nevertheless, though the primary interest in formalization might no longer have been there, formalizing for its own sake continued and increased as a full-fledged professional activity. The Logical Positivist school of philosophy provided a rationale for this approach; it saw formalizing as a kind of anti-metaphysical prophylactic designed to produce a sterilized science and so to prevent the generation of unwanted metaphysical entities. 'It became commonplace for philosophers of science to construe scientific theories as axiomatic calculi which are given a partial observational interpretation by means of correspondence rules' (Suppe 1979, 3). Under the slogan of the 'Unity of the Sciences', formalization became a programme of Positivist reductivism to which most scientists subscribed, especially after the triumph of Positivism in the immediate post Second World War period. Formalization for its own sake then became academically respectable and even de rigueur in many disciplines. It functioned almost as a professional shibboleth used to separate the formalist sheep from the informal goats, and, so it was thought, the tough minds from the soft ones and strong students from weak ones.

Another development in the period since the Second World War has seen formalization transformed into computation under the impact of computer technification; the invention of the computer has thus led to a merging of formalization and technification. The proliferation of research on Artificial Intelligence is displacing the older formalizing work in logic and mathematics. A sub-speciality of this research called theorem proving carries on directly from mathematical logic. Some mathematical and logical theorems are only provable in computer terms. The method of logic programming has established the predicate calculus as a computer language and so brought mathematical logic and computation together. Another approach seeks to programme even 'natural' languages.

Formalization has had a decisive influence on the practice of nearly all World sciences. This is why it must be treated as a key thematic category in the transformation of science. It has affected the practice of the sciences as well as the interpretations the sciences have received. Formalization has almost invariably been given a reductivist interpretation, especially by Logical Positivism which took formalization as the method of its reductivist programme. Positivism supposed that to formalize a science meant to reduce all its concepts and objects to the basic terms figuring in the axioms of the formal system or calculus. And its attempt to unify the sciences came down to trying to reduce them all eventually to physics and logic. The sociological effect was to endow physics and formal logic with an extraordinary aura of respect as the ultimate sciences. Little attempt was made to separate formalization from this Positivist reductivist interpretation, to argue that formalizing a science in no way determined its interpretation because the formal system that resulted also had to be given an interpretation and that need not necessarily be a reductivistic one. Nor was there much success, despite some attempts, to show convincingly that the formalized branches of any science, those rigorously formulated and made systematic, were thereby not in the least superior to the branches presumed backward because they were merely informal.

Formalization also had the ideological effect of fixing sciences in an unalterable canonic form and stifling any conceptual dispute that made for opposition and change. Formalization was extensively used to defend entrenched theories in many sciences and put them beyond question by presenting them in a finished, closed form which only those with the necessary formal abilities were even competent to understand. And in any case, any argument over substantive issues itself had to be formalized as it had to be expressed in the language of formal systems; so in any such dispute it could be made to appear as if what was at stake was nothing more than the issue of whether to adopt one symbolism or another. Thus substantive disputes became nominalist and pointless. 'Where mathematization of relations in a closed, coherent system is reified as the basic goal of a discipline in educational curricula, reward systems and career structures, any controversy over fundamental ontological problems will be short lived' (Whitley 1977a, 154). An example of this, discussed at length in an article by Pinch (1977), is the attempted challenge by David Bohm of the orthodox Copenhagen interpretation of quantum mechanics, which was successfully turned aside by the physics establishment simply by an appeal to von Neumann's purely formal proof. 'Bohm was making a contribution to the research problem of the validity of von Neumann's proof and, more generally, to the problem of axiomatisation of quantum theory'; 'the response of the elite to Bohm's articulation was also to articulate von Neumann's proof and to dispute Bohm's challenge to it' (ibid. 187). Whitley (1977a, 157) states the issue even more pointedly: 'by reopening the whole issue of the physical meaning of formalisms and threatening the authority of pure mathematics, Bohm was, perhaps, seen as a danger to the authority structure of physics'.

Thus the ultimate sociological effect of formalization is to affirm authority structures. Theories satisfactorily formalized are regarded as closed and assume a canonical status. All that remains is for such theories to be applied in research that is usually of the technical kind, requiring direction from outside. In this way formalization furthers technification and finalization: 'knowledge is finalized when it is expressed in a coherent, closed formalism' (ibid. 150).

Abstraction

The eventual upshot of extensive formalization within any discipline is a certain kind of abstract simplification as concepts and ideas are reduced to a restricted range of formal meanings and as the 'semantic content' of theories becomes limited. A high order of abstraction also ensues because formal objects are by definition far removed from the real object to which they refer, the relation between these objects only being established through interpretations and correspondence rules. Thus, formalization gives rise to abstraction, our next thematic category of contemporary science. However, abstraction is not necessarily bound to formalization since it can also ensue in the absence of any formalization or technification, purely as a process of redefinition.

In a certain basic sense, of course, all science involves abstraction, for, as Ravetz (1971) argues, all science deals with what he calls 'intellectually constructed objects' or 'ideal' objects and it departs from the objects of everyday commonsense. Bachelard (1949, 101) had made this the point of departure to his approach to science and spoken of a '*rupture avec la connaissance commune*'. In a basic sense, therefore, even Galilean mechanics calls for a degree of abstraction from commonsense insofar as it abstracts the so-called secondary qualities. However, abstraction did not go very far in the first epoch of Classical science, which lasted to the end of the eighteenth century. Bachelard points out that even Lavoisier employed the everyday implements of weights and measures to assay the chemicals he ordinarily dealt with: '*dans la chimie lavoisienne on pese le chlorure de sodium comme dans la vie commune on pese le sel de cuisine*' (ibid.). On another level of abstraction chemistry starts to determine atomic weight by means of mass spectroscopy and various types of isotopes are separated out. And so, analogously, in the history of the science of light, the eighteenth century was still bound to naive realism, and the decisive epistemological revolution only took place when Fresnel first instituted optics on an abstract basis and established in it the 'government of mathematics'. Mathematics itself took an abstract turn at this point when geometry abandoned its Euclidean intuitive notions for the formalisms of non-Euclidean geometry.

According to Bachelard the level of abstraction reached a new dimension in most of the sciences at the start of the nineteenth century, when an epistemological revolution occurred which inaugurated what we have here called the second phase of Classical science. At that point science for the first time departed from intuitive and common-sense notions. We can study this development in a number of constellations of sciences, to begin with in the mathematical and physical sciences. According to Scharlau, the early nineteenth century saw the origin of 'pure' mathematics, an abstract mathematics for the first time freed from any inherent physical application.

> The 18th century is characterized by a remarkable continuity and uniformity: in the foreground stands analysis and its application to mechanics, in particular to celestial mechanics. In this sense, the mathematics of the 18th century is applied mathematics, i.e. primarily aligned to the natural sciences and subordinate to the description of physical phenomena. . . . What we understand today as pure mathematics, namely theoretical mathematics in which mathematical theories are developed for their own sake and then applied to particular mathematical problems for their solution, first existed around the beginning of the nineteenth century (Janke and Otte 1981, 332).

The examples Scharlau gives are the new areas of abstract algebra: elliptic functions, the work of Abel and Jacobi; group theory, the creation primarily of Galois; algebraic number theory, complex analysis, mathematical logic, non-Euclidean geometry and even Fourier series. The last example relates closely to the parallel rise of pure physics in this period, which Cannon (1978, 111) in fact calls straight out 'the invention of physics'. Cannon does not consider Newtonian mechanics or optics a physics in the required sense and therefore claims that 'physics itself was invented by the French around the years 1810–30. . . . I would name Ampère, Carnot, Fourier, and Fresnel as among the first physicists' (ibid. 115). Whether or not one ought to consider their work the start of a new science, it is clear that a new level of abstraction had been reached which amounted to a veritable Bachelardian epistemological break.

From that point on the level of abstraction in mathematics and physics continued to rise through the second epoch of Classical science. In the twentieth century it reached its climax in pure number theory, in the symbolic logic of set theory, in the formalistic constructivism of Hilbert, and in Cantor's transfinite numbers—perhaps the ultimate in pure abstraction. Classical physics, too, reached its culminating abstraction in the work of Einstein and quantum theory. In this new physics all contact was finally abandoned with the ordinary concepts of human experience so that even space and time, cause and effect, continuity and identity assumed new abstract meanings far removed from the concrete objects of common reality. However, not all relation between theoretical abstraction and concrete reality was abandoned since it was always possible to translate by means of transformation rules from the one to the other. Only in certain branches of contemporary science have such difficulties in fact arisen, with the result that the relation between the abstract 'objects' of science and the real objects of experience is no longer apparent.

These branches of contemporary World science have, therefore, undergone a still further level of abstraction as compared with Classical science. Thus, for example, Steven Weinberg's proposal, previously noted, 'that the really fundamental laws of nature are not, in all cases, directly manifest . . . that nature, as we observe it, is but an imperfect representation of its own underlaying laws' (*Science in the Twentieth Century,* 79), constitutes a level of abstraction more rarified than anything encountered in science before. Other branches of theoretical physics also display that degree of abstraction in which theory and hypothesis take the form of nothing more than a purely mathematical formalism. Such a mathematical description might no longer have any clear physical meaning—in fact, in a literal sense it is description of nothing specific at all, though obviously it can be used as a calculating devise for the behaviour of real things.

And in turn, mathematics itself has developed in a 'pure' direction where it no longer seeks any application to the real world. The reason Kline (1980, 304) gives for this development is that contemporary mathematicians have moved even further in the direction of abstraction and generalization than during the previous epoch of Classical science: 'they have turned to fields such as abstract algebra and topology, to abstractions and generalizations such as functional analysis, to existence proofs for differential equations that are remote from applications, to axiomatization of various bodies of thought, and to arid brain games'. Although these developments are largely based on classical work, the further abstraction to which they have been subjected is largely new; it is at least no earlier than this century. Thus Marshall Stone writes in 1961:

> When we stop to compare the mathematics of today with mathematics as it was at the close of the nineteenth century we may well be amazed to note how rapidly our mathematics has grown in quantity and complexity, but we should also not fail to observe how closely this development has been involved with an emphasis on abstraction and an increasing concern with the perception and analysis of broad mathematical patterns (Kline 1980, 296).

Not all mathematicians are as sanguine as Stone that this is 'the true source of its tremendous vitality and growth during the present century' (ibid. 297). Abstraction in pure mathematics has meant its separation from science, the realm of applied mathematics. Many mathematicians opposed to this trend feel that it leads to the pursuit of recherché and trivial problems and to the neglect of interesting and important ones which emerge from application in science. Thus von Neumann warned against what he called 'baroque mathematics':

> As a mathematical discipline travels far from its empirical source, or still more, if it is a second and third generation only indirectly inspired by ideas coming from "reality", it is beset with grave dangers. It becomes more and more purely aestheticizing, more and more purely l'art pour l'art. . . . In other words, at a great distance from its empirical source, or after much "abstract" inbreeding, a mathematical subject is in danger of degeneration (Ravetz 1971a, 229).

Kline would obviously agree with this conclusion for he bases his main case against pure mathematics and for applied mathematics on just such an argument. He seeks to explain what he takes to be a very pernicious trend in largely academic political terms, pointing out that it relates closely to the recent professionalization of mathematics and its departmentalization as a self-contained discipline. Excessive specialization, narrow definition of problems with the resultant restrictions of communication and understanding to small specialist cliques, empty axiomatization that is no more than 'postulate piddling', selection of problems because they are easily solvable and publishable—all these are the symptoms of abstraction and professionalization in mathematics.

Abstraction and professionalization are found together in many World sciences, and not only in sciences but also at the other extreme in the humanities. Wherever there has been a tendency to constitute a pure discipline, abstraction and professionalization have been the cognitive and political means whereby this has been accomplished. Thus the attempt to institute a pure philosophy has meant its professionalization and the imposition of abstract forms of discourse. Rorty (1979, 131) points out that the beginnings of this development go back to Kant and that it was carried on by the neo-Kantians during the course of the nineteenth century as part of the transformation of philosophy into an academic discipline in the German university system. This tendency towards pure philosophy was furthered by Husserl's phenomenology as well as by Logical Positivism. The culmination and completion of this academic-intellectual process are not encountered until after the Second World War when philosophy became a self-contained discipline with little relation to any other and when abstract and abstracted forms of philosophizing were developed, such as linguistic analysis, which had no bearing on and no relevance to any other intellectual discourse. An analogous development can be traced also in literary studies, beginning much later and still not as complete. The need to give literary studies the dignity of an autonomous discipline led to the foundation and propagation of abstract aestheticizing schools such as New Criticism and is now promoting the Deconstructivist movement.

In the social sciences, too, abstraction and professionalization have gone hand in hand. The most professionalized social science, economics, is also the one most prone to purely abstract mathematical theory spinning without any reference or relevance to application in the real world of production, exchange and consumption. At the same time, as seen in relation to Klein's work, abstraction can be the effect of a misconceived abstracted empiricism that seeks to incorporate every detail of every business transaction in a great computer model with 'billions of equations each with many parameters' (Judson 1980, 126). If such a computer model does not give results which match those of the real world, governments are sometimes prevailed upon to ensure that the world conforms. And it is but a small step from this to the argument that the equations are always correct; only reality sometimes makes a mistake. So, too, in experimental psychology Nature is made to conform to theory when animals are carefully bred and reared to make them behave as learning theory predicts they should. The relation between the abstract terms of that theory—stimulus, response, drive, reward—and the observed activities of an animal in its natural surroundings is no longer apparent to animal ethologists. In sociology, too, the abstract objects of functionalist description or of systems theory are at a great remove from the real events of history and society. Wright Mills has satirized the tendency of Parsonian functionalism towards what he calls grand theory: 'the grand theorists . . . are so rigidly confined to such high levels of abstraction that the typologies they make up—and the work they do to make them up—seems more often an arid game of Concepts than an effort to define systematically—which is to say, in a clear and orderly way—the problems at hand, and to guide our efforts to solve them' (Wright Mills 1970, 43).

Thus without some degree of abstraction there could be no science, but too great a degree of abstraction places science out of touch with the Nature or the reality it is intended to explain or serve. 'More seriously, its practitioners can come to take their system of artificial objects as the basic reality, ignoring its differences from the external world which it was originally intended to represent' (Ravetz 1971a, 114). As Ravetz points out, the seriousness lies in the dangers that arise when the real problems encountered in society are solved by scientists solely in terms of their own abstractions in the artificial setting of their own formally redefined problem-situation. And when a problem does not fit the available abstract formulations it tends to be abandoned as not scientific.

Problem-Solving

Problem-solving is by no means an exclusive characteristic of World science. According to Kuhn, it is a feature of all 'normal' science following a paradigm revolution. Ravetz, too, insists that problem-solving through abstract terms in an artificially defined problem situation is a sine qua non of most sciences at all times. However, such problem-solving features dominate the contemporary sciences to a degree that neither Kuhn nor Ravetz takes fully into account for they do not realize that it marks a break with the Classical science of the past. Problem-solving is a very different task in the context of universalizing sciences that are theoretically unifying and progressively developing as compared with sciences that are narrowly specialized because they are technified, formalized, abstracted and finalized. The very nature of the problems that arise is going to be different; in World science these are mainly specialized problems to be solved by applying set technical procedures. But even when the problems to be solved call for considerable ingenuity and sometimes even for creativity on the level of genius, the science this activity promotes will have a different character from the Classical science of the past. For, as Ravetz (1971a, 232) is aware, 'the continuous increase in the number of solved problems is not at all the same as the deepening and enrichment of scientific knowledge'.

World science is a problem-solving activity par excellence in a way that no previous science was. Whereas previously problems arose almost in passing from other more important aspects of scientific research or method, now they are one of the key determinants of new scientific knowledge. When the elaboration of theory or the discovery of laws was the main preoccupation, problems appeared at the periphery as difficulties to be overcome in order to establish the theories or laws in question. Kuhn assigns problem-solving to his second phase of scientific activity following the creation of a new paradigm, the phase of normal science. In the

Classical sciences problem-solving was clearly a secondary activity, for the most part undertaken by those who were less than great minds. The problems arising out of Newtonian celestial mechanics preoccupied a host of subsequent mathematicians and physicists. Kuhn is surely right in drawing some such distinction even though the division between paradigm creation and the problem-solving of ordinary science never reached the degree Kuhn postulates. However, in contemporary science there is almost no such division. The aim of attaining new knowledge is frequently presented as a proposal of a problem to be solved. In fact, the greater achievement often is not the solution of a known problem but the proposal and definition of a new interesting problem—though that never wins Nobel prizes.

Science assumes a different character when its knowledge is gained through a process of inventing and solving problems. It becomes an activity that can be undertaken piecemeal, requiring the collaboration of many participants, which means that frequently it is a large group effort. For example, the problem of deriving the complete set of all possible simple groups involved the team effort of some 100 mathematicians under the 'leadership' of Gorenstein and resulted in 500 scientific papers covering 10,000 pages in the journals. The problem was pre-determined and a programme for its solution could be planned in advance. The more difficult and interesting the problem, the more it requires insight and imagination for not only is the solution unforeseeable but even the approach to the problem and the method of tackling it have to be discovered. The definition of the problem might require ingenuity amounting to genius. However most problems are not of this order of creativity; they simply arise out of having to fulfil ends and goals from outside science.

In a situation of finalization, the scientist has to exercise ingenuity in deciding whether the particular science is at a stage where it is capable of solving a given problem or whether there is a cognitive deficit and more pure research still needs to be done. The problems of building nuclear and thermonuclear devices were considered to be, in Oppenheimer's phrase, 'technically sweet' or ripe for solution because the scientific knowledge then available in physics, chemistry, and technology was judged adequate to the task. The solution to the second of these problems found by Teller— and presumably almost simultaneously by his Russian counterpart Sakharov—was greeted with delight in scientific assemblies as a 'neat trick' on Nature, one which, as Sakharov has since realized, has also tricked its inventors. In this case we can only hope that the engineers will not be hoisted on their own petard. Since these 'great' problem-solving achievements scientists have very often been mistaken about what is 'technically sweet' and within the contemporary competence of science to solve: controlled plasma fusion to produce unlimited energy was long promised but is as far as ever from fulfilment; a cure for cancer also seems beyond the present reach of science despite work on the largest scale; the social sciences have had even less success with their problems. It is obvious, therefore, that there are limits to the problems science can at present solve. Selecting the right problems and abandoning the impossible ones are perhaps the most urgent critical tasks of science. Unfortunately, there is almost no problem that some scientist will not attempt provided the funding is available. In weapons research, as Ryle (1981, 24) states, 'if the device includes a problem for which there is at present no solution, so much the better—it must be investigated, funds are needed ("too soon to know")'. Scientists' attachment to problem-solving makes them ripe for exploitation for almost any end whatsoever. Many scientists are, fortunately, still engaged on beneficial problem-solving. But nearly all scientists are routinely solving pre-determined problems whose answers can be foreseen in general terms. It is therefore easy to tell whether their answers are right or wrong. Students in science are trained by having to do research to find answers to problems which are already known in general terms apart from the details or exact numbers. Problem-solving is, thus, the standard fare of work in most sciences at most levels.

Even some of the greatest theoretical achievements of contemporary science have some of the hallmarks of problem solutions. The threshold of the contemporary era in genetics was crossed by the solution of the decoding problem of the structure of the DNA molecule by Watson and Crick. The definition of this problem took considerable time and was mainly carried out by biochemists belonging to an earlier scientific tradition, above all by Avery and Chargaff. The problem was defined with great difficulty and much patient research, for only gradually and with effort could it be proved that DNA was the carrier of heredity and that heredity was 'coded' in a structure made up of four basic chemicals. Once defined and posed the problem could be solved relatively easily for it showed itself to be one of decoding, that is, akin to a conundrum or puzzle for which many clues were available, above all some outstanding crystallographic x-ray photographs made by Franklin. Hence, no sooner was the problem defined than the solution was forthcoming with brilliance and panache arising from the personal style of the discoverers. Its style carried all before it. The old style work, such as that of McClintock, was relegated to a backwater, and ever newer problems were generated requiring their own solutions.[1] Eventually, molecular genetics became a routine problem-solving activity, which is now of a largely technical nature. As a prominent biochemist Cavalieri comments:

> For example, the recent manufacture of insulin through recombinant DNA technology by Walter Gilbert and his co-workers at Harvard and by William Rutter and Howard Goodman at the University of California, involved procedures which had already been established; no new basic scientific information came from this work. It was a sophisticated engineering feat, with results readily transferable to industrial processing (Cavalieri 1981, 133).

The concentration on problem-solving in this, as in any other science, came to exercise an extremely wide-ranging influence on the whole character of the scientific undertaking, affecting the general goals of the science, its specific research programmes and the methods and techniques employed. As Yoxen points out, the attitude of molecular biologists to life changed as a result of the problem-solving impetus:

The effects of this increasingly intense drive for results was to enforce an exclusive concentration on just these problems, phenomena, or aspects of an organism that filled the needs of specific research programmes. Molecular biologists learnt to take an increasingly instrumental attitude to the living material with which they worked and were forced through the pressures of international competition to intensify the degree of specialization in the problem-solving skills required to stay in the field. As a result, their relationship with, and conception of, nature changed. Life came to be viewed in information terms (Yoxen 1982, 136).

A concentration on solvable problems in turn affects and is affected by all the academic political aspects of science in a vicious circle of cumulative causation. The need for publishable results means that only those problems are tackled which promise to be solvable with the available techniques in the period of time for which funding is allocated. Any deeper problems or ones that do not lend themselves to quick solutions tend to be avoided. In any case, research which undertakes such problems will almost certainly cease for lack of funds. Funding tends to be given for problems where results are forthcoming, not ones which seem interminable. As Cavalieri (1981, 78) notes, 'the contemporary scientist is more than ever aware that in order to stay in the business of science he must produce; and it helps immensely if his discoveries are laced with public relations'.

The division of any serious scientific problematic or research program into a series of specialized and restricted problem packets is an almost inevitable approach to science given the prevailing authority structure. It helps to sustain the hierarchy of scientific authority and the bureaucratic management of departments and institutes. Doling out pre-packaged problems to be solved in a given time is a division of labour that has the same effect in the laboratory that it has in the factory. It enables managers as superiors to maintain authority without doing the work, and it enables workers as subordinates to do the work without being responsible for the overall results. This approach is further reinforced where the solution of problems is of a purely technical nature for in such circumstances the scientific workers assume the role of a technical proletariat and the separation of the worker from the means of production is complete. Industralized science eventuates.

Problem-solving of this kind pushes science ever further in the direction of technology. Any distinction between a scientific research laboratory and a technical institute disappears. Both specialize in solving useful problems on contract. Thus once molecular biology had gone in the direction of genetic engineering it assumed the problem-solving propensities of a technological enterprize.

The human hormone somatostatin was the first functional protein to be synthesized by gene-splicing, and with its synthesis for the first time in the field of molecular biology, science and technology coalesced. The scientific goal was to show that a human gene could be expressed (i.e., make protein) within a bacterium, whereas the technological aim was to show that it is feasible to manufacture a protein in this new way for the commercial markets of the world (Cavalieri 1981, 71).

From that point onwards genetic engineering has continued with its problem-solving routines, utilizing known techniques for externally determined
ends increasingly of a commercial nature.

Many contemporary sciences have gone through such a process, driven
deeper into technification and finalization by their problem-solving propensities and the example of a few definitive successes. Some of their
problems are extremely difficult and will only be solved with outstanding
brilliance, and they will be heralded in the usual way as fundamental
break-throughs. Nevertheless, it is unlikely that such solutions will uncover
anything fundamentally unknown. Weingart (1978, 276) reports that in the
National Academy's evaluation of eight subfields of physics 'only Elementary Particles and Astrophysics and Relativity theory are granted definite
potential for discovery of fundamental laws'. He concludes that 'most of
chemistry, solid-state physics and systematic biology are examples of extensive research, in which the fundamental principles are understood and
the task of research is to discover how they apply to real objects or
systems' (ibid.). In other words, the task of research is to solve problems.

As Lindblom and Cohen (1979) have shown, problem-solving in the
social sciences has reached almost pathological dimensions, with the result
that no difficulty is considered beyond the scope of policy sciences to put
it right. The effects in many cases of a premature and presumptuous
misapplication of social science have been the serious aggravation of existing social difficulties. Alternatively, the neglect of real problems by the
social sciences has rendered them non-existent in professional and public
consciousness. 'An example is the exclusion from academic economics of
the problems of the under-developed countries until after the Second World
War. . . . A remarkable feature of American political science, shared to
some extent with other social sciences, was its long-time implicit denial
of the existence of a large population of blacks in our society' (ibid. 94).
There is a widespread reluctance to recognize that most problems do not
have a readily formulable scientific solution. The fact that we have so
many problem-solving sciences and hosts of problems almost inevitably
brings the two together. The mixture is sometimes explosive, as in the
practice of strategic studies in applying the problem-solving methods of
games-theory to the intractable non-mathematical problems of the arms
race—leading to their exacerbation.

Finalization or the Ends of Science

Finally we arrive at finalization, a term recently introduced to refer to
the extrinsic ends of science which builds on and develops further the
political direction of science which became generally prevalent after the
Second World War. The practice of research for military ends during the
war and the huge influx of funds for all kinds of externally stipulated
purposes after the war had already produced the idea of mission-oriented
research. Finalization, however, goes much further for it shows how this
process is furthered from within science itself by its own autonomous
theoretical development. Harvey Brooks came close to the idea in the
early 1960s when he defined what he called 'basic research in engineering':

The term "basic research in engineering" causes a great deal of confusion, since engineering is ordinarily thought of as, by definition, "applied". Nevertheless, a number of basic scientific disciplines have become traditionally associated with engineering in universities. These are pursued largely for their own sake and are just as fundamental as the disciplines associated with the natural sciences. The basic sciences associated with engineering are primarily those concerned with the behaviour of man-made systems—information theory, the theory of structures, the theory of feedback and control systems, computer and systems theory—but they are nonetheless fundamental. Moreover, subjects such as fluid mechanics, solid mechanics, and thermodynamics—what might be called macroscopic or classical physics—have been largely taken over as basic engineering sciences (Brooks 1968, 61–2).

But even this idea of basic engineering sciences does not go far enough, for it does not show how such sciences differ theoretically from the Classical sciences. This difference must be explored in order to explain what is meant by finalization in the World sciences.

Finalization was made possible by the fact that many Classical sciences were already mature in the sense that they had arrived at closed theories (Schäfer 1983, 133), having discovered the basic laws at least in the non-fundamental sciences, and so could explain almost anything within their scope in principle. But from these generalized laws, which applied only to abstracted objects and simplified models, it generally proved impossible to derive specific explanations for complex phenomena, especially those involved in technical systems or useful problem situations. In other words, technology and the other useful and applied sciences could only utilize the general and abstract results of the pure Classical sciences as overall specifications within which their specific answers had to fall, but not as formulae from which these answers could be derived. The logical point, made much of by Positivist philosophers, that practical problems could be reduced to general laws did not entail the converse, that answers for them could be derived from these laws. As we saw in Chapter 1, the issue of complexity intervened. The theoretical reduction of objects X to more basic objects Y did not entail, as the Positivist philosophers of science imagined, the derivability of X from Y, for example, of biological entities from chemical substances. The only way of overcoming this problem of complexity was to devise special intermediate theories specifically designed to solve problems arising out of the application of general laws in concrete situations, usually in areas of technology and the useful and applied sciences. Thus arose many of the specialized theories which Boehme, van den Daele and Krohn regard as early instances of finalization: in chemistry, Liebig's agricultural chemistry, dating from the mid-nineteenth century; later in chemical engineering and in fluid mechanics, where Ludwig Prandtl developed a specialized theory; and now in contemporary fields such as plasma physics, heavy ions, environmental research, educational research, computer science and cancer research.[2]

What accounts in such cases for the feature of finalization—the word is to be understood more in the Aristotelian sense of directed to a final end as telos rather than in any sense of finality—is that research is promoted and guided by external ends and purposes rather than by the intrinsic explanatory goals of science itself, as in the Classical sciences. Once a Classical science had arrived at a mature state, in Heisenberg's sense of the term as discussed in Chapter 2, and had developed a relatively complete and closed theory governing its specific field, such as Newtonian mechanics or Maxwell's theory or Quantum mechanics, then any further research in this field could no longer be guided by the intrinsic disciplinary goal of seeking more basic laws. Instead research would tend to proliferate and expand horizontally into sub-fields of application of the already known basic laws. But which sub-field to choose for further detailed investigation or which problem situation or even object to address could not be decided solely by reference to the basic theory. At this point criteria of choice based on needs, purposes and other values extrinsic to natural science had to enter to guide the further development of finalized special theories.

> The social interest in specific themes has induced the development of the general theory into various directions. Thus, technical and military interests have promoted the aerodynamics of aircraft construction, the environmental problem of noise pollution fostered aeroacoustics, and the needs of cardiac research will eventually lead to the development of some physiological theory of fluids (Boehme, van den Daele and Krohn 1976, 316).

In fact this kind of direction by interests and ends had always obtained in the social sciences, so in that way finalization in the natural sciences marks a new convergence in the sciences. But ironically for the philosophers of science, this convergence is in the opposite direction to a reduction of the social sciences to the natural sciences.

In brief then, the finalization thesis applies at the stage of mature science when theories are complete so that the further development and elaboration of theories cannot take place as a matter of inner articulation according to inherent norms of the science itself. The driving force of theoretical explanation that was operative before the science was mature is no longer there; in other words, the work of bringing ever wider dimensions of reality under one general theory and of unifying the divergent theories under still more general ones has already been largely accomplished. At this stage a science becomes open to external value direction in its further theoretical development. Finalization, then, is a matter of the 'openness of science to external purposes becoming the guide-line of theory' (ibid. 310). Under contemporary conditions of research such external purposes are predominantly political, for this is the era of political funding of science, of science planning and policy direction, and of mission-oriented research. Finalization, therefore, results from a two-fold confluence: the development of a science to a stage where 'it implies openness to the social or political determination of the course it is to follow' (ibid. 312), due to its own process of maturation; in parallel with that process within science there is a process within society and politics where problems are seen to be open to scientific solution. These politically stipulated problems then take on the role of external purposes around which the science develops; they become the presuppositions of its further theoretical articulation. Thus at this stage 'problem-orientation and the "internal" dynamics of disciplinary development can be co-ordinated' (van den Daele, Krohn and Weingart 1977, 234).

Thus the process whereby external ends become internalized in a science takes two complementary paths: first, the downward expansion and extension of pure research itself, away from the intensive search for ever greater unification and more general laws, towards the particularity of detailed working out of specific sub-fields guided by final ends; and, second, the upward intensification of applied research or technology through its own inherent problems into areas of relatively pure research where theory elaboration is required. In the second trend, as van den Daele, Krohn and Weingart put it, 'the strategic direction of science may assume such complexity that problem-solving can no longer depend on the application of advances made in basic research but instead implies the production of new forms of fundamental knowledge' (ibid. 220). The downward trend from pure to applied science and the upward trend from applied to pure are simultaneous and congruent. And what results from this mutual approximation is no longer either pure or applied science but an amalgam of the two in which the distinction disappears. The authors previously quoted have made extensive studies of many contemporary compound pure-applied fields in the natural, formal and social sciences. Some analogous developments go back a long way into the past, for example, agricultural chemistry, chemical engineering and theoretical engineering which all date from around 1850. But most such developments were only in their infancy till after the Second World War.

These authors make it quite clear that in such a finalized discipline research is not simply a matter of deducing special applications from already known laws and fundamental theories. As Boehme (1979, 116) points out, 'it has turned out that to make a fundamental theory applicable to specific practical problems the former must be developed into a special theory oriented to these practical problems'. Such a special theory gives rise to a new sub-field which has many of the features of pure research, such as theoretical models, special laws and boundary specifications of applicability; but at the same time, the whole of this special theory and the sub-field it promotes is subsumable under an already known general theory. 'Special theories are developed out of fundamental theories by means of kernel expansions' such that 'the concepts which engender these expansions are determined by intended applications which are of practical relevance' (ibid. 117). Boehme gives the example of fluid mechanics, where within a mature but practically useless general theory, classical hydrodynamics, Ludwig Prandtl developed a special theory based on the concept of boundary layer which made the general theory applicable to practical problems (ibid.). Many such examples in which problems of application, themselves determined by ends to be served, guide the theoretical development of special theories and produce sub-fields of research. Johnston and Jagtenberg (1976) show how such sub-fields can be set up as a result of goal directions outlined in government policy, or through public demand, or economic needs; thus, for example, the new specialized sciences of tribology or lubrication engineering, environmental research and solar energy research arose in these ways.

Thus far in their writing the finalization thesis theorists have given little attention to finalization in the social and behavioural sciences. In this vast and rich field of sciences guided by external ends something like finalization has obviously occurred not because of any presumed 'maturity' of theories leading to theoretical closures. The general theories available in these sciences are far from mature; they are invariably the subject of intense disputation and are usually in conflict with each other. Even the supposition that the relation between general social theories and their social application is like the relation between the pure and applied natural sciences is a seriously mistaken one. There has been considerable confused talk of 'social engineering' sciences but these are nothing like physical engineering proper; nor did they originate because 'pure' theory became capable of concrete application. Finalization in the social sciences, which has been extensive, has to be explained in different ways from finalization in the natural sciences. It had to do with the external imposition of ends deriving from the needs of mass society, industry, complex organization and State administration, frequently for the purpose of waging total war. At the same time, what made it scientifically feasible for these ends to be served was the autonomous development within these sciences of a large body of procedures and techniques which were capable of general social application outside the experimental situation, the scholarly research task, or the individual therapy in which they may have originated. I have already mentioned the rise of such techniques in earlier sections; they are bound up with technification which is closely related to finalization. None of this has much to do with the 'maturity' of theories in the sense that the finalization thesis theorists intend.

Thus in one form or another finalization is a feature of most World sciences, and few of them can any longer function without external goal directives. This is clearly demonstrated by the present situation in the large research institutes where Big Science is practised. The incidental discussion among key scientific luminaries and administrators during a symposium on the present state of science, entitled Civilization and Science, shows clearly that despite the formal content of the official papers this question of goal direction is the main source of their worries in science. How to keep establishments, such as the Oak Ridge Laboratory or the Euratom Laboratory at Ispra or Harwell, running and busy with research when their initial tasks have been played out is the theme to which the influential scientific administrators Weinberg, Thiemann and Lord Todd keep returning time and again. According to Thiemann, these establishments are now floundering 'like sailing boats with no wind'; Lord Todd puts it very directly: 'finding big new tasks is a tremendous problem. One is starting at the wrong end: instead of finding something that one can work on, one is starting out with a set of facilities and people and trying to find a problem to match. Unless continually changing economic objectives can be found, research institutions die' (Thiemann 1972, 85). One wonders what will be the fate of NASA once Star Wars ceases to be promoted on a big and expensive scale or of the big nuclear establishments at Los Alamos and in the Soviet Union, Britain and France, once the production of bombs ceases. The importance of finding new goals for scientists to work on becomes politically crucial if they are ever to be weaned from their present addiction to war production, which if continued much longer will lead from the finalization to the finality of science and much else besides. In all these cases the problem is finding new worthwhile ends without which the sciences will wither, for they can no longer be expected to develop through their own inherent theoretical advance as they did in the past. New ends are called for to promote alternative sciences.

The Scientific Establishment

I have shown that contemporary World science is characterized by a constellation of defining features, including technification, formalization, abstraction, problem-solving and finalization. This is not to say that every science now necessarily displays all these features at once, nor does it even mean that there are no instances of scientific work that evince few if any of these characteristics. Although there are numerous cases of exceptional sciences, these are the exceptions that prove the rule. The major or dominant disciplines or fields within science at present are those which display some combination of most of these characteristics.

The foregoing distinguishing characteristics of the contemporary sciences correlate closely with their organizational dispositions and institutional arrangements. Sciences that are highly technified require large-scale organizations, with teams operating high-powered machinery requiring an extensive division of labour. And vice-versa, where such organized institutions exist, the scientific work they will tend to undertake and the results they will tend to produce will be mostly highly technified. Funding of specialized projects through institutes or designated teams will almost invariably produce 'finalized' scientific research. And vice-versa, the tendency towards finalized research, where it is already pronounced, will seek support from outside agencies which will direct it towards their own ends. Problem-solving will almost inevitably be the character of such works, since there will be a predisposition by the scientific organization itself as well as by outside bodies to subdivide functionally any task to be accomplished and allocate it in small parcels as specific problems to be solved on contract. Thus there is an elective affinity between the various cognitive, instrumental and organizational aspects of contemporary science. In general terms it may be roughly concluded that sciences which deal with complex objects must be organized in a complex way: putting it another way, a human system is often required to cope with a system in Nature.

Such a human system needs to be directed as well as organized, and such direction entails authority and control. Invariably the small groups that exercise controlling authority will become an establishment. As in a church, so in science, an establishment enforces a belief-system together with orthodox practices, institutional arrangements, status hierarchies and an authority structure. Whitley (1982, 316) claims that 'establishments in the sciences acquire, control and allocate resources for the production, validation and extension of particular knowledges by awarding reputations to individuals, groups and employment organizations on the basis of their contributions to the intellectual goals of the organizations as interpreted by the establishment'. Elias (1982a, 40) adds that 'by virtue of their monopolistic control of an existing fund of knowledge and the skills needed for developing it, for producing new knowledge, they can exclude others from access to these resources or admit them to their use selectively'.

Such exclusions or restrictions are directed not only against individuals but also against whole fields or even disciplines which do not satisfy the requirements of the dominant sciences—generally those not sufficiently technified, formalized, abstracted, problem-solving and finalized. In such cases one can perceive the workings of a super-establishment which directs the course of science as a whole. This general Establishment is largely made up of the leading members of the specific establishments of the dominant disciplines, above all physics, for these disciplines mutually cohere and reinforce each other. Scientists from other disciplines who have run afoul of this Establishment insist that it exists and that it operates in an exclusionary manner. Barry Commoner asserts: 'You understand that there is an Establishment . . . and you either have to decide that you are going to bend yourself to do the right thing and conform, not upset people— or if you don't, you just turn your back on it' (Goodell 1977, 60), which given the power of the Establishment is easier said than done. From another point of view, Eisenhower was referring to such an Establishment in his 'Farewell Address' when he spoke of a scientific-technological elite which represents science as far as the State is concerned. Through its control of funding and top appointments this elite largely manages the whole research program of the United States.

This group is surprizingly small in number. The Roses state that 'in the United States, for example, it has been estimated that some 200–300 key decision-makers—primarily scientists—constitute the inner elite out of a total scientific work-force of some two million' (Rose and Rose 1980, 33). They go on to comment that 'the restricted membership of this elite stratum is evident in the management of the entire research system' (ibid.). The political dominance of this elite stratum also has not escaped attention; Goodell (1977, 48) comments that 'too much power in Washington seemed to be concentrated in a few influential scientific advisers, a self-perpetuating, self-selecting elite, in which new members were carefully screened for political pliability'. The situation in Britain and the other major scientific countries is similar in this respect though the make-up and role of the scientific Establishments differ, largely due to the cultural and social differences of the societies involved.

In all countries the scientific Establishments closely resemble the society of which they are a product. And in general the all-pervasive Rationalization of modern society has its counterpart in that of science as well. Science tends to become permanently fixed and set in its ways just as does the bureaucracy, the State or industry. Nevertheless, this Rationalization is not yet complete; other principles of rationality are also at work. Exponents of one or another mode of critical reason, ranging from the conservatives to the radicals, are to be found disputing the Establishment's hold on science and calling for a scientific reformation. The main barrier standing in their way is the prevailing authority structure of science or what might colloquially be called academic politics. Thus before we can proceed, in Part 3, to examine these demands for a reformation of science and the existing trends towards an alternative future science, we must first in Part 2 consider in general the place of authority in science. Without this understanding we cannot overcome the present authority structures, and no scientific reformation can even be contemplated.

Part Two

Knowledge and
Authority

4

Knowledge and Authority: An Introduction

By these three, namely the priesthood, the empire and the university (studio), the holy Catholic Church is spiritually sustained, increased and ruled as by three virtues.

—Alexander of Roes, *De Translatione Imperii*

Sacerdotum, Imperium et Studio

Political, spiritual and intellectual modes of authority have been ubiquitous almost throughout civilized history. Typically they have been embodied in functionally separate governmental, ecclesiastical and academic polities—*imperium, sacerdotum* and *studio*—that is, in forms of State, Church and School. In contemporary societies the dominant and governing school polity is a complex system of education whose upper stratum is composed of universities and research institutes; within these the intellectual loci of authority are the scientific and scholarly disciplines. This school polity is formally separate from State and Church, though it is wholly dependent on the former for its economic maintenance, just as in the middle ages it was reliant on the latter. In other periods and in other civilizations State, Church and School were not as functionally distinct as they are now; one need only recall the role of priests in governmental and educational establishments at earlier times.

However, although they are now functionally segregated, the authority structures of State, Church and School are still in many respects homologous. Thus, a highly centralized, hierarchical and bureaucratically organized regime in the State will have close structural parallels in some churches and even closer authoritarian analogues in the regimen of the university and research-institute complex, as well as in the very disposition of intellectual authority of many scientific disciplines. It is not my prime purpose in this context to explore such parallels nor to trace the causal sequences in which they arise and develop, but they should always be borne in mind since they frequently suggest broad sociological explanations for the development of forms of authority in the sciences.

Thus it is possible to show in broad terms that the transformation of the older universities and academies into contemporary multiversity and research-institute complexes results from causes parallel to those involved in the transition from absolutist monarchies to bureaucratic states. Previously the sciences were more like 'schools' in the old sense; the forms of authority governing them were personal, simpler and less institutionally organized than at present, when research is often centrally planned and hierarchically directed in large organizations of Big Science. Whitley puts this change in authority structure in rather simple, but basically correct terms—albeit with some exaggerations and omissions:

> In pre-professional sciences, prestige and authority was a personal possession which could not really be reproduced, except perhaps through a few disciples and provided one lived long enough it was possible, at any rate in principle, to successfully challenge the orthodoxy. . . . Contrarily, in professional sciences, authority becomes institutionalized in employing organizations which educate neophytes, provide resources and generally control the conditions of scientific work. Orthodoxies become reified in textbooks, courses and organizational commitments; the death of an eminent individual no longer opens up new possibilities and challenges from outsiders. . . . Authority develops into an organizational form of property (Whitley 1977a, 147).

In this chapter I shall explore at length the effects on the system of the sciences of such changes in the structure of their authority forms in order to show that scientific methods, practices, and ideas—indeed the intellectual content of whole sciences—change as a result.

Such a conclusion will come as a surprise only to those who still think of scientific research as inherently an autonomous rational procedure governed by the abstract and impersonal logic of the one and only scientific method, by which a few individuals of genius discover new truths about Nature or humankind and add them to the cumulatively progressing store of knowledge. It will be less surprising to those who have already considered what it means to make an acknowledged discovery in the present scientific dispensation. First, it means getting a paper or book accepted by an editor or referees and so attaining to the minimum of authorship. Second, it means that the results, style of work and ideas of the published piece are legitimated in the specific discipline if and when they are accepted by other workers in the field as results to be cited, work to be followed up in the same style, and ideas to be treated as yielding further potential working hypotheses. Third, it means that scientists in other disciplines are willing to acknowledge that the established results, style of work and confirmed hypotheses of the discipline are also binding in their own disciplines. And last, if all these steps are successful, the general public is told authoritatively that this is now a truth of science. The discovery of truth is thus a cycle of authorship and authority; at each stage of this process there are issues of authorization at stake.

And even before this public process of authorization can begin, when authorship alone is sought or claimed, there are organizational authorizing procedures to be undergone. An individual has to be certified and hold the approved qualifications and positions before he or she can gain access to the tools of scientific research and so begin to work. The individual's specific proposed research project has to be approved authoritatively at every step: as he or she is granted funding, and assigned students or assistants and recruits collaborators. Most of the time such institutionally supported scientific work is conducted in direct competition with that of other teams of scientists in parallel institutions engaged on the same or similar work; this competition constitutes a struggle for authority or mastery of the scientific field in question in every sense of that term. As Bourdieu (1975, 19) sees it, in every scientific field a struggle takes place for 'the monopoly of scientific authority, defined inseparably as technical capacity and social power, or to put it another way, the monopoly of scientific competence, in the sense of a particular agent's socially recognized capacity to speak and act legitimately (i.e., in an authorized and authoritative way) in scientific matters'. Such a field is bound by a network of different kinds of authority forms—a point Bourdieu tends to overlook—constituting a regimen of research for which the old words 'school', 'scientific society' and even 'discipline' are now all-too-quaint anachronisms.

However, this complex contemporary scientific polity is no unprecedented departure from purely personal authority, as Whitley almost makes it appear; the schools of the past also had impersonal authority structures peculiar to themselves. Each of the historically distinguishable scientific eras had a different polity and economy of science: a specific subdivision of the field of knowledge into subjects or disciplines, an appropriate division of labour within them, unique goals and values, tacit rules of competitive struggle and conditions of success and failure, ethical and professional norms governing permissible behaviour, and in general a sui generis scientific ethos. Science was practised quite differently in the period immediately preceding the World science epoch.

In the second phase of Classical science, from the early nineteenth century till almost the start of the Second World War, science was mainly, though not exclusively, the preserve of professors with their almost 'privately' owned laboratories attached to academic chairs in the newly reformed German-style universities, which became nearly universally prevalent. Scientific work was still highly decentralized and largely individualistic. Independent researchers could produce acceptable scientific results, usually in the newer or less prestigious sciences, while remaining outside the universities, which at that time provided only tiny research institutes. Within the university the authority of the individual professor was paramount in his own chair, which was not yet a department; the collective authority of the professoriate of each university decided what specific sciences were to be studied there, and the 'republic of professors' ruled over broader fields of science. Yet each professor, if capable, could develop his own brand of science almost from scratch and nobody was entitled or felt free to interfere. There was as yet no disciplinary association to bring professors to heel if they strayed beyond the accepted confines.

In the first phase of Classical science, preceding that of university-based science, from approximately the mid-seventeenth century till the late eighteenth, science was practised largely outside the unreformed and antiquated universities still dominated by scholastic philosophy; the new 'scientists' were amateur natural philosophers, who were usually gentlemen of leisure, including a sprinkling of lower class 'mechanics' and a few other banausic types. The ruling authoritative bodies were the newly established academies of science, some of which were royal academies under monarchical charter. These were the earliest of specifically scientific research organizations, though the Renaissance academies of seekers after the 'secrets of nature' had prepared their way. Prior to the Renaissance, scholastic science— usually based on Aristotle and as yet not formally separated from metaphysics and theology—was pursued by masters in the universities founded all over Europe from the early middle ages onwards.

This system of university authority was decisive and formative for the subsequent development of science and scholarship, although the universities temporarily fell into desuetude later. The universities made learning, and eventually the sciences, an 'academic' process, that is, an accredited, continuous and full time enterprise practised jointly by groups of masters and their common students. This form of authority was a quite different form of authority from that of both the general and the differentiated schools, with their charismatically revered heads, found in high cultures outside Europe. In the ancient classical world schools had also usually been based on the work of great teachers and their successors. The philosophic schools of Athens, such as the Academy, Lyceum, and Stoa, had begun and continued in this way. Only the great museum-libraries, such as that at Alexandria, were state establishments funded to carry out research and so were the sole historical anticipations of modern scientific royal academies at least in their earlier stages.

Science has been successfully practised under a wide diversity of regimes and regimens of sacerdotum, imperium and studio. Hence, it is not possible to stipulate that one kind of disciplinary authority structure is in some sense best for science. Each form of authority and its associated institutions can successfully produce a corresponding kind of scientific knowledge and would be unable to produce other kinds. Thus, a highly decentralized, fully competitive and free-market-like mode of scientific production—which is still the prevalent 'liberal' ideal of most philosophers of science—would be incapable of producing the results of the contemporary large-scale highly organized science. But by contrast, the more authoritarian discipline of science has forfeited the individualistic qualities of scientific creativity associated with the previous more liberal era of free competition in a marketplace of ideas. It would be pointless to try to recover those qualities, to turn back the clock to an earlier scientific era—but this does not mean that specific reforms modelled on the past are not to be attempted. Each age has its own qualities. So it is never possible to generalize about what kind of scientific authority or political involvement or the lack of authority is best for scientific advance. For sometimes in its history science has profited from political guidelines and sometimes it has been cramped by them. The setting up of royal academies was one of the first of many expressly political acts which have furthered the cause of science. But at present the political redirection of science for destructive and sometimes repressive ends cannot but harm it.

The scientific polity is at present extremely well integrated into the State, and it functions largely at the State's behest and direction. The production and reproduction of scientific knowledge are now indispensable to the functioning of society at every level; the economy, health and social services, work, leisure and above all defence, as well as all the other State agencies, are dependent on scientific research. Research is itself merely the apex of the total pyramid of scientific knowledge with its base in the educational system of training and enculturation. This is what we mean when we say that science has entered a stage of organized production of knowledge. The parallels between political authority and scientific authority are now very pronounced; both rely on bureaucratic hierarchies, on technical expertise, on planned routines, on disciplined and disciplinary work; both are in some fundamental sense authoritarian.

To emphasize authority structures in science in this way is not to discount cognitive norms of methods, ideas, theories, modes of testing and logics of argumentation, which have their own relative autonomy and do not simply consist of imposed authoritative pronouncements or regulations. Neither does it discount technical instrumentation and technique, namely the technological dimension of science which also has its own partial autonomy. It is, however, to insist that authority structures, instrumentation and cognitive norms are aspects of the one social process of scientific work and hence are so intimately related that changes in the one will invariably bring about changes in the other; contention or disputation in the one dimension almost invariably brings about conflict in the other. Thus, cognitive differences over theories, testing procedures, the direction of research, or any other such basic disagreements are almost always linked to competition for authority, with the result that it is difficult to disentangle the one from the other. Any separations and distinctions are not based on some supposedly logical difference between a presumed 'context of discovery' and a 'context of verification or falsification', as the Positivists imagined. Since authority structures and cognitive norms are two facets of the one complex social and intellectual process of scientific work, it is possible to distinguish them for heuristic purposes of comparison and so separate them up to a point. Inevitably such distinctions must break down at the interface where these facets merge. And any distinction will always be merely provisional, for if made in one way it will no longer be useful for other purposes in other contexts where different criteria will have to be invoked and the distinction redefined. To call one feature of science a matter of ideas or method and another a matter of authority is always relative to a given sociological perspective and the concepts and categories elaborated within it.

Consider, for example, the situation in the newly burgeoning science of Artificial Intelligence as outlined by James Fleck. He speaks of 'the range of, often conflicting, views within the field itself' and goes on to specify how these conflicts involve at once differences over ideas, programs, plans, power and funds:

Something of this has already become evident in the differences between Longuet-Higgins and Michie, one favouring the cognitive science definition of AI, and the other the Machine Intelligence approach. There are other divisions: those supporting a theoretical formal approach, such as McCarthy, for instance, and those supporting the exploitation of practical applications, such as Feigenbaum; those who see no problems with accepting military funding (McCarthy and Feigenbaum) and those implacably opposed (Melzer, while Michie was opposed to classified work). These divisions, which are legion in the area, are coupled with a rather amazing state of substantive partisanship, or scientific ethnocentricity, in which proponents of the various different research areas each tend to see their own approach as the real AI approach—to the theorem provers, theorem proving is central, for the natural language proponents, language is the basis for reason, and so on. Many of these differences can be related to the background competencies of the practitioners, and can be interpreted as competition between groups on the research area level for resources and authority within AI as a speciality, constituting perhaps the primary locus for competition over cognitive commitments (Fleck 1982, 206).

Competition over cognitive commitments—that is, over ideas, methods and research programs—is in this case inseparable from competition over authority. Since both involve issues of legitimacy, it follows that both are on the same level and that there are no intrinsic 'logical' differences between them.

Nevertheless, it would be a mistake to identify these aspects, even in the theoretically sophisticated way that Bourdieu seems to do so. Intellectual ideas, methods, techniques of discovery and norms of research always have their own relative autonomy apart from authority structures. They cannot be considered merely the 'ideological' results of what Bourdieu calls the 'scientific field'; or as he goes on to say, that which 'constitutes the basis of the practical consensus on what is at stake in the field, i.e. on problems, methods and solutions immediately regarded as scientific, is itself based on the whole set of institutional mechanisms which ensure the social and academic selection of researcher (through, for example the established hierarchy of disciplines) the training of the selected agents, control over access to the instruments of research and publication, etc' (Bourdieu 1975, 34). The scientific field seen in this way does not determine the content of scientific ideas, though it does rule over their acceptability. Young Einstein's original ideas on relativity can be considered the outcome of a particular perception and response to the whole intellectual problematic of the discourse of physics in his time, and his ideas were facilitated, though not determined, by his uniquely eccentric position in the field of institutional science. This problematic had an intellectual content that was not 'politically' determined, though it was subsequently 'politically' legitimated. Ideas have their own raison d'être.[1]

Bourdieu is, however, correct in stressing that legitimacy is what is at stake in any issue of scientific authority and cognitive commitment. Whose ideas are better is frequently a matter of whose ideas are more legitimate; and whose ideas prevail is at least initially the same as who has more authority to make them current. The two aspects are interlocked: ideas legitimate authority, and authority legitimates ideas. Whitley (1977a, 164) shows conclusively how the cognitive norms of the so-called arithmomorphic ideal legitimate an organized professional authority structure, and, vice-versa, such an authority structure institutionalizes and legitimates these cognitive norms. Accordingly he states that 'the institutionalization of this ideal as a major aspect of professional science has had important consequences for the organization of science' (ibid. 148) because 'abstraction and mathematical complexity come to be seen as the hallmark of scientificity' to such an extent that 'if a science deals with phenomena that are not amenable to representation by such formalism then it is much less of a science. Similarly, within restricted sciences this view implies that there is a hierarchy of prestige and authority resting on abstraction and formality' (ibid. 149). According to Whitley, the ultimate upshot of legitimation by means of the arithmomorphic ideal is that 'radical changes in knowledge are ruled out as is the rationality of any substantive challenge to established authority and beliefs' (ibid. 150). Authority is in this instance indissolubly both cognitive and institutional.

Authority structures are not necessarily always conservative in their effects, as the previous example implies; they can be, and have been in the past, also innovative and radical. Sometimes when a new authority structure arose in the sciences—for example, the authority of new academies or that of a new role for the professor—the effect on the development of the sciences was startlingly invigorating, even more so than the introduction of new ideas and theories. Whole new disciplines were differentiated and were able to develop in ways that would have been impossible under earlier authority structures. In any case, science practised with any degree of organization will always require authority in some form. And it is difficult to see how the sciences could have developed to their present stage without organization. Science is in this respect very different from art. The arts can be practised by individuals in relative isolation from each other, provided they have a common public. The sciences do not require such a public, but they do call for joint collaborative arrangements, which demand some degree of organizational cohesion. The exercise of authority in science is one of the requirements of collective scientific work; it is not pathological, disfunctional, or a matter of wrong norms. This is not to deny that a corrupt and false exercise of authority is always possible and that some authority structures stultify rather than advance the cause of science as usually understood.

The individual scientist, too, works to attain authority; he or she strives to become the authority in a given field in all the senses of that word, senses inherently fused and not mere equivocations. Furthermore, authority in science is conjoined in numerous ways with authorship, for the one makes for the other. The possibility that an individual genius can arise out of nowhere and make a fundamental contribution which will be instantly recognized, accepted and appreciated is a fairy tale of science which on rare occasions in the past—when science was still much more of an art—might have been fulfilled in real life. The young Einstein was in this respect one of the very last of the Cinderellas of science. In the present climate of scientific organization such an achievement is a near impossibility. This is why scientists have to aim for authority first in order to achieve authorship and recognition for their work. To aim first for rec-

ognition through some free, spontaneous and independent achievement is
to risk almost certain failure.

Even at the time of Einstein, achievement in itself was no guarantee
of recognition or attainment in science. For lack of the necessary political
skills, or because of his high-minded refusal to exercise these, the great
scientist Pierre Curie, denied a professional appointment at the Sorbonne
which would have eased his labours, was left to work himself to death.
His daughter, Eve, wrote movingly of his 'awkwardness' in this respect:

> The fact was that Pierre, so beautifully fitted for puzzling out mysterious
> phenomena and for the subtle struggle against hostile matter, was awkwardness
> itself when it came to canvassing for a place. His first disadvantage was that
> he had genius, which arouses secret, implacable bitterness in the competition
> of personalities. He knew nothing about underhand methods or combinations.
> His most legitimate qualifications were of no use to him: he did not know
> how to make them valued (Curie 1939, 187).

Close to the present time, as great a mathematical genius as Alan Turing
could not get very far or receive adequate recognition for his work because,
in a high-minded spirit, he refused to fight for authority and possibly
lacked the necessary academic-political skills to do so. His biographer
Andrew Hodges, himself a talented mathematician, puts it that Turing
'rather expected truth to prevail by magic', that is, of its own accord, and
he draws the general lessons from this concerning the relationship between
the truth of ideas and their efficacy:

> In another sense, it was that very bridge between the world of logic and the
> world of human action, that Alan Turing found so difficult. It was one thing
> to have ideas, but quite another to impress them upon the world. The
> processes involved were entirely different. Whether Alan liked it or not, his
> brain was embodied in a specific academic system, which like any human
> organization, responded best to those who pulled the strings and made
> connections. But as his contemporaries observed him, he was in this respect
> the least "political" person (Hodges 1985, 125–6).

Since Turing's time science has become even more 'political' in this sense:
now little can be attained without the necessary string pulling and connections. This is even true for the ultimate accolade that a scientist can
attain, the Nobel prize, for as another active scientist, Cavalieri, explains,
it must be prepared for long in advance:

> To "win" the [Nobel Prize] one needs, in addition to scientific achievement,
> a modicum of political manoeuvering, and good public relations. The scientist
> may start by moving to a well-known university with a bustling department
> filled with members of the National Academy of Sciences and a few Nobel
> laureates thrown in for good measure. Here the Big Scientist has all the
> opportunities for becoming a science potentate, for the power exercised by
> Nobel laureates and science academicians is legendary. The Big Scientist can
> now enter the politics of science (Cavalieri 1981, 109).

The Philosophy of Science and the Sociology of Science

To have raised the issue of authority in science is to be involved in all the old philosophical quandaries of the relation between knowledge and authority—or even more starkly put, between truth and power—which go back at least to Thrasymachus the Sophist. These questions cannot be avoided, but neither can they be answered with any simple formula which asserts either that truth is power, or conversely that truth is one thing and power something utterly different and that they have nothing to do with each other. It is not even possible to identify truth with knowledge too readily or power with authority. Knowledge is a much more social— linguistic as well as cognitive—matter than truth, which has connotations of logical absoluteness; and authority is certainly far more symbolically meaningful than mere power, for it entails legitimacy and legality. Thus knowledge and authority are far closer and more intimately related as concepts of social symbolic systems than truth and power. And whatever the relation between truth and power, it is mediated by that between knowledge and authority; so it is the latter which needs to be studied in order to say something about the former.

The traditional philosophy of science, from Bacon and Descartes through Popper, has invariably asserted that knowledge and authority are logically distinct, and it generally tended to insist that any intrusion of authority into science constitutes an unwarranted interference with knowledge. Knowledge was seen as the outcome of a supposedly logically foolproof scientific method; authority at best was the institutional context in which science could be practised and hence was merely circumstantial to the validation of new knowledge. In one of its last versions, that promulgated by the Positivist philosopher Reichenbach, this distinction was interpreted as the separation between the context of discovery and the context of justification or verification: the latter a necessary rational procedure, the former merely socially contingent and incidental. 'The philosopher of science is not much interested in the thought processes which lead to discovery', said Reichenbach (Schilp 1959, 289). The other Positivist philosophers of science echoed this view and insisted that as philosophers they were themselves solely concerned with the context of justification, with the purely rational standards and logical procedures of verification or falsification. The context of discovery they were content to leave to sociologists of science, most of whom were initially prepared to accept this division of labour and not intrude into areas reserved for the philosophers.

The demise of Positivism is, however, being acknowledged even by some philosophers; Suppe (1979, 3), for instance, speaks of the 'swan-song of Positivism in the philosophy of science'. That it has not been more widely recognized by philosophers can only be due to the insularity of philosophy departments. Outside philosophy it has already become obvious that even apart from the intellectual difficulties and shortcomings in the narrow reductionism of Positivism, it has proved itself ineffective and useless for working scientists. As von Bertalanffy declared:

It needs to be said that modern positivism has been a singularly sterile movement. It is paradoxical that the declared "philosophers of science" have neither contributed any empirical research nor new idea to modern science—while professional or half-time philosophers who were justly censored for their "mysticism", "metaphysics", or "vitalism", indubitably did. Eddington and Jeans in physics, Driesch in biology, Spengler in history are but a few examples (Buckley 1968, 19).

As the sterility of Positivism made itself felt, the pendulum swung the other way, and, as is usually the case with such swings, it has now gone too far. Whereas the Positivists were most intent on totally separating truth and power, some of the newer sociologists of science are identifying them. Something like this was already implicit in Kuhn's conception of scientific revolutions, but it was left to still more radical Frenchmen to go all the way and identify truth with power. Foucault has followed Nietzsche in this respect. Nietzsche had already asserted that will to truth is nothing but will to power and that truth itself is merely the error that is powerful enough to prevail: 'Truth is the kind of error without which a species of life could not live' (Nietzsche 1967, 272). 'The criterion of truth resides in the enhancement of the feeling of power' (ibid. 240). For Foucault, too, will to truth is will to power. Already in his inaugural lecture at the College de France (Foucault 1971) he referred the will to truth *(volonté de vérité)* to power and desire; he asked rhetorically: 'if, since the time of the Greeks, true discourse no longer responds to desire or to that which exercises power in the will to truth, in the will to speak out in true discourse, what, then, is at work, if not desire and power?' The same question is raised at the opening of his work *The History of Sexuality* (Foucault 1978, 11): 'what are the links between these discourses, these effects of power, and the pleasures that were invested by them? . . . the object in short is to define the regime of power-knowledge-sexuality that sustains the discourse on human sexuality in our part of the world'. Perhaps the clearest statement on the relation between truth and power is to be found in an interview entitled 'Truth and Power' (Foucault 1980, 133):

> "Truth" is linked in a circular relation with systems of power which produce and sustain it, and to effects of power which it induces and which extend it. . . . It is not a matter of emancipating truth from every system of power (which would be a chimera, for truth is already power) but of detaching the power of truth from the forms of hegemony, social, economic, cultural, within which it operates at the present time. The political question, to sum up, is not error, illusion, alienated consciousness or ideology, it is truth itself. Hence the importance of Nietzsche.

Bourdieu has also come close to identifying the struggle for truth with the struggle for power; the scientific field is 'the locus of competitive struggle in which what is specifically at stake is the monopoly of scientific authority, inseparably defined as technical capacity and social power' (Bourdieu 1975, 19). Although Bourdieu uses the term 'authority', he implicitly slips into identifying it with power or some such function of power as influence, as when he states that 'scientific practices are directed towards the acquisition of scientific authority (prestige, recognition, fame, etc.)' (ibid. 21). And he explicitly identifies authority with a quasi-economic power which he calls 'symbolic capital': 'scientific authority is thus a particular kind of capital, which can be accumulated, transmitted, and even reconverted into other kinds of capital under certain conditions' (ibid 25). Blume expounds a similar view when he asserts: 'scientists are seen as competing to impose those definitions of science, those paradigms, those theories which are likely to bring them individually the maximum "symbolic profit". It would not be difficult to show that in such struggles recourse is had to all available resources of power (not necessarily excluding political power or influence in its traditional sense)' (Blume 1977, 13).

As against such views it can be contended that though in scientific struggles recourse may be possible from all available resources of power, this does not mean that these various kinds of 'power' are all the same. From an heuristic point of view the exercise of discursive power in scientific disputation is no better 'logically' than the exercise of the power of persuasive argument—though it has to be backed by all the relevant evidence as determined by the standards of significance current within a given scientific discipline at a given point of its historical development. Also the same evidence might have been nugatory or worthless in another discipline or in the same discipline at another period of its development and within the context of another authority dispensation. But from all this it does not follow that the compelling power of scientific argumentation is mere rhetorical persuasive power. The appropriate corroboration by the available evidence—as determined by the current norms of a given scientific discipline and the context in which they operate—gives a theory or idea an authoritative status that no amount of any other kind of power can bestow on it.

It is true in general terms, as Bloor puts it, that, 'in so far as any particular theoretical view of the world has authority this can only derive from the actions and opinions of men. . . . Authority is a social category and only men can exert it. They endeavour to transmit it to their settled opinions and assumptions. Nature has power over us, but only men have authority' (Bloor 1978, 35). It is also true, as he states, that 'scientific theories and procedures must be consonant with other conventions and purposes prevalent in a social group. They face a "political" problem of acceptance like any other policy recommendation' (ibid. 37). However, these statements must not be taken to mean, as Bloor implies, that the politics of science and scientific authority are exactly like the politics and authority of other spheres of life. What makes for scientific legitimacy differs markedly from the legitimacy criteria of other spheres. This is not to say that there is one universal rational procedure, a scientific method, that is the one and only court of rational appeal to rule on matters of legitimacy. Legitimating and validating procedures might differ from one science to another or at different times within the history of one science. Nevertheless, there always are such authorized procedures, in general implicitly accepted and agreed on by those pursuing research in a science in a given historical period. Changes in these authorized procedures constitute veritable revolutions in ideas and institutions; though it rarely happens that they emerge suddenly as one complete Kuhnian paradigm, like Athena from the head of Zeus. More usually such conceptual shifts occur gradually and even go unnoticed over a long period as many partial, subtle adjustments that have continually to be made. The theory of evolution, for example, seeped in very gradually over at least a century before Darwin and Wallace independently formulated it in a scientifically complete form. This suggests that throughout this period there was a steady development of a new mode of argumentation, of a new way of ordering the available evidence, and of new standards of validity. Without these prior changes in the intellectual climate of a whole group of sciences, neither Darwin nor Wallace would have conceived his theory; if either of them had done so by some act of inspiration, it would not have been understood by anyone else and certainly could not have been immediately accepted as valid by the whole scientific world. The contrary case of Mendel's untimely discovery bears this out and shows that there can be no inherent separation between a context of discovery and a context of justification.

Such changes in the authorized procedures of argumentation belong to the changes in the cognitive norms of a science; they can only be achieved through a process of acceptance that can rightfully be called rational or dialectical, not through the dictate of any authority or as an imposition effected by power alone. This process of acceptance can be seen as guided by a social logic and is no mere fortuitous sequence of events; it must be explained socio-logically rather than merely sociologically (Redner 1986). However this must not be taken to mean that rational acceptance is logically compelled by a supposedly universal rational norm, such as a scientific method. On the contrary, the immediacy, force of adhesion and certitude of conviction with which authorized procedures of argumentation are accepted are also the result of the extent to which they are linked to the authority structure of the institution within which the research in a given science proceeds.

A scientific 'polity' of a given kind demands—and will in turn be demanded by—the cognitive norms authoritative within it. Thus authorized cognitive norms and authority structures constitute two distinguishable facets of scientific authority in general. Both these facets must support and maintain each other, for otherwise science would be in disarray. This concordance gives science its authoritative aspect and makes it compelling both intellectually and socially, both socio-logically and sociologically, both cognitively and 'politically'. One kind of authoritativeness without the other is either an aberration or a pathology in science. Thus the assertion of 'political' authority in science without reference to and not in defence of a given cognitive content—such as a scientific paradigm, or a method, or critical standard, or some set of intellectual ideas—constitutes a scientifically illegitimate and illicit exercise of hegemony or politics in the usual sense. By contrast, to affirm a cognitive content without invoking or establishing any legitimating authority structure on its behalf—without institutionalizing it in some way—would make the scientific project speculative or philosophical, or a form of art, and subject therefore to style or fashion. Science must be authoritative in both respects, both cognitively and institutionally compelling; otherwise it ceases to be science. But these two aspects of the scientific process, though in practice inextricably bound up with each other, must not be theoretically identified. The one legitimates the other in ways which must be uniquely specified in each given case. There are no general laws in the sociology of science stipulating how intellectual authority and 'political' authority support and sustain each other or how 'contradictions' arise between them. Such 'contradictions' are of great importance for explaining major historical changes in the sciences; but they are never law-like or even predictable, and this is why science does not simply change in a linear, cumulative developmental sequence. Tracing the specific agreements and 'contradictions' between cognitive authority and institutional authority has become one of the major tasks of the sociology of science.

This task was explicitly undertaken by Whitley (1977a, 163) in extensive and detailed studies designed to demonstrate that 'the way in which a particular ideal, and its associated form of organization, comes to dominate professionalized science has major consequences for the development of the sciences'. He argues that 'scientific authority rests on the dominance of particular approaches, phenomena and beliefs' (ibid. 146) and that these will promote certain corresponding authority structures. He addressed above all the relation of mutual legitimation in the contemporary sciences between the cognitive norms of the arithmomorphic ideal and the authority structures of professionalized and organized scientific disciplines. Once instituted, authority structures tend to maintain their associated cognitive norms, with the result, for example, that 'where mathematization of relations in a closed coherent system is reified as the basic goal of a discipline in educational curricula, reward systems and career structures, any controversy over fundamental ontological problems will be short lived because it could threaten the whole structure of organisational authority and disciplinary identity' (ibid. 155). What are regarded as legitimate work and authoritative practices will, therefore, depend on the authority disposition of the discipline in question; for example, 'in a discipline based on the ideal of conceptual closure and reticular theories the development of sophisticated formalism will be seen as authoritative practice' (ibid. 154). Any developments or changes in this direction will tend to promote a move towards corresponding organizational forms; thus, as Whitley (1982, 345) puts it elsewhere, 'the development of standard techniques and/or theoretical consensus and coherence change relations between scientists and the organization of the reputational system and its relation to employment agencies'.

When such changes were not merely gradual adjustments but drastic upheavals caused by fundamental contradictions, the whole scientific field was altered in all respects. A prominent example was the introduction of the 'mechanical model' in the seventeenth century, which fits best with Kuhn's notion of a paradigm revolution. In this and allied cases a veritable revolution in the authority system of science took place, changing the legitimate methods, practices and procedures as well as the standing and roles of scientists in relation to each other, including the position of outside influences allowed to impinge on science. During the turmoil of such major disputes it was never possible for the participants even to agree on how to separate cognitive from political differences. All kinds of issues were hopelessly intermingled as one side accused the other of rebelling against the established authority structures in the guise of promoting new ideas, and the other invariably retorted that resistance to the new ideas is solely conservatism designed to maintain the prevalent authority dispensations. A scientific dispute of this kind, if serious enough, is equally a dispute about what constitutes a legitimate as distinct from an illicit recourse to authority.

Only in retrospect, following the resolution of the conflict and on the basis of the already established course of science, is it possible to separate the real cognitive issues of the time from mere 'political' interference. The historian of science can adjudicate a past scientific dispute and assign praise and blame to those who can be seen retrospectively as furthering or blocking scientific progress, as judged in relation to subsequent developments. But in the heat of the scientific contention such assessments are mere rhetorical weapons that both sides will use against each other. Conventional Positivist philosophers of science, including even the unconventional Lakatos, could make rational reconstructions of the progress of science on the basis of the authoritative norms of science current in their own time, norms which were themselves the outcome of successful struggles. But the contenders of these struggles in the past had no way of knowing what would be looked on in the future as progress or as rationality. They had to prosecute the case as they saw fit with the means available to them at the time, which did not include the norms retrospectively used to judge them.

This kind of historical uncertainty and indeterminacy affects all ongoing research. In the context of research still in the making, or in disputes on the frontiers of knowledge, judgements based on cognitive principles, together with those stemming from positions of reputation or from authority standing, are nearly always inseparably joined in the minds of scientists. Whether one scientist accepts the results and theories of another depends on what the first thinks of the second in general, whether the first regards the second as a sound and reputable member of the discipline, or whether the first scientist treats the second as something of a crackpot, to put the matter at its simplest. And this, in turn, will crucially depend on the authoritative standing of the second scientist in the discipline. As Bourdieu (1975, 20) puts it, 'judgements on a student's or researcher's scientific capacities are always contaminated at all stages of academic life by knowledge of the position he occupies in the instituted hierarchies (the hierarchies of the universities, for example, in the USA)'. The philosopher of science or sociologist of science is in no position to step in and ex cathedra tell the scientists engaged in research what is really a cognitive and what a 'political' matter. If the philosopher tried to do so, without also being a scientist contributing to the research, he or she would be bound to be wrong or off the point. A god's eyeview, enabling one to foresee how history will judge, is impossible. The working scientist must proceed without the benefit of historical hindsight. This means that the personal trust a working scientist invests in a rival's work in general—as a result of such factors as its authoritative standing and the scientist's almost intuitive estimate of its future prospects—determines whether he or she also believes in the cogency of the rival's research and even trusts the rival's specific research findings. Latour and Woolgar, who have carried out extensive fieldwork on this issue, report their conclusions as follows: 'firstly, evaluative comments made by scientists make no distinction between scientists as people and their scientific claims. Secondly, the main thrust of these comments turn on an assessment of the credibility which can be invested in an individual's claim' (Barnes and Edge, 1982, 36). Commenting on an actual incident that arose in an on-going research dispute they state: 'this incident underscores the common conflation of colleague and his substance: the credibility of the proposal and the proposer are identical' (ibid.). One of the main reasons for this is that some proportion of a scientific claim in the form that it is published in a current paper has to be taken on trust. Since experiments are only very rarely replicated, because of the sheer impossibility of duplicating the exact instrumental arrangement from published accounts and the expense in labour and money involved, it follows that the reliability of an experiment is in large measure a function of the presumed reliability of the experimenter. Disputes in science frequently turn on just this kind of issue. Of course, after the event, when the dispute is over and the issue settled, it will be possible for the historian of science to separate out those factors in the matter which—from the later point of view—can be subsequently judged as having been 'political' and extrinsic to rational science from others which were really cognitive and 'scientific'. But contemporaries and participants in the dispute cannot do that since they do not have the advantages of hindsight.

The advantage of hindsight is obvious when one considers any contentious scientific case still sub judice. A good instance is the ongoing dispute surrounding the work of the immunologist Ted Steele and his colleagues, among them Reg Groczynski and Jeffrey Pollard. At first hailed as a potential refutation of neo-Darwinianism and a partial vindication of Lamarck, it is now authoritatively dismissed as a grave mistake or worse. As originally published in a short book *Somatic Selection and Adaptive Evolution* (Steele 1980) and subsequently republished in papers of the proceedings of the National Academy of Sciences and in *Nature,* the work seemed to involve strong experimental evidence that acquired immunological tolerance or resistance could be passed on to succeeding generations. Mutations which occur outside the germ line could be incorporated into the genetic endowment and so inherited by offspring. In a carefully orchestrated campaign, copies of the book were sent to Koestler, Popper, Temin and Burnet, a judiciously chosen group of highplaced supporters and their support was elicited. Subsequently an offer came from Medawar for these experiments to be repeated at the Clinical Research Centre in London, an offer too good to refuse. There, Leslie Brent attempted and failed to get the reported experimental results. This failure elicited a savage attack on Brent by Steele in a twenty-five page paper entitled 'Criticism', in which he called Brent's work 'shoddy, dishonest and bloody-minded' (Roberts 1983). Brent retorted in kind, and Steele was sent packing under a dark cloud. He now states, 'the nature of the attacks on me was so strong, that by the normal rules of the game I shouldn't be working in science at all . . . things got very nasty there for a while' (ibid.). He is now continuing his work on his own, with very meager resources, in Canberra and hopes to get more and better results to prove his case, which is of great importance not only for the theory of evolution—it threatens the whole neo-Darwinian establishment—but also for such current medical problems as AIDS.

It would be foolish and foolhardy for an outsider not engaged in this scientific battle to express an opinion as to who is in the right or to have anything to offer to help settle the dispute. This also goes, of course, for philosophers of science. As the case shows, it is not even possible to judge purely objectively whether an experiment has been repeated or not; that, too, is a moot point. All the elements of a scientific dispute previously outlined are involved in this case, and they are all hopelessly entangled so that while the dispute remains unresolved it is impossible to separate the cognitive elements from those which are merely technical or a matter of authority, politics and even ideology, since a whole worldview is at stake. However, this much might be said: given the rebuff he has received from such established authorities, it is doubtful Steele will ever be able to make a comeback, no matter what his future experiments are like and what he claims they demonstrate. Even if he is proved right, someone else in better standing will have to redo the work for it to have a chance of being accepted. Oddly enough, this was the case, when the science of genetics first began, with the work which is now being so tenaciously defended by the neo-Darwinian establishment, as the well-known story of Mendel demonstrates.

The Mendel story also shows how the significance, place, standing and the very meaning of the one theory or the same piece of scientific research— that is, the same cognitive content—change, depending on the context of authority into which the theory enters at different periods of its scientific lifetime. Thus, Mendel's work, commonly known as Mendel's law, has changed repeatedly in all these respects from the time he first promulgated it till now. At first it was the work of an obscure, amateur horticulturalist monk published in a provincial journal; it was hardly worth considering and its experimental evidence counted for nothing.[2] This interpretation was not altogether without justification, if anyone had bothered to repeat his experiments, for in fact we now know that he could not have got the exact findings he claimed, that his figures must have been adjusted—most probably by his assistant—to fit his theories. R. A. Fisher (1937) the statistician concluded that 'the data of most, if not all, of the experiments have been falsified so as to agree closely with Mendel's expectations'. However, by around 1900 when Mendel's discovery was independently arrived at by de Vries, Correns and Tschermak, the context of its redis- covery ensured a very different reception. Among the very first to hail it was Bateson, a junior Cambridge botanist, whose own research trail had already prepared him for the paper he received from de Vries, which also referred to Mendel. De Vries, himself a professor of considerable standing, had prepared for the publication of his novel ideas very carefully with preliminary publications over a period of many years (Olby 1966, 127). Nevertheless, even at this stage the reception of Mendelism was neither instantaneous nor universal; all that had so far been accomplished was that it had to be taken seriously and could not be dismissed as Mendel's work had been originally. So there ensued 'the fight to legitimize genetics', as Carlson (1966, 9) calls it, to give genetics the authoritative status which was being denied it by other hostile approaches, among them the biometric school of Galton and Pearson. This fight continued for a considerable time; in the Soviet Union it went on till very recently for there it had become purely political. However, even when the struggle was first engaged in, it would have been difficult if not impossible for the participants, the pro and anti Mendelians, to distinguish purely cognitive issues from those of scientific authority and even from ideology. All these factors were at play when early in the century Bateson, on behalf of the Mendelians, took on Weldon, his senior at the Cambridge biometric school, and they are evident in Bateson's decision to write a book, *A Defence of Mendel's Principles of Heredity,* instead of a journal article. As Carlson remarks, 'here, free of an editor's censoring pencil, he could form his case for Mendel . . . he would return sarcasm for wrath' (ibid. 12).

But the fact that any clear differentiation between one kind of authority and another in current scientific work cannot be made except as a matter of parti pris does not mean that it ought not to be made retrospectively. The history and sociology of science have developed analytic tools for separating out what was initially inextricably conjoined. And there are many reasons for distinguishing different aspects of scientific work and, on the basis of later science, for categorizing some as intrinsic and rational and others as extrinsic and circumstantial, identifying some as cognitive and others as social, and for marking off those which are communitarian from those which are authoritative or 'political'. Work of this kind is not merely of historical interest; it also has contemporary relevance for it serves to make scientists more aware of what is likely to be involved in current scientific disputes and to alert those who are opposed to the reigning scientific dispensation to what they are up against. In general, it will make scientists more critically self-conscious.

Unfortunately some of the new sociology of science has already been co-opted by the current scientific establishment and used to bolster the ideological defense of its position. Kuhn's seminal work has in some respects lent itself to this purpose. Kuhn elaborated two models for the social organization of science, neither of which is very relevant to contemporary science, though both can be partially exemplified in past ages of science. The first is the radical political model of a 'paradigm revolution' when authority is overthrown, the second is the contrasting communitarian model of 'normal science' where everyone is in agreement and no authoritative imposition is required. By holding out the ever present theoretical possibility of a paradigm revolution, Kuhn makes it seem as if science could drastically change at any moment, even though at present such a possibility seems to be out of the question in most sciences. The notion of a 'paradigm revolution' is probably historically limited even where it does apply, and it is possible that those sciences which are in a mature contemporary state, at the post-paradigm stage of Big Science, may no longer be subject to such drastic upheavals. At the same time, for Kuhn, barring a paradigm revolution, the present course of 'normal science' would seem to call for complete adhesion to the norms now prevailing. This has distinctly authoritarian consequences, as Bloor notes: 'the theme of "community" is a pervasive one, with its over-tones of social solidarity, of a settled way of life with its own style, habits and routines. This theme is only reinforced by its contrast to the controversial imagery of the "revolution" which periodically overtakes the community. There is in Kuhn no campaign against the notion of authority' (Bloor 1978, 51). There can be no such campaign because Kuhn showed little awareness of the role of authority in science in all its various differences and historical trans-formations.

The strongly communitarian emphasis of 'normal science' in Kuhn is possibly derived from the work of Ludwik Fleck, which was published in 1935 at a time when science was far less of an organized enterprise and when the Gemeinschaft aspects still might have predominated over the Gesellschaft ones. Fleck characterized the scientific enterprise as much more like an artistic one; his basic concepts, 'thought style', 'thought collective', 'esoteric and exoteric circles', were drawn from the sociology of the arts. At one point he advocated this explicitly when he stated that 'a good example of the general structure of a thought collective is provided by the thought community of the world of fashion' (Fleck 1979, 107) and pursued the analogy at length. His general characterization of a thought collective was modelled on the relationship between artists or schools of art, their followers and the general public: 'the general structure of a thought collective consists of a small esoteric circle and a larger exoteric circle, each consisting of members belonging to the thought collective and forming around any work of the mind (Denkgebilde), such as a dogma of faith, a scientific idea, or an artistic musing' (ibid. 105). There is no denying that such a characterization is extremely illuminating; neither is there any need to doubt that there are thought collectives of this kind in the sciences (I shall discuss such clusters eventually in Chapter 7) and that communal groupings exist, so that 'communistic' values, to use Merton's old term, are relevant in some instances. They were certainly much more important in past stages of science than they are now. Even now not all relations in science are 'political' or mediated by authority; there are all kinds of other relations: collegial, cooperative, conspiratorial, in-spirational, emotional, devotional, ideal as well as base. Authority relations are only one kind governing the myriad interactions prevalent in scientific work.

However, in the present stage of the scientific enterprize, the non-authoritative relations—though never absent and occasionally still very prominent—are less decisive than the authoritative structures for these are necessitated by the high level of scientific organization. As Whitley has noted:

The more there is an apparatus to be organized, the more important administrative authority becomes. Whereas previously prestige based on past achievement was the main form of "capital" in science, the development of a professional hierarchy and elaborate training facilities meant that control over resources used in scientific production constitutes an additional major form of capital. While prestige may be a necessary condition for obtaining such control—or at least of denying resources to deviants—it is not always sufficient and, correspondingly, administrative control need not imply scientific authority in terms of current work and approaches (Whitley 1977a, 165).

Whitley's stark contrast between the previous stage of prestige and the present one of authority—that is, an 'artistic' followed by a 'political' phase—is a simplification; however, the point behind it is correct. It needs to be amplified by a detailed study of the modes of authority and their role in the different historical stages of science. Sociologists of science, with some notable exceptions, have tended to neglect or completely overlook the need for such a study, which will begin here and continue in Chapter 5.

The Instituting of Authority

Scientists tend to be averse to any attempt to make them face up to the role of authority in science. This reaction is a continuing legacy of the whole movement of modern science, from the time of the Scientific Revolution, the ideology of which was almost precluded from recognizing the role of authority because it began as a struggle against authority. It was a revolution against the old authority of the scholastic universities and the ancient authors, rejected in favour of what seemed like the anti-authoritarianism of pure reason, experience and individual conscience. 'Truth is the daughter not of authority, but time', said Bacon. *Nullius in verba* was the motto of the Royal Society. This ideal was upheld by all the new scientists or natural philosophers of Europe among whom the trial and condemnation of Galileo evoked fear and righteous rage. Scientists have used the case ever since to warn of the nefarious effects of authority in science. As van den Daele states:

> The battle for the emancipation of learning was not confined to the rejection of philosophical systems. It implied contests with the classical ideals of scholarship and education and of classical style with its emphasis on eloquence and logic. Above all, it implied opposition to laws, statutes and privileges by which schools and universities and the monopolies of knowledge exercised by the corporate professions (medicine in particular) were shielded from the freedom of philosophic thinking (van den Daele 1977, 32).

Textual interpretation, the staple of learning in the schools of all civilizations, was overthrown, perhaps not for the first time but certainly more decisively than ever. The authority of the keepers of the texts was thus directly challenged, even though eventually a compromise with them had to be reached. Instead a science sans texts was promulgated, one that promised a rational method for the direct access to the book of Nature and truth without the mediation of human authority.

The old authorities were dethroned, and just as surely new ones were instated. But these usurpers ruled more covertly: the new royal academies were not authorities that prescribed texts and methods of interpretation; rather they controlled nominally free research by certifying its results. As the Royal Society declared:

> The business of the Society in ordinary meetings shall be to order, take account, consider and discourse of philosophical experiments and observations, to read, here [sic], and discourse upon letters, reports, and other papers containing philosophical matters; also to view and discourse upon rarities of nature and art; and thereupon to consider what may be deduced from them or any of them; and how far any of them may be improved for use or discovery (Blume 1974, 100).

Although this was the program, in practice it meant that the business of the Royal Society became to rule on claims and disputes of priority; in other words, it was a scientific property-assigning institution serving an analogous role in science to that which the absolutist monarchy served in the new mercantile early capitalist economy. But beyond this business function, the society also instituted a new kind of scientific authority, for the acceptance of papers and their publication became the new test of scientific orthodoxy and the main regulative function of authority. By an exclusive right to give its imprimatur of scientificity, it also instituted and enforced certain approaches and methods—roughly those corresponding to the mechanistic model—as valid and objective and eliminated others as either above science or beneath it, designating these as theology, metaphysics and logic, or alternatively as empiric quackery and rhetorical charlatanism. Thus everyone, everywhere, could freely engage in scientific research on almost anything, except in those areas which impinged too closely on the preserves of State, Church and university such as politics, morals, religion and grammar. Thought was declared free, but only those thoughts would pass which happened to fit the new prescribed norms.

In the succeeding scientific polity, that of the revived university as modelled on the German academic reforms of the nineteenth century, the authority of the academies was not challenged, as might have been expected, but on the contrary even more strongly reinforced. The academies became the upper tier of the authority structure as the most successful professors became academicians, and their function was to oversee in general the whole scientific establishment. In this new university-based establishment of science authority was extended downward to the very production process itself (Redner 1987). Scientific research could no longer be freely engaged in by amateurs, or only as rare exceptions; it was now controlled by the fully accredited professors and reserved for their students. But at this stage each professor was still free to research what he saw fit. The scientific field was still relatively open so that each innovative professor could establish himself as the authority over some particular domain, and each such pioneer could extend the frontiers of knowledge. New areas of science were continually being opened up by individual professors, and in time many of these became our present closed disciplines.

This regime of professorial authority was loose and decentralized compared to that of the present organized disciplines because access to many kinds of publication was still freely available. A professor could circumvent the refusal of the few officially accredited journals to publish a work by appealing directly to a scientifically interested general public. Or the professor could launch a new journal very easily with a few followers. Many subversive scientific theories and approaches and quite a few new scholarly sciences were launched and maintained in this way in the teeth of official opposition. Scientists regarded themselves as independent scholars who shared the same ethos as their humanistic colleagues. Thus there flourished what Ben-David (1971, 171) calls 'a decentralized common market for researchers, students and cultural products'.

This open market disappeared when the liberal era of the scientific polity concluded, together with the liberal laissez-faire capitalism of which it formed a part. In the age of advanced capitalism characterized by giant corporations, multinational combines and bureaucratic state controls, science, too, has entered into an authoritarian phase in the new institutions of the multiversity–research institute complex. The professors of the old university have ceased to be independent agents or even the main exponents of authority. The individual professor is only loosely and frequently only nominally attached to a place of work or university. The professor now depends on funding agencies made up of what Weingart (1982, 74) calls 'hybrid communities of experts' in relation to whom he or she acts as a client. The professor's main external attachment is to the State agency or the industry that funds the work, and the main internal attachment is to the discipline which has become an organized institution. The discipline as an organization controls the direction of on-going research by its sponsorship of journals and steering of publication through assigning editorships, arranging peer-review panels and planning conferences; through these activities it marks out the course and allocates the division of labour within the specific science in question. The individual has no choice but to be available for whatever the discipline requires. This usually means becoming more expert in an ever narrower sub-division of a field, for 'in pure science, the more expert an individual is on a topic, the more he can be trusted as an authority' (Dolby 1982, 257). Within organized science the struggle for authority becomes crucial, so much so that it tends to dominate every step of a scientist's career. The rewards are bigger than ever; when successful, such a career assumes an international scope for disciplines are now world-wide. Hence organizational and personal competition for authority, as well as the more co-operative activities of communication and exchange, have become global.

The reasons that science has become authoritarian in the era of world civilization are a function of the nature of World science and the institutions in which it is produced. Big Science and organized science cannot function without well-demarcated lines of authority. The huge government funds channelled into science necessarily create controls. The transition from the earlier university polity to the present multiversity–research institute complex continually requires and brings about more direction and steering, that is, more scientific authority (Redner 1987). The very bulk of research undertaken on contract and the resultant publications call for prearranged divisions and assigned projects, in short, for rationalization and all the other measures of control to prevent excessive duplication and waste. Hence, all the features of World science, the cognitive character of research as well as its institutional setting, conspire together to bring about an expansion in the role of authority and to establish the disciplinary character of all research and employment.

Obviously the factors making for authority differ from discipline to discipline. Each has its own authority structure, and in each a different mode of authority can predominate, for authority is never all of one piece, as we shall see in Chapter 5. Some disciplines in the sciences and especially some in the humanities function with very weak authority structures, or they still maintain authority structures that hark back to an earlier polity. In that sense there are strong or well-formed disciplines and weak or ill-formed ones, that is, disciplined and undisciplined ones. Moreover, the tendency in the present academic polity is for well-formed disciplines to be assertive in relation to the ill-formed ones and to act as dominant disciplines. Thus an extremely well-formed discipline like physics in the natural sciences or economics in the social sciences will be in a commanding position compared to ecology or anthropology. In this way disciplines themselves form status and even authority hierarchies. This is also true for specialities or subdisciplines within disciplines which can usually be ordered in precise grades of status standing (Ward 1972, 10). Such hierarchies of authority are important not merely in institutional respects but in cognitive and theoretical respects as well. As is well known, in the period of the triumph of nuclear physics and atomic energy the methods and procedures of physics were imported into or imposed on most other scientific disciplines, including a few even in the social sciences. Elias states that 'as a rule, higher ranking and more powerful disciplines can impose upon those who rank lower their own method and categories of thinking as a model to be imitated. They can effectively stigmatize deviants, who do not or cannot comply with their prescriptions, as "non-scientific", "non-philosophical", "non professional", and in other ways' (Elias 1982a, 23). The same phenomenon is found in the influence that higher ranking sub-disciplines exert upon those lower in the hierarchy, for example, in the impact of mathematical economics and econometrics on all the other economic specialties.

Disciplines are made up of numerous sub-disciplines or specialties whose definitions cut across that of the discipline itself: the specialty tends to be defined more in cognitive terms, the discipline itself in terms of authority structure and institutional character. Whitley defines a specialty as follows:

> A specialty may be considered as an agglomeration of research areas or a set of sets of problem situations. It also implies, however, a mode of understanding which structures and integrates different problem situations, e.g. field theory in plasma physics. Such integration is not necessarily by means of monistic models, or explanatory schema, but may occur through the

common application of a particular instrument to a number of research areas (Whitley 1974, 77).

A research area may, in turn, be defined in terms of the problem situations which constitute it; each problem situation is characterized by some such principle of unity as a technique or mode of instrumentation, or specific issue covering similar phenomena, or the application of the one cognitive model. As Whitley states: 'a research area can be said to exist when scientists concur on the nature of the uncertainty common to a set of problem situations. . . . The more consensus on the definition of phenomena, application of appropriate techniques and the meaning of results, the higher the degree of cognitive institutionalization' (ibid. 80). The terms we have introduced—'discipline', 'specialty', 'research area' and 'problem situation'—are not completely mutually defining as categories, sub-categories and sub-sub-categories, nor as genus and differentia; they are to some extent incommensurable, being determined by the context for their specific application. Thus it is not possible to subdivide a discipline into exactly so many specialties, research areas and problem situations; each of these terms is applied on a somewhat different basis, some more by reference to authority structures, others more by reference to instrumental techniques or cognitive models.

The discipline is the most institutionalized category and is most subject to an authority structure. Different disciplines are constituted in different ways but always in terms of some authoritative function: some in terms of the authority of a reigning cognitive paradigm, others in terms of a sense of status and belonging stemming from a common educational background, still others almost purely organizationally where there is very little cognitively in common between the members of the discipline. Some specialties are joined into one discipline solely for fortuitous historical reasons. But once so joined it becomes almost impossible to separate them or for a specialty to break away because of the ensuing loss of status and power, unless the specialty is strong enough to build up a discipline of its own. Disciplines among themselves, specialities within disciplines, the departments within which these are located, as well as specialist factions within departments, are locked in a continual struggle for authority, status and power. The outcome of this struggle is, as Elias notes, that

> at a given time, every department and every laboratory has its place within the academic status hierarchy at a variety of levels—locally at its own university, nationally, and in some cases internationally, among representatives of its own and related fields. The whole figuration is animated by a continuous competitive struggle for preservation, avoidance of loss or rise of status and power chances. It is a controlled form of competition subject to certain, mostly unwritten, rules and often if not always, compatible with a measure of co-operation (Elias 1982a, 39).

There are thus two basic levels to this struggle and hence also to academic authority: the universal level of the discipline as a whole, which will sometimes transcend national boundaries, and the particular, local level of the department, institute or laboratory. In a well-formed, or really well-disciplined, discipline these two levels are well integrated, so that only members of the discipline have the sole and exclusive right to direct the departments and institutes, and, vice-versa, only those who graduate from its departments have the right to enter the discipline. A well-formed discipline comes to exercise a total monopoly over the knowledge produced in its field. The discipline controls all the resources, material, intellectual and organizational, necessary for the production of knowledge and for its accreditation and acceptance. No outsider can gain access to these resources, and if by some chance one does succeed in producing knowledge independently, then in only very rare cases is it accepted by the discipline. Many disciplines in the natural sciences are well formed in this sense and constitute monopolistic establishments. As Elias sees it:

> Scientific establishments are groups of people who collectively are able to exercise a monopolistic control over resources needed by others. They control, and engage in, the production of a particular type of knowledge. . . . That is to say, they are establishments only in so far as there are groups of non-established people, of outsiders, who need the resources monopolized by them and who depend on them for access to, or use of, them (Elias 1982a, 40).

A discipline does not merely monopolize the knowledge needed by others; it also controls the knowledge needed by its own members. Only certain kinds of things known count as knowledge. As the historian Hugh Stretton explains:

> A discipline of study, especially when practised by a profession, develops social characteristics. Rules define membership, including the "member" type of knowledge. Even where the methods and subject-matters of neighbouring disciplines overlap, they may have very different rules for the use of similar knowledge. A political scientist or a theorist of economic growth may present without penalty "facts" about eighteenth century society which would make a historian blush; the historian may present better certified facts in an ungeneralized disarray that would disgrace a political scientist or economist. When the facts are figures the roles may be reversed, and the scientists measure and count what the historians are still content to guess at (Stretton 1969, 63).

The discipline is represented at the local level by the department. The department carries out the crucial authority roles of initiating and training neophytes into the discipline and subsequently hiring and promoting them. Richard Ohmann, a literary critic, explains how 'departments carry out their extraordinary powers of appointment' in the discipline of English:

(1) hiring is generally done by special field. . . .

(2) departments in large universities are much more likely to hire at the top. . . .

(3) though teaching ranks first or second among stated criteria for advancement in 86% of the institutions, and scholarship in 35%

only, those departments concerned with reputation value scholarship more highly, so that success is defined by publication and the notice that accompanies it. In brief, the division of rewards in this system lends support to the values that faculty have made pre-eminent in American higher education: specialization, research, visibility among peers, loyalty to the guild rather than to the college or university (Ohmann 1976, 220).

Brown (1982, 41) reports that 'Dresser and his associates were able to verify in their survey of 1200 faculty members that it is indeed the department which receives the basic loyalty of the academician'. This finding has to be qualified by noting that it is not a department in any specific university or college that is in question, but generally the department that pertains to the discipline wherever it may be located. Changing lower status departments for higher status ones is crucial to career advancement. It is also likely that this loyalty becomes more diffuse in the higher reaches of the discipline. As the academic rises and acquires many alternative modes of employment, his or her loyalty to the department becomes more attenuated. The discipline itself remains the universal focus of belonging, like the party to the politician or the Church for the believer. But to start with the department is indispensable, as Diana Crane reports:[3]

> It is usually necessary for the graduate student to be identified with a single department. In cases where joint programs have been developed, the new hybrid often has difficulty finding a job and usually has to take a job in a department representing one rather than both his disciplines. Since research facilities are controlled by departments, it is difficult for young men to obtain their use in order to take the first step in a borderline field (Crane 1972, 108).

Out of such borderline fields new disciplines arise, usually with great difficulty as a result of protracted struggles with the matrix disciplines out of which they are born. The absence of departmental facilities makes the process of recruitment and training nearly impossible. But one of the great attractions for the young in joining a newly forming discipline is that it will at first inevitably be ill formed, or really not disciplined, with a weak authority structure and a strong sense of personal collegiality. Thus young scholars can make contributions to knowledge in the field without having to establish themselves first as authorities. As James Fleck notes for the newly forming discipline of Artificial Intelligence: 'the high number of important contributions to the field at Ph.D. level seems to have been the characteristic of AI, and has combined with the very fluid and informal nature of the organization of work in the area, to maintain a very shallow internal hierarchy with no elaborate vertical division of labour' (Fleck 1982, 201). As the discipline becomes established and better formed this fluid situation will evaporate and stricter authority controls will be introduced preventing the young academics from entering the most advanced research in the field. Some evidence indicates that this is already starting to happen in Artificial Intelligence as the most senior men have occupied the available professional posts and have begun to build up circles of client students around themselves. In time they will establish themselves as what Elias calls a 'hegemonic generation', as has happened in other disciplines:

> Representatives of a scientific view who have gained recognition in their own field or in society at large for their work can establish themselves as a hegemonic generation. As high status persons they can assume the attribute of an established authority, discourage criticism, however well founded, and no longer teach the rising generation those scientific techniques and strategies which would enable them to examine effectively the "paradigm" of their teachers (Elias 1982a, 50).

It is not possible to provide rules for or even generalize about what kinds of discipline will be well formed or ill formed. The cognitive content of a discipline—or even whether it is a strict science, a natural or social science, or an humanity—is not of itself decisive. Some humanities, linguistics, for example, can be well disciplined, whereas some strict sciences, for instance, symbolic logic, can be poorly disciplined to the point of scarcely being a discipline at all. Nevertheless, as Whitley (1977a) has demonstrated, there is an understandable tendency for the so-called restricted sciences, those which practise the arithmomorphic ideal, to be professionally organized and to make up well-formed disciplines. There is a contrary tendency for the looser, 'configurational' and 'unrestricted' sciences to be less well disciplined. Physics, with its horizontal and vertical divisions of labour and its resultant hierarchies best exemplifies a well-formed discipline. Most of the earth sciences are by contrast ill formed. Disciplines become better formed when they are unified under one cognitive goal, the same techniques and instruments, and an exclusive membership within one organization, in other words, when all the aspects of scientific authority coincide (Whitley 1975). There is, of course, no value judgement implied in calling a discipline well formed or ill formed; it is purely a sociological designation.

It is also not possible to generalize about or provide laws for how disciplines are initially constituted and how they develop later into well formed or ill formed structures. The history of each discipline has to be studied separately for in each case it follows an unique course of development. Sometimes a discipline develops out of a seceding group in the course of a struggle amounting to a 'civil war' within a larger discipline; sometimes it simply grows up quietly in a neglected space in between other disciplines; sometimes it is founded by government fiat to meet a new need; sometimes it forms itself around a new cognitive paradigm; and there are many other possibilities. Hagstrom describes at length the first of these processes, which he sees in socio-political terms as one of deviance, attempted suppression, rebellion followed by expulsion and secession, leading to a separate foundation:

> Differences between specialties may be viewed as deviance by members of specialties that are traditional or central to the discipline, and attempts may

be made to sanction such deviance. Initially attempts may be made to establish conformity by the use of formal sanctions—with regard to appointment, instruction of students and access to communication channels. The exercise of these sanctions tends to be implicit. Unsuccessful candidates for jobs may not be told specifically why they were not appointed, papers may be rejected by journals for vague reasons, and a professor may find his students failing because of their "incompetence" or their "attitudes". Whether or not the recipient of the sanction is informed of the standards used in judging him, the matter does not become public.

Further development of the deviant specialty leads to overt conflict. Those likely to be sanctioned publicly question the legitimacy of the standards used. Thus goals and standards are made explicit, and scientists and others will be made aware of the conflict. Dissatisfaction with these failings may stimulate formal differentiation of disciplines. Such differentiation requires special communication channels, the development of a disciplinary utopia, and successful appeals outside of existing disciplines.

Later on, separate departments for the new discipline may be established. This represents an almost irreversible differentiation, for universities are strongly committed to departments of instruction and through their graduates the departments have reproduced themselves and established ties with groups in the larger society that employs them (Hagstrom 1965, 122–6).

This quotation illustrates many of the issues concerning the relation of science and authority. A large-scale struggle of this kind will be a conflict for authority, power and influence at all levels—at the cognitive, instrumental, institutional and personal levels at once. A difference over ideas, standards or procedures becomes indistinguishably intermixed with questions of authority, propriety and sheer power and money insofar as issues of funding will inevitably be involved. In such cases it is hard to distinguish an exercise of legitimate authority from an illegitimate misuse of power. However, the initial steps in the suppression of a deviant specialty outlined by Hagstrom, and apparently accepted by him as normal, are themselves clearly deviant and constitute pathologies in science. To reject candidates for jobs and papers for journals and to fail students for no other reason than their refusal to conform cannot but be taken as corrupt. As will be shown in Chapter 6, such corruptions are frequently condoned tacitly throughout the academic establishment, but this acquiescence does not make them any the less corrupt.

The system of authority that I have previously outlined applies only to the contemporary context of the sciences and humanities within the institutions of the multiversity–research institute complex. Only there does the key relationship of the discipline to the department operate, and only there can well-formed disciplines be found. In Chapter 5 I will examine more specifically the contemporary disciplinary structures of authority.

5

The Forms of
Scientific Authority

I've often thought about developing a talk on the politics of geology for students. Sometimes I get cynical enough to want to tell grad students what they're really getting into—a competitive world where success is not necessarily dependent on how good a scientist you are. . . . It would be interesting for students to hear more about the politics of science. It would help them to be better scientists from the start.

—Anonymous geologist (in Mitroff 1974)

Politics and Politicking

The 'politics' of science has not as yet received adequate theoretical treatment, despite some creditable empirical endeavours. One reason is the widely prevalent misidentification of academic politics with politicking in the narrow and 'dirty' sense, as exemplified in the quotation. Although the difference is as crucial and as great as that between business and racketeering, it does not follow that the two can always and in all circumstances be sharply differentiated. Academic politics is the open exercise of legitimate authority without subterfuge and subject to accepted ethical norms; politicking is the illicit trafficking in influence and courting of favours that can only be done covertly. In the present context, academia and above all the scientific establishment could not function without politics, that is, without a recognized authority structure. It could, however, certainly do with less politicking, for this is one of its pathologies.

Legitimate academic authority is properly exercised on behalf of a cognitive standard or ideal; it functions to uphold and maintain a given paradigm or method in science or set of critical norms in the humanities, or some such general intellectual interest. The interest that is furthered by politicking is usually closer to the commercial one. Once again it needs to be pointed out that it is not always possible to distinguish and disengage the two kinds of interests, especially when controversy intervenes, and it is a well known psychological fact that many academics are prone to treat them as one, to consider what is good for themselves as also good for their discipline or for science as a whole. Nevertheless, it is in the interest of science that such a distinction be made and enforced wherever possible.

The contemporary academic system is institutionally a multiversity–research institute complex broken up into numerous disciplines, each governed by its own distinctive authority structure. An exhaustive description of the authority structure to be found in every discipline is almost beyond a single work or a single person; the field is too vast. And the descriptive task cannot even be begun without a general theoretical typology. Solely for this descriptive sociological purpose and with no critical intent, I first postulate a general typology of academic authority. It is not, of course, postulated a priori, but derived from the field work studies that have already been undertaken. And it must prove itself by providing a fruitful yield in further field research expeditions.

Three basic forms of authority are to be found to varying degrees in all disciplines, whether scientific or humanistic: formal-professional, collegial-elite and patronal. These forms are intended purely as ideal types in Weber's sense, analogous with his three modes of legitimation: rational-legal, traditional and charismatic, though there is no one-to-one correspondence between the two sets. At best, the formal-professional and rational-legal types relate to one another; the other two correspond more closely to Weber's collegial and patrimonial forms, respectively. In the academic polity these are legitimately recognized forms of authority. Formal-professional authority obtains its legitimation from officially recognized positions and appointments, and it constitutes the hierarchical academic order within departments and disciplines as well as in the multiversity–research institute complex as a whole. Collegial-elite authority is more informal authority of the ruling group of a discipline, who constitute an 'invisible college' of intercommunicating participants among whom collegial relations of nominal equality and the cameraderie of the aristocracy of science obtain. Patronal authority is that of some individual of recognized high standing and status who is called upon legitimately to exercise authority, through personal judgement, powers and prerogatives, on behalf of others.

These are quite different authority forms from those found in previous educational and research institutions or in the older-style university, though the newer modes of authority have evolved historically from the older ones and the latter can still be found as vestiges in modern institutions. One of the oldest intellectual authority relations is that of master to disciple; an affective and purely personal relation which is in rare instances in evidence even now. Some exceptional masters were considered charismatic teachers or writers by a whole group of disciples or followers. Nowadays such relations develop very rarely and are more likely to take place outside academia and lead to a very different intellectual politics, as the examples of Marx and Freud show (Turkel 1978). The combined authority of teachers or professors as a guild corporation is also rarely in evidence now since they are divided by disciplines that do not co-operate. Even the old-style god-professor is no longer as prominent as in the recent past. Examining boards and accrediting bodies still retain something of their older authority status, but they tend now to be purely formal authorities, merely confirming decisions reached elsewhere.

Although other kinds of relations in academia besides the 'political' or those mediated by authority have survived from the past, they are not the subject of this study. It is not the purpose of this work to examine affective, personal, inspirational, or wholly cognitive relations and the social forms based on them, yet this omission must not be taken as a denial of their presence and importance. Political relations are emphasized here because their importance has tended to be denied or underplayed. In contemporary academia their role is so crucial that one might speak of the sciences as overly 'politicized' and use this aspect as a focus for criticism and a call for reform. This is not, however, the intention of this chapter, which is primarily designed to be sociologically descriptive in the ideal-type manner.

Formal-professional, collegial-elite and patronal forms of authority apply only as ideal types to actual disciplines, departments or individuals. They are rarely likely to be encountered in a pure form; more often than not they cross and interpenetrate and are mixed with other non-authoritative relations. It is very difficult to delimit the sphere in which academic authority alone operates and influence, prestige, social status and sheer domination are excluded. Nevertheless it is possible to describe disciplines, departments or even specific situations or transactions where one or more of the pure forms of authority apply. As a very rough approximation it might be said that formal-professional authority is paramount in disciplines that are strongly 'job' oriented, where the work organization is everything; such disciplines tend to be found in highly technified but decentralized sciences such as chemistry and the applied sciences. In such situations, the individual is completely dependent on the facility, but since each facility is a separate unit to itself, no controlling elite can arise. By contrast a collegial elite does develop in centralized and technified disciplines where an extensive division of labour is practised and the top practitioners control the work of all others. Such control requires gradation of difficulty of work; some tasks will be theoretically abstract, problem-solving and difficult, whereas most are routine and humdrum. A discipline like physics exemplifies this distinction to perfection. Patronal authority is prevalent where all these features of the 'hard' sciences are absent, where the individual can rely on personal resources to do his or her work and does not require technical facilities or much co-operation with others, but also where a leading personality can establish a near-monopoly on some corner of the field or dispute it with only a few contenders. Anyone else who wants access to this corner must rely on the recognized authority to act as patron for admission and protection. This pattern tends to occur in the humanities and some of the 'softer' social sciences.

The three ideal-type forms of authority provide useful criteria for distinguishing types of discipline. Since nearly all disciplines are likely to feature all three forms to some degree, in order to distinguish one discipline from another one must establish the proportion in which each is present. This criterion matches distinctions arrived at on other grounds, for example, those provided by Whitley (1982, 340), who gives a systematic analysis of all disciplines in terms of the two key parameters—levels of task uncertainty and levels of mutual dependence. His account of types of discipline fits well with the theory of authority here elaborated. We can distinguish basically four types of discipline: that in which formal-professional authority predominates, for example, chemistry; that in which collegial-elite authority predominates, for example, physics; that in which patronal authority predominates, for example, the humanities and the 'soft' social sciences; and that where all three forms are evenly balanced, for example, parts of mathematics, biology, psychology, and economics. These are also the four categories which Whitley separates on the basis of task uncertainty and mutual dependence. Whitley's subsequent elaboration of this four-fold schema into a seven-fold categorization of scientific fields, or what he calls 'reputational organizations' (Whitley 1984), could also be accommodated if authority forms were matched with cognate types of cognitive content and instrumental dispositions. Relating the three basic forms of authority to the previously outlined features of World science—technification, formalization, abstraction, problem-solving and finalization—would produce a very precise mapping of scientific disciplines and fields. Clearly there are elective affinities between certain forms of authority and certain types of cognitive content and unlikely relationships between others. There is no need to spell out exhaustively all the possible and impossible combinations.

Authority structure and cognitive content, as stressed in Chapter 4, need to be kept separate when one is analysing disciplines even though they are closely interconnected: the 'ideal' and 'political' dimensions of a discipline are not the same. It is possible for the authority structure to remain the same and for the cognitive content to vary, though only within strict limits imposed by their mutual constraints. There is therefore no way to deduce the cognitive content of a discipline from an account of its authority structure, or vice-versa. Nor is there any way of judging the one solely by reference to the other, no way of telling whether the cognitive content of a given scientific polity is interesting or trivial, scientifically sound or bogus, making great advances or standing still. All such judgements require independent evaluations. It follows that there is no simple way of prescribing in general the kind of authority structure that will make for good science or avoiding the one that makes for bad science. This complication does not make science policy decisions impossible, since in any given concrete situation specific reforms in the authority structure designed to further a given kind of scientific emphasis or programme, or in general to facilitate advance, can be formulated, but it does preclude the formulation of general laws on which to base policy decisions.

Formal-Professional Authority

Formal-professional authority is the easiest to identify as it pertains to rank, office or status attained by promotion through a graded and sequential hierarchy. Such grades usually entail salary differentials, rights and pre-rogatives in decision-making and such status marks of authority as titles, though these are not as obviously displayed as in the Church, the army, or business corporation. On the contrary, some attempt is made to purvey a sense of collegial equality, as Ohmann notes for departments of English in the United States:

> Yet surely, this is a strange hierarchy. Orders do not move down along its conduits, as in a military line of command or even a corporation. The assistant professor does not report to an associate professor or give daily assignments to the instructors below him. On the contrary, most departments try to avoid a strong sense of subordination within the regular ranks and even suppress the order of hierarchy in daily tasks. . . . Rank is not power, so much as it is a background condition largely ignored in the daily work of the department. But if rank is not power, it is status (Ohmann 1976, 215).

Departments in scientific disciplines do not usually feel it necessary to maintain such subterfuges and assert authority more openly. In any case authority tends to be more open on the national level of the discipline and between universities whose precise status rankings are zealously maintained.

In academia, as in real politics, there tend to be two parallel hierarchies of formal-professional authority: that of the institutional organization, which usually is located within some specific multiversity or research institute, and that of the disciplinary organization, usually the national professional association. The distinction corresponds roughly to that between government and party in real politics. As in politics, the positions pertaining to the institutional organization are much more precisely defined than those pertaining to the professional organization; in the latter there is only an approximate hierarchy of statuses, such as panelist, conference organizer, referee, grants advisor, editor of core disciplinary journal, president of the association, and so on. And overall the various conferences, journals and seminar meetings are themselves ordered in a hierarchical relation and entry to them is controlled. In some disciplines the 'party' side is poorly organized and is something of a chore or 'joke' as it is only mobilized for specific events, as are U.S. political parties; in other disciplines this side is thoroughly organized, as are British parties. There is always close correlation between these two sides of formal-professional authority, with the result that elevation within the one side requires and entails promotion within the other. But this correlation can be as loose as that between party and government in the United States, or as close as that between the two in the USSR: in the former case the top jobs need not go to the top people in the professional association; in the latter case only those top people are eligible for the top jobs. All these issues have so far received too little attention from organizational theorists.

The relative strength of the 'government' or 'party' side of a discipline varies, depending on numerous factors, above all on the national university system as a whole. The existence of high mobility, as in the United States during the post-war period, will tend to strengthen the disciplinary professional association as against any 'local' authorities. The individual who is moving quickly from job to job is less bound by any specific employment agency, whether a multiversity or research institute and its hierarchy of authority, than by the national disciplinary organization and its hierarchy. The latter claims the individual's primary allegiance for through it he or she can hope for promotion, which usually entails moving from a lower position in one university to a higher position in another one or simply from a lower to a higher university according to the national status grading. This association maintains disciplinary standards and controls intellectual expectations, characteristically through two major devices: journals and publications, and conferences and meetings. An academic's standing within a professional association can frequently be assessed exactly in relation to his or her role in these two forms of disciplinary institutions. The role of the journal is obvious, but the ritual authority-conferring function of the conference is not well understood. The conference serves numerous authorizing functions: it reaffirms the solidarity of the elite and enforces the currently authorized work of the discipline; it bestows prestige and honour so as to establish the ranking within the discipline; it is the venue for establishing new client-patron relations; it initiates the neophytes to the discipline; and sometimes it serves as the forum for casting out disciplinary dissidents and ritually anathematizing and excommunicating them. In the treatment of dissidents there are close similarities between sacerdotum, imperium and studio.

By contrast to the situation in the United States, in the national university system of Italy the 'government' side of academia seems all important whereas the 'party' side barely functions, which makes the system more like real politics in the United States. There are hardly any disciplinary associations in Italy; the formal hierarchy is all embracing and totally dominating—in law if not in practice. Formally all Italian academics above the level of unpaid assistant are members of the civil service and are ranked nationally according to seniority, person by person, in a document published by the Ministry of Public Instruction. All appointments to chairs are filled through a national competition (*concorso*) staged by the ministry. The whole university system is thus highly centralized in public service style and apparently totally bureaucratized. But actually, as Burton Clark (1977) shows, behind the screen of formal authority an extensive patronal system is run by the individual chair holders to whom real authority pertains in the absence of departments. According to Clark the 'bureaucratic centralism' of the formal Italian system is at the opposite pole to the decentralized and formally autonomous universities of the United States, each having its own administrative arrangements and free appointment procedures. Closest to the Italian is the French system of formal authority, both having originated from Napoleonic legislation. The German system is allied to both these systems insofar as appointments to chairs have to be approved by the government at the state (*Land*) level, but otherwise it is much more decentralized. The British system is decentralized almost equally to that of the United States, except that all British universities are at least partly funded by the State so none is completely private. The closer a university system approaches that of the United States, the more important do disciplinary professional associations become as a mode of authority that cuts across the formal hierarchies— the 'party' side is strengthened at the expense of the 'government'.

The different national systems were variously advantageous or disadvantageous for the development of particular sciences and humanities at particular periods in their histories. Hence, there is no a priori way of asserting that one system is better or worse for science than another. Nevertheless, the present U.S. system is best adapted to the contemporary stage in the development of the natural sciences, even if it is less so for the social sciences or humanities. The other national systems, deriving from an earlier historical period, are less suitable at present for the natural sciences, though they retain some distinct advantages at least for the more theoretical aspects of the social sciences and for some humanities, those which still depend on the work of autonomous 'great masters' or independent scholars. In no sense can one take the U.S. system as normative for the formal authority structure of science and by reference to it criticize that of any other nation, though obviously critical comparisons in both directions on more specific grounds cannot be avoided. Terry Clark (1973) implicitly slips into this error when he criticizes the French system for being unlike that of the United States because it lacks professional associations; on this basis alone he tries to account for the failure of the social sciences to develop in France after very promising beginnings in the nineteenth century. This argument is akin to ascribing the failings of U.S. politics to a failure to develop party 'machines' like those of France.

Academic 'parties', that is, disciplinary professional associations, vary as widely as do political parties. Some are no better than clubs of gentlemen led by a loose partnership of the leading notables in the discipline; others are highly organized party 'machines' designed to safeguard all the vital interests of their members. As in political parties, there are always two sides to any disciplinary association—a vocational side and a more strictly professional side—and the nature of the association will differ depending on which of these predominates. The vocational side corresponds to the interests of the members insofar as they might be said to be living for science and the strictly professional side, to their interests insofar as they might be said to be living off science—to adopt Weber's two categories. And just as political parties are in varying degrees both job procurement agencies and ideologically motivated sects, so that their 'struggles are struggles for the patronage of office as well as struggles for objective goals' (Weber 1971, 87), so, too, disciplinary associations are job security associations and intellectually motivated concerns. Increasingly the former is assuming predominance over the latter as the basic motivation for scientific work shifts away from a sense of vocational calling and more towards a sense of performing professional tasks, as John Maddox, the editor of *Nature*, notes:

Many people in the scientific community still have the ideals of the old-fashioned academic scientist. They want to make discoveries that are in themselves important, and they aspire only incidentally to Nobel Prizes. Many do good work without any wish for worldly recognition. But most view their occupation as a way of earning a salary. They do good work, much of it important, but they do not consider that among the products of their activity will be excitement and intellectual satisfaction. Some are increasingly concerned with getting grants so they can have lots of research students and appear important to the institutions that employ them (Maddox 1983, 31).

Disciplinary associations whose interests are predominantly intellectual correspond close to what Blume calls 'scientific or learned societies'. Those whose interests are predominantly occupational, 'those specially concerned with bolstering the professional or employee variants upon the scientific role', he terms 'professional associations in the first instance, trade unions in the second' (Blume 1974, 99). But it is always a matter of proportion since most disciplinary associations are all of these at once to some degree. Blume brings this out in his historical account of chemistry societies in Britain and the United States; he notes that 'of all sciences, chemistry was the most rapidly "professionalized"', and in this area 'relevant phenomena were best developed' (ibid. 102). In Britain the Chemical Society broke away as a specialized science from the Royal Society in 1840. By 1867 the opposition between the vocational and strictly professional wings had already become evident: 'Some held that the Chemical Society should establish itself as an association of eminent men of science . . . others held a contrary view: the charter required that the society exist for promotion of interest in chemistry, and this could be done by attracting to membership all with an interest in the subject' (ibid. 105). The Chemical Society tried to straddle both these interests and to 'recognize the rival demands of scholarship and professionalism' (ibid. 111) through numerous tactics and institutional expedients. The American Chemical Society, formed in 1874, which was unwilling or unable to overcome this contradiction, eventually found itself surrounded by secessionist organizations such as the more professional Institute of Chemical Engineers, formed in 1908.

Chemistry is the pre-eminent example of a discipline in which formal-professional authority predominates, and as a result its authority structure is like a 'smoothly functioning formal bureaucracy' (Whitley 1982, 340). Whitley has spelled out the cognitive paradigms and institutional structure of such sciences and shows how these relate very closely. Work in these sciences calls for an extended and precisely specified educational background, usually of a highly technical or formal nature. The research is itself technified, utilizing throughout such a discipline common techniques and technological devices but always to different specific ends, as, for example, when applied to different materials or problems. This is why such disciplines are decentralized and have strong local controls but not necessarily any over-all direction for the whole discipline. These local controlling bodies set goals for specific problems to be solved, and tasks for this purpose are allocated, for 'a high degree of division of labour is possible and overt conflict over goals unlikely' (ibid. 344). Thus work is planned and proceeds smoothly on a regular day-by-day basis with little chance of major theoretical disputes interrupting the process. The total upshot is that 'a common educational background which develops similar skills and ensures that practitioners share technical procedures here leads to a common professional identity and enables the community to exclude outsiders from jobs without centralizing control over facilities' (ibid. 333).

Thus cognitive paradigms are closely integrated with authority structures. As Whitley (1977b, 29) argues, 'where research tasks can be relatively closely specified and appropriate ways of proceeding are clearly constrained, the possiblity of formal control systems and authority structures is enhanced as compared with sciences where objects are less "obviously" specified'. In general, all sciences that are technified, problem solving and finalized will tend in the direction of formal-professional authority structures. In such cases 'the whole science operates like a smooth machine'. And vice-versa, the more a science embraces such an authority structure the more will it tend towards intellectual norms and work procedures and approaches of the formal, efficient kind where task outcomes are highly predictable in general terms.

> Establishments in these fields control both work goals and procedures to a high extent through largely impersonal and formal means. . . . Within an elaborate and formalized body of knowledge and skills which defines and orders tasks, and evaluates the significance of results in a relatively uncontested manner, different groups develop research programs in a variety of directions which are integrated through the commonly accepted rule (Whitley 1982, 334–5).

The level and nature of integration in such disciplines are diffuse and general, and the establishment in such cases never constitutes a controlling elite. Sciences where an elite predominates are very different in their cognitive and 'political' character.

Collegial-Elite Authority

A collegial-elite form of authority is very different from formal-professional authority though the two types either have not yet been distinguished or have been confused. Much work in the sociology of science has gone into identifying, locating and measuring ruling elites in different sciences. Such elites are called establishments, hierarchies, reputational organizations, and so on, and thus they are not distinguished clearly from formal-professional authority. The differences are by no means clear cut for frequently the same personnel occupy both authority positions. However, even in such cases an analytical separation may be made. The distinction can be seen most clearly in those situations where the disciplinary elite constitutes a distinct group separate from the professional authorities. Typically these will be arrangements where the 'brilliant young men', who determine collectively the way the discipline is proceeding, are distinct from the grey eminences—the established elders—occupying the formal and administrative positions of power.

A clear separation of formal-professional from collegial-elite authority emerges from Merton and Zuckermann's study of acceptance rates of articles in the prestigious journal *Physical Review* (Merton 1973). These authors note that in 'science, as in other institutional spheres, positions of power and authority tend to be occupied by older men. (Indeed, it has sometimes been said with mixed feelings that gerontocracy may even be a good thing in science; it leaves the young productive scientists free to get on with their work and helps occupy the time of those who are no longer creative.)' (ibid. 488). By the phrase 'positions of power and authority' they clearly mean formal-professional authority. At the same time these authors note that

> at least in physics . . . it is not the older scientists whose papers were most often accepted but the young ones. And these age-graded rates of acceptance obtain within each applicable rank in the hierarchy of esteem. Both eminence and youth contribute to the probability of having manuscripts accepted; youth to such a degree that the youngest stratum of physicists in the third rank had as high an acceptance rate as the oldest stratum of eminent ones whose work, we must suppose, was no longer of the same high quality it once was (ibid. 488–9).

From this they seek to conclude that 'it would seem that if the sheer power and eminence of authors greatly affected refereeing decisions, then the older eminent scientists should have the highest rates of acceptance. But . . . this is not what we find' (ibid. 488). Perhaps that conclusion is a little over hasty. Although formal-professional authority does not determine acceptance rates of articles in physics, those whose articles are most readily accepted, frequently without any outside refereeing, might constitute another kind of authority group distinct from the formal-professional. The distinction in physics between those who hold official positions and those who contribute most in authorship, and so determine the research course of the discipline, suggests that such a group might indeed be a reality.

We know from other sources that physics possesses an elite not simply composed of its office holders. Derek Price, as early as 1959, spoke incidentally of 'power groups' in such sciences as physics as an already acknowledged phenomenon and clearly did not identify them with the official establishment figures but rather with those who were 'getting on with the job, making serious advances in their field', and who 'substitute personal contacts for formal communication'. 'In many of these fields, it is now hardly worth while embarking upon serious work unless you happen to be within the group, accepted and invited to the annual and informal conferences, commuting between the two Cambridges, and vacationing in one of the residential conference and work centres that are part of the international chain' (Price 1961, 99). This vivid description could now apply to many sciences, but it has particular relevance to physics. It was perhaps the first science to develop the authority structure of a collegial elite; Schrödinger saw this as early as 1935 though he tended to think that it was also true for other sciences, which may not yet have taken this direction. 'These men practically form a unit. It is a relatively small community, though widely scattered, and modern methods of communication have knit it into one. The members read the same periodicals. They exchange ideas with one another. And the result is that there is a fairly definite agreement as to what opinions are sound on this point or that' (Hagstrom 1965, 18). The old term 'invisible college' aptly characterizes such an elite, both because its members are only informally linked through chains of communication and because those so linked maintain relations of collegial equality. The authority of such a collegial elite also functions informally and 'invisibly' in the sharpest contrast to formal-professional authority. Even at such formal proceedings as conferences, where the role of an elite in managing its discipline is most clearly revealed, the actual deliberative decisions taken are more a matter of accepted arrangements than of explicit stipulations. Diana Crane notes: 'an informant in high-energy physics described how prestigious members of that area attend annual conferences where they confer about the important problems to be solved in the area and make decisions about the research that needs to be done in the immediate future' (Crane 1972, 53).

The discipline of high energy physics is by all accounts an extreme case of the authority of a ruling elite, as Gaston's (1973) work reveals. Diana Crane reports on an unpublished paper by Zaltman and Blaue who locate a small group of thirty-two high energy physicists as the key communicants in the whole world-wide network of the discipline and the ones responsible for the trend-setting research. The authors refer to this group as 'a highly elite invisible college' (ibid. 53). Blume (1974, 68) states categorically that 'control of the field by the elders of high-energy physics is exceptionally clear, the selection procedure extremely rigorous' (the term 'elders' must here be interpreted metaphorically). He explains that this development is a result of the extremely high cost of the facilities involved in research and their centralization in a few localities under the control of small groups. However, he does not show why the small groups in control of this kind of research should have come to dominate the whole field of physics with its myriad types of research and tens of thousands of workers.

The sociological explanations for the fact that physics has come to be ruled by a collegial elite have to do with the whole cognitive and authority development of the discipline during this century. The pre-eminence of one specialty, particle physics, had long come to be accepted because of its significance in disclosing the ultimate nature of matter and consequently its attraction of the best minds. As Schrödinger reports, this part of the discipline was already conscious of its elite status in the inter-war period. Even before the First World War, the famous Solvey conferences conveyed the impression of a physics elite. When particle physics inevitably became high energy physics after the Second World War the sense of elite status and collegial camaraderie was strengthened by the successful war-time work by the leaders of the discipline and their students at Los Alamos. After the war these students became the next generation of the collegial elite of physics. Increasingly this elite tended to assume the role of elite of all elites in science, as physics became the major scientific discipline and as physicists invaded and 'colonized' many other fields. During this process lesser physicists were dispersed throughout other sciences bringing with them not only the methods and techniques of physics but also its characteristic authority structure. Thus a super-elite—the Establishment— was partially constituted for all sciences: 'Killian estimated the consistently influential group at no larger than 200. The insiders tend to be leaders of the Los Alamos generation, predominantly physicists who had taken their Ph.D.'s at about a dozen graduate schools and held faculty positions at a handful of universities' (Kevles 1979, 394). Much the same kind of situation holds true in Britain where the theoretical physicists of the Oxbridge universities dominate the scientific establishment; as Whitley (1977a, 154) writes: 'these universities, it should be noted, also dominate—and again physicists appear to be to the fore—the British scientific advisory system'.

Physicists dispersed not only into adjacent disciplines but also into more distant ones where the arithmomorphic ideal could be applied, initially at least, with stunningly revolutionary results. Physicists moved into such fields as biophysics, molecular biology, neurology, economics and econometrics, strategic studies and artificial intelligence; numerous famous people in these fields had formative educational beginnings in physics and then branched out. In each new field they sought to recreate a collegial elite and with it to propel their host discipline into the precipitate rush for break-throughs in fundamental research to which they had become accustomed in physics. The more slowly paced research traditional to these disciplines was usually relegated to a backwater. At times, an almost manic striving for problems to solve and for quick results appeared as a side-effect of a collegial-elite authority structure. Yoxen notes this effect in molecular biology:

> Throughout the world, the control by research elites over money, status and access to research opportunities within an increasingly specialized set of biological disciplines has intensified the degree of competition and assisted the formation of a very esoteric, introspective research culture. . . . The effect of this increasingly intense drive for results was to enforce an exclusive concentration on just those problems, phenomena, or aspects of an organism that filled the needs of specific research programs. Molecular biologists learned to take an increasingly instrumental attitude to the living material with which they worked and were forced through the pressures of international competition to intensify the degree of specialization in the problem-solving skills required to stay in the field (Yoxen 1982, 136).

The method of physics applied to any other discipline puts a premium on formalization and abstraction and on high levels of mathematical ability. An elite forms out of the few who have undergone rigorous enough training to acquire such skills, and it excludes all those who lack them. It becomes an obvious recruitment device for new members. The elite tends to conduct its discourse on behalf of the discipline as a whole in its own preferred symbolism and formalized language. Such a discourse closes off intercourse with the uninitiated and with outsiders. The ultimate effect is to push the whole cognitive content of the discipline in the direction of ever greater formalization and abstraction, usually based on the arithmomorphic ideal. This approach has far-reaching cognitive and intellectual effects, as Whitley notes:

> The elevation of highly abstract, logically closed conceptual systems to definitive status as science results in attention being focused on purely formal properties of concepts and relations and the exclusion of all those that are not susceptible to treatment by the current most "elegant" and "simple"

formalism. It also directs attention away from substantive problems towards esoteric manipulations which may or may not have any physical meaning. Abstraction and mathematical complexity come to seem as the hallmark of scientificity (Whitley 1977a, 136).

A clear example of this development can be seen in economics, as Benjamin Ward notes:

> They are probably no more than a hundred economists who have been making important contributions to this part of the field, developing the basic ideas of mathematical economics and econometrics. They are the science's elite. For practitioners within this area of economics there can be no appeal other than to their peers in the field; no one else knows what they are talking about when they are talking the language of their science (Ward 1972, 12–13).

As an accompanying development, the very same social process that produced elites in some sciences produced a system of elite sciences and 'elite' methods and approaches within most sciences. The authority standing of the elites within each science helped to legitimate that of the elite sciences, and in the same way the cognitive side furthered the 'political' and vice-versa in a mutually supporting and reinforcing manner. Out of this development arose an 'elite' view of what constitutes science in which the arithmomorphic ideal and its associated authority forms took pride of place. Whitley notes how emergent elites in different sciences were able to establish themselves by appealing to the norms of scientificity held by the supreme elite or Establishment of the academic system. By presenting themselves as the only ones in a discipline who worked toward these norms, the members of a potential elite within a discipline could gain recognition and legitimation for themselves from outside the discipline, sometimes even against the interests of most of the other more traditional-minded members.

Once an elite is constituted within a discipline the almost inevitable effect is that it institutes a division of labour so that its work becomes definitive for all activities within the discipline. The work of the ruck of researchers is then graded according to its role in relation to the work of the elite. Whitley states that 'fundamental concerns and principles are remote from day-to-day tasks of most scientific workers, and may become the preserve of a distinct group. . . . Since the way in which work in a field is "made sense of" or "rationalized" reflects and institutionalizes research goals and priorities, this group is obviously influential in directing interests and allocating rewards' (Whitley 1977b, 29). Chubin and Connolly (1982, 304) speak of an 'advising, consulting, reviewing elite' that acts as a 'gatekeeper' to allocate rewards and grant or withhold information required to carry out the more prestigious research within a discipline. In this way 'the elite can . . . determine what problems are chosen and what (research) trials sustained' (ibid. 304). And through this mechanism the elite can also maintain and enforce the division of labour, allowing each researcher only the kind of work that his or her standing in relation to the elite allows. Anyone who attempts to innovate from a position outside the elite will usually find little support, or worse, positive hostility for only those within the elite are granted the prerogative to undertake novel departures and only if the innovation does not threaten the elite position. As Whitley notes, 'once a particular view of the discipline has become institutionalized and legitimate topics and approaches specified, reformulations and novel developments will be strenuously opposed since they imply a reordering of priorities and threaten the existing distribution of expertise and property rights' (Whitley 1977b, 32).

An elite asserts its authority through its control and co-ordination of the influential work within the discipline and not through organizational direction. In this crucial respect collegial-elite authority differs from formal-professional authority, and it explains why these authorities can in some disciplines be exercised by different groups. The role of elite authority cannot be completely taken over by the formal hierarchy if the work of the discipline is not to degenerate into planned routine. An elite is required to innovate and integrate without being bound by overly rigid formal rules and status hierarchies. As Whitley states, echoing Bourdieu, 'if a science is not to disintegrate into an unco-ordinated set of narrow research tasks, which cognitive and social barriers combine to separate, integrative tasks have to be undertaken and these require confidence and prestige. By focusing on this sort of work, elites are able to maintain their authority and superiority. They renew and expand their "cultural capital" by risking it on major problems' (ibid. 44). Some disciplines that were unable to evolve such an authoritative elite have indeed disintegrated into unco-ordinated groups carrying out unrelated research.

A collegial elite derives its authority and power from its position within the discipline and the many recognized and legitimate prerogatives this position carries. But its capacity to exert influence on the level of specific research derives from its restricted access to and control of the vital channels of informal information without which no serious work in science can be done. The elite is first an intercommunicating network of researchers informally passing on among themselves the latest news and information, including all the incidental tips, suggestions, advice and instructions only circulated by the grapevine and not found in printed sources. As the work of Collins and others has shown, contemporary scientists cannot repeat an experiment or imitate a technical device on the basis of printed sources alone. Without a large and almost verbally unspecifiable context of 'tacit' knowledge, in Polanyi's sense, and implicit information, the data set out in an abbreviated paper or technical report cannot be reconstructed or even fully appreciated. Someone with no access to the background knowledge cannot join a new line of scientific research and is effectively excluded from the field. As an anonymous laser researcher quoted by Collins states: 'what you publish in an article is always enough to show that you've done it, but never enough to enable anyone else to do it. If they can do it then they know as much as you do' (Barnes and Edge 1982, 54). Collins' account of the numerous failed attempts by British laboratories to build a TEA laser—first constructed by a Canadian defence laboratory—from fully published specifications amply bears out these conclusions. 'The major point is that the transmission of skills is not done through the medium of the written word' (ibid. 54). The power of an elite intercommunicating network is simply its capacity to be in the know and by implication or design to keep everyone else in the dark. Access to the elite is thus the same as access to essential information.

An elite must not, however, be seen simply as a conspiracy of exclusion barring general access to vital information or to resources necessary to work at a certain level in a field, though that can be one consequence of its position. It derives its position from the positive functions it performs, which can be essential for a discipline. These functions of control and integration are now unavoidable and requisite in many disciplines even though they might have been absent during the development of disciplines. As Whitley (1984, 22) notes: 'collegiate groups in the sciences . . . also have to monitor research results and co-ordinate task outcomes in a systematic way. . . . Without the formal communication and control systems, the pursuit of originality could fragment scientific fields'. Though it is questionable whether 'pursuit of originality' is the real problem, some disciplines fail to develop further for want of an elite. Without a means of exercising internal direction and control a discipline can become fixated in unco-ordinated, repetitive work. This seems to have occurred in the field of small human groups research as studied by McGrall and Altman. Diana Crane reports their findings as follows: 'the (typical) study is done more or less in isolation from other small group endeavours, in the sense that it seldom attempts to replicate the findings, variables, or studies of others. . . . Lack of theoretical emphasis, lack of ties to other work, and lack of replication all are very general problems of the field' (Crane 1972, 54). As a result each researcher aims to 'apply the (same) procedures, task or piece of equipment over and over, introducing new variables or slight modifications of old variables' (ibid.), with the aim of generating as large a volume of research publications as possible. Nobody is prepared to invest the time and effort or take the risks of undertaking broad theoretical work for the discipline as a whole. Instead each research group stakes out its own territory and is unconcerned with what other groups are doing. Such a situation can only be remedied by introducing a collegial elite to distribute tasks within the discipline and to co-ordinate the results around a central body of commonly accepted theory. But, of course, such an authority structure cannot be simply imposed or willed; it must grow organically from the needs of the discipline. It can be encouraged by general review papers that assess the state of the discipline as a whole and make the necessary advisory judgements about its current state of research.

The presence of an elite in a discipline does not necessarily mean a consensus on everything. An elite can be riven by factional in-fighting around major disagreements, as in party politics. Also some disciplines, usually those in the social sciences and humanities, can be divided into competing elites. Competing elites indicate a cognitive situation where there is no uniform disciplinary paradigm or set of standards but rather a number of these challenging each other. Thus in the field of literary criticism, an older elite of New Critics is being challenged by a newer elite of Deconstructionists. There is no reason to believe that one will ever win out conclusively over the other or that a third force will not enter the fray. From an international viewpoint, in literary studies many elites are clearly in power, though when these do not engage with each other or even communicate it becomes difficult to consider them as rival elites of the one discipline. Such complexities have not as yet been adequately studied, even though the study of elites has so far been one of the most extensive preoccupations in the sociology of science.

Two main methods have been employed for this purpose: the citation index has been tabulated to locate the papers referred to most frequently, and survey information has been sought from scientists to ascertain with whom they correspond, so as to locate those who stand centrally in the communication network. It is not fully established whether these methods completely correlate with each other or whether they uniquely determine a collegial elite. It might be necessary to test them against other criteria which better exclude the interference of other authority forms—for example, attendance and crucial roles at elite conferences or publication of key review papers. Although these more evaluative criteria cannot be applied in a quantifiable social-scientific way, they may be more adequate to the task. The sociology of science is itself beginning to suffer from an elite which dictates too rigidly the methods and approaches of the field. This rigidity has led to many omissions.

Patronal Authority

If elite authority has been studied almost too extensively, patronal authority has hardly been studied at all. Apart from incidental remarks, only three substantial pieces on the subject are available in the literature: a chapter in Terry Clark's book *Prophets and Patrons* (1973), which deals largely with patronage in the French University system prior to the Second World War, and analogous chapters in Burton Clark's *Academic Power in Italy* (1977) and Bourdieu's *Homo Academicus* (1984). The sociology of science has yet to discover patronal authority or assess its importance. Perhaps one reason for this neglect is the widespread opinion that patronage is not a matter of legitimate authority but of undue influence or preferential treatment, something morally reprehensible and against the supposedly 'impersonal' and 'objective' criteria governing science.

That this view concerning patronage is mistaken is obvious from the legitimate role played by referees and refereeing processes in all aspects of a scientific career, from receiving a Ph.D. to getting an appointment or promotion or to having work accepted for publication. The legal stipulation to nominate persons as referees in all kinds of applications for all kinds of different purposes legitimates the role of patrons in acting on behalf of their clients. Obviously the degree of legitimacy of kinds of patronage differs between university systems. In Italy it is considered legitimate for a patron to act on behalf of a client on an appointments board; in one case reported by Burton Clark (1977, 99), during an appointment procedure when subject to criticism 'the majority replied that it was everyday practice for a professor to become a member of the evaluating committee in order to safeguard the correct evaluation of his own student'. Clearly this approach would be considered illegitimate and even corrupt elsewhere; but other patronage practices would nevertheless

be accepted as perfectly valid. Everywhere the more authoritative the patron
the greater weight is carried by his or her reference or recommendation.
According to well-known and 'legitimate' practice, the recommendation of
a powerful patron in the discipline can permit (or at times prevent) the
publication of articles or books, sometimes to the exclusion of every other
consideration. And regardless of whether the patron's view is solicited or
arrives unrequested, it still carries the same weight. Hence, to consider
patronage as anything but legitimate authority in academia is almost to
be guilty of academic double-think.

Terry Clark's, Burton Clark's and Bourdieu's works show beyond doubt
that patronage can be legitimate authority and that it may have been the
dominant form of authority for all disciplines within a whole university
system for over a century. The Clarks have no hesitation in speaking of
the legitimate authority of patrons and of the legitimating function of their
journals. For example, Terry Clark states with reference to Durkheim and
his journal: 'finally, Durkheim's authority was extended and legitimated
through the Année. . . . Division of labour led to elaboration of Durkheim's
ideas by others who in turn enforced the master's authority. . . . Beyond
these manifest goals . . . the Année performed four more latent functions:
recruitment, training, social integration, and the exercise and legitimation
of authority' (Clark 1973, 183). The patron's authority was recognised both
by clients and by other patrons who acknowledge his exclusive right to
act on behalf of and in respect of the members of the patron's cluster—
Terry Clark's neutral designation, instead of the more accurate word 'clique',
for the group of followers surrounding a patron: 'each was considered the
legitimate and total master of his particular constituency, and whenever
possible, constituency decisions (for examinations, promotions, appointments, and so forth) would be referred to him by his colleagues and his
judgement accepted without question. Monopoly remained the unquestioned organizational principle' (ibid. 72). This case is by no means exceptional in France or any other country, though there are special reasons
that patronal authority should have become so all pervasive in French
and Italian academia. Terry Clark notes that 'legitimation for patronal
authority may be found in French culture' (ibid. 83) in a tradition that
goes back to Roman times. He also identifies the special features in the
French official centralized formal-professional authority structure and the
peculiar role of Paris as the centre that make patronage mandatory in
most other dealings; without his Parisian patron no provincial can achieve
anything.

Burton Clark argues analogously that in Italy the highly centralized and
bureaucratized system of formal academic authority has produced of necessity an informal patronal system as its counterweight. As he states,
'professors are so often academic barons in Italy because a unitary administrative framework has helped to make them so' (Clark 1977, 108).
A full sociological explanation for this complex symbiotic relation between
formal-professional and patronal authority would also be concerned largely
with Italy's tradition of local particularism, by which any imposition from
the centre is resisted, as well as with the age-old traditions of patronage
inherited from Roman times that are prevalent in all Mediterranean so-

cieties. 'Clientela' and 'parentela' relations are endemic to Italian government and business. These particular features found in France and Italy do not hold true elsewhere, and, consequently, patronal authority is not so prevalent. Nevertheless, in every academic system there are relationships which necessitate this kind of authority form to a greater or lesser degree depending on the total authority structure.

The French system of patronal authority was particularly well organized in that the clients of a patron formed a unified and mutually co-operating cluster: 'an association of perhaps a dozen persons who shared a minimum core of beliefs about their work and who were prepared to collaborate to advance research and instruction in a given area' (Clark 1973, 67). Terry Clark recognizes that such ideal cognitive interactions were less important than those crucial necessities of academic life which could not be satisfied without the intercession of a patron; hence 'probably the most important mechanism uniting the cluster was the patron's influence on the careers of lower status members' (ibid.). The members of a cluster varied widely in status, including many rankings ranging from students to professors in provincial universities. It is unlikely that such varied and well-organized clusters will be found outside France; it is more likely that only tenuous links join together the clients of a patron, independent of the shared relation itself. Nor is it likely that most clienteles can survive as a unit the demise or retirement of their patron, unlike many French clusters which developed mechanisms for grooming a 'dauphin' and helping him succeed to the 'throne' when the sovereign master died or had to abdicate. One of the few examples of a fully developed French-style cluster in the United States is the school surrounding the psychologist B. F. Skinner. As Diana Crane describes it:

> Many Skinnerians are former students or collaborators of Skinner or students of his former students. Skinnerian psychologists have their own journals that publish only material using Skinner's theoretical approach to the study of learning. Skinnerians seldom publish in other psychological journals . . . these findings suggest a group that is closed to external influences and in this sense has some of the characteristics of a school (Crane 1972, 87).

However, this case is exceptional; as Terry Clark (1973, 89) remarks: 'American academic despots are small fry compared to their French counterparts'.

Because the French system of patronal authority was so well established and so permanent, extremely well defined and understood relations governed the behaviour of patrons to clients and patrons to each other. In the latter case 'a system of exchange of favours served to regulate the system. Over time favours performed among patrons would tend to balance out. Those most adept at arranging favours would tend to benefit most, while those in relative isolation would benefit least from the exchange system' (Clark 1973, 72). Since a patron's resources for generating such exchanges of favours were by no means equal, some patrons had to present themselves as clients to others better endowed. In this way the system produced what Terry Clark calls 'patrons' patrons'. These top patrons used their resources of 'scholarly creativity, contacts, money, political acumen' to run the whole system in a balanced way; 'what they had in common was a capacity to structure the supply and demand of resources so that exchanges could approximate market characteristics' (ibid. 74). It is unlikely that patrons' patrons can develop outside a system of patronal authority approximating that of France; this system is rarely found elsewhere, with the possible exception of the British Commonwealth universities where the main patrons in the academically dependent 'colonies' must have their own patrons in Britain, usually at the Oxbridge universities, the latter approaching the role of patrons' patrons.

As Terry Clark shows, the key to the French patronal system is the role exercised by the schools of Paris and their dominance of the provincial universities. Provincial academics, as well as those aspiring for positions in the provinces, must have their Paris patron, who because of location and contacts with all the other patrons is in a position to negotiate posts, promotion and all other advances for his or her clients. The clients serve their patron by identifying themselves with and furthering his or her intellectual authority: 'patrons would be expected to present general programmatic theories, while followers would tend toward more narrow scholarly activities, often testing and extending hypotheses implicit in the patron's theory' (ibid. 81). Hence, much depends on the intellectual competence of the patron; an incompetent patron would lead the whole school into 'blind alleys and inconsequential results' (ibid.). A whole scientific field could be rendered sterile in France by one dominant senile patron. There could never be any question of the clients rebelling, for the hold of the patron over them was total.

On the other hand, a brilliant patron could revolutionize a whole field almost single-handed. Yet, as Terry Clark argues, this situation, too, could have some drawbacks, for 'students, outside witnesses and even many participants, observing the almost revolutionary introduction of new paradigms and the redefining of entire subfields or disciplines following a coup d'université often led to an uneasy feeling that no knowledge was legitimately established' (ibid. 88). This particular criticism seems to depend too much on anecdotal psychology. Institutionally considered, the disconcerting effect of rapidly changing approaches in the sciences does not necessarily affect the legitimacy of the new knowledge, since that is always far more a matter of the legitimacy of the authority maintaining it. Once a coup d'université was carried out, the new authority figures would quickly establish themselves and so legitimate their innovations in knowledge.

This tradition leads to a different pattern of change in the sciences, one that would approximate closer to changes in the humanities or in other fields where patronal authority is dominant even outside France. The power and brilliance of single personalities have typified the development of the social sciences in France. The very same sciences, for example, sociology or economics, have developed quite differently outside France—in Germany, England, or the United States. And these differences can be largely attributed to difference in the structure of authority. The growth of a solid scientific organization with departments and a professional association, a division of labour affirmed by journals and conferences, with no one individual being able to determine the course of the discipline, such as one finds it in the United States—all these are absent in France. One must not assume, as Terry Clark does, that this pattern of authority constitutes some kind of institutional scientific norm by which the French patronal system can be criticized.[1] However, since 1968 the French system is in crisis: the old ways of patronage can no longer be maintained first because the sciences in France have expanded beyond personal control and now involve institutional allocation of large-scale state funding for specialized research projects and second because the universities are changing and expanding on the model of the mass-education multiversity. Numerous attempts at reform designed to bring about developments in an American direction have been made. However, the old ways inevitably reassert themselves (Cohen 1978).

A patronal system in the sciences can be subject to the specific deformation that Terry Clark identifies: 'but without strong professional norms inside the national system, leading patrons have sometimes deviated considerably from international standards. In such instances the level of private discontent has often been so high but that of public criticism so low that patrons and observers, especially younger observers, have seen their standards erode' (Clark 1973, 240). Clark believes that such a situation cannot arise where there is a professional association made up of many 'autonomous individuals', and a large 'middle-level' personnel with 'clear criteria of professional evaluation' and mechanisms for 'the informed evaluation and criticism of supposedly original contributions and for allocating proper rewards' (ibid.). But a professional 'machine' is no proof against corruption, and once in place its dictatorial power can be even greater than that of any one despotic patron. A professionalized discipline, like a political party, can enforce its norms far more effectively than an individual, and even less recourse can be had against it by anyone in opposition. Even such seemingly ideal scientific norms as 'the differentiation of social scientific roles and the definition of ethical neutrality' are by no means a pure gain for scientific objectivity, though Clark believes them to be highly desirable in the social sciences and ascribes them to the professionalization of these sciences in Germany and America. The failure of such norms to develop in France—explaining, for example, 'resistance to the separation of the scientific and moral components of his work' (ibid. 216) by Durkheim— is by no means a simple failing. Ethical neutrality or *Wertfreiheit* can be used as a professional shibboleth to enforce 'methodism' in the social sciences and to proscribe work that displays any social concern or moral relevance.

Obviously France will have to introduce other authority forms (as it has tried to do since 1968) to make up for the lack and failures of its traditional patronal system; the student unrests have shown that the old system is unworkable under changing conditions of research and teaching (Bourdieu 1984). In the sciences the move has been towards the professionalization of research in specialized research institutes funded by direct government grants. But the old patronal system has also continued to prevail beside the new; it still operates particularly in the social sciences, especially for those who want to enter teaching careers in which connections to a powerful patron are much more important than research accomplishments, as Bourdieu (1971) reports. Clark (1973, 235) concludes that despite all the changes and reforms none of the social sciences has 'developed strong disciplinary communities'.

Since so little research has been conducted on academic patronage, one cannot avoid turning to work which focusses on patronage elsewhere in the social system and bring it to bear on academia. Though this research is invariably carried out by academics, its relevance to academia is never remarked on by them nor utilized for this purpose. Ironically, only in academia does patronage constitute legitimate authority; elsewhere its legitimacy is usually doubtful. Nowadays patronage is most commonly found in landlord-peasant relations in the Mediterranean area in Europe, Africa and the Middle East, as well as in Latin America and the Philippines where Spanish feudal influences are still prevalent. Criminal organizations of Mediterranean provenance tend also to be organized along patronal lines; a formal sociological kinship can be noted between the dons of the Mafia and those of academia for which the Italians have coined the expression 'la Mafia delle cattedre' (Clark 1977, 100). Patronage is ubiquitous in politics, for example, in the system of U.S. party bosses. But everywhere outside academia patronage and clientelism are on the decline and perceived to be less legitimate as rational-legal forms of authority become more prevalent and as the free-market relations of a developed economy take over from more personal traditional arrangements. Only where land is in extremely short supply, leading to subsistence farming, must the peasants safeguard themselves by acquiring patrons as landlords who will see the peasants through bad times and protect them in emergencies. Where jobs are abundant and education improved, patronage tends to wither away and be perceived as corrupt, as Scott notes: 'thus patron-client exchange falls somewhere on the continuum between personal bonds joining equals and purely coercive bonds. Determining exactly where between these two poles a particular patron-client system should be placed, or in which direction it is moving, becomes an important empirical question in any attempt to gauge its legitimacy' (Gellner and Waterbury 1977, 22).

The identical question can be posed for academic systems of patronage and the degree of legitimacy with which they are perceived. Among academics, as among landless peasants, the job situation is the key to the prevalence of patronage and to its perception. Where many jobs are available, where mobility from one appointment to another is easy and can be accomplished by relatively impersonal means, patronage does not tend to be extensive and is frowned on as corrupt. This has typically been the case in the United States and very much so since the Second World War and the huge expansion of education. In European countries, by contrast, job opportunities, especially at the higher levels, have tended to be restricted for many reasons, among them the reluctance of existing patrons to allow positions to be opened up that would challenge their authority. Hence the ratio of students to professors has risen in the postwar years in France, Germany and Italy, till finally only the student explosion of 1968 revealed it to be an untenable situation (Driver 1971).

Since the 1970s, however, as the number of academic job opportunities has shrunk in the United States and as mobility has almost ceased, patronage has probably grown and is likely to become more readily accepted in American disciplines where it was marginal before. If job opportunities become very restricted in given disciplines, informal arrangements between patrons are likely to emerge in order to monopolize the few openings; for instance, in governing appointments in fields such as classics in Italy, where less than half a dozen patrons monopolize all available appointments, each patron takes a turn to fill a vacancy with a designated protégé, so appointments can be predicted years in advance. All these are at present mere hypotheses that will need to be empirically tested by research on academic patronage and clientelism.

Landless peasants, ward heelers and godfathers are perhaps too far removed from the genteel conventions of academic patronage. A closer analogue is the patron-client relations of antiquity, especially in the late Roman republic and early empire. Saller's work provides a rich source of comparative examples. In Rome, as in present-day academia, patron and client were social roles that could be played interchangeably by social unequals or equals. The actual status of being a *patronus* or *cliens* tended not to be openly acknowledged: 'Fronto never referred to himself as a *patronus* of his protégés and used the word *cliens* only once' (Saller 1982, 9); instead, the real relationships were disguised behind the politer language of *amicicia* or friendship. In academia one observes the same phenomenon of reluctance to spell out connections, resulting in an obligatory false consciousness. 'Since patron-client relationships were essentially instrumental—that is, based on the exchange of goods and services—the words which describe the exchange are perhaps the best pointers to patronage . . . : officium, beneficium, meritum and gratia' (ibid. 15). These words basically refer to different modes of obligation and debt accrued in the exchange of favours. It would be worth ascertaining their modern equivalents in the parlance of academia; the references, reports, recommendations and commendations academics exchange will have to be studied with the scrupulous care and attention with which classical scholars now peruse the letters exchanged by Roman senatorial or imperial benefactors and aspirants for proconsular office. Terry Clark has already made a start in this direction by quoting from the letters concerning appointments, which were exchanged by French professors in the last century, which included such famous names as Binet, Comte and Worms.

Each country will probably have its own linguistic conventions for expressing *officium, beneficium, meritum* and *gratia*. The very important role of patronage broker, which was extremely well developed among the Romans since access to the emperor enabled a person to act as go-between for others, will also find its equivalent in academia in the use of contacts on behalf of others. The amassing of influential contacts is a widely cultivated activity in academia. Harriet Zuckermann quotes an anonymous Nobel laureate in chemistry on this topic:

I've accumulated over the years a lot of what I call wealth. Many, many connections. I keep them all active. All for one purpose: to do my research and teaching better. Science in this day is a world-wide proposition. I have three worldwide empires which I can call on: research, teaching and industry. So if it's necessary to send my students to Bangkok or somewhere else, I can do it easily. If it's necessary to get someone to teach one of them who isn't here but in Europe, I can do it. All of this is done for this reason, taking care of the students. There aren't many people "rich" enough to do that: rich in the sense of connections, power, financing for research, influence (Zuckermann 1977, 134).

It would be naive to assume that 'taking care of the students' does not at the same time entail taking care of oneself, though it is unclear what *officium, beneficium, meritum* and *gratia* are exchanged in chemistry.

However, it does not follow that patronage per se is corrupt or that sound science must avoid it. On the contrary, it is doubtful that anything worthwhile could have developed in science without the exercise of enlightened patronage in support of original work before it could prove itself. For example, molecular biology might not have arisen or developed so rapidly except for the patronage of Warren Weaver and Francis Crick. Weaver, who was not even a biologist, became the director of the Natural Sciences Division of the Rockefeller Foundation where he set up a vital processes program in 1932. Through the funding and encouragement of on-going work of a reductive type, he propelled biology research in the direction of what eventually became molecular biology. Yoxen describes the political process by means of which the methodology of biology was redirected:

> Weaver's task as patron was to evade or transcend the divisions of existing disciplines, not least because it would shift the balance of power in his favour, and to strengthen the analytic and methodological rigour of biological research, according to criteria operating in physics and chemistry. What he chose to do was to cluster together a set of projects of a transdisciplinary character amongst them Pauling's structural chemistry of biological macromolecules, Astbury's crystalography of DNA and protein, Schoenheimer's use of radio-isotopes in biochemistry, Beadle's work in biochemical genetics, Svedberg's development of the ultracentrifuge, Perutz's X-ray studies of haemoglobin. The intention was to intensify research, to allow people to travel to more progressive labs, to promote the use of physical theories and methods in biology and to interest physical scientists in the life sciences (Yoxen 1982, 133).

Having thus acted as the godfather of molecular biology in its early stages, Weaver was later to perform a similar office for information theory; but he also contributed to it personally as a scientist, not merely as a patron. In molecular biology a more active leadership and patronage role was subsequently taken on by Crick, who emerged as almost the research director of the entire discipline. As Cavalieri reports:

> A significant portion of these "think-tank" activities occurred at the famous Gordon Research Conferences, which take place every summer in New Hampton, New Hampshire. . . . Each year, Francis Crick would attend the conference and fire up all nucleic aciders with his imaginative and usually correct

hypotheses about DNA functions. It seemed as though the entire scientific community was at his disposal for him to direct their experiments from his podium; it was almost a kind of remote control research. He was unique among the ring-leaders, and I guess that his "sermons" encouraged the many hopeful global thinkers who were always trying to emulate him. Endless series of experiments and theories had their inception at New Hampton (Cavalieri 1981, 107).

Patronage is not always so far sighted, selfless and enlightened; frequently it can lead to the ruination of science in a whole university system, particularly when it becomes institutionalized. The French and Italian systems are bedevilled by patronage, but perhaps nowhere is its influence worse than in Japan where it is institutionalized as the so-called *kozasei* system. As Sibatani reports, *kozasei* is the practice of doling out limited funds equally to small research teams headed by a professor. This process is meant to be democratic and egalitarian, but the consequences are the very opposite:

> The *kozasei* often gives each professor power over a small number of people. It may render some professors immune to review by peers and thus it undermines the traditional mechanism of maintaining high scholarly and moral standards among scientists—the concept of external examiners is unknown in Japanese universities, for example. Given a social institution which strongly favours a life-long commitment to a particular job, the breaking of a relationship between a student and the professor he or she has chosen to work under could therefore ruin his or her academic career (Sibatani 1972).

This system is found in the social sciences and humanities in many of the universities of the world, and the effects are not unlike those experienced in Japanese science. The life or death powers of professors over their students and their immediate entourages inhibit any tendency to individuality or innovative originality. The overcoming of such corrupting influences should constitute a key project for any reform movement in science. However, it must be recognized that patronage must remain an inherent part of personal relations in academia.

As Zuckermann (1977, 99) shows, patronage is extremely important at the start of a scientific career. It is almost a sine qua non for winning a Nobel prize; more than half of the prize winners have been pupils or followers of other Nobel laureates. Some Nobel dynasties of teachers and pupils extend over many generations, as for example, the succession of J. J. Thompson, Rutherford and Bohr which was productive of whole teams of laureates at each generation in physics (ibid. 103). This succession extended into other fields as Bohr in turn was the patron of Delbruck, who then became a kind of patrons' patron in molecular biology, forming two successive clusters—a phage group and a phycomyces group; interestingly, the two groups did not overlap. 'The alumni of the phage course (which ran for 26 years) were to include many of the most prominent figures in the later landscape of molecular genetics', as Stent (1982) in his obituary on Delbruck notes; the phycomyces group was far less successful. Zuckermann (1977, 133) quotes extensively from the correspondence between Einstein and Bohr through which they sponsored each other's students and speaks of 'the expanding network of sponsorship and its impact on scientific careers'. The evidence presented shows that this practice was an extensive and quite commonplace procedure in no way considered underhand, against fair competition, or counter to the objective spirit of science.

However, some of these relationships were probably not 'pure' cases of patron-client links since they cross with an older form, that of the master-pupil relationship. The master-pupil relation is a much more permanent and intellectually forming attachment than that of patron and client; the latter is exclusively or predominantly an exchange relation in which intellectual influence plays a lesser part. The difference is not merely a matter of interest as against affect, since patron-client bonds can also produce intense loyalties on both sides, rather it has to do with the terms on which the relationship is entered into and maintained. The master-pupil relation is elective on both sides; it is maintained on the basis of a shared activity and common beliefs persisting through the life stages of apprenticeship and maturity (Bourdieu 1984, 140). The patron-client connection is more intellectually casual, more definite in the obligations incurred and expected on both sides, and in general more calculating (ibid. 125). The difference is analogous to that between entering a marriage, which can be either monogamous or polygamous, and engaging in numerous affairs either sequentially or simultaneously. But the one shades into the other, especially in science, and it is impossible to provide strict criteria for separating them. As Waterbury remarks: 'the concept of patronage and patron-client relations offers all the analytic frustration common to most attempts to categorize social action and human motivation. One cannot advance irrefutable generally accepted criteria by which to establish what patronage is and when (not to mention how) it has become something else' (Gellner and Waterbury 1977, 329).

Not only the client but also the patron benefit from a patronage relationship. Indeed, a key to scientific success at any level is the capacity to attract clients, as collaborators and subordinate researchers, and especially as doctoral candidates. A well-developed cluster of followers multiplies a patron's output of papers and redounds to his credit as he can usually claim the lion's share of any joint work—and besides, a clique can also double as a claque. At the same time the development of clusters serves the more substantial purpose of establishing and maintaining a program of research. Whether or not a given line of research will continue depends to a large extent on whether it can be parcelled out and packaged into neat problem bundles, each of approximately three years' duration, which can be assigned as Ph.D. topics. The capacity to attract doctoral candidates, apart from the intrinsic interest of the work, also depends on the patronage powers of the supervisor, that is, whether he or she can ensure his students publications—generally with the patron's own name first—and subsequent appointments on completion of their theses. Chubin and Connolly consider 'training capacity' one of the key factors in the pursuit and success of a 'research trail' in all sciences in the United States after the Second World War.

Graduate students, for example, are likely to seek dissertation advisers who can provide well specified projects, with a high probability of successful completion and publication. Upon receipt of the Ph.D. the new entrant is faced with the urgent need to establish a reputation and publication record within local promotion and tenure timeframes. Again, both participants gain from the arrangement: the professor maintains his reputation by further work on a problem which he pioneered earlier, keeping alive a research trail; the student benefits by the safety and legitimacy of competent extension and publication, carrying forward the banner of the professor's seminal work (Chubin and Connolly 1982, 303).

Patronage is thus a key determinant in what scientific research is undertaken and how it is continued. As Whitley (1977b, 33) sees it, 'in general patronage remains an important means of control and influence over work choices and styles'.

Patronage in science is itself very varied; it operates quite differently in different sciences, and it enters into different stages of a scientific career and different phases of the process of research. Whitley remarks particularly on the differences inherent in the restricted and the unrestricted sciences, utilizing a distinction elaborated by Pantin (1968) to refer to those sciences that work on simple, abstracted objects with few parameters as against those that have to tackle complex objects and situations, for example, physics as against geology, or chemistry as against biology. In the former, 'hard' sciences patronage will be extended within clearly specified organizational conditions and unambiguous research methods, disciplinary boundaries and goals of given fields of study. 'Research priorities become "rationalized" so that important topics and "fruitful" models, etc. are firmly separated from "marginal" or uninteresting ones' (Whitley 1977b, 31); directives are firmly given as to what is right and wrong, done and not done. Generally, patronage tends to shade off into hierarchical direction and control by the leaders of research over all the others on their staff. In the unrestricted or 'soft' sciences, by contrast, no such precise boundaries can be drawn or directives given; 'formalized procedures are not so prominent in these sciences and acts of personal judgement are more commonplace' (ibid. 34). As a result the style of collaboration and the mode of patronage are different for 'in this situation there is a low limit on the number of students any individual scientist can adequately supervise' (ibid.). It is extremely difficult simply to package research projects suitable for Ph.D.s and let the students get on with them in accordance with standard procedures, so 'the supervisor may have to become much more involved in the student's work than originally intended', and as a result the link between supervisor and student is likely to be more intense and personal involving a 'higher degree of commitment to the basic problem and approach adopted' (ibid. 42). The relationship begins to approximate that in the humanities.

Patronage is much more prevalent in the humanities and social sciences than in the natural sciences. Patronal authority is clearly the dominant mode of authority in the humanities, where collegial elites tend not to exist and where professional associations are weak and only formal academic ranking within departments and an informal hierarchy of departments at different universities constitute the authority structure. Under such conditions the power and hold of the patrons over clients—students, independent scholars, or lower professors—are particularly pronounced. The followers of really powerful patrons form whole schools or fully self-contained cliques or clusters, and the patrons determine completely the fate of members. There is no way of appealing outside the cluster for usually there are no general or independent intellectual norms or impersonal authorities in humanistic disciplines. The method of study, the subject to be studied, and the study team are wholly determined within the cluster, which in practice means by the patron X or Y. Hence, members identify themselves as an X-ite or a Y-ite, and that identification determines their intellectual predilections as well as their career chances. Not to be an X-ite or Y-ite, to try to go it alone, usually means being bereft of support, sponsorship and guidance and of any way of identifying oneself in relation to others. Since the pressures for joining a cluster are very strong and the dangers of leaving one very high, patrons have a strong hold over the members of their groups. The condition in these circumstances is more or less like that found in France, as Terry Clark (1973, 82) puts it, 'with theoretical inspiration, career advancement, and intellectual and social control largely concentrated in the individual patron, he would understandably become both adored and feared by his followers'. It has not escaped Clark's notice that there are strong Freudian elements in any such relation, with the patron taking on the role of authoritative 'father' and the client that of dutiful 'son' or more rarely 'daughter'.

The clusters prevalent in some of the humanities, particularly in literary studies, extend beyond the bounds of academia, forming circles around leading critical journals, select publishers and nowadays even the electronic media. Such circles can be castigated, as F. R. Leavis (1968, 160–2) did those of England, as metropolitan cliques, clubs, coteries and even literary rackets. Whether or not the condemnation was merited in this particular case, it must be recognized that clusters are an inherent feature of literary politics and that Scrutiny itself was such a group under the patronage of Leavis. The remarkable sociological insight, shown in particular by Q. D. Leavis, into the sociology of academia and literary politics was unfortunately often marred by an over moralistic identification of politics with politicking, as when she writes 'that the academic world, like other worlds, is run by the politicians, and sensitively scrupulous people tend to leave politics to other people, while people with genuine work to do certainly have no time as well as no taste for committee-rigging and the associated techniques' (Leavis 1968, 3). An analogous fault suffuses the extensive and well-documented study of literary politics in America by Richard Kostelanetz (1974), which was influenced by the Leavises. Kostelanetz almost takes literally Leavis' metaphor of a 'literary racket' and speaks in rather crude terms of the 'New York Literary Mob' to whom he ascribes the morals and manners of the Mafia. This approach might be acceptable as literary satire but not as the sober sociology it claims to be and to which it makes a contribution. Whatever purely formal analogy there might be between the authority structures of the two kinds of 'dons' and 'godfathers', this similarity must not be portrayed as if there were substantive likenesses.

Nevertheless the Mafia metaphor has obvious appeal in America, as Lentricchia's (1980, 215) rather tart application of it to the Yale deconstructivists shows.

Clusters and patronage in the social sciences take a form somewhat inbetween those found in the humanities and those in the natural sciences; they are usually more like those in the 'unrestricted' or 'soft' sciences than the 'restricted' or 'hard' ones, depending on the discipline and its particular authority structure. A discipline with a single intellectual source can have quite different authority structures in different university systems, and this makes a great difference to its subsequent cognitive development. For example, sociology has a humanistic patronage pattern on the European continent; it is more like an unrestricted 'soft' natural science in some departments in England and the United States and like a restricted 'hard' science in other departments—in each instance with quite different modes of patronage. These differences in authority structure correlate quite closely with differences in intellectual approach and cognitive content and with the scientific method of the discipline. The historical reasons that a discipline such as sociology should have developed quite differently in different university systems are usually very complex, depending on the disposition of leading members of the discipline at a crucial time in its development, on outside pressures and opportunities—funding, for example, and competition with other disciplines for the available niches in the intellectual 'ecosystem' of academia. It would be necessary to write extended histories of economics, politics, psychology, education and so on to explain why they developed so differently in different countries and academic systems and why some disciplines, such as economics and parts of psychology, attained to near universality and others did not. Usually the authority structure plays a prominent part in explaining these developments.

Authorship and Authority

Authorship as a measure of academic achievement and ability is generally acknowledged as the basic criterion for attaining each of the three forms of authority: formal-professional, collegial elite and patronal. But in each case it is also possible to invoke other criteria which to a greater or lesser extent, depending on the accepted practices and rules, obviate the need for authorship. Thus something referred to as administrative skill or managerial ability can be invoked in the case of promotions within the formal-professional hierarchy; being a useful member of the team, or really 'one of us', 'one of the boys', can be referred to informally as justifying co-option into the collegial elite, and being a great teacher or, more informally, being able to provide students and clients with jobs, can serve as a claim to exercise patronage. None of these alternatives is strictly speaking illegitimate, but all are open to corruption—though probably no more so than is authorship, since publication can often be arranged for mediocre work that can muster backing. In any case, since almost everyone has some publications, how can their relative merits be assessed? Studies of the specific criteria for attaining authority in different systems or even individual universities have not as yet been carried out. Thus the most crucial dimension of academic life is sociologically speaking terra incognita, though every academic knows the lie of the land from a personal point of view since on this knowledge depends his or her career strategy and chances of success. Every academic, like every business-person, knows from experience how to amass some 'symbolic capital', but nobody has any theoretical 'economic' or 'political' knowledge about how this quasi market mechanism functions; as yet there are no 'political economists' of academia.

The role of authority in education in general has remained largely unexplored and frequently unacknowledged. Often authority is confused with discipline and treated as a matter of sheer domination, which authoritarians demand and libertarians abhor. At lower educational levels the issue of corporal punishment is sometimes regarded as a question about whether to institute or abolish authority. The libertarian approach to education, emphasising self-development and free expression, has tended to deny or obfuscate the presence of authority relations. Yet, as Lord Balogh (1982, 86) remarks, 'in practice, and even under the most progressive conditions, education will involve some degree of persuasion and compulsion', and that means some degree of authority. It is a paradoxical irony, one that Lord Balogh relishes, that the educational institutions which most inculcate the libertarian ideals are sometimes those which are themselves most authoritarian:

> It is therefore interesting to observe that it is the most libertarian authors who are among those to have been subjected to the most thorough process of intellectual conditioning (which in other institutions they would describe as brain-washing) which it is possible to encounter outside the most stringent Communist elite schools of propaganda or the Roman Catholic Church—the English preparatory and public schools, followed by Oxbridge (ibid. 86-7).

In a footnote Lord Balogh gives a possible sociological explanation for this surprising fact: 'this system—which produced the monolithic ruling class to oversee the Victorian empire—has been one of the most totalitarian or "directive" educational experiments ever witnessed' (ibid. 233). It hardly needs pointing out that Lord Balogh, as a long-time fellow of Balliol College, Oxford, was in a good position to supervise the 'educational experiment' that made 'men of Balliol'.

In the present context it is not possible to embark on a study of authority in education in general. However, it would be an interesting hypothesis to test the extent to which the three basic modes of authority or versions of them also apply at levels below the academic. They clearly have considerable application at the level of post-graduate study, usually but not always the Ph.D. level, which acts as the stepping stone to a formal appointment and a career in academia. There are crucial differences at this level in different national systems: in England a Ph.D. is not mandatory since a B.Phil. from Oxbridge—a special degree for aspiring academics comprising mainly course work sometimes differing little from an undergraduate degree and designed partly as a schooling in obedience— outranks a Ph.D. from anywhere else; in France the start towards a career is taking the Agrégation and teaching in a provincial lycée, followed much later by the exhaustive and exhausting *doctorat d'état* which is increasingly being displaced by the simpler *doctorat de troisième cycle*; other countries have other variants.[2] But everywhere at this level there is something akin to promotion within a formal hierarchy, being groomed for an elite at an elite institution and having to rely on a patron usually called a supervisor. This is why the arts and skills of career strategy have to be learned at this make-or-break stage. Those who do not learn them or do not wish to practise them are usually broken for life, since failure at this level can only very rarely be compensated for or made good.

Almost everywhere authority is severely exacted and repressively applied at this level. Undergraduates are indulged, but post-graduate aspirants to an academic career are strictly disciplined as if in preparation for the authority they will themselves have to wield later. As a group they stand in the most invidious position in the whole multiversity system, between the students who are cared for and the faculty who are feared or revered. They tend to be the most ill treated, abused and exploited, but they are the least capable of asserting their rights or defending themselves since they aspire to the very positions of authority and power which are exerted against them. Even though their numbers have risen astronomically in the postwar years to constitute at times up to 20% of the student body, their power has not grown proportionally. Becker and Kogan find it puzzling, 'that the postgraduate's marginal status remains virtually unchanged'. They offer two explanations for this, 'the one couched in anthropological terms and the other in political':

First, it can be suggested, the institution sees its doctoral postgraduates— and indeed they see themselves—as initiates to academia. So it is under-standable that a rite of passage should be devised—in the doctoral disser-tation—which is deliberately given the features of an ordeal. To make things too easy would be to fail to put disciplinary devotion to a proper test.

Second, the continued physical and intellectual isolation of those students who are most likely to be politically active—social scientists and those working in the humanities—renders them ineffective as a pressure group; in contrast, the norms of the scientists require them to accept hierarchical authority, and not to reason why, so their continual presence on campus does not constitute much of a threat. Since, as we suggested in Chapter 5, academic institutions share many of the characteristics of political systems, it is understandable that underdogs who neither bark nor bite are—albeit unconsciously—treated as if they were dumb and toothless (Becker and Kogan 1980, 119).

Above the post-graduate level the accredited academic is formally in-dependent and autonomous, though nevertheless subject to authority. Fur-thermore, the attainment of authority constitutes—to a greater or lesser degree, depending on the person's ambition—his or her academic raison d'être. What the academic aims and works for is one or another of the forms of authority. Hence, the three basic forms of authority apply not merely to the macro-structure of whole disciplines but also to the micro-structure of individual careers. A career in academia usually entails wield-ing all three forms of authority either concurrently or simultaneously. The success of a career is to be judged by the sum total of authority attained in all the three ways. To attain a large measure of authority requires skill at utilizing strategies of conversion whereby one form of authority is transformed into another form with maximum profit in the transaction. Thus Zuckermann reports: 'most prospective laureates elect to transform the esteem in which they are held—symbolized by the awards and prizes so many of them receive—into positions of influence and responsibility. They accept offices in scientific societies, editorships, and a variety of other gatekeeping posts that require them to decide how resources are to be allocated and to whom' (Zuckermann 1977, 200). Lesser luminaries at lower levels of science simply aim to acquire as many posts as possible and to produce as much research as necessary for this purpose. Such career strategies can best be analyzed as transformations of one of the three forms of authority into the others and back again. A career becomes a cycle of conversions and reconversions of authority. Obviously, different individuals, depending on their ability and ambition, will aim for different kinds of authority at different stages in their career, and this objective will also vary relative to the authority structure of their disciplines. But, typically, in the natural sciences the young academic aims to be in touch with or to be co-opted into the elite; the middle-aged academic aims for patronage influence in order to build a following for his or her work; and the elderly professor retires into prestigious formal-professional posts. The typical successful career pattern tends to be different in the humanities and the social sciences; there the academics strive for formal-professional posts as soon as possible to escape complete dependence on a patron and just as quickly aim to establish themselves as patrons for others.

Most often in science the typical successful career pattern can be described as an ascending or descending path from truth to power—depending on one's perspective. Cavalieri sees the path as descending:

> The path from truth to power, at least in the early stages, is apt to be tortuous. A scientist's euphoric feelings about a discovery he has made, and his enjoyment of peer approval, impel him to investigate the subject more deeply; this may lead to the "need" for more staff, say, another postdoctoral fellow in the laboratory. Usually this can materialize only if the investigator can manage another grant. If he obtains additional funds, he then finds the need for more space and equipment. Soon there follows the need for promotion to a higher rank, which may be a prerequisite for further expansion of his research effort or nomination to an honorary society. And so the seed is sown; and it is nurtured by the system. . . . These extraneous matters claim the scientist's attention and cause him to become a manipulator of programs, funds and space. The Big Scientist is thus caught up in a power structure in which he is forced to participate if he wishes to remain viable. Concomitantly, the cherished activity—research in pure science—has been dealt a heavy blow (Cavalieri 1981, 108-9).

Such a career path ensues when all the conversions are from truth to power, but for a really successful career both truth and power must be aimed for, one as a means for the other. Successful research opens the door to grantsmanship; grantsmanship leads the way to further research.

And always this process entails a conversion of one form of authority into another.

A successful career calls for subtle skill and timing in transacting such conversions, always with as much profit and as little loss as possible. Hence it encourages role multiplicity as the careerist attempts to hold on to his previously attained authority positions and simultaneously gain new ones. The careerist aims to extend his authority as far as possible, so that at its most expansive, almost grotesque, version there is the 'married, urban-based Italian professor who runs a chair, an institute, and a journal, commutes between several faculties and universities; writes a column in a newspaper or a weekly magazine; appears on television; advises publishing firms; serves in the top management of one or more public and private agencies; and participates formally or informally in the formation of government policy in the legislature and the executive branch' (Clark 1977, 87). Such a career makes for a very hectic life. Elsewhere most academics recognize that to acquire one kind of authority they have to give up another. The profit and loss calculation of the conversion is always decisive.

There are safe and risky strategies of conversion. Depending on their prior positions, their current chances and their sense of themselves, academics will tend to adopt the one or the other kind. Thus, for example, to take up an official post is not always a safe thing to do, since at certain stages in a career it can mean diminishing or abandoning research work without which a subsequent conversion might be made very difficult. Conversely, to carry on research work or scholarship beyond the point at which it pays can be very dangerous. As Burton Clark points out:

> The Italian professor who narrowly restricts his role to the search for pure scholarship is likely to suffer many punishments. To the question (posed in interviews in this study), "Why can't a professor, securely tenured, crawl off in a corner, do his research, and write books?" knowledgeable Italians, whether junior or senior and inside or outside the system, told of how much damage he would do to himself, his discipline, his colleagues and his students, in a system that pressed for role accumulation. He would throw away the power to assist others; students cannot afford the foolishness of allying themselves with a professor who cannot help them in academic and external careers. And, as he lost control of resources as well as the attachment of students, he would in time not even be able to help himself (Clark 1977, 88).

Conditions for continuing to do scientific research or scholarship are not so inhibiting outside Italy. But everywhere in almost every discipline there is a point of diminishing returns where further work, no matter how brilliant or original, can only be undertaken at a loss to one's career and authority standing. A person who wants to succeed must divine that point, which might come early or late in a career, depending on the discipline and the individual.

There are analogous considerations of career strategy involved in deciding what kind of research to undertake: there are safe projects which carry a predictable, narrow reward, and there are risky projects which if successful multiply one's investment and boost one's standing and reputation in all respects. Once again it is a matter of authority conversion:

those with little authority standing will usually not gamble on converting it rapidly by staking it all on a risky project; they will tend to aim for safe ones. Only those with considerable authority already can take the risk of staking some of it on a difficult venture where the returns are high. Even failure in a risky research project by someone with high authority is not the total disaster it would be for someone lesser placed: for the former it is looked on as a heroic loss, for the latter as sheer folly. This is why only scientists with much 'symbolic capital' behind them, as Bourdieu (1975) notes, dare undertake really innovative research. One must be in a position of considerable authority even to risk supporting or taking up new and difficult ideas, theories and experiments. As Mullins notes:

> Scientists change their theoretical positions according to status. Some active, highly rewarded scientists change more rapidly than anyone else as, over time, they adopt innovations that may have started at many different places in the field. Others do puzzle-solving but retain their high status through operation of the ratchet effect. Middle-rewarded scientists generally remain locked into normal science patterns. Low-rewarded scientists have little to risk and usually lose when they do; they therefore drop out. Students begin their careers by reflecting their professors' status, but most soon lose it (Mullins 1975, 195).

Presumably only those students who are able or clever or lucky enough to rapidly transform their original stake into some other form of authority—for instance, a position or publications or more highly placed patrons—who then begin the cycle of conversion that leads to a successful career. Bourdieu puts this in terms of his 'economic' model of symbolic capital:

> in order to understand the transformation of scientific practices (as that has frequently been described) which accompanies advance in a scientific career, we must relate the different scientific strategies—e.g. massive, extensive investment in research alone, or moderate, intensive investment in research combined with investment in scientific administration—not, of course—to age classes, since each field defines its own laws of social ageing, but to the amount of scientific capital possessed, which by defining at any given moment the objective chances of profit, defines "reasonable" strategies of investment and disinvestment (Bourdieu 1975, 28).

Career success is largely a function of this process of authority conversion from one form into another with a net gain. This is why successful people, highly skilled in such strategies, tend to be perceived as 'operators'. According to a study by Ladd and Lipset (1972), 'half of the respondents accepted . . . the charge that the most successful men in their fields gained their positions more as "operators" than as "scientific achievers"'. Obviously, there is usually a close link between being an 'operator' and being an 'achiever' in most sciences, so that successful scientists are in these cases to some degree 'operators' and to some degree 'achievers'. The separation of 'operators' from 'achievers' is not like that of sheep from goats: in most cases it is difficult to make because it requires skills at 'operating' to achieve anything. Without a considerable capacity for the conversion of authority, it is difficult for anyone ever to be in a position to achieve anything or to get that achievement recognized and accepted. And alternatively, without some measure of achievement it is very difficult to begin 'operating' or to continue to 'operate' successfully in most sciences.

This cyclical relation between 'operating' and 'achieving' is illuminated by applying Latour's and Woolgar's 'economic' model of a 'cycle of credibility'. The cycle operates through a continuous conversion of what they call 'credit' and 'credibility'. The credibility scientists gain from producing results and information useful for the work of other scientists in the field is transformed into credit, and with this they obtain the means for further work to further increase their credibility. They 'invest' their resources, both intellectual and 'economic', so as to 'facilitate the rapid conversion of credibility and the scientist's progression through the cycle': 'for example, a successful investment might mean that people phone [a scientist], his abstracts are accepted, others show interest in his work, he is believed more easily and listened to with greater attention, he is offered better positions, his assays work well, data flows more reliably and forms a more credible picture' (Barnes and Edge 1982, 41). Latour and Woolgar seek to correct the 'primitive' model of scientific exchange propounded by Hagstrom as well as the more sophisticated 'capitalist' model offered by Bourdieu. Hagstrom's model is drawn from the gift-giving exchanges of primitive societies, like the kula practised among Melanesians, and first theoretically discussed in anthropology by Mauss. But it is hardly applicable to modern scientists who practise a rational investment of effort and resources and expect highly specific returns which will rapidly turn over their initial 'capital'. Bourdieu's model, which is based on the 'capitalist' notion of an investment and reinvestment of 'symbolic capital', does not according to Latour and Woolgar account for the mutual exchanges between scientists, for it does not explain the demand side of scientific productivity as well as the supply side. Latour and Woolgar thus plump for a neo-classical 'economic' model of scientific exchange in which each scientist is like a 'small corporation' dealing with others like itself on an open market governed by the laws of supply and demand (ibid. 40-1).

The problem with all such 'economic' models of scientific exchange is that they are bound to postulate some concept of 'symbolic capital' as a measure of exchange and to treat this concept with full literalness and not merely as a revealing metaphor. Unfortunately, symbolic capital cannot be taken as real, in the way of capital in economics proper, because there is no way of quantifying scientific exchanges or even working out rough equivalences. There is no way of stating what a certain given kind of scientific authority or achievement is 'worth' in terms of other kinds of authority or achievement or therefore in terms of a medium of exchange such as symbolic capital, since no quantified exchange values are possible. How a given individual converts authority into other types depends largely on imponderable factors, such as opportunity, luck, skill, cunning, and personal relations. A certain level of authority is not marketable at a fixed ratio of exchange. Hence, all talk of symbolic capital must be largely metaphoric.

Undoubtedly, all these economic models of scientific activity capture some aspects of the micro-realities of scientific work. However, none is capable of dealing with the macro-realities of institutional arrangements which require political models based on authority rather than economic ones based on exchange. Models of exchange work well in assessing specific scientific and academic transactions: in explaining the cost-benefit calculations that decide whether a certain piece of research is undertaken, whether a colleague's work is read and followed up, whether a certain collaboration is sought, and so on. But a whole scientific career cannot be explained in this way as if it were no different than running a small business. The aim is not a cumulative sequence of small advantages that can be added together as a 'profit'; rather it is positions of authority and standing institutionally defined and legitimated. The micro-realities of economic exchanges and calculations are only the means towards the macro-realities of authority. This relation is like seeking to earn the money necessary for a political career which cannot simply be bought for money alone. Hence, the scientific polity and its authority structure provide the context in which specific economic exchanges are made and credits accrued. Outside of the politics, the economics would be meaningless.

However, in one area the politics and economics of academia interact very closely: the relation between authorship and authority—the key determinant of an academic career. Clearly, authorship or publication and authority or standing form an interlocking cycle of mutual conversions. That authorship is convertible into authority is the recognized and prescribed sequence; however, it is less often admitted that authority is also convertible into authorship. Nevertheless, numerous studies of science and scholarship have revealed the multiple ways in which authority makes for authorship, both in enabling the production of knowledge and in guaranteeing its publication, dissemination, and recognition once it has been produced.[3] Such conversions of authority and authorship will be very different in the 'hard' natural sciences from those in the humanities, given that the modes of production of knowledge and the authority structures are so diverse; it will be different again in the 'soft', 'unrestricted' natural sciences and in the social sciences. In the discussion that follows I shall concentrate on the two extreme poles—the 'hard' natural sciences and the humanities—supposing that the others can be filled in as intermediate cases.

The main mode of publication in the 'hard' natural sciences is journal articles which appear very soon after submission; that is the mechanism by which the latest and newest research is reported. Book publication has a secondary place, unlike in the humanities where books are more important than articles. Journals in most scientific disciplines are graded according to their authoritative standing. Hence, the acceptance of an article for publication is an act of authorization that varies very much depending on the journal in question and its status ranking. As Ziman (1976, 111) sees it, 'an article in a reputable journal does not merely represent the opinion of its author, it bears the imprimatur of scientific authenticity, as given to it by the editor and the referees he may have consulted'. Acceptance by a prestigious journal is itself an act of selection which means that the work falls into the top 5% bracket of scientific work. In physics only four journals have top world repute: *Physical Review, Physical Review Letters, Physics Letters* and *Nuovo Cimento*. Authority plays an important part in their process of selection, even after the self-selection of daring to submit a paper to one of them.

Merton and Zuckermann's study (Merton 1973, 482) of the most prestigious physics journal *Physical Review* reveals that 'of the manuscripts submitted by the physicists of the highest rank, 87% were judged exclusively by the editors, in contrast to 73% of those coming from the intermediate rank, and 58% of the rest'. In addition, 78% of manuscripts of high ranking physicists had an immediate acceptance, as against 70% and 58% respectively for the intermediate and lower rankings. They thus conclude that 'the higher the rank of physicist-authors, the fewer the judges involved in accepting their manuscripts' (ibid. 488). It is clear from these and other figures that the ranking of authority standing of physicists has a major effect on the acceptance of their work, provided that it is borne in mind that authority in this context is very likely of the collegial-elite variety rather than formal-professional. Whitley reports a similar conclusion with respect to British social science journals: 'over half of the journal editors interviewed made decisions on most of the submissions to their journal on the basis of their own judgement or in consultation with departmental, usually junior colleagues' (Blume 1974, 70). Elsewhere Whitley (1977b, 33) writes that 'in some departments papers are screened before submission and, equally, fast publication for some can be secured by personal contacts'. A good instance of this use of patronage authority to facilitate publication is reported by Watson in his account of the role played by Sir Lawrence Bragg in the publication of his and Crick's epoch making paper in *Nature*: 'Sir Lawrence was shown the paper in its nearly final form. After suggesting a minor stylistic alteration, he enthusiastically expressed his willingness to post it to *Nature* with a strong covering letter' (Watson 1980, 129). It is just conceivable that without that 'strong covering letter' an article from two relative unknowns might have suffered the fate of the 'very original paper by Lord Raleigh (the president of the Royal Society) to which he had forgotten to affix his name' (Blume 1974, 78) and which was rejected until, 'when the authorship was discovered, the paper was found to have merit after all' (Merton 1973, 487). *Nature* has a good record of such rejections; 'Hans Krebs' first description of the citric acid cycle, Urey's work on heavy hydrogen, and Fermi's research on beta decay were all rejected by *Nature*' (Manwell and Baker 1986, 274); when subsequently published elsewhere these researches helped obtain Nobel prizes for their authors.

The part played by patronage in publication in the humanities is certainly much larger than in the natural sciences. The reason is that publication in the natural sciences is very easy to obtain whereas in the humanities it is very difficult. Once work is actually produced in publishable form in the natural sciences the probability of its being published somewhere is virtual certainty. The proportion of journals to available papers is larger, and the lesser journals are always in need of material. The acceptance rate for submitted manuscripts is also very high; even such a

top journal as *The Physical Review* ultimately published 80% of all single
authored papers submitted (Merton 1973, 477). The principle on which
the editors operate is 'when in doubt accept' (ibid. 486). In the humanities
journals the principle is the opposite one: 'when in doubt reject'. The
rejection rates are the inverse of those of the natural sciences: in history
10% of papers are accepted, in language and literature 14%, in philosophy
15%, in political science 16%, as the tables provided by Merton and
Zuckermann show (ibid. 471). The law of publication seems to be that
the more like a natural science a discipline or specialty is, the higher is
the acceptance rate; the more like a humanity it is, the higher the rejection
rate. Typically, the social sciences fall in the middle; and those composed
of different specialties reflect exactly this law with the more humanistic
segment suffering humanities rejection rates and the more scientific segment
enjoying scientific acceptance rates. For example: '*The American Anthro-
pologist* devoted largely to social and cultural anthropology, approximates
the high rejection rates of the other social sciences with a figure of 65%,
while the *Americal Journal of Physical Anthropology* with a figure of 30%
approximates the low rates of the physical sciences' (ibid. 471).

The difficulties of publication in the humanities are compounded by
many other factors. There are usually few journals per discipline, and
these journals can accommodate only a few articles per issue. The upshot
of these factors is that a humanistic scholar will publish during a career
only a fraction on average of the number of papers published on average
by a natural scientist. The publication rates of successful scientists run
into the hundreds, those for leading scholars at best into the tens. Scholars
publish books, if they are successful, and in book publication the rejection
rates must be even higher than for articles; no exact figures are available,
though verbal reports suggest that only a few per cent of all submissions
are accepted.

The extreme ease of publication in the natural sciences suggests that
authority needs to be invoked less in achieving acceptance, though it
nevertheless plays some part. Authority standing probably counts for more
after publication in determining whether the published work exerts an
influence, is cited or discussed, and even whether it is read. The few
studies available suggest this conclusion. Thus Diana Crane 'found that
highly productive men at major universities were considerably more likely
to have gained recognition for their work than were equally productive
men at minor universities. Indeed, the latter were no more likely to have
won recognition than very much less productive ones at the major school'
(Blume 1974, 81). Authority thus acts as an amplifying medium; the same
recorded message might be heard as a whisper or a shout depending on
its volume boosting. And, as we shall see, authority in the natural sciences
plays an even larger role in the production of work.

In the humanities, the extreme difficulty of publication suggests that
authority is exercised most stringently at the editorial level. Since editorial
policy emphasises rejection, it follows that those subject to it will try to
utilize every possible advantage to ensure acceptance. To wield high authority oneself or to command that of powerful patrons must be a crucial
advantage for some over others. Book manuscripts must be accompanied

almost de rigueur by covering notes from authoritative personages in order to achieve even the distinction of being noticed and sent out for refereeing. To what extent this is true for journal articles is not known, but one assumes it must be much more extensive than in the natural sciences. Certainly in literary publication, as Bourdieu (1977) notes, 'the manuscripts that will be published hardly ever arrive directly, but almost always through recognized go-betweens'. Among publishers, the expression 'unsolicited manuscript' is almost a term of contempt and refers to all those submissions, relegated to the bottom of the heap, which might not even be looked at.

How is one to explain these remarkable discrepancies between publication in the natural sciences and humanities? Why should there be high acceptance rates in the former and the opposite in the latter, rather than vice-versa? Is there anything inherent in the intellectual content of the humanities that ensures that most articles are rejected and vice-versa for the natural sciences? What aspects of the system of these disciplines and their authority structures produces these effects on publication? Clearly, maintaining high or low rejection rates is in some respects conscious policy on the part of editors and disciplinary associations, with a view to limiting or expanding the number of journals available in a given field. However, these policies are not arbitrarily arrived at; they reflect the underlying features of the basic *modus operandi* of disciplines. We must therefore seek explanations that go beyond conscious policies and decisions.

It is important to note that publication serves a quite different purpose in the natural sciences than in the humanities. In the sciences it has an essential informing function, conveying to the whole discipline the latest results, methods, theories and ideas. This information is eagerly awaited by those engaged in similar work as well as by those in neighbouring fields; without up-dated information they could not continue their work. Publications mark out the front line of research, enabling researchers to advance to the next position and the new problems thus opened up to be attacked. Without publication this co-ordination of research could not be maintained. Publication also establishes priority and prevents the duplication of work, effort and cost in other scientific establishments all over the world. Without speedy publication, disseminated quickly all over the world, most discoveries probably would be duplicated two or more times, which would lead to endless wrangling over priority.

Once published new work is immediately read, discussed and very quickly cited in the next sequence of articles along the same lines. But because it is so quickly absorbed, new work becomes obsolete just as fast as other articles presuppose its results and go beyond it. The citation lifetime of an article is typically less than two years, after which it is forgotten and relegated to the archives, unless it happens to be the rare path-breaking piece which is cited in review articles over a ten year period. Because publication serves this crucial role of information, the latest and newest articles must be published as quickly as possible in as large numbers as possible in case some vital results are omitted. For this purpose there have even developed pre-publication networks for the circulation of the very latest results. If the acceptance rates for journals were not very high, such informal methods of the circulation of information would even further proliferate. Hence, a scientific journal rejecting articles would be like a newspaper rejecting news.

In the humanities publication serves a very different purpose. There is no flow of information on which everybody depends for further work nor—usually—priority disputes to worry about, for most of these disciplines are fragmented into clusters of patronage networks, each doing its own work. The purpose of publication is therefore to grant public authoritative recognition and accreditation to the work deriving from a given cluster or more rarely from an independent individual. Publication acts as an imprimatur certifying a given kind of work as acceptable within the discipline. It would therefore defeat the whole purpose of the publishing system to publish too many articles; on the contrary, it is essential that most be rejected so that the few accepted stand out by contrast. Articles need not be accepted or published quickly; a long waiting time makes for a greater sense of urgency. Once published there is no expectation that the article will be quickly or widely read or that it will exert any kind of general influence. In the humanities nobody is going to change an approach as a result of the latest publication in a journal. Nevertheless, published work does have an effect on the discipline at a slower rate and over a longer period in that it provides exemplary models of the new and on-going lines that the journal wants to convey and the styles that are recommended. In this respect a journal's selection of articles is much like a fashion collection at which the latest articles of clothing are displayed. The editorial authorities act as arbiters elegantiarum, setters of standards, moulders of taste and sometimes even of manners and morals. Something analogous to this function of setting styles and standards is not unknown even in the natural sciences, as Bourdieu (1975, 30) notes when he speaks of 'the scientific journals which, by selecting their articles in terms of the dominant criteria, consecrate productions faithful to the principles of official science, thereby continuously holding out the example of what deserves the name of science, and exercise a de facto censorship of heretical productions, either by rejecting them outright or by simply discouraging the intention of even trying to publish them by means of the definition of the publishable which they set forward'. But this is not the main function of science journals.

There are even deeper causes for the emergence of such different systems of publication in the natural sciences and humanities and for the striking contrast between the authority structures governing authorship in each. Basically, the underlying 'economic' realities of the production of knowledge are decisive. Scientific knowledge is very costly and very difficult to produce. It requires extensive funding for plant, materials and machinery; a very complex laboratory organization has to be in place, and technical staff, graduate students and collaborators must be trained, organized and assigned to each project. In the humanities, by contrast, knowledge is cheap and easy to produce. Usually only libraries are required, which are expensive to set up but once available cost little for the individual to use; their upkeep does not rise significantly as more scholars use them to extract material for publishable pieces. Hence, there is no way of controlling or supervising the production of scholarship in the humanities apart from the informal controls exercised within the clusters, and there is really no effective control over the independent scholar. Once the scholar has an official position he or she can more or less produce at will. In the natural sciences, by contrast, authoritative controls on the production of knowledge are very stringent. At every step in the complex and costly production process authoritative approval must be sought and without it the work cannot proceed. Hence, before the work even gets to the publishable stage, it already has been extensively vetted, checked and supervised, and numerous authorities at different stages of the production process have ruled on it. In the humanities there is relatively little authoritative vetting or control in the production stage.

These differential features in the economy of the production of knowledge explain much about the systems of publication. In the natural sciences authority has already ruled on and approved of a given project in its production stage. Hence, there is little need to exercise many checks once the work has been produced and written up for publication. The very difficulty in producing work ensures the ease of its publication. It would make little sense to deny the publication of work that has been bought so dearly by the whole scientific organization. In the humanities the process works the other way: the ease and lack of authoritative controls on the production of work are compensated for by the difficulty of achieving its publication. Authority is exercised at the point of publication rather than before as in the sciences. There is every reason to deny publication to work which has till the point of submission in no way been supervised. These economics of production also explain to a considerable degree why the authority structures in the natural sciences and the humanities are so different. Work that is costly and difficult to produce will inevitably be controlled by gatekeepers: formal-professional hierarchies usually in conjunction with collegial elites which decide who does what by dictating the division of labour within disciplines. Work that is economically easy to produce by anyone but hard to publish will encourage patronage as the basic authority form.

The other economic factor underpinning these 'laws' is the relative availability of resources in the natural sciences, as compared within the humanities, in the multiversity–research institute complex since the Second World War. The sciences have been continually expanding as the State, industry and the foundations have been pouring in finance for research. By comparison the humanities have dragged behind, profiting only indirectly from the affluence of the sciences, feeding off the crumbs from the rich man's table. Consequently, over-all there have been far fewer rewards available in the humanities than in the sciences. Competition for the few available rewards in the humanities has nevertheless been very keen, partly because of the sheer numbers of students, especially women, going through these disciplines and partly because of their traditional prestige. Hence, with few rewards and many contenders it has been necessary to restrict publication, which serves as the official claim on which rewards are based. In the sciences with many avenues of reward available it has been possible to expand publication.

The situation in the social sciences, as well as in the 'softer' 'nonrestricted' natural sciences is half way between the 'hard' natural sciences and humanities. Those specialties or segments of a discipline that lean closer to the former will show marked features of that type and those which incline to the latter will evince its characteristics. Obviously, it is impossible here to undertake a discipline by discipline review, so these conclusions must be treated as mere hypotheses to be confirmed by detailed empirical analysis.

These broad authority and authorship conditions within the two extremes of the 'hard' natural sciences and the humanities are the forces determining the typical career patterns of individuals. They also influence strongly the attitude and approach to work and the psychological mental set of individuals and their relations in departments and other places of work. By and large, the natural scientist is subject to authority in a more 'catholic' manner and the humanities scholar in a more 'protestant' one. The scientist perceives authority as external, regulative and relatively predictable with expressly spelled out rules and conditions. He or she therefore knows exactly what approach will succeed and what kinds of good works will ensure salvation. The scientist has firm expectations that once he or she has done good work it will be accepted with good grace and credited to its author and that he or she can thereby build up credit worthiness and amass 'symbolic capital'. The humanities scholar has no such certainties and works in perpetual fear of failure, full of self-doubt, anxious and afraid. Since no one supervises the scholar's work, he or she must guess at the requirements to get it accepted, knowing that the chances of rejection, as exercised by an inscrutable editorial providence, are very high. The humanities scholar scans the journals and publishing houses, trying to discern the signs of what editors and referees are looking for, since this is never openly spelled out. Alternatively, he or she must seek reassurance from patrons, which is rarely freely forthcoming. All these authorities are internalized and act as an inner conscience; the scholar hears their voices of disapproval even when writing the work. According to these inner promptings he or she exercises an almost unconscious self-censorship in what material is included or excluded, or what final position is adopted on any issue, if success is the only aim. The scholar must believe that he or she is one of the elect deserving of reward to go on working for any time, but he or she can never be sure.

The attitude to work and the working environment of scientists and humanities scholars is consequently very different. Scientists assume a much more work-a-day approach to their task; they generally have a positive attitude because they can count with certainty on some degree of continual success as evinced by a steady publication rate and a gradual upward climb. Though authority might at times be openly authoritarian, it is never inscrutable and tends to be more impersonal and 'objective'; the individual rarely feels the curb of having to depend on the whim of any one single person. If the scientist's career is blocked in one direction he or she can always find another in which to proceed; there are many laboratories, many fund-granting agencies, many journals, and if all this fails there are always high-paying jobs in industry. Hence scientists' relations with each other and the whole temper and ethos of scientific departments are matter of fact and formally regulated; everybody knows who is in charge, what work to pursue, and how to go about it. Conflicts are usually only over the use of facilities and staff, and these are adjudicated by higher authorities. One of the few occasions when scientists experience inner anxiety is when they are waiting for their grant applications to be processed and they experience an acute sense of failure when a grant is denied.[4]

Humanities scholars, living with an almost perpetual sense of failure and oppressed by unrelieved anxiety, are far less able to get on smoothly with their work or with each other. In a humanities department characteristic animosities fester as a result of rankling envy, jealousy and ego struggles as every scholar believes he or she is much better than his or her usually meagre achievements show and certainly better than those slightly ahead as a result of better fortune or patronage. Co-operation under such circumstances is extremely difficult, the atmosphere poisoned by petty strife. The incidence of mental instability and break-down is probably higher than in the sciences. Little, if any, research has been done on the mental health of staff and none on comparisons between different faculties, but it is a fair assumption on the basis of circumstantial evidence that the humanities are much more troubled than the more placid, if not complacent, sciences.[5]

Such differences between career experiences in the natural sciences and humanities are already fully evident at the Ph.D. stage. The student scientists relate to their supervisors in terms of an implicit contract whose terms can be crudely set out as follows: I shall perform so much work and learn your methods on a project provided by you, and in return you must ensure that sufficient results are produced for my Ph.D., which you must also guarantee I get in the allotted time. The supervisor can exercize authority over students directly in telling them what is required and whether they are up to the mark at every stage. In the humanities the supervisors relation to students approximates more to the traditional *Doktorvater* role. Though circumstances vary widely as between countries and universities, nevertheless it is generally true that the old academic ideals tend to be officially maintained in the humanities, and the fiction is sustained that the student is an independent scholar working with the help of a supervisor, who cannot openly dictate how the work is to proceed. Consequently authority has to be aserted through a high screen of mutual self-deception. As Bourdieu (1984, 118) states, in the *disciplines canoniques* in France— which correspond to arts subjects in the Anglo-Saxon systems—authority is maintained through '*un art de manipuler le temps des autres, ou, plus precisement, le rythme de leur carrière, de leur cursus, d'accélérer ou de différer des accomplissements aùssi différents que le succès aux concours ou aux examens, la soutenance de thèse, la publication d'articles ou d'ouvrages, la nomination dans des postes universitaires, etc.*'

Thus the process of internalizing authority goes on in the humanities for most of the duration of a career because the dependence on a patron simply continues the student-supervisor relation of the earlier stages. Only those sufficiently successful and powerful to set themselves up as patrons finally become authorities themselves, but even then they are still likely to depend on patrons' patrons. Publication, especially for books, is difficult to obtain and frequently must be sought through personal intervention; the whole submission-acceptance procedure is fraught with anxiety. The acknowledgement pages of books frequently bear the marks of the struggle to get them accepted, like the scars of a successful operation. A serious study of acknowledgement pages in books has yet to be undertaken; it might reveal networks of allegiances and alliances and tell much about the realities of authorship if the aesopian language in which acknowledgements are couched were to be decoded. The acknowledgements in scientific books are much more straightforward because books in science serve an obvious purpose: they are either specially commissioned texts for teaching purposes or popularizations of current scientific findings for a more general public, also usually commissioned by publishers. In both instances the publication of a book is a further recognition of an already established scientific reputation and can be looked on as a fringe benefit of a successful career. No one has yet studied the typical course of a career with a view to discovering at what stage and for what motives scientists undertake to write either type of book. Perhaps a careful reading of acknowledgements might reveal this. Interestingly enough, when a scientist attempts to write a book which philosophically expounds a discipline and takes critical issue with its unthinking assumptions, one usually finds in its acknowledgements all the signs and scars of a struggle to get it accepted into print, as in the humanities.

An excellent recent instance is one of the very few thoughtful books on computer science and artificial intelligence, Joseph Weizenbaum's *Computer Power and Human Reason* (1976). Weizenbaum, a professor at MIT and an acknowledged expert in the field, writes as follows in his Preface:

> The writing of this book has been an adventure for me. First and most important, I have been cheered beyond my power to say by the generosity and the intellectual and emotional support given me by people who owe me absolutely nothing. But now I am very greatly in their debt. I am thinking primarily of Lewis Mumford, that grand old man, of Noam Chomsky, and of Steven Marcus, the literary critic. Each of them read large sections of the manuscript in preparation (Lewis Mumford read all of it) and contributed the wisest and most useful kinds of criticism. But more than that, each encouraged me to go on when I despaired. For there was often cause for despair (Weizenbaum 1976, p. X).

We are not told explicitly what the cause for despair was, but perhaps we can glean it from the acknowledgements. None of the individuals thanked so profusely is a computer scientist, and no computer scientist is referred to in the rest of the preface with the exception of Thomas Cheatham; pointedly, no colleague from among the many at MIT is mentioned. The phrase 'people who owe me absolutely nothing', said in a tone of surprised wonder, speaks volumes about what one would normally expect to be the case. If one remembers that the people referred to are an old and distringuished free scholar, a radical and unconventional theorist of linguistics and a relatively unknown literary critic, then perhaps the exceptional nature of this indebtedness will be realized. The publisher of the book, though a reputable scientific press, nevertheless is not one of the recognized university or Boston or New York presses. Clearly even a person as authoritatively placed as Weizenbaum has experienced enough difficulty with this kind of a book to be driven to despair.

Authorship and authority should normally be intimately related and mutually supporting. The cases where this is not so are normatively exceptional though very common, since the relation between publication and position is very indirect. There is something anomalous in academia about authorship without any authority or authority without any authorship—though both possibilities are not unknown. The incidence of both is perhaps highest in Italy. Burton Clark (1977, 99) reports that critics 'have pointed to noted researchers and scholars who, they claim, have been denied chairs because they were outside the circle of sponsorship, or who have finally, after much squabbling, been given a chair in a minor university, as in the case of a Nobel Prize winner in medicine (Bovet)— which is roughly equivalent to telling an outstanding scientist in the United States that the only appointment open for him as full professor is at a specified third-level university'. On the other hand, prestigious chairs can be filled by academics with little or no independent publication. In England, too, high authority with next to no authorship and extensive authorship with no authority are frequently encountered because of the dominant and commanding position of Oxford and Cambridge in the British university system. Appointment, promotion and general standing within the Oxbridge semi-autonomous colleges are very much internal matters relatively unaffected by outside achievements or outside reputations.[6] Publications need not be required or can count for little in attaining a high place within Oxbridge, which is tantamount to the highest authoritative standing within the British system. The personal qualities that count in Oxbridge have sometimes little to do with research ability or with publication. By contrast, very high publication rates in a British provincial or 'colonial' university might not gain one any authority standing within Oxbridge and so equally— almost by definition in the British system—no authority commensurate with authorship. Individual examples that spring to mind are legion.[7] To what extent Italian and British practice is exceptional is hard to assess since no sociological studies have yet been done, so detailed comparisons between countries are unavailable. Insofar as these examples transgress a universally acknowledged academic norm, requiring that authority must to some degree be commensurate with research ability as determined by authorship, they constitute instances of corruption and are pathological rather than normal. Normality and pathology are thus the next topic of investigation in this book.

6

Pathologies of Science

Most of my colleagues are also old prostitutes and we don't mind supporting ourselves that way. Indeed, we will continue to lie, cheat, embezzle, and pimp as is the custom, in order to keep our laboratories going and our students financed.
—Lettvin (1971)

Pathology and Normality

What is normal and what is pathological in the present polity of science? What are the inescapable institutional realities of the multiversity–research institute complex and what are avoidable corruptions of it? Such questions have often been raised by sociologists and critics of science. For example, Elias has stated:

> The question evidently is to what extent does the knowledge produced by scientists suffer a professional deformation because it also serves as a means of preserving and enhancing their power ratio and status intra-murally as well as extra-murally, because, in other words, it also serves as a weapon of defence against the encroachment of others upon their own field of work or, alternatively, as a weapon of attack in attempts at imposing their own model of scientific work as authoritative on other fields (Elias 1982a, 51).

To what extent and at what point does the mode of production of scientific knowledge become deformed? When and how is scientific authority suborned? When does it degenerate to illegitimate power and influence wielding? To answer such questions requires making nice sociological discriminations as well as critical value judgements. Elias is perhaps not fully alert to this necessity when he declares:

> there are recurrent tendencies of some groups, or of some individuals among scientists themselves, to set themselves up as authorities whose views cannot be doubted or criticized. Again and again, the organization of scientific work creates conditions which allow some scientists, collectively or individually, to claim and to establish effectively a hegemonic position either within their own field or in relation to other fields. They achieve, in other words, the position of a firmly entrenched scientific establishment (ibid. 50).

Elias clearly has corrupt practices in mind when he castigates such scientists. Yet he does not distinguish clearly between 'established authority', which is legitimate in science, and 'hegemony' which is not. The former is normal, the latter pathological. Without such a distinction not only are value judgements of the quality of scientific work useless, but also no practical proposals can be made for the reforms of science. Short of a total scientific 'revolution', which at present is highly improbable, the sanctioned practices of scientific work and the established authority forms of science must, at least prima facie, be considered normal and accepted as part of the unalterable reality of the present regimen of science. Only the hegemonic practices and the illicit deviations can be castigated as corrupt and so capable of being eradicated or reformed. The proposals one is to make at least for the immediate future of science depend very much on one's judgement as to where such distinctions fall and what can be taken as normal, which is not simply that which is current.

The usual difficulties in making such judgements are at present compounded by the transitional stage in which the sciences and the whole academic complex are still found. The transformation of science from its pre-1945 epoch is not complete. And academia is on many levels and in many countries still caught between the old university system and the new multiversity–research institute complex. In such a situation of transition, old values, beliefs and ideals tend to be officially invoked as if they were valid in the old way, though the realities to which they are now referred are no longer the same. Hence the officially fostered expectations no longer match the known practices, which tend to breed either fond conservative hopes that things should return to the good old days or disillusionment and cynicism that they will not. The old university values, beliefs and ideals are maintained partly as an ideological cover in order to present to the outside world, the public as well as government, a seemingly unchanged face of science and to prevent outside interference with supposedly old-style, autonomous 'pure' scientific research. The old ideals are also maintained because nothing has as yet been developed to replace them. As Ravetz comments:

> it was the dominant self-consciousness of academic physical science in Germany in the latter part of the nineteenth-century, where it spread to other fields and other nations. As such it is important, for it is such an ideology that provides the only existing foundation for an ethic of science which is distinct from technological development or commerce. The danger is that this ideology will be kept in a fossilized state for particular public-relations functions, while becoming less and less relevant to the experience of those who live in the world of industrialized science. Then the inherited ethical principles of scientific work will become increasingly divorced from reality, and under pressure of present conditions, they could no longer survive as effective controls on action (Ravetz 1971a, 43).

As Ravetz argues, such ideological distortions are a potent source of corruption, leading to demoralization and loss of commitment among the scientific personnel as they perceive the wide gap between the officially preached standards and the actually condoned practices.

It is crucial, however, not to confuse this failure to live up to the approved ideal standards with corruption, as at times even Ravetz tends to do. The normal is no less so when it fails to live up to the ideal; it does not thereby become pathological, especially when this ideal is mere ideology. The present regimen of science and the multiversity–research institute complex must not be judged by the old ideals of the university and academic science which are still the officially recognized standards. What is normal and what is pathological ought to be judged in relation to present realities alone. However, since present realities are transitional and have not yet completely outgrown the past, it is necessary to ascertain to what potential state they are tending before any judgement is made. This interpretation entails critical and sociological assessment. In critically judging the present, one must attempt to foresee realistically what science at its best might become in the future; only then can one assert what is normal for it to be now. Chapter 8 will attempt to locate what there is in present science that might enable it to realize its best alternatives, without indulging in utopian visions of a totally alternative science. Normality in science—as elsewhere in personal or social development—is a normative concept, not simply a descriptive one. On such a critical standard, 'normal' science in a Kuhnian sense might be judged pathological.

Inherent in all such complex judgements is the danger of a confusion of standards. Without a clear grasp of the standards invoked, pathologies cannot be diagnosed, normal growth cannot be distinguished from cancer, or metamorphoses from metastases; characterization can become caricature and criticism mere satire. Sound, sociologically and historically informed criticism requires the determination of what is to be expected and at least provisionally accepted as normal, not in the sense of what is typical or average but of that state towards which present changes point. This approach does not exclude the possible criticism of the whole drift of science or of major scientific fields—that is, radical reformist criticism that does not invoke the simple opposition of pathology to normality or remain content with proposing institutionally sanctioned corrective action for the eradication of what is generally judged to be corrupt. However, the distinction between ethical and radical criticism is relative and a matter of degree for the one subtly shades into the other. Ravetz adroitly modulates from the one level of criticism to the other, as in the following extract:

> Should morale decline among the ordinary members of a scientific community, then it becomes impossible, either by sanctions or rewards, to restore it through action taken at the top. And without morale, what good work is done will fairly soon be driven out by the bad. . . . If this degeneration occurs in isolated fields, it can still be checked through the system of controls across fields. But if corruption spreads to this highest level as well then whole areas of science can become gigantic confidence games, producing pseudo-property at a feverish pace, and resembling a stock exchange in a bull market rather than a collective endeavour on behalf of the highest human goals (Ravetz 1971a, 311).

The initial criticism of a loss of morale is already beyond the scope of corrective action undertaken at an institutional level. The final criticism of the degeneration of whole fields of science is no longer on the level of diagnosing mere corruption and suggests that only a radical transformation will be adequate. But as Ravetz intimates, and as shall be explored in Chapter 7, there need be no break between these rising levels of criticism; the call for reform can lead to demands for a reformation. Our discussion in the present chapter will also follow a rising level of criticism, starting with relatively uncontested ethical judgements and concluding in a radical critique.

Corruptions of Scientific Ethics

Ethical criticism is exemplified in the range of pathologies in the sciences and humanities which arise from a refusal to countenance openly and make the necessary adjustments for the fact that the authority structure in the multiversity–research institute complex is very different from that previously prevalent in the university. A good case of this may be seen in the pathologies attendant on the transition from the older master-disciple relation of authority to the present patron-client relation. In the older relation it was scientifically fair and ethically just for the master to claim a large share, perhaps even the preponderant share, in the work of a pupil since the master usually suggested the thesis or the research project, supervised its on-going procedure and sometimes designed the method and instruments used. In such circumstances it was not inappropriate for the master's name to appear first on the resultant joint publication. But in the present relation a patron can no longer fairly or justly claim the major share in the work of numerous clients to which the patron has cognitively or instrumentally contributed nothing apart from extending a generalized *protectsia* by providing the financial and human resources. The patron who affixes his or her name to the papers of clients while knowing little or nothing about the work that went into them is simply appropriating the work of others in a way no different from that of the landlord who takes the lion's share of the produce of peasant tenants. Yet this practice is condoned as acceptable in the sciences. Nobody inquires into or ever complains about the personal contribution that a laboratory chief makes to the innumerable papers put out in his or her name. The pretence is maintained that a master-pupil relation still obtains, even though in most cases it does not. If it were openly admitted that a patron-client relation is now the norm then it would be more difficult to condone the practice of work appropriation by the patron, which is, indeed, the patron's principal reward in the exchange relationship.

This simple criticism opens up a more serious contradiction in the attribution of scientific work. If the relation that obtains in joint research is actually a patron-client exchange relation, it flies in the face of the whole ethic of scientific attribution. For the present operation of the system this fact must be kept hidden or unacknowledged. To acknowledge it openly would mean either that the patron must cease signing the client's work, in which case the patron would not receive the reward that provides the motive for extending patronage in the first place, or if the practice continued, though the work was recognized as being in no way his or hers, then the patron could no longer claim the reward attendant on publishing papers. In either case the patron-client relation would break down. Hence it is in the interest of both patrons and clients to keep secret the fact that such a relation operates and to maintain the pretence of the older master-pupil relation. Both can share in the rewards of publication, which the patron's name can secure, without openly infringing on the other accepted scientific norm that no one should claim credit for work done by others. Thus the patron-client relation as it operates at present is inherently pathological since it is based on a widely-known and condoned deception. It would be very difficult to bring this basis to light and institute reforms for it would require revision of all the interlinked norms of scientific collaboration and attribution: it would require a major institutional shift, if not a thorough reformation.

The prevalence of the practice of laboratory chiefs and others in authority or in a position to act as patrons affixing their names to joint or multiple authored publications is well attested in numerous instances documented by Broad and Wade. The case of Vijay Soman and Philip Felig of the Yale University School of Medicine—apart from the plagiarism and fraud perpetrated by Soman of which Felig was wholly innocent—reveals much about the attribution practices of senior scientists. Felig co-authored the joint incriminating paper and claimed credit for work carried out solely by Soman, which as later investigation revealed was plagiarized and fraudulent. Felig could justly say that he was innocent of these charges because he took no part in the actual research carried out by Soman; yet he did claim credit for it as co-author. Broad and Wade remark that of 'his claim to 200 papers, Felig is sole author of only 35'. 'On the other papers his name is surrounded by co-authors. In the early days of his career, these fellow authors were undoubtedly senior researchers who at best made minimal contributions to the published work. In the later days, the situation was reversed, the Somans of the world were undoubtedly giving Felig's career something of a lift' (Broad and Wade 1982, 165). The same kind of conclusion is applied by these authors to the work of Robert A. Good of the Sloan-Kettering Institute for Cancer Research, 'the epitome of a well-organized lab-chief': 'in a five-year period he had co-authored almost 700 scientific reports, a feat aided by establishing a large empire of research workers under his personal banner. Far from puffery, the papers he signed were highly regarded. Over a fourteen-year period, work with Good's name on it was cited by other scientists more than 17,600 times—making Good the most frequently cited author in the history of research' (ibid. 153). So much then, for reliance on the citation index, as Broad and Wade (ibid. 222) themselves advocate, for assessing the quality of scientific work, although it may be useful for quantifying authority and reputation standing. Felig and Good are only exceptional in being more successful than most other scientists with large publication records. The method whereby these are achieved is almost invariably the same. As Broad and Wade note: 'the appropriation of credit can expand to the point that large teams of junior researchers work almost exclusively for the glorification of a lab chief, even though the master has little or no day-to-day involvement in the work. Despite such remoteness, it is not unusual for the name of a prominent biomedical researcher to appear on as many as 500 to 600 papers produced by his juniors' (ibid. 144).

Even more serious cases of the pathology of scientific authority arise when the patron appropriates sole credit for work done by a client and refuses to share it at all. Such occurred in the case of Antony Hewish and Jocelyn Bell concerning work done partly by Bell (Judson 1980), then a Ph.D. student supervised by Hewish, in the discovery of pulsars for which Hewish alone claimed the credit; on this basis he obtained the 1974 Nobel prize for physics specifically for the discovery of pulsars. Hewish is quoted as excusing himself as follows: 'Jocelyn was a jolly good girl, but she was just doing her job. She noticed the source that was doing this thing. If she hadn't noticed it, it would have been negligent' (Broad and Wade 1982, 148). The attitude this statement evinces is indicative. Although Fred Hoyle, senior astro-physicist at Cambridge, denounced Hewish for 'pinching the discovery from the girl' (ibid. 147), his criticism made no difference to Hewish's Nobel. An analogous situation had already arisen in relation to the 1959 award of the Nobel prize to Segré and Chamberlain for work on the anti-proton to which Ypsilantis, Wiegand and Piccioni originally also contributed. Years later, when he felt no longer threatened by his superiors, Piccioni initiated a court case to publicise the issue but without any other result.

Broad and Wade ascribe these pathologies to 'the breakdown during the past few decades of the relationship between master and apprentice' (ibid. 144). And they go on to intimate that a patron-client relation is appearing in its place: 'the bond today is often based on material needs such as the purchase of equipment and the getting of grants' (ibid.). They spell this out almost in the very sociological terms proposed in this work:

> In the contemporary science, the solemn bond of the master-apprentice relationship is often abused. Instead of being content with founding a research tradition, some professors seek the shorter-term goals of instant fame and recognition. The intellectual bond tends to be diminished, sometimes almost entirely replaced, by the elements of a business exchange. The lab chief trades job slots and patronage for the right to take credit for his subordinates' achievements (ibid. 149).

All the elements of the transition from a master-disciple to a patron-client relationship are implicitly there. However, this transition is not just a matter of abuses, even though all kinds of pathologies can be inherent in it; it is a transition necessitated by the changed conditions of the production of scientific knowledge from a more artisanal stage to a more industrial stage, as already extensively described. Broad and Wade set it out as follows:

> Earlier in the century, research was still for many a calling, and the necessary ingredients for doing science were a sharp mind and perhaps some apparatus from a hardware store. With the professionalization of science, and the increasing expense of equipping a research laboratory, young researchers setting out on their careers must now find not just an intellectual master but a patron with command of a large government grant. For his part, the

patron, simply to keep the grants flowing and to meet his payroll, must busily cultivate the appearance of success (ibid. 150).

Clearly, a new authority relationship obtains, one that must be kept in the dark for it contradicts other established norms of science, and this secrecy more than anything else causes pathologies to be generated.

The other ideal-type forms of authority in the sciences, viz., formal-professional and collegial elite, also generate pathologies, but of a different and ultimately less insidious kind since these authorities are more openly acknowledged. Formal-professional authority promotes the more obvious pathologies of hierarchic authoritarianism; collegial elites bring about an exclusivity of the group that suppresses the outsider or the individual as such, anyone who is not 'one of the boys'. There is hardly any need to document such cases; every academic has exemplars in abundance. In what follows my initial concern shall continue with such ethical pathologies, but I shall go on, by gradual stages, to a critique of the whole institutional context of science.

Perhaps the most obvious of the 'diseases of science', one already diagnosed in 1959 by Derek Price (1961, 97), appears almost 'demographic' in nature, namely, the population explosion of scientific papers, personnel, and the hypertrophy of the whole scientific and academic establishment. Price has shown that the number of journals in science has doubled about every fifteen years and increased exponentially to a power of ten every fifty years, reaching 10 in 1750, 100 in 1800, 1,000 in 1850, 10,000 in 1900 and 100,000 in 1950, threatening at this rate the demographic calamity of 1,000,000 by the year 2000. 'The number of journals has behaved just like a colony of rabbits breeding among themselves and reproducing every so often' (ibid. 100). With far less statistical rigour and much more dubious methods of evaluation, Price regards the 'quality of research as opposed to its quantity' as increasing exponentially, so that 'the actual stature of science, in terms of its achievements, appears to double within about one generation (some thirty years)' (ibid. 119). The idea of treating the products of different scientific ages as if they were members of the one population which can be compared for quality has about as much validity as treating all works of art as if they were demographically alike regardless of whether they were produced by medieval craftsmen, Renaissance virtuosi or modern industrial design teams. If one then plotted increments of the increase of artistic quality over the ages, that is, of artistic progress, one would have about as reliable a graph as the one Price provides for scientific quality and scientific progress. The undertaking is highly dubious, and it brings into question the reliability of quantitative statistics of scientific population growth in general, since the judgements involved are at least partly arbitrary: what is to count as a member of the species 'science' or 'scientist' or 'scientific journal' or 'article' is partly a matter of stipulative definition (for example, when should electricians or electrical engineers count as scientists).

Science is not a natural species, as Price's statistical methods almost force him to believe. The demographic model is largely a metaphor. There is nothing 'natural' about the growth of science, and though 'exponential growth . . . is very common in nature' (ibid. 113), this fact has nothing to do with growth of science. The latter is much more like an instance of economic over-production than of population explosion. In fact, it exemplifies a trend that is much larger than the economics of science; it might be called the hypertrophy of knowledge or information, resulting from and closely reflecting the transition from a handicraft to an industrial society and subsequently from an industrial to an information society, a far from 'natural' exponential process of growth. We are witnessing an institutionally generated process, not one intrinsic to the expansion of science or knowledge itself.

Broad and Wade point to some of the real reasons for this expansion of knowledge:

> A problem that affects research in general is the excessive proliferation of scientific papers. Too many scientific articles are published. Many are simply worthless. Moreover, the worthless papers clutter up the communication system of science, preventing good research from receiving the attention it deserves and protecting bad research from scrutiny. . . . As the system now stands, researchers are rewarded for extracting the maximum number of separate articles out of a single piece of research, so as to amplify the list of their published work. This pernicious habit makes reviewing the literature almost impossible (Broad and Wade 1982, 221–2).

As Broad and Wade intimate, this contemporary hypertrophy of knowledge is symptomatic of many different diseases of science, depending on the scientific and academic context in which it occurs. It is clearly not the same phenomenon in the natural sciences, where it is most developed, as it is in the social sciences or humanities, where it is least developed. In the former case, apart from the problems it causes librarians in storing, cataloguing and abstracting an ever rising flood of information, there is also the graver problem that too much information brings diminishing returns for the development of knowledge. The individual scientist is drowned under masses of specialized papers of ever narrower scope even in an already narrowed field. Not only can scientists no longer oversee the general picture of their fields, but frequently they can no longer be sure whether the details on which they are working are already in existence elsewhere, perhaps in another language or slightly different form, stored away in the libraries of the university. As in Borges' fabulous library of the universe, all that can be known seems to be there somewhere but no longer capable of being retrieved. It is often simpler to make a discovery again from scratch than to try to locate it in the books—it is cheaper to read the book of Nature. It is difficult enough to determine whether the same paper has been published once or several times.

As a result of this hypertrophy of knowledge, some work certainly repeats work done elsewhere and already on record. Duplication on an even larger scale occurs when methods, theories and ideas in one discipline, already long familiar if not forgotten, are apparently rediscovered anew much later in another one. As Norbert Wiener noted:

There are fields of scientific work . . . which have been explored from the
different sides of pure mathematics, statistics, electrical engineering, and
neurophysiology; in which every single notion receives a separate name from
each group; in which important work has been triplicated or quadruplicated;
while other important work is delayed by the unavailability in one field
of results that may have already become classical in the next field (Wiener
1965, 2).

This kind of confusion is symptomatic of much more than excess of
knowledge, but the conditions of the over-production and over-publication
of knowledge make it well nigh incurable. Such duplication is almost a
permanent condition in the social sciences and humanities where a forgotten
trend in one discipline is a new line of research in another: what is a
truism in the former becomes a truth in the latter.

The inflation of knowledge leads inevitably to a devaluation of the
currency of truth. A new variant on Gresham's law makes itself felt: bad
knowledge drives out good knowledge. Where too much of the work being
published is standard and pedestrian, it becomes even more difficult for
any unusual or really original work to gain recognition and acceptance.
The sheer pressure for publication permits the entry of non-intellectual
criteria of selection, and it also makes authority as a measure of quality
almost inevitable. The harassed editor or reader, innundated by material,
even with the best intention has almost no other recourse than to go by
previous reputation or position in making judgements. The pressure of
publication, like blood pressure, aggravates all other organs of the body
politic of academia. It can not be permitted to go unchecked; some ways
must be found of reducing it.

An indication of a possible cure for this disease of science lies in the
fact that it results from a reversal of previous ethical inhibitions against
over-publication. Over-publication, like over-population, is not a natural
condition resulting from an inevitable demographic law of population
growth. Both over-publication and over-population were partly kept in
check by ethical norms, as well as by other inhibiting factors. Marvin
Minsky can still maintain the following views on publication: 'I felt that
a successful scientist might publish three or four real discoveries in his
life-time and not load up the airwaves with partial results. I still feel that
way. I don't like to take some little discovery and make a whole paper
out of it' (Bernstein 1982, 35). This attitude is clearly old-fashioned and
is now honoured more in the breach than the observance. But in the
previous epoch of science such self-restraints must have been operative
more generally and been partly effective in keeping the gross level of
publication down. For accompanying the self-censorship by one's scientific
conscience was the public censorship of one's peers making one ashamed
to bring out anything trivial or unworthy, and this approach contained a
more robust motive of self-interest since a poor publication was held
against one. The general public of scientific connoisseurs to whom scientific
works were addressed also acted as a break against too specialized, recherché or trivial publications which could interest nobody, and such a
public still existed in many sciences till relatively recently.

In the contemporary scientific situation all these inhibitions have broken down, and instead encouragement and reward are given to the sheer bulk of publication. The injunction 'publish or perish' is as potent as 'populate or perish' in increasing the scientific birthrate. Promotion is now frequently assessed on the weight of published material or some equivalent quantitative measure, such as that deriving from the citation index, despite the proven unreliability of this index as an indicator of quality. Increased competition for priority ensures that everyone must rush into print as soon as possible even with incomplete studies and partial results. The haste to get into print is a condition of survival for there are now only weak inhibitions or ethical restraints on appropriating other people's research projects, 'scooping' at the last possible moment their painfully won results or even 'filching' their ideas. The very processes of policing research provide new opportunities for theft: 'peer review situations—whether of theses, manuscripts submitted for publication, or proposals submitted for research grants—are frequently criticized for providing the opportunity for the plagiarism of data or ideas' (Manwell and Baker 1981, 155). The quantity of published material is also artificially swollen because the art of extracting as many papers as possible as quickly as possible from the one idea, experiment or method and of using one's quickly growing reputation to place them in as many journals as possible, has now become the art of survival and success. This corrupting set of practices and procedures will have to be curbed sooner or later by instituting and enforcing anew ethical norms against excessive publication if science is not to be buried under its own self-generated avalanche of papers. If nothing else works perhaps draconian measures—such as those enforced in China against over-breeding—limiting each scientist to a fixed number of papers a life-time will ultimately have to be introduced. But one hopes such measures will not be necessary.

The breakdown of ethical restraints in general is a corrupting influence in the sciences and in academia. It involves not so much practices which are outlawed and punished if discovered as connivances which are now condoned.[1] The former, as with any crime, are not as dangerous for the well-being of science or as morally disturbing as the latter, the real corruptions. But inevitably the one shades into the other, and as the transgressions merge they become harder to distinguish from each other and eradicate. This situation is well illustrated by the much-publicized case of the fraud perpetrated by Sir Cyril Burt, who is to British science what Philby is to British intelligence. Burt's fraudulent statistics were only exposed after his death by Leon Kamin, an outsider to intelligence testing till then, whose attention was directed to Burt's papers by a student. In retrospect, the fraudulence of Burt's work should have been obvious to anyone in the field. It was apparent to some, such as D. F. Vincent as early as the 1950s, but he was unable to publish his criticisms because of Burt's eminence and power within psychology (Gieryn and Figert 1986, 72), which was the decisive factor in the case all along. It might be objected, now that the crime has been revealed, that there is no evidence of damage to science in the long run. This kind of rhetorical retort was made by succeeding pupils and friends such as Hans Eysenck, the present doyen of British psychology, who at first rejected all allegations against Burt. Eysenck goes to some length to make Burt's fraud understandable and almost excusable from a human-all-too-human point of view—Burt lost forty years of experimental data because of bombing in the war, his wife left him, and so on—though there is evidence that he began his frauds prior to these events. However, in the process of exculpation, Eysenck reveals details of Burt's previous activities which are ethically far less excusable from a human point of view; he does not seem to realize this and obviously never exposed these breaches or protested against them during Burt's life-time, in company with many other prominent scientists of the time.

Eysenck (1982) reveals that 'a very well-known British statistician' told him ten years after the event that a favourable review he wrote of Eysenck's first book for 'Burt's journal'—the *British Journal of Statistical Psychology* 'which he regarded as his own personal property'—was surreptitiously replaced by Burt with a vitriolic review but published under the statistician's name without his approval. Neither the 'well-known statistician' at the time nor Eysenck when he learned of it protested against this deception. All Eysenck can say even now is that 'this surely is not normal behaviour in academic circles'. Perhaps not, but it must have been considered normal enough by those such as the statistician and Eysenck if they were not willing to speak up about it. Eysenck now reveals that Burt made Eysenck's students 'rewrite their conclusions so as to be critical of myself; he also altered the papers they published on their work. On occasion he was not above inventing studies which did not exist, in order to support his views' (ibid.). Some of this must have been known to Eysenck and his students at the time, yet allowed to pass without demurral. Does this not make them complicit in some of Burt's misdemeanours? He also writes that 'Professor L. L. Thurstone, perhaps the leading psychometrist of his generation, told me in confidence that he refused to take anything Burt wrote seriously, or to pay attention to any claims he made. Professor Penrose in this country has been quoted in a similar vein' (ibid). What is one to make of this kind of silence by scientists of such eminence in the face of patent scientific corruption? Eysenck obviously thinks of some of these misdeeds perpetrated by Burt as mere peccadillos, 'hardly crimes in the sense that his later fraudulence was'. What kind of ethical insouciance does this verdict unwittingly disclose? And worst of all, many people owe their positions at least partly to Burt's patronage. Burt's journal for over a generation purveyed studies, experiments and conclusions falsified to conform with Burt's personal prejudices, which in turn had a profound influence on a number of sciences based directly or indirectly on Burt's 'data', ranging from educational psychology to sociobiology, and these sciences had a very strong influence on educational practices, subjecting a generation of British school children at secondary and primary level to spurious evaluations.

Most worrying is the fact that so many suspected Burt's frauds for many years before his death and did nothing about them. Manwell and Baker (1981, 155) ask: 'why did it take so long to be detected?', and they point out that the erroneous statistics were obvious and not hard to locate.

None of his papers, it seems, whether published in his own or other journals, was ever checked or properly refereed. They answer all these questions in the words of Philip Vernon, 'an eminent student of human intelligence': 'there were certainly grave doubts although nobody dared put them in print, because Burt was enormously powerful' (ibid). The corrupting face of power and misused authority, so prevalent in science as Manwell and Baker document, is here glaringly revealed.

The Burt case uncovers other more subtle abuses prevalent elsewhere. Those in positions of as high authority as was Burt in British psychology are generally insulated from all criticism. It would be considered suicidal for anyone of lower authority status to dare criticize the work of anyone of a much higher status. As Manwell and Baker (ibid. 156) claim, 'scientists who have criticized authority—either that within science itself (i.e., challenges to disciplinary dogmatism) or powerful vested interests which are outside science but which finance it—are often subjected to dismissal or similar serious harassment'. But such condign punishments need not always be applied for discouragement of criticism to be effective. In many disciplines even peers at the top tacitly agree not to meddle with each other's work or findings. In anthropology a tacit agreement prevails to the effect that the leading field workers appropriate their own tribe of native people as their exclusive research 'property' and nobody else dares poach on their preserve. Hence cross-checking of findings is almost unknown. In the rare cases where it does occur its results frequently are not published.[2] This creates ready conditions for the abuse of authority.

Nevertheless, the Burt case is extreme in all respects and certainly in respect to journal editing: rarely do journal editors behave like Burt; most would not dream of altering findings in submitted papers, faking reviews or inventing studies. However, most do make snap judgements about what they will unhesitatingly accept or reject, and generally only when an editor is in doubt will a paper be sent to outside referees. And most editors demand changes to make the new contributions conform with the general style, line and policy of their journals. Thus the historian Theodore Zeldin (1982) writes: 'I began my career as a historian by publishing one article in each of the major learned journals, and each demanded some changes. The price of publication is conformity'. And even the process of refereeing—anonymous and objectively impersonal as it seems from the outside—has built-in potential for corruption. Anonymity is a fiction that can rarely be maintained in practice since it is almost impossible to disguise the author or source of a paper. It is, therefore, very easy for editors or other authorities sending out work to be refereed to stack the likely outcome for or against. As Michie, a prominent British scientist and leading exponent of Artificial Intelligence, reports:

A fairly senior official of a non-British agency whose nationality I shall not disclose, once told me that if for any reason he felt justified in short-circuiting the system in order to get a given result, he would make a judicious selection of referees—either the scientist's friends or his particular enemies, according to which result he wanted. He needn't have told me. I knew it already. In his heart of hearts so does any scientist who has been in the game any length of time (Michie 1978).

Manwell (1979), who quotes this, provides in his own article a telling case history of how peer review can be biased. The unreliability of peer review, which is based on secret reports, in any highly competitive field has been shown up by many researchers.

Repeatedly one encounters instances in all sciences and humanities where the reviewing system for journal publication functioned to reject highly original work. Chomsky (1977) reports that his early original work was not accepted and not publishable in journals of philology. Barbara McClintock gave up trying to publish her late and very original work in journals of molecular genetics (Fox Keller 1984). The founder of mathematical chaos theory, Mitchell Feigenbaum, had the same experience with his early papers, as Gleick (1985) reports: 'the scientific journals wouldn't touch the articles he offered them. . . . Feigenbaum's first papers from Los Alamos, in 1976 and 1977, were returned unpublished'. One of the roles of journals almost appears to be to sift out and reject really original contributions. One editor states frankly that 'a primary function of the referee system is to make sure that any given vehicle of publication remains as limited a way of expressing truth as it always has been, so that its readers may feel secure' (Cannon 1978, 137). This rhetoric is not altogether ironic when one remembers that another of the roles of journals is to enforce disciplinary authority, and that means disciplinary conformity. For this and other reasons many scientists have given up publishing in the regular journals. Feigenbaum remarks that 'the dissemination of information no longer goes through journals. It all goes through a well-supported reprint system' (Gleick 1985, 62). As a result being in touch with the right people is more important than publishing: 'in the age of photocopying, scientists have mailing lists for their papers, and staying current is very much a matter of making sure you are on the right mailing lists' (ibid.). But this expedient remedy for the ineffectiveness of journals is no solution to the real problem and could itself give rise to worse pathologies.

In the humanities the situation is probably even worse. It is next to impossible to publish original work in the leading, long-established journals. Some editors have even remarked that no journal of literary criticism would now publish such masterpieces of criticism as D. H. Lawrence's essays on American literature. Yet commentaries on this classic text—couched in the right scholarly jargon, adequately footnoted, and making the appropriate obeisances to the 'authorities' in the field—appear regularly in all journals. This paradox of publication is not peculiar to criticism; it is also very much in force in philosophy and other subjects. The noted Spanish philosopher Julian Marias notes that

> in the "technical" publications in which the doctrines of the great philosophers are studied, certain requisites are commonly considered ineludible, among which are some that, obviously, the philosophers who are being studied themselves never observed. And here we come to the unexpected and paradoxical conclusion that, if one of those great thinkers were to present an

original manuscript to the editorial committee of one of those journals, this committee would probably reject it, considering it "beneath" the required standard. (Strictly speaking, I could very well remove the conditional mood from the two preceding sentences and rewrite them in the present indicative with a few proper names added) (Marias 1971, 50).

Experiments along these lines to test the system of publication under controlled conditions ought to be attempted. Perhaps something like Doris Lessing's hoax on literary publishing might be tried for academic publishing, especially in the humanities. Lessing wrote a new novel, *The Diary of A Good Neighbour,* under the pseudonym of Jane Somers and submitted it to both of her usual publishers; they rejected it, as did many other publishers. Eventually it was accepted and reviewed without anyone, including the official Lessing academic critics, recognizing it as her work or having anything good to say about it. It sold poorly, until it was republished under Lessing's name, whereupon the sales suddenly shot up dramatically. The experiment proves that most frequently names and positions, not books, are published and bought. Chuck Ross (1982) has confirmed this conclusion by demonstrating that a book, which won the National Book Award for fiction in 1969, resubmitted unchanged under another name in 1977 to fourteen major publishers and thirteen literary agents was rejected by all without being recognized as a plagiarism even by its original publisher. Peters and Ceci (1982) performed an analogous experiment on journals of psychology. They resubmitted twelve articles to the same journals which had published them eighteen to thirty-two months earlier, changing nothing but the authors' names and prestigious institutional affiliations for lesser ones. Only three of the articles were recognized as plagiarisms, and of the remaining nine, eight were rejected.

Thus, in general, the system of publication and peer review tends to work against original research. This is reasonable because the reviewers chosen for a doubtful paper, especially one written by someone without standing in the field, are invariably the recognized authorities in the field; but these are precisely the people with the most to defend against any challenge; otherwise they would soon lose their authoritative standing.[3] Hence, even without conscious bias, the process is slanted against originality or radically new departures. According to the terms of reference of peer review, those already in authority, whose own ideas and theories are the authoritative standards in the field, are being required to rule on new theories and ideas, some of which will inevitably render their own obsolete. Human nature being what it is, it is difficult for those in authority to see the point of new theories and ideas which are likely to undermine that authority. As Ravetz notes:

The pioneer whose work lies outside the common experience of the field must expect not only technical incomprehension by his colleagues, but also a failure on their part to appreciate the value of his endeavours. To the extent that the initiation of research in a field requires the investment of funds, and hence social approval, then the field may find itself becoming ingrown and eventually stagnant through the entirely natural working of these social judgements of value against deeply original projects (Ravetz 1971a, 162).

In such fields originality is stultified by many devices, even by such seemingly innocuous ones as the conventions of citation. As Whitley (1984, 27) notes, 'it is also a way of exerting social control over novel ideas. By insisting that authors refer to particular scientists and currently established evidence, reputational organizations ensure that work is not too far removed from the aims and procedures of the dominant groups'.

The system of peer review—whether for publication or grants or any other scientific awards—only functions fairly if those engaged in the reviewing process are imbued with ideal scientific ethical standards. Failing that, the system can easily degenerate into a technique for preserving the status quo and maintaining those already in authority. As Ravetz states:

> Unless the referees are indeed committed to something more than the protection of property, control and direction from above is very necessary for the prevention of a rapid decline in standards. . . . If their concern is no more than the creation of intellectual property which can be cashed in for material and social benefits, then there are no internal barriers to the rapid degeneration and corruption of a field at all levels. . . . In a single generation, the style of leadership can change from that of genuine scientists, who are greatly enjoying unexpected material benefits, to entrepreneurs in the business of production of results on contract (ibid. 306).

It is evident from the comments of many practising scientists that this kind of degeneration is already starting to occur in many fields. Cavalieri notes that '"safe" projects, targeted studies in circumscribed areas designed to support a popular assumption or settle an already half solved question, tend to find favour. This policy discourages innovative and original ideas, which might be considered "chancy"' (Cavalieri 1981, 28–9). Physicist Levy-Le Blond concludes from such developments that

> the correlation between the hierarchy of power and that of competence is becoming weaker as the very notion of individual competence tends to lose all meaning. When experimental work becomes explicitly collective (scientific papers bear more and more signatures), when theoreticians themselves often do no more than progressively improve on a common idea, then individual recognition is largely due to factors outside scientific activity, such as good public-relations, easy access to experimental instruments, membership of a rich and prestigious institution (Rose and Rose 1976, 289).

As the work of Ravetz and others makes evident, there are various ways of accounting for a loss of morale and eventual demoralization in many fields in contemporary science and scholarship. The most obvious and simplest causes are the intrusions of external power demands and market values into scientific work. The almost universal pressures to engage in arms production and join the military-industrial complex, operating in science through the agency of funding organizations, have proved almost irresistible; military-industrial aspects of science now occupy almost half of all scientists in many disciplines, above all in physics and mathematics. Milton Leitenberg (1971) shows that all sciences are involved, since 'there probably is no area of scientific research that is not now of interest to the military'. The methods of waging war have so diversified, and now involve whole societies at all levels of social existence, that no scientific knowledge is any longer 'pure' or untainted. Nevertheless, the main military effort is still located in physics. In a more recent article Woollett argues that 'the physics enterprise has become a (largely) silent partner in the evolution and acceleration of the arms race. Anyone trained in physics who reads the Annual Reports of the Secretary of Defence will recognise the essential way in which progress in science has become linked to "progress" in modern weapon systems' (Woollett 1980, 109). At the same time, as Woollett shows, any acknowledgement or awareness of this fact is suppressed in the textbooks by which the young are inducted into the discipline. He concludes that 'it is intellectually dishonest, we believe, to emphasise the intellectual beauty and excitement of physics, and the many practical benefits we owe to scientific progress, and at the same time to ignore the present technological predicament of mankind' (ibid.).

But despite the continual preoccupation with war technology, some aspects of waging war have received little attention; a curious myopia has affected scientists in areas of war where military funding has not directed their gaze. Perhaps one of the greatest and gravest of the scandals of science was the lack of any sustained effort till recently devoted to the study of the after-effects of nuclear war; only recently have such studies appeared with any regularity, above all from teams led by Carl Sagan (Turco et al. 1983) and Paul Ehrlich (1983). Such studies have revealed the full extent to which the effects of even small-scale nuclear detonations can block out the sun, a potential capable of exterminating animal life on most of the earth. It is unlikely that any new fundamental knowledge was necessary to discover this fact, though Sagan et al. do speak of 'using new data and improved models'; the past failure to study this aspect was in large part a function of a paucity of interest on the part of scientists themselves. The main previous study, one that was evidently inadequate, was published in 1975 by the National Academy of Sciences and entitled 'Long-Term Worldwide Effects of Multiple Nuclear-Weapon Detonations'. This and a few earlier studies failed to consider the long-term effects of smoke and soot on climate.

The first published intimations of the severe atmospheric smog effects following a nuclear war appear in 'The Atmosphere after a Nuclear War: Twilight at Noon', by Paul Crutzen and John Birks, published in *Ambio* late in 1982; that issue, the *Ambio* editorial notes, 'was carried out with limited financial resources and called for extraordinary commitment on the part of the *Ambio* staff'. Considering what is spent on military science, such a comment does not bear consideration. Crutzen and Birks stress that 'many of these effects have not been evaluated before' and that 'such effects have been largely overlooked or not carefully examined in previous considerations of this problem' (*Ambio* 1982). This oversight is perhaps one of the most scandalous in the whole history of science. It is hard to explain since the effect of smoke on the atmosphere has been known for many years, and the relevant calculations, as Crutzen and Birks show, are not difficult to make. Ultimately the oversight must be put down to a lack of involvement and interest on the part of the vast majority of the world's scientists in the most urgent problem of the human race.

The corrupting effects of the world-wide involvement of so many sciences with military matters are all-pervasive, touching on all aspects of scientific work—institutional, technical and cognitive. These exceed by far the corrupting effect of the market on those sciences too closely involved with it. However, the market, too, bears its share of blame, for in those sciences where there is money to be made through research academic ethical standards are loosened and the ethos of science is replaced by that of private enterprise. This has been particularly the case in two new sciences of immense commercial potential: molecular biology and computer science.

Molecular biology has for some time had a reputation as a risk-taking go-ahead science in which a nice observance of proprieties is no longer mandatory, an impression made public since the publication of Watson's book *The Double Helix*. The fine details of his surreptitious inspection of the x-ray diffraction photographs of DNA in the so-called B form made by Rosalind Franklin, without her knowledge or approval, have already received extensive critical scrutiny.[4] The rights and wrongs of this issue apart, the fact that this book became a best-seller and a kind of vade mecum for young scientists bespeaks a freer and looser attitude to scientific research and its ethical norms. By the time genetic engineering developed, with its enormous market possibilities for individual enrichment, the ethical groundwork of research in this field had already been eroded. With entrepreneurs like John Baxter and Peter Seeburg contesting patent rights and accusing each other of bad faith, chicanery and straight-out theft, one must conclude that all this is no longer in the realm of scientific ethics but of commercial enterprise with its quite different norms (Stockton 1980). A similar situation prevails in medical research and in some branches of computer science for analogous reasons.[5]

A more subtle source of demoralization in science arises through no fault of individuals themselves but merely from the altered conditions of research and from the introduction of large-scale team-work. As Cavalieri notes:

> Team effort has the same consequence for the scientist as mass production has for an assembly-line operator: the separation of effort from end product, with its psychological price. In addition, the necessity or urge to produce scientific results in a hurry leads in many instances to an almost frenzied atmosphere. In this milieu, the scientist often passes up the opportunity to follow a new lead, frequently manifested by an inconsistent result, a fluke. This is a profound loss, for that is the way much "pure" knowledge is born. The mass production of contemporary science is not really efficient (Cavalieri 1981, 80).

Ziman comments on the effects this style of work has on individual ethical responsibility:

To the extent that a team is self-governing and impersonal, it lacks ethical standards of behaviour, and may be driven by institutional desire to survive at any cost. A large laboratory, whether organized around a particular machine or merely created by administrative fiat, is potentially immortal. It can continue indefinitely by drawing in new people to replace the old. The natural selection processes of age and human mortality no longer act against out-of-date problems. There is enormous human resistance to any administrative action to push such an institution along new roads, whether for the benefit of pure science or human welfare (Ziman 1976, 238).

The big nuclear physics establishments, such as Calder Hall or Ispra, exemplify these problems in their full extent. Under such conditions individual ethics gives way completely to organizational politics. All decisions as to research topic, duration, direction and team become political decisions of the directorate. Insofar as such conditions obtain in science generally, Ravetz's conclusion holds good:

> In the conditions of industrialized science of the present period all these bases for the maintenance of a scientific ethic have been eroded; philosophy and religion have become irrelevant; the applications of science are not a matter of simple benefit; and one can earn a living and indeed become rich in a career in science. The great pronouncements of the noble ideology of science of the earlier period would sound false or hypocritical in this new context. These changes produce many difficulties in the preservation of an enlightened ethical code in science (Ravetz 1971a, 310).

Once a situation has become as corrupt as that, how can it be reformed?

Problems of Big Science and the Scientific Babel

The hypertrophy of knowledge and the ethical corruption of science relate closely to other pathologies resulting from the new mode of scientific production typified by team-work, large-scale organization and industrial methods of the division of labour. Known as Big Science, this method of production received an enormous boost from the Second World War: 'in all wartime projects, scientists were exposed for the first time to large-scale team research, to big science, and to applied science, not to mention access to almost unlimited funds' (Kimball-Smith 1970, 36). Some scientists believe, as does the British physicist Sir Rudolf Peierls (1970, 101), that 'it was perhaps a fortunate accident that the time of increased support for nuclear physics happened to coincide more or less with the time when the nature of the subject forced a change from the traditional string-and-sealing-wax method to "big science", with accelerators and highly sophisticated detection devices'. This development was neither as fortunate nor as accidental as Peierls believes; it was deliberate policy that totally changed the character of this science. Peierls seems to retract at least part of his conclusion elsewhere: 'the development of accelerators and other equipment therefore represented years of hard work by too few, and a preoccupation with hardware, largely to the exclusion of the other important task of following the rapidly growing new ideas and principles of basic physics' (ibid. 102).

This kind of elephantine growth also affects other sciences which try to match physics in the size of their projects. The well-known Mohole experiment in the earth sciences—the ill-fated attempt to drill through the earth's crust to the mantle—was inspired and launched by scientific entrepreneurs whose main aim seems to have been to instigate a great project that would match the Apollo mission to the moon and bring them an equal share of public and political attention (Greenberg 1969). The social sciences are not immune to such delusions of grandeur. In the behavioural sciences the short but sad tale of Project Camelot, undertaken in the early 1960s, was a case in point.[6] Others have gone in for vast model building; in econometrics models have steadily grown in size and computer power until econometricians such as Lawrence Klein are envisaging super-models of 'a thousand-equation system' to embrace the economy of the whole world in the one giant formula (Judson 1980, 125). Whether such a model would serve any useful purpose, even if it were possible to devise it, is an unexamined question.

Many of these preoccupations with sheer size and with hardware in the social sciences are also due to the 'fortunate accident' resulting from the Second World War that Peierls mentions in regard to physics. As Chomsky recollects:

> In the intellectual milieu of Cambridge (Mass.) there was a great impact of the remarkable technological developments associated with World War II. Computers, electronics, acoustics, mathematical theory of communication, cybernetics, all the technological approaches to human behaviour enjoyed an extraordinary vogue. The human sciences were being reconstructed on the basis of these concepts. It was all connected. As a student at Harvard in the early 50s all of this had a great effect on me (Chomsky 1977, 128).

Other writers have also remarked on the sources of the contemporary sciences in the exigencies of war and war technology. Anatol Rapoport sees this relation as the start of a new industrial revolution: 'the Second Industrial Revolution came into being with the appearance of machines designed to process not energy but information. . . . The origins of this technology are rooted in the military problems of World War II' (Buckley 1968, p. XIX). The main features—cognitive, instrumental and institutional—of most contemporary sciences and some humanities evidently derive from their war-like provenance and continued application to war. These are the features of science already discussed: technification, finalization, mission-directed research and problem-solving.

Problem-solving typified much scientific work as most sciences were directed to the solution of problems that arose as a consequence of the exigencies of war, armaments for the Cold War, and post-war reconstruction. Problem-solving leads to proliferating rates of publication but not necessarily to the emergence of anything basically unforeseen. Polykarp Kusch (1977, 43) remarks that 'increasingly the university sees itself as a collection of problem solvers; although problems can be solved only if there is knowledge, their solution may offer very little new knowledge'. For example, in economics, as Sumner Rosen (1968, 88) states, 'the major innovations of recent years have been quantitative methods, highly useful for problem-oriented research and for practical use'; these arose largely out of the involvement of economists in wartime government agencies and in post-war government regulation of the economy to create rising productivity and full employment. The theoretical basis of most of this had already been laid down by Keynes prior to the war. The post-war emergence of the welfare state has had a decisive impact on all the social sciences:

> The social sciences increasingly become a well-financed technological basis for the Welfare State's effort to solve the problems of industrial society. Above all, what one sees is a vast growth in the demand for applied social science; the policy-oriented use of social science by governments, both for welfare and warfare purposes, and by industry, though on a considerably smaller scale, for purposes of industrial management. The rate of institutional growth of the social sciences in the past decade, has, in consequence, approached revolutionary proportions (Gouldner 1970, 345).

Gouldner goes on to outline the effects on the scientific practice of sociology of the vastly increased level of government investment with its 'increased governmental commitment to intervene deliberately in society' (ibid. 349). This commitment must also be justified, and the job of the social sciences becomes 'to persuade resistant or undecided segments of the society that such problems do, indeed, exist and are of dangerous proportions' (ibid).

As a result of all these post-war developments most sciences are now beset by pathologies. Among the most widespread are those arising out of the division of labour and the ever narrower specializations that this division produced. Every team or scientific enterprise is made up of numerous experts, each of whom only performs a specialized task in the overall design and none of whom can function without the others. It usually requires a director to assign these specialists their roles before they can even communicate together. The most basic of the separations of function is that between the theorists and the experimentalists or empirical researchers. A version of this split is to be found in every science or field of scholarship; everywhere a wide gulf exists between theory and experiment, between mathematical model and measured data, between method and application, procedure and problem, critical standard and textual reading, and different people become experts in the one or the other. Thus in economics 'the mathematical economists and econometricians, by contrast, function at two other extremes—that of systematic abstraction in the one case and data manipulation in the other' (Rosen 1968, 88). If left to themselves theorists tend to spin abstract models in a void and empiricists to accumulate data without relevance.

In every Big Science where theorists and empiricists are separated difficulties in relating theory to empirical findings have arisen. Frequently theories are developed in an ad hoc way, and experiments performed, statistical data collected, and scholarly facts unearthed without any theoretical consideration or evaluative relevance. In the natural sciences experiments are frequently mounted not to test theories but to utilize the capacities of the available equipment and expensive technological devices, which otherwise might lie idle; the institutional imperative compels the work and so produces the findings. Weinberg's assertion that 'the somewhat bureaucratic imperative to exploit expensive machinery circumscribes the direction of scientific growth' (Weinberg 1972, 125) is a modest understatement in many areas of natural science. In the social sciences surveys are undertaken and assessments made because some government authority believes or can be made to believe that this information will be of use to it or that it will help solve some social problem (Lindblom and Cohen 1979). In the humanities mountains of scholarly work pile up on some monument of knowledge, often with enormous duplication of effort— witness the proliferation of the Shakespeare industry—from which no new perspective or judgement or revaluation emerges because no critical stance is questioned or disturbed.

The difficulties of squaring theory and practice are not merely practical ones that can somehow be overcome by more efficient liaison work but theoretical difficulties at a more fundamental level, at the level where each science is in need of the kind of philosophical help philosophers are so rarely able to supply. In psychology Wittgenstein diagnosed the problem as follows:

> The confusion and barrenness of psychology is not to be explained by calling it a "young science"; its state is not comparable with that of physics, for instance, in its beginnings. (Rather with that of certain branches of mathematics. Set theory.) For in psychology there are experimental methods and conceptual confusion, (as in the other case conceptual confusion and methods of proof). The existence of experimental methods makes us think we have the means of solving the problems which trouble us; though problem and method pass one another by (Wittgenstein 1956, 232).

Unfortunately, the kind of conceptual clarification that Wittgenstein's linguistic philosophy can offer hardly serves to overcome the conceptual confusion in the theory of a highly sophisticated science; for this the capacity to elaborate better theoretical concepts is required, a requirement that linguistic philosophy is in no position to meet. Many other sciences are suffering from a similar difficulty of problem and method passing one another by: hypotheses and experiments, models and findings, assumptions and proofs, judgement and scholarship, in short, the theoretical and empirical do not cohere.

One of the most far-reaching and extensive of all such incoherences is the separation between mathematics and the sciences in general, which has taken place despite the continuing mathematization of the sciences. Mathematics has continued to develop in an ever 'purer' form divorced from the 'applied' mathematics of the sciences. The result has been the proliferation of specialized mathematical researches that are useless and insignificant, mere problem-solving of artificial problems. Although it is never possible to rule out completely the future utility of any development in pure mathematics—the best of which has its own inherent interest and worth even when useless otherwise—nevertheless, it is difficult not to agree with Kline, a somewhat idiosyncratic mathematician, when he comments:

> Blinded by a century of ever purer mathematics, most mathematicians have lost the skill and the will to read the book of nature. They have turned to fields such as abstract algebra and topology, to abstractions and generalizations such as functional analysis, to existence proofs for differential equations that are remote from application, to axiomatization of various bodies of thought, and to arid brain games (Kline 1980, 304).

Kline speculates that, 'though no precise statistics are available, about ninety per cent of the mathematicians active today are ignorant of science . . . the trend to abstraction, to generalization for the sake of generalization, and to the pursuit of arbitrarily chosen problems has continued' (ibid. 303). Paralleling this trend is the tendency to specialization within mathematics itself, to the point where a mathematician in a given specialty can no longer even understand those in others; as the French mathematicians of the Bourbaki school state: 'mathematicians . . . are unable to understand the language and the terminology used by colleagues who are working in a corner remote from their own' (ibid. 284). The reasons for this degree of specialization and the isolation of mathematics from the sciences are partly institutional and have to do with the authority structure of the discipline. This structure encourages the tendencies towards purism and discourages 'applied' work. Thus 'generalization and abstraction [are] undertaken solely because research papers characterized by them can be written' and published, even though they are 'usually worthless for application' (ibid. 283).

> Another inducement to take up problems of pure mathematics is the pressure on mathematicians from institutions such as universities to publish research. Since applied problems require vast knowledge in science as well as in mathematics and since the open ones are more difficult, it is far easier to invent one's own problems and solve what one can. Not only do professors select problems of pure mathematics that are readily solved but they assign such problems to their doctoral students so that they can produce theses quickly (ibid. 282).

Unfortunately, Kline has not backed up his assertions by studies in the sociology of mathematics—a subject that barely exists—but they seem plausible because they match what sociological studies of other sciences have revealed. The widespread practice of only engaging with those problems that are solvable in a set period of time while the research money lasts and which can be parcelled out into so many neat Ph.D. bundles can be found throughout the arithmomorphic or 'restricted' sciences. As Whitley shows, it is a feature of contemporary research in physics; he reveals how the abstract and 'restrictive' cognitive paradigms of physics work in with its institutional 'political' structures to result in a division of labour that proliferates disparate research findings that can no longer be integrated in a coherent way:

The more specific objects become, the more easily they are separated and can be organized as foci for distinct tasks but, equally, the more difficult it may be to relate them coherently and make sense of some more general phenomena, as Bitz suggests is happening in particle physics. Processes of specification and refinement of instruments may outrun the development of integrative theories or models, especially if work does become organizationally distinct so that cognitive boundaries are reinforced by social ones. Rather than research tasks being derived from distinct aspects of a single problem, they may develop in a very ad hoc manner from every-day organizational and technical exigencies. What may be regarded as "efficient" in the sense that work can continue in ever narrower directions may lead to "inefficiency" in terms of making sense of increasingly disparate topics and problems (Whitley 1977b, 28).

The pathologies deriving from this vertical division of labour within one subject are accompanied by the pathologies deriving from the ever narrower 'horizontal' separation of one subject from another. Scientific subjects have fragmented into disciplines, disciplines into specialities, and specialities into fields and fields into sub-fields. And each separate fragment tries to become institutionalized as a self-contained unit with its own technical jargon, journals and associations and, if it is fortunate and powerful, its own department or centre or institute. Even within the still nominally single department, communication between scientists or scholars working in different fields has become impossible; one of the ironic commonplaces of the multiversity is that few can talk seriously to their colleagues in adjacent rooms. To be reminded of the large-scale failures and gigantic waste of effort this lack of communication brings about it is necessary to turn again to Norbert Wiener:

These specialized fields are continually growing and invading new territory. The result is what occurred when the Oregon country was being invaded by the United States settlers, the British, the Mexicans and the Russians—an inextricable tangle of exploration, nomenclature and laws. There are fields of scientific work . . . which have been explored from the different sides of pure mathematics, statistics, electrical engineering, and neurophysiology; in which every single notion receives a separate name from each group (Wiener 1965, 2).

This babble leads to all kinds of problems of mutual incomprehension which makes it seem as if a kind of Babel had befallen the sciences. Boulding identifies this new 'fall' as the main danger threatening all the sciences:

The crisis of science today arises because of the increasing difficulty of such profitable talk among scientists as a whole. Specialization has outrun trade, communication between the disciplines becomes increasingly difficult, and the Republic of Learning is breaking up into isolated subcultures with only tenuous lines of communication between them—a situation which threatens intellectual civil war. The reason for this break-up in the body of knowledge is that in the course of specialization the receptors of information themselves become specialized. Hence physicists only talk to physicists, economists to economists—worse still, nuclear physicists only talk to nuclear physicists and econometricians to econometricians. One wonders sometimes if science will not grind to a stop in an assemblage of walled-in hermits, each mumbling to himself words in a private language that only he can understand (Buckley 1968, 4).

A good example of how subdivision leads to incomprehension is Boulding's own science of economics which arose early in the nineteenth century as a broad field called political economy. But by about the middle of the century this discipline had already split into classical or 'bourgeois' economics and Marxist or socialist economics, two groups that could no longer communicate. By the end of the century the former became neo-classical economics as a result of the Marginalist 'revolution' and was quickly engaged in a *Methodenstreit* with the Historicist economics of such people as Roscher and Schmoller. By the 1930s Keynes broke away from the neo-classical school to establish a new variant, since called by his name. A little earlier formalization and mathematization had been introduced into neo-classical economics, leading to the insistence that all discourse be couched in mathematical formulae. Since the end of the Second World War some of these divisions, even further divided, have become institutionalized as separate disciplines, frequently in separate departments, each with its own language. By now Benjamin Ward has identified at least a dozen different economic disciplines currently taught in the United States, which he orders in groups of three according to their hierarchical status in the economics establishment:

A - Microtheory, macrotheory, econometrics.
B - International trade, money and banking, public finance.
C - Industrial organization, labour, economic history.
D - Economic development, history of economic thought, comparative economic systems.

For purposes of status ranking these fields are divided into four classes. Essentially the idea is that the highest status fields, those in class A, define the nature of acceptable research problems in economics and the appropriate procedures to use in attempting to solve them. . . . Some of the class C fields are occasionally referred to as the 'slum fields of economics'; the class D fields face even more serious problems (Ward 1972, 10).

This status hierarchy determines the lines of communication: who is willing to talk to whom and in what language, whose methods will prevail and who will be treated as an untouchable outcast, not to be spoken to at all. 'Thus the economic orthodoxy is reinforced by ideology, by the sociology of the profession, by the politics of who gets published or promoted and whose research gets funded', as Kuttner (1986, 71) puts it.

Similar differentiations and a status hierarchy of disciplines, leading to restricted lines of communication, have also arisen in the subject of psychology which is of about the same age as economics. There are now in existence numerous branches of psychology whose current status position is determined more or less according to how 'hard' and scientifically rigorous or how 'soft' and humanistically diluted they are. Liam Hudson puts it that in psychology 'the experimental, usually physical or biological in back-ground, look down on the social, industrial, clinical and educational. The psychologist of high status works in a laboratory, and studies either a sub-human species—rat, pigeon, monkey—or some simple aspect of human skill. The psychologist of low status works with human beings in their natural habitat, and studies them in their full complexity' (Hudson 1972, 54). This kind of status disposition of disciplines is symptomatic of numerous pathologies wherever it is to be found in science.[7] It indicates that positions have become hardened and institutionally entrenched, that certain methods—usually those to do with technification, finalization, formalization and problem-solving—can no longer be questioned and that authority structures have become fixed and irremovable.

Given such pathological developments it is little wonder that some contemporary scientists are questioning the present achievements of their disciplines. Thus the economist Robert Heilbroner (1979, 193) concludes that 'modern economics is disappointing in comparison with the economics of earlier periods', and he speculates 'that the intellectual puzzle of some future time will be to account for the failure rather than the success of the period in which we have lived'. He believes that many economists have mistaken the purely technical advances of the subject for its intellectual progress. He lists the following developments of technique: 'econometrics is the child of this era. So is the full-fledged application of mathematics to economic theory. So is vectoral analysis, linear programming, input-output theory and practice. Everyone knows that we owe the descriptions of oligopoly to these years as well as the formulation of imperfect competition in general' (ibid.). But despite these impressive new techniques, the basic ideas of economics have remained relatively unchanged since Keynes, with the possible exception of the highly theoretical work of Sraffa. This lack of new ideas has become patently obvious since the current crisis hit the world economy and economists have been caught out with no new approaches to deal with it or account for it. The very fact that it has provoked a regression to such earlier theories as Monetarism is proof enough of this fact. As Lord Balogh (1982, 159) puts it: 'the recrudescence of monetarism now stands out as an incomprehensible aberration, which may be likened only to the Lysenko episode in biology'.[8]

The introduction of new ideas and innovation in general has become very difficult in the present scientific dispensation. 'The consequences of "big science"—elitism, competitiveness, "grantsmanship", bureaucratisation, business management mentality, and the concentration of economic and decision-making power—have entered the field along with the government money. They have stifled spontaneity, independence, originality, creativity, and even objectivity' (Yaes 1974, 462). The prevailing ideas have become institutionalized and are looked on as 'paradigms'; institutional authority can guarantee their continuance no matter how intellectually obsolete they may become. Although sooner or later all theories must become obsolete as science moves on, the reigning ideas of our time have been rendered almost irremovable. A new approach cannot take over an old discipline; it must develop on the margins or outside the departmental framework and from that precarious position seek to build up its own institutional base. Thus, for example, Chomsky (1977, 132–3) makes it clear that his new departure in linguistics, called Generative Grammar, met with wholesale indifference and hostility from the old practitioners and that it could only have arisen outside the departmental framework of the discipline: 'there was little interest in the work I was doing, at least among linguists. . . . I had little hope of seeing any of this work published, at least in a linguistic journal . . . [only because] there were no entrenched strongholds in the areas that interested me . . . [was it] made possible for linguistics to flourish at M.I.T. in a way that for us would have been virtually out of the question elsewhere'. The unfortunate side of this kind of development, precisely when it succeeds in instituting a new approach, is that it inevitably means establishing a new discipline cut off from its original parent. Eventually the original and the new discipline learn to live in mutual hostility or indifference, unable any longer to communicate with each other sufficiently even to disagree. In time still further secessions will occur—and so the pathology of fragmentation and incomprehension deepens.

As numerous sociological studies have revealed, the introduction of new ideas usually results in these being at first treated as 'deviant' and forced out so that eventually when the deviant specialty has become established this effectively entails the segmentation of the original discipline (Hagstrom 1965, 122–6). The process of horizontal segmentation cannot go on indefinitely or be allowed to spread throughout the sciences; eventually when this process can no longer be permitted to proceed ways will be found of eliminating 'deviance' altogether. Those academically marginal individuals, the so-called 'role hybrids', from whom so much innovative work derived in the past, will then no longer have any scope in which to manoeuvre (Ben-David 1964). The exclusion of innovators who challenge the established ideas is also made easier by the authoritative institution of highly technical or formalistic cognitive norms, those usually associated with the arithmomorphic ideal. Whitley (1977a, 157) concludes that once such a mathematical formalism 'has become institutionalized and professionalized, it is no longer simply a question of individuals and battles of ideas, but a social hierarchy of organization is based on and legitimated by this ideal which makes any radical change unlikely'. In what follows we shall consider how relevant this conclusion is for the social sciences and humanities.

Failings in the Social Sciences and Humanities

Philosophy is strictly speaking neither a science nor a humanity. It is an august subject of great antiquity, one that has only since the nineteenth century been professionalized in an academic setting. Such an abstruse and other-worldly subject might be expected to be little affected by the pressures of academic politics. In fact, the very opposite has proved to be the case, for precisely because philosophy is not bound by scientific criteria of utility or by humanistic ones of cultural interest and relevance, it has become all the more readily subject to the determinants of disciplinary authority. Since philosophy is relatively unconstrained by any need to be accountable to other interests and is free to pursue whatever aims it sets for itself in its departmental fastness as a minor academic backwater, it has in fact lent itself all the more easily to the free play of internal academic politics. Thus, Richard Rorty, a prominent philosopher and critic of philosphy, who because of his criticisms is being treated as something of an outcast, explains that the subject matter of philosophy has largely been determined by the outcome of political struggles within the discipline: 'the topics and authors which fall under the care of philosophy departments form a largely accidental, and quite temporary hodgepodge—determined mostly by the accidents of power struggles within universities and by current fashions' (Rorty 1982, 30). In his account of current academic philosophy Rorty stresses the struggles between the reigning paradigm of the discipline in Anglo-Saxon universities, analytic philosophy, and the other brands challenging its dominance, usually collectively called continental philosophy. The history of contemporary philosophy is largely 'a story of academic politics . . . one of struggles between kinds of professors' (ibid. 228). Rorty tends to be rather nonchalant about this because he believes that 'problems created by academic politics can be solved by more academic politics' (ibid.). But, as we shall see, it is not easy to reform a disciplinary paradigm, no matter how empty it has become, or to introduce another elsewhere in the university system, since the struggle for academic survival ensures that only the one subject-species can fill the available academic niche.

Elsewhere in his work Rorty (1979, 132–6) explains how philosophy became a *Fach* or professionalized discipline, beginning with neo-Kantianism in the nineteenth-century German university. The process was completed after the Second World War in the American university system where philosophy acquired a professional organization with journals, a peer review system, grants, Ph.D. training and all the other paraphernalia of the sciences. The earlier preponderance of patronal authority—which is still more the norm on the continent—gave way within the Anglo-Saxon system to formal-professional authority with a strong collegial elite of elderly eminences grises. This authority rules with a very strong hand, excluding and outlawing any philosophic perspective other than that which falls within the analytic spectrum. Occasional open rebellions against this draconian rule attest to this fact. Thus at the seventy-sixth annual meeting of the American Philosophical Association in New York in late December 1979, a group of rebels, among them such prominent figures as William Barret and John Smith, 'charged that the American Philosophical Association has become a monolith and intolerant, that its programs neglected basic philosophic issues and that its leadership has lost contact with other philosophers' (Lask 1979, 23). The academic political reasons for the dominance of analytic philosophy are openly acknowledged, and the upshot was 'that the A.P.A. was dominated by people espousing analytic philosophy, preventing those with other perspectives from having an effective say in the organization' (ibid.). As John Lachs puts it, in philosophy 'power is an important and lucrative matter' (ibid.). 'It was made clear that differences between the European Continental, historical position and the Anglo-Saxon Analytic position were not merely an abstract matter but touched on such practical matters as grants, government support, endowments, publishing and the placing of students and friends in faculty positions' (ibid.). It remains to be seen how this particular insurrection will fare, though one cannot be sanguine about one that seeks openly to assault an entrenched organizational position.

Perhaps because of previous failures at open reform, there have been many attempts to infiltrate continental philosophy into Anglo-American universities by the backdoor of other departments. Thus the so-called 'deconstructive' movement in literary criticism is partly such an attempt to smuggle in continental thought—mainly that of Derrida and his predecessors such as Heidegger and Nietzsche—through departments of comparative literature, English, French and German. This tactic has caused an inordinate amount of confusion and bitterness among the older style literary critics who cannot understand how and why their theories are being outflanked by something that claims to be more sophisticated than mere criticism but which they see as less interested in literature than in literary philosophy. The battle lines are being drawn, with the opposed literary camps organizing in cliques and possibly to become rival professional bodies. If the deconstructivists succeed in taking over some departments completely, two kinds of philosophy will be taught in Anglo-Saxon universities which have nothing to do with each other. This is already the situation at Sydney University in Australia. Rorty's (1982, 328) rather blasé view that all this is 'not much more, in the long run, than a matter of what sort of professors come under which departmental budget' seems mistaken because once departmental divisions are set up there is no way of breaking through them and the discipline becomes fragmented, narrowed and impoverished.

Analytic philosophy and continental philosophy are already narrow, puristic subjects, the one stemming largely from the ideas of Wittgenstein and his predecessors Russell and Frege, the other from those of Heidegger and his predecessor Husserl. Both versions have by now become highly abstruse and almost empty of substantive content (Redner 1986). Both shun involvement with the sciences, the arts or politics or with any other extra-mural thought. Practitioners of analytic philosophy have even gone as far as to show a disinterest in history, including the history of philosophy itself, so that they have almost lost touch with the metaphysical traditions of philosophy. The younger practitioners are little interested in the classics and are almost solely preoccupied with the latest issues of the journals, as set out by the prestigious figures of the field. The result, as Rorty sees it, has been as follows:

> Analytic philosophy was thus left without a genealogy, a sense of mission, or a metaphilosophy. Training in philosophy turned into a sort of "casebook" procedure, of the sort found in law schools. Students' wits were sharpened by reading preprints of articles by current fashionable figures, and finding objections to them. The students so trained began to think of themselves neither as continuing a tradition nor as participating in the solution of the "outstanding problems" at the frontiers of a science. Rather, they took their self-image from a style and quality of argumentation. They became quasi-

lawyers rather than quasi-scientists—hoping an interesting new case would turn up (Rorty 1982, 227).

Like philosophy, politics is a subject of great antiquity which was transformed beyond recognition to become present political science. A brief sketch of this metamorphosis is offered by Habermas:

> In Aristotle's opus the *Politics* is part of the practical philosophy. Its tradition reaches even into the nineteenth century, till it is finally broken off by the critique of Historicism. And its course dries up even more completely the more its currents are diverted into the channels of the specific sciences. Thus, since the end of the eighteenth century, the newly emerging social sciences and the disciplines of jurisprudence have drawn off the waters of classical politics. This process of separation from the body of practical philosophy has ended for the time with the establishment of political science on the model of the modern experimental sciences, having little more than the name in common with the old politics. Wherever we still encounter the latter, it seems hopelessly old fashioned to us (Habermas 1974, 41).

The discipline of politics has also experienced an insurrection against its current reduction to the 'science of political behaviour'. As long ago as 1967 a Caucus for a New Political Science was founded to work within but against the American Political Science Association. Essays critical of the instituted discipline appeared subsequently in a representative publication by members of this new caucus (Green and Levinson 1970). Once again the main burden of the criticism is against the organized conformity of the discipline and its attempt to institute the behaviouralist paradigm as the sole intellectual content and method of politics. This disciplinary prescription was frequently buttressed by reference to Kuhn's idea of a single paradigm per science. Peter Euben sums up this approach:

> A paradigm must be "enforced". To achieve a science of politics, we need enforcers, we need those whose authority in a community of political scientists would function in ways comparable to that in the community of science. Tolerance for diversity within such a community, as within the "normal political science" it would be there to defend, would necessarily be limited in order to guarantee cumulative knowledge (Green and Levinson 1970, 43).

Euben predicts that such a paradigm community would soon cease to have much to do with real politics and become an ivory tower discipline: 'the community of political science will be fairly small, embrace the concept of professionalism maintained by one or two core journals and the key textbooks, provide opportunities for closeness, common purpose etc.' (ibid.). This course, however, has not been followed since the pull of real politics is too strong to resist, especially by leading professors called to political office or advisory capacities. The converse danger is that the discipline will be staffed by ready apologists for the regime and its policies.

This evolution has been steadily taking place since the 1950s, especially in American universities where politics is now frequently the study of what politicians are currently engaged in doing, mainly with the purpose of offering them acceptable academic advice and so making the scholars indispensable to the politicians—the example of Kissinger and Brzezinski looms large in the aspirations of political scientists. Long before he had assumed office, Brzezinski had already proffered such a program for political studies:

> As engagement in the world is encouraging the appearance of a new breed of politicians-intellectuals, men who make it a point to mobilize and draw on the most expert, scientific, and academic advice in the development of political programs . . . , (so) the largely humanist-oriented, occasionally ideologically-minded intellectual-dissenter, who saw his role largely in terms of proffering social critiques, is rapidly being displaced either by experts and specialists, who become involved in special governmental undertakings, or by generalist-integrators, who become in effect house-ideologues for those in power, providing overall intellectual integration for disparate action (Brzezinski 1958).

He has been as good as his word, both as academic and politician. Most other academic mandarins have followed suit. The result has been that foreign policy, diplomacy and international relations studied at present are mainly concerned with the balance of power in the period since the end of the war, with nuclear deterrence as a technical speciality and with the major power blocs as areas of specialization. The study of domestic policy, government and institutions has become focused on the current workings of corporatist representative democracy, concentrating on parties, pressure groups, administration, and the strategies and tactics of electioneering— the last even going to the ludicrous extreme of attempting to become established as a special science with the name of psephology. One-party systems are the preserves of specialists calling themselves Kremlinologists and China men. To this body of studies at the top of the status ladder are sometimes added bits and pieces derived from other sciences, such as political sociology or psychosocial politics, or the occasional subjects dealing with issues such as totalitarianism or Third World politics. An outline of the main modern ideologies is presented largely for undergraduate teaching purposes, though since the 'end-of-ideology' thesis these are looked on more as historical curiosities. Only the ex-student radicals, with their influx of new Marxisms, have altered this development a little here and there. Political theory is frequently presented only for teaching purposes as a potted history of political philosophy. Political theorists have gone to the length of trying to establish a separate association called the Conference for the Study of Political Thought. But such secessions do not improve the discipline as a whole, which now suffers from an absence of integrating theories. There is usually nothing of what used to be considered the main staples of politics: no comprehensive theory of the State (*Staatslehre*), no theory of sovereignty, right or law, no ethical political philosophy or morality of power, no comprehensive theory of representation or power and authority, no utopian speculations, no comparative study of political systems in different countries and epochs, no political economy, no study of politics in relation to culture, no study of the 'spirit' of politics, such as the classical concern with the civic virtue of citizens. In short, there is hardly anything left of what was thought worthy by classical political thinkers, as indeed Habermas declares.

History is also an 'intermediate' subject, situated somewhere between the social sciences and the humanities but of late tending more to the social sciences, so much so that much historical writing is no more than applied social science. This position, coupled with period overspecialization, the endemic disease of historical scholarship, produces those cherished titles of historical monographs which are regularly paraded for the amused delectation of other academics, titles such as the perhaps apocryphal, 'the economic consequences of the wooden peg in Norwegian shipbuilding 1311–1388'. The historians sometimes embrace with pride this view of themselves as applied social scientists. Thus Le Roy Ladurie declares: 'we historians form the rearguard of the avant-garde. We leave it to researchers in more sophisticated disciplines to carry out the dangerous reconnaissances' (Zeldin 1982). But the ultimate consequence of this attitude is that history simply becomes antiquarian social science. The problems dealt with in the social sciences might be relevant and important when applied to contemporary society, but they lose their purpose and become in a certain sense anachronistic when referred to a distant age. The economic consequences of using one kind of rivetting technique rather than another in modern shipbuilding are certainly worth studying, but 'the economic consequences of the wooden peg in Norwegian shipbuilding 1311–1388' are almost certainly not worth pursuing. What interests us in relation to our own society need not necessarily have any importance in relation to past societies. Historians of the *Annales* school and many other schools have gone to great lengths to compile mountains of data on past societies of the kind we possess of our own. Even the work of Braudel at times reads like an encyclopaedic survey compilation not sustained by any overarching historical conception. It is as if the catalogue of ships had swallowed up the epic of history. The effect of all this is that, seen in the mirror of the social sciences, the past becomes a ghostly reflection of the present.

Some of the other humanities still suffer from an older form of antiquarianism; to them the present appears as a reflection of the past, for they ensconce themselves in museums of past culture where they live off the remains of the dead. But although they are mostly preoccupied with dead culture, the spirit of scholarship is conducive to a denial of this fact because of the academic sense of objectivity and impersonality and its attribution of ever-presentness to dead artifacts, treating these as if they were living things and dead texts as if they were live deliverances. Some humanities departments give the impression of being mausoleums in which death is denied. This image can have its ludicrous side, as when scholars and critics identify with their antique objects of study and deck themselves out with the trappings of the past, pretending to finer feelings, higher moralities, greater culture than their more humdrum colleagues in the sciences. Some are capable of forgetting themselves to the extent of transporting themselves imaginatively into their favourite period as if to escape the grim realities of the unideal present. At that point such antics cease to be amusing and become harmful to present culture, for a delusory denial of the past as dead can lead to a forgetfulness of the present which loses all sense of living realities. The ideal objects and texts that are the subject matter of humanistic study are usually far removed from the culture of the present; only through a difficult mediation that is fully aware of them as dead and past can they be meaningfully related to present life.

The remains of the dead can be meaningfully integrated into the present and made life enhancing provided they are directed to living ends. In the past such ends have varied, depending on how the particular culture in question was related to its own past or to history in general. An unhistorical relation to the past was to see it as timelessly continuing in the present, so that the past was a perpetual present. Out of this undifferentiated mingling of present and past derived the traditional relation to the past which saw the present as different from the past but maintaining unbroken continuities with it. A more explicit historical relationship to the past arises when a lost past is deliberately revived for some present end, such as to initiate or justify a renaissance, reformation or revolution, since in culture, art and even politics all innovations seek to refer back to past precedents, that is, to look for ancestors. In a living culture the past is continually being relived and rethought; and this in turn makes demands on scholars to rewrite the past but at the same time provides them with perspectives for continual re-interpretations and revaluations, for as the present shifts its interests it forces changes in the whole focus on the past.

The continuing development of the humanistic disciplines was premised on such interactions between the living present culture and the dead cultures of the past. The onset of the nineteenth century saw a flowering of these disciplines, with history, philology and comparative literary studies in the vanguard, partly because the decisive changes then taking place— for instance the various revolutions, political, economic and intellectual— provoked a need to rethink the past. Out of this emerged the Historicist attitude to the past, which was intellectually productive as long as changes in culture continued to stimulate changes in perspective on the whole of the past and gave rise to new ways of interpreting history. When, however, the present uses and relevance of history no longer mattered, when it became merely scholarly, then a purely Historicist antiquarian mentality set in and dominated the universities. A crisis of scholarship ensued in the late nineteenth century in all cultural studies, which had become increasingly fixated in their own past since the present was incapable of generating changes of viewpoint in terms of which the past could be re-examined. As Weber warned at the time: 'the points of departure of the cultural sciences remain changeable throughout the limitless future as long as a Chinese ossification of intellectual life does not render mankind incapable of setting new questions to the eternally inexhaustible flow of life' (Weber 1949, 84). Such a 'Chinese ossification' has indeed ensued, but it was arrived at by a round-about route that at first sought revital-ization from the very fount of presentness and modernity.

The cultural movement known collectively as Modernism provided the last vital, living impulse for the redirection of the humanities. Although the Modernist masters arose and developed in an avant garde environment of metropolitan culture, usually neglected and shunned by academics mired in the Historicism of cultural studies, they were quickly absorbed into university curricula once their modern-classics status had been established. All the great writers, composers, painters and architects of the pre–Second World War period became accepted academic cynosures after the war. Academics thrived on this discovery of the modern geniuses and busied themselves in incorporating them into the traditional canon. On this basis modernist aesthetics were developed and established as schools of criticism and programs of instruction in all the humanistic disciplines. It seemed as if the humanities were still in touch with living culture.

However, the impulse proved short-lived. Once Modernism as a move-ment collapsed and the avant garde of artists gave themselves over to ever narrower, more extremist and outrageous experiments, academics who followed suit or even tried to keep up found themselves having to propagate a cultural nihilism in total contradiction to their professional role. The artists could create reputations by attacking the cultural expectations of their audiences, but the critics could not similarly assault their readers, mainly their students. As broad cultural movements in the arts gave way to fickle changes of fashion, frequently manipulated in the metropolitan centres by dealers, impressarios, publishers and media advertisers, it be-came increasingly more difficult for the academics to treat these changes with the seriousness their academic approaches by definition demanded. Some tried and found themselves swept up as apologists for every passing fad or fancy. What Hilton Kramer, ironically echoing Susan Sontag (1966), has called the Camp aesthetic was the coup de grâce of criticism; as practised by Warhol, Cage, Ashbery and the post-modernist architects, the Camp fashion sought to treat art as a sophisticated in-joke and ridiculed every pretension to serious meaning. This predilection for style without meaningful content could not lend itself to academic critical treatment or interpretative discussion.

Camp art was preparation for the final joke of all, the artificial revival of the very excrescences of nineteenth century Historicism and Victoriana against which the Modernist movement had been launched in the first place. At this point the antiquarianism of the market-place could join hands with the traditional antiquarianism of academia. Academics could now with good conscience extol the virtues of the very outdated art they were earlier forced to abandon by the Modernists but which in their heart-of-hearts many of them must have preferred all along.

Thus like a ghost the museum has re-entered living culture; the antique has come alive. The Modernist movement, together with the general cult of progress it subserved, was itself responsible for this outcome. In the name of modernization and rationalization it sought to clear away all the accretions of the past, to sweep away the rubbish of history and put in its place the bright, clean, functional and new. Thus architects razed the supposed slums of the older urban environments and surrounded the historic cores of the old cities, which they dared not demolish, with the high-rise habitations in which few of them preferred to live themselves. The historic buildings left behind were preserved as museum relics. A similar process ensued in respect of old objects so that in the face of mass-produced disposable goods every old-fashioned artifact assumed the status of a treasured antique. Thus the antiquarian-become-antique has taken on the aura of the irreplaceable, the cherished, and in time will be something to be reproduced and imitated. The old becomes the new. Art nouveau imitated again is made over into new art.

All this inevitably means that the humanities will be without the cultural stimulus from the outside world that they need in order to re-orient themselves. A 'Chinese ossification' is upon them; it is doubtful whether they can escape it. The humanities in the universities are doubly isolated: they are cut off from contact with an outside cultural world by the commercial desert of the culture industry, and they are immured within the prisons of university departments by the sciences surrounding them. Without stimulus from outside, without sources of reference, without new standards of value and significance, without any kind of living relevance, they quickly degenerate either to sheer antiquarian scholarship or to critical bickerings in a void, forever revaluing or re-interpreting the few accepted masterpieces. The attempts to overcome this impasse by a direct importation into the university of present 'relevance' by the radical movements has only aggravated it. To bring raw ideological and political issues or social problems into humanities research trivializes it even further. Thus, for example, pop culture, ethnicism or feminism can hardly provide a re-orientation of literary studies which will prove fruitful in a re-thinking of the major authors or a discovery of new ones. Even if some of these movements are undoubtedly just causes, it does not follow that they will prove to be intellectually innovative. There is no way of revivifying a humanities discipline short of a new approach to its subject, one that cannot be politically willed or concocted; it must be painfully worked for and attained as the outcome of a new orientation of the present on the past.

For similar reasons, the direct importation into the university of artists, political intellectuals or even bohemians by giving them academic jobs—which they usually gladly accept as they represent the only security they can hope for—is debilitating for them in the long run and does nothing for their more professional colleagues. Their own artistic or intellectual work must inevitably suffer in an academic setting, which is both too constricting and too demanding, and is mentally and emotionally wearying without offering the stimulus of new experience. For these reasons some artists and writers have preferred menial jobs to the comforts of the university. Political intellectuals must give up all hope of political effectiveness in academia where their only potential followers, the students, are too fickle and too transient for any lasting political commitments. Inevitably the professional academics come to look on the artists and pseudo-politicians in their ranks with suspicion and resentment, and sometimes not without justice they see them as pretenders, charlatans and panderers. In the institutional setting where all are competing for the same rewards, even those who might have started off differently soon become absorbed. The proper setting where academics, artists, political-intellectuals and journalists can meet on an equal footing with no fear of competition is not the staff room of a department. Unfortunately, however, there are now no public scientific societies, no political debating circles, no salons and even no literary cafes where such disparate people can meet. An occupationally stratified and status ordered society makes it more difficult for intellectual intercourse to take place than does one merely divided into classes. As a result 'the intellectual vocation . . . is largely obsolete, an archaic profession; the intellectual has gone the way of the cobbler and the smithy', as Atlas (1986, 45) puts it.

The problems besetting the humanities are very different from those confronting the natural or the social sciences. Nevertheless, they all come together to make up the complex predicament which constitutes the crisis of knowledge and the university. And that crisis in turn relates to the critical situation of culture and society and the dangerous state of humankind in a technological civilization. Each of the issues we have encountered in the university has its analogues in the social world as a whole. Overproduction, specialization, the division of labour, bureaucratic hierarchy, and so on in knowledge are parts of a general economic and social condition. Technified instrumentalism in science is one dimension of the general technological reification. Quantification, abstraction, and formalism in methodology relate to the rationalization of life as such. All the problems of language in relation to knowledge have their correlates in the fragmentation and separation of languages in all modes of discourse, public and private. The difficulties in the relation of present to past that we encountered in the humanities are inherent in the relation of an advanced technological civilization to its own more traditional ancestors, as well as to the whole of human history which it is displacing. Thus the crisis of knowledge and the university is part of a general crisis of world culture, one of whose main symptoms is the cultural meaninglessness of science.

The Cultural Meaninglessness of Science

Of all the pathologies besetting the sciences the most general are those resulting from the fact that the sciences are becoming purely technical enterprises without any cultural, that is to say, really 'human' relevance. The problematic of the 'two cultures' introduced by C. P. Snow actually begs the question on both sides of the divide. The world of knowledge is fragmenting into a set of technified sciences on the one side and a preserved museum 'culture' on the other. Neither is a living culture. Science is no longer a culture because the languages of the sciences have ceased to have any meaning in common human life. The usually mathematized languages of the sciences are becoming culturally 'meaningless' for they are without significance in relation to the cultural languages within which human life is interpreted. Thus, any 'object' described in purely scientific terms loses all its comprehensible significances and appears reduced to an abstraction or technical item.

At its most extreme the meaninglessness of scientific language is exemplified in a formal sense in the languages of physics dealing with the smallest and largest of things: sub-atomic particles and the universe as a whole. Gunther Stent (1979, 8) has explored the formal meaninglessness of these concepts of physics, noting that 'the meaning these concepts have in the scientific context is no longer consonant with our intuition', and he considers this to be a 'semantic limit' of science 'beyond which the world of things can no longer be understood by the use of our intuitive concepts'. He traces back the origins of this 'semantic limit' to Einstein's theory of relativity which 'cannot be reconciled with the intuitive concept of time' and which, furthermore, 'dissolved the fundamental conceptual independence of space and time, whose intuitive development in the mind of every child Piaget had discovered to be a biologically given, natural process' (ibid.). Quantum theory and Heisenberg's 'Uncertainty Principle' also eroded the ordinary conception of a particle as a thing existing at a given time and place and subject to cause-effect interactions. Subsequently, as Stent writes, 'nuclear physics has taken further steps toward the conceptual alienation of science from intuition' (ibid 9). The terms invoked in the so-called chromodynamics of quarks, such as 'up', 'down', 'strange' and 'charm', 'have nothing in common with their everyday meanings and cannot therefore evoke any picture of the world' (ibid). He concludes that 'these words are purely formal, semantically meaningless symbols' (ibid).

Such a form of meaninglessness is very common in the theories of contemporary physics. At the sub-atomic level there are theories that presuppose that time moves backwards. At the level of the universe questions are asked as to what happened in the first ten-thousandth second of the beginning of the Big Bang. Alternative universes of anti-matter are postulated at the other end of black holes which have shrunk into non-existence in our universe. These are but a sample of the many conceptual monstrosities spawned in the language of physics. As Stent states, 'attempting to orient ourselves with our means of speech in realms of space and time a billion times smaller or larger than those of our direct experience' gives rise to 'linguistic images of phenomena belonging to domains far beyond the middle domain that we can directly experience [and these] contain contradictions, or lead to mutually incompatible pictures of the world' (ibid. 7). This must not, of course, be taken as an argument for abandoning physics in favour of ordinary intuitions.

Stent does not deny that theories embodying such 'semantically meaningless' concepts are useful in physics, that they can 'predict the results of high-powered experiments' and that they may lead to practical advances. Although a purely technical meaning may be indispensable for advances in technology, it need not be significant for culture or ordinary human life. As Schrödinger had already warned some time ago:

> there is a tendency to forget that all science is bound up with human culture in general, and that scientific findings, even those which at the moment appear the most advanced and esoteric and difficult to grasp, are meaningless outside their cultural context. A theoretical science unaware that those of its constructs considered relevant and momentous are destined eventually to be framed in concepts and words that have a grip on the educated community and become part and parcel of the general world picture—a theoretical science, I say, where this is forgotten, and where the initiated continue musing to each other in terms that are, at best, understood by a small group of close fellow travellers, will necessarily be cut off from the rest of cultural mankind; in the long run it is bound to atrophy and ossify however virulently esoteric

chat may continue within its joyfully isolated groups of experts (Schrödinger 1952, 109).

This conclusion holds true for all sciences whose concepts and theories have only a technical meaning. Hence the tendency towards ever more technically specialized languages in many sciences since at least the Second World War threatens to render all the sciences semantically meaningless in this sense. Such a meaninglessness constitutes a profound cultural crisis even though it is technologically highly productive.

Couched in their mathematic, technical formulae, many of the latest discoveries in the natural sciences are without clear cultural or social relevance: from that point of view they are also meaningless. Thus all the latest disputes in cosmology concerning the origin and nature of the universe, which ought to be of soul-searching importance, sound no better than technical wrangles; nobody's attitude to the universe is touched in the slightest; no beliefs are affected in this respect; it makes no difference who is right. How different it was when Newtonian physics, or even later the theory of relativity, burst on the world! The reason must be that the language in which cosmological disputes are now conducted has lost contact with our other languages or with other problems outside its own specialized ken. Hence, the efforts of scientific popularizers to render this technical language into common-sense terms does not really clarify it but only falsifies it, since this language is too abstract for translation. A language capable of being translated must have translatable meanings built into it, and these are precisely what mathematical scientific languages deliberately eliminate. These problems of translation will govern the future relation of science and culture for a long time to come. Their solution is at present only dimly foreseeable.

This wholesale technification of science and its merging with technology to give rise to a new compound techno-science have been considered by some critics of science as constituting a pathological development on the largest scale of civilization itself. Techno-science has come to be seen by such critics as the instrument of technocratic domination of both Nature and humankind. Many recent extreme critiques of science, ranging in their attitude from the radicalism of the Frankfurt school thinkers, Adorno and Marcuse, to the conservatism of Heidegger and Ellul, have stressed this domineering and controlling role of science and technology. Such criticisms obviously apply where science simply serves the power needs of technocratic elites, which at present embraces a good proportion of scientific work.

But the fact that such criticisms apply to World science per se is not as evident. Much of it appears merely utopian when voiced by the radical thinkers and merely reactionary when voiced by the conservative ones. It harks back to the traditional philosophic view that science was a matter of theoria or essential truth which could have nothing to do with power. Its prime motive was wonder not power; as Aristotle put it: 'for it is owing to their wonder that men both now begin and at first began to philosophize' (McKeon 1968, 692). Some took exception to this view— Bacon, for instance, who believed in 'scientia propter potentiam'—but even he distinguished between the truth of science and its uses. However, at least since Nietzsche and the Pragmatists, such a distinction has no longer been so clearly made. Truth and power, knowledge and authority cannot be completely separated even in theory. Power is an ineradicable part of the curse of the blessings of science. It is not possible to return to the state of innocence of an original philosophic wonder untainted by power.

The question still remains, however, whether the kind of power afforded by the present practice of science is one that humankind can tolerate. Do we need technological power of such immensity, or would some other kinds of power serve us better? Is this kind of power a pathology of science and not its true aim? Now that it is available, how can this power be controlled? How might the institutions of science be reformed to enable science to take another direction? Can its pathologies be cured?

We began by asking 'what is normal and what is pathological in the present epoch of science'. By now it should be clear that this question cannot easily be answered because the distinction between the normal and the pathological disappears when the whole of modern science is put in doubt. Needham questions the normality of European science as a whole when compared to Chinese science.[9] And to extreme radical critics as well as to extreme conservative critics, who claim that the whole of present science is perverted, nothing is acceptable as normal. For them no piecemeal reforms are possible; only a total transformation amounting to a revolution or wholesale rejection can be adequate to the task of saving science. Unfortunately, their proposals to this effect tend to be utopian or retrograde; rarely are they realistic.

However, there have been and continue to be realistic attempts to reform science which to some degree entail accepting its basic direction as irreversible. On these views World science cannot be abandoned or totally transformed, but it can be changed and its pathologies can be diagnosed and cured. There are moderate conservative and moderate radical, as well as those that might be called 'liberal', proposals to this effect. In Chapter 7 I shall examine the various kinds of revolutionaries and reformers of science.

Part Three

A Scientific Reformation

7

The Main Movements
of Reform

*A real rejuvenation of science would have to be based on a radical modification;
it would be based on a new ideology of science, and realized in debate and
institutional struggle.*

—Ravetz (1971b)

A Scientific Reformation

Reforming science involves a struggle for authority at the highest level
and broadest scope. Just as in the State or Church, such a struggle is
usually waged against an entrenched Establishment jealous of its prerogative
and power. If it succeeds then what eventuates can amount to a veritable
reformation or revolution. There are close analogues between the reforming
or revolutionary movements to be found in sacerdotum, imperium and
studio. If the usual everyday competition for authority carried on in every
science and every university department and between every laboratory can
be called 'little academic politics', then the battle against the whole of the
present scientific dispensation must be called 'great academic politics' in
something like Nietzsche's sense of the term.

At present there are incipient signs of a struggle for authority at this
level which might in time amount to a scientific reformation. As in the
religious Reformation, the fight is against the Establishment of science
which, like the old Church, is everywhere buttressed by the State in the
alliance between the scientific-technological elite and the military-industrial
complex against which Eisenhower warned. It is firmly instituted in the
multiversity–research institute complex and enjoys the support, both material and moral, of every agency of society. Thus any battle against
Establishment science cannot be sanguine of success, despite the symptoms
of failings and pathologies that even the lay public can now perceive and
the very evident need for reform in so many respects outlined in Chapter
6. But neither is it ineluctably doomed to failure. It clearly will go on for
a long time, perhaps as long as it took to bring about the religious
Reformation from the point when the decay of the medieval Church first
inspired calls for change at the time of Wycliffe and Huss, if not before.

A Reformation in science, if it were to eventuate, would be something very different from anything attempted hitherto. However, it might fruitfully be compared, both for its similarities and differences, to the Scientific Revolution. This was the initial movement for the establishment and institutionalization of science, carried out in the teeth of fierce opposition from the older schools, above all the universities, and against pre-scientific metaphysical, theological and rhetorical modes of thought; by contrast, the present movements for reform in science are directed against the very scientific institutions—some now grown to monstrous proportions—and scientific paradigms which had their origins in the Scientific Revolution. Nevertheless, there are some historical analogies as well for the Scientific Revolution also involved a struggle for scientific authority at the level of 'great academic politics' where a whole school system was at stake. As the work of van den Daele (1977) brings out, it was no foreordained conclusion which proto-scientific trend would be institutionalized and enforced as the dominant paradigm of science. The mechanical model was not accepted unquestioningly as the only rational one; it had to win out over numerous other contenders for authority in science. The chemical philosophy as propagated by Paracelsian iatrochemists and many others, including such 'orthodox' scientists as Robert Boyle, was a strong rival to the mechanical philosophy. It is futile, but by no means historically senseless, to speculate on the counter-factual possibility as to how science might subsequently have developed if the chemical philosophy had succeeded in attaining institutional authorization. It is no less interesting to wonder what physics might have looked like if it had begun with the electro-magnetic theories of Gilbert rather than the mechanical ones of Galileo. Those who even now contend that the mechanical paradigm had to win out because it was inherently more rational or scientific are in effect arguing an ex post facto case. In retrospect it might be taken as the one and only possible paradigm for science and in line with its rational development. But looked at prospectively from the historical point when the issue was still in the balance, it is possible to visualize a different kind of scientific development which, had it eventuated, would also have come to be considered the norm of science and rationality. Of course, one can see such a development only in very vague and general terms, for it is now not possible to reconstruct counterfactually putative discoveries that unknown geniuses of the past would have had to make in order to initiate science on a different paradigm.

But the general lesson to be drawn from this historical *Gedankenexperiment* is clear: alternative courses in science are always in principle possible. Whether or not they will eventuate in practice depends on numerous factors at a given historical juncture in science, including struggles for intellectual supremacy which spill over into struggles for scientific authority. At this level of historical explanation, it is always contingent how such a struggle will work itself out, and one can imagine that it could have gone otherwise with incalculable consequences for the course of science. Now, as during the period preceding the Scientific Revolution, there are numerous contenders for scientific authority. Just as then the fight was between all contenders for science and against the established schools of learning opposed to science so now it is against the established schools of science as well as between the various rival movements for reform in science.

As we showed in Chapter 3, it is possible to speak in general terms of an Establishment in science. It is constituted by the dominant institutions, the dominant disciplines and the wielders of authority who through their prestige, position and control of resources dictate to all others their place in the hierarchy, their prospects for advancement and even their styles of research and discovery. The Establishment controls the cognitive, instrumental and institutional norms of most sciences. Any mode of research or study which fails to live up to its stipulated expectations risks being branded a lesser science or even a non-science and excluded from all positions carrying with them entitlement to the rewards of science. A number of such candidates for scientific status have in the past temporarily suffered complete demotion, notably psychoanalysis and Marxism, but many others even now only subsist in a marginal way, such as ecology and sociology in many university systems. As argued previously, there are close correspondences between the cognitive, instrumental and institutional norms of the dominant disciplines that constitute the Establishment. Whitley has shown how the norms of arithmomorphism, deriving largely from physics, together with its associated hierarchical forms of professional authority have been imposed upon many other natural and even social sciences. As in physics, high technification has almost become de rigueur for acceptable scientific work—though the type of technification employed can vary from the high-powered, high-technology machines of Big Science to the complex and painstaking survey and statistical techniques of the social sciences. Because of such technified research methods, a tendency towards a fusion of science and technology is everywhere evident within the Establishment. This fusion in turn encourages cognitive norms that are problem-solving and finalized; external values and purposes, frequently of a political provenance, assume the role of guiding directives for research and even of determinants of theory formation.

The Establishment tends to be authoritarian, for to the ordinary and inevitable exclusionary propensities of scientific authority it has added a degree of intolerance not countenanced before. As Ludwik Fleck notes, science has always excluded that which does not fit its norms and thereby promoted 'a characteristic intolerance':

> The organic exclusiveness of every thought commune goes hand in hand with a stylized limitation upon the problems admitted. It is always necessary to reject or ignore many problems as trifling or meaningless. Modern science also distinguishes "real problems" from useless "bogus problems". This creates specialized valuation and a characteristic intolerance, which are features shared by all exclusive communities (Fleck 1979, 104).

However, in the era of Classical science these intolerances were kept in check by the whole liberal and individualist cultural temper of which science was only a small part. In the era of the World sciences when science has become intellectually dominant throughout society and an

Establishment has been formed within science, there is little to restrain these otherwise normal self-protective exclusionary tactics. For the individual scientist this means conformity or isolation, for as Lewontin and Levins note:

> The academic community is as quick as any small town to declare someone a crackpot and not quite believable. The disabilities attached to such a judgement may be anything from smirks to difficulties getting published, even greater difficulties getting read, to unemployment. . . . Thus a whole scientific community may be personally aware and yet intellectually unaware of dissident currents (Rose and Rose 1976, 187).

Pleas for toleration for the sake of maintaining diversity within science are frequently voiced on solemn occasions by prominent figures but usually to no avail. Thus in his Nobel Prize address Feynman makes a plea for alternative theories and views even when these do not differ in their predictive content and so cannot be distinguished by the canons of experimental testing:

> theories of the known which are described by different physical ideas may be equivalent in all their predictions, and hence are scientifically indistinguishable, [however] they are not psychologically identical when trying to move from that base into the unknown. For different views suggest different kinds of modifications which might be made, and hence are not equivalent in the hypotheses one generates from them in one's attempt to understand what is not yet understood. . . . If, on the off-hand chance, [the truth] is in another direction—a direction obvious from an unfashionable point of view . . . who will find it? (Easlea 1973, 84).

Invariably such appeals fall on deaf ears for institutional imperatives are at issue, not the good will of people. Only a broad-based reform movement able to carry the fight to the Establishment has any chance of sustaining alternatives in science.

At present any call for reform in science is directed in the first place against the evident corruptions stemming from practices condoned by the Establishment and only implicitly against the Establishment itself. At this stage the reformers are themselves divided and isolated; rarely are they united in a broad frontal assault on the whole Establishment. They are still in the pre-reformation phase of partial criticism. The Establishment tends to deal with these critics in the way that the medieval Church dealt with its well-meaning opponents: they are branded as the equivalent of heretics and are denied any authoritative voice and frequently also authorship; furthermore any small recognition they are granted is of marginal status. This is particularly evident at the large scientific conferences where all departures from strictly professional business are shunted into out-of-the-way corridors to be frequented only by a few sectarians. Thus the Establishment guards itself against insurrection as do all well-entrenched and well-endowed institutions.

The Establishment's stance is made all the easier because the reformers do not speak with one voice. They often do not even recognize each other as partisans of the same cause or identify their opponent in the same way. Frequently they exert more of their effort denouncing each other than their common enemy. This in-house fighting is not unlike what took place during the Reformation. Then as now the opposed reforming groups can be roughly divided into the radicals, the moderates and the conservatives. The radicals in the Reformation were those who followed the Swiss reformers Calvin and Zwingli. The extreme radicals were the Anabaptists who were denounced by everybody. The moderates, or liberals according to our political vocabulary, were the Lutherans and Anglicans who maintained a position somewhere in between the radical Protestants or Puritans, as they came later to be called, and the Catholic Church. The reformers who stayed within the Church and eventually constituted the counter-Reformation we can call conservatives. Each of these three groups was in turn divided within itself. A very similar situation obtains now among the scientific reformers who also constitute three analogous groups each internally split. The oldest is that of the conservatives who wish to call science back to its ideal image as elaborated during the nineteenth-century Classical era of science. A more recently formed group, which might be designated as moderate or liberal, is made up of those who see in the systems sciences a new post-Classical basis of reform for all sciences. Finally, the newest group is the radicals who demand more revolutionary changes, frequently of a political nature, and are mainly intent on attacking the present misuses of science. This last group even contains a wing of extreme radicals, who might be referred to as anarchists for they are antinomian in the sciences and who might, therefore, be seen as roughly paralleling the Anabaptists.

The conservative reformers of science can be divided into two mutually hostile factions that might whimsically be dubbed Methodists and High Churchmen. The Methodists, as the name suggests, are exponents of scientific method in one or another form; in the post-war period the form usually espoused is a Positivist methodology of science or a 'logic' of scientific rationality. During this period Methodism has tended to degenerate into a scholastic philosophy of science quibbling over logical trifles and out of touch with the actual developments in the sciences. Such Methodist variants of logical Positivism became entrenched within philosophy departments in Anglo-Saxon countries.

Partly in opposition to these Low Church Methodists arose a group of High Church conservatives averse to scientific method and methodology, regarding them as specious forms of idle philosophizing; instead they advocate an approach to science based on a study of traditions of informal procedures or the art and craft features of practical scientific work. The High Churchmen have tended to be practicing scientists, such as the little-known medical researcher Ludwik Fleck or the well-known chemist Michael Polanyi and biochemist Erwin Chargaff. A few philosophers with a similar disposition have come from the school of Wittgenstein, for example, Toulmin and Winch.

Despite the fundamental differences that divide the two wings of the conservative movement, they hold in common a basic adhesion to the essential principles and modes of procedure of the 'pure' sciences as developed during the previous epoch of Classical science. These they take to be universal principles and practices of science per se, holding true for all approaches to knowledge as a rational enterprise. Thus the conservatives see scientific methods or basic practices as essentially unchanging and reject the attempt to historicize science or make it subject to changing values or socially determined norms. Science is the only rational way of apprehending an objective reality, and though its theories and concepts change as old ones are refuted or displaced, its inherent relation to reality or truth remains the same. Thus in the conservative view contemporary science can be intrinsically no different from the science of the past. The changes which brought about World science have been for the worse; present science has fallen away from the purity of practice and intent of the great founders of the past epochs of science, especially that of the nineteenth and the early twentieth centuries. Contemporary science has been corrupted because it departed from these traditions and became merely utilitarian, given to industrial and commercial ends, and allowing itself to be subject to direction, regulation and planning by outside bodies. Useful science is anathema for the conservatives. Science can be recovered from its fallen state by bringing it back to its essential self, to its unchanging nature as the rational pursuit of truth. And for this to ensue scientists must be called back to their true vocation. The onus is on them as individuals to uphold the truth of science.

If the conservatives are the uniformitarians of science, then the more liberal systemists are its evolutionists. They see the history of science as an evolutionary sequence from simpler and lower to complex and higher grades of scientific organization. The Classical sciences figure in their historical scheme as an already superseded epoch made up of the sciences of organized simplicity, such as the Newtonian science of clockwork celestial mechanics. Following that, they distinguished two further stages in the evolution of science: the sciences of unorganized complexity, such as the statistical sciences of large masses (e.g., thermodynamics); and the sciences of organized complexity, the present stage of systems sciences, the most advanced level of all. First proposed by Warren Weaver, this evolutionary schema of different levels of science has been taken over and elaborated by all other exponents of systems sciences which they present under a bewildering variety of 'trade names': systems analysis, systems engineering, systems methodology, systems theory. The proponents of these overlapping approaches can be divided into two rival groups: those who expound a mechanist approach to systems and those who regard this approach as reductionist and instead advocate an organicist, holistic approach. This basic opposition is spelled out by von Bertalanffy:

> there are within the "systems approach" mechanistic and organismic trends and models, trying to master systems either by "analysis", "linear (including circular) causality", "automata", or else by "wholeness", "interaction", "dynamics" (or what in other words may be used to circumscribe the difference). While these models are not mutually exclusive and the same phenomena may even be approached by different models (e.g. "cybernetic" or "kinetic"

concepts) it can be asked which point of view is the more general and fundamental one (von Bertalanffy 1968, 25).

I shall be taking up this issue later.

One of the first and leading exponents of mechanist systemism was Norbert Wiener whose seminal work, *Cybernetics,* appeared in the immediate post–Second World War years heralding other outstanding departures in this approach in a movement centering mainly on Cambridge on the Charles, but with some cognate departures in the other Cambridge on the Cam. Some of the more prominent scientists involved were Alan Turing, Claude Shannon, Warren Weaver, Herbert Simon, John McCarthy, W. R. Ashby, Marvin Minsky and Russell Ackoff. Information theory and game theory together with operations research and systems analysis became closely allied trends within the general mechanist systemist movement, whose basic techniques and concepts are 'feedback', 'servo-mechanism' and 'circular systems and processes'. Utilizing these methods and the theories built around them, the mechanists consider machine principles as basically adequate for the explanation of all complex processes including organic and neural ones. Most of their efforts have been directed at trying to construct mechanical analogues of life activities, especially those of a self-directed and intelligent nature.

The organicist systemists regard this goal as unattainable because they hold that complex organic wholes cannot be reduced to machine processes whose principles are limited to such simple operations as feedback and self-adjustment. Instead they seek to elicit higher-order principles of complex wholes, such as the equifinality of open systems, and to develop new systemic sciences that are not reductive. Ultimately, they see themselves inaugurating a new scientific dispensation based on the systems movement whose fundamental principles they seek to unify in an overarching General System Theory. This schema has largely come from the initiative of Ludwig von Bertalanffy, who is the main exponent of organicist systemism and around whom have gathered many other distinguished scientists, including Kenneth Boulding, Anatol Rapoport and Ervin Laszlo. According to Richard Mattessich (1978, 283), even prior to von Bertalanffy and unknown to him, the basis of an organicist systemist approach was established in the work of the Russian Alexander Bogdanov, whose main book entitled *Tectologia* appeared in three volumes during the years 1912 to 1927.

The last group, the scientific radicals, differ fundamentally from the conservatives and systemists not so much in their sense of the nature of scientific research per se—indeed in this respect they often appropriate the ideas they need from the others—as in their view of the purpose and direction of science. They see science as inherently value guided and value determined at every stage of its procedure. Thus, for example, Ravetz (1971a, 166) insists that he is 'clearly arguing that complex judgements of value which are in principle highly fallible, condition and even determine the selection of those facts that actually come to be'. By contrast, both the conservatives and systemists had sought as far as possible to make science value-free, subject only to methodology or formal criteria such as simplicity and comprehensiveness, or to a teleology inherent in natural systems themselves. The radicals see science as inherently a social process governed by social purposes, and most of them consequently adopt a social constructivist attitude to scientific entities and theories. In fact many of them tend to be sociologists of science rather than philosophers or scientists. Holding science to be a process of social construction, they see it as subserving social needs and therefore as subject to political direction and control. Consequently they seek to transform science by propounding one or another version of 'critical science', as Ravetz (ibid. 425) puts it, 'critical science is inevitably and essentially political'.

The radicals too are split into two opposed groups who might be called conservationists and revolutionists, or Greens and Reds for short. Both subscribe to the notion of a scientific revolution or a radical break in science which distinguishes them from the uniformitarianism of the conservatives and the evolutionism of the liberal systemists. One of the first exponents of the notion of a scientific revolution, which he called a paradigm change, was Thomas Kuhn, to whom all the radicals look back—though in other respects Kuhn had more in common with High Church conservatives like Polanyi. The other inspiration for the radicals, especially for the revolutionist wing, was the work of Marcuse with its call for a critical or dialectical science of negation as against the positivist one-dimensionality of the current techno-sciences—though Marcuse also had a naive faith in the utopian political potential of the new technologies which was not unlike that of the mechanist systemists.

The conservationist radicals have tended to adopt an organicist systemist approach, speaking of irreducible wholes and open systems, and have taken the ecological sciences as paradigmatic of their new scientific dispensation. However, many of them are less interested in pure scientific research than in furthering a new scientific movement based on conservationist values and ultimately in expounding a new world-view sometimes with quasi-religious pantheistic overtones. Their emphasis is more on the applied sciences and technologies and on the social and environmental effects of science and technology. As part of a radical populist movement, they frequently address themselves to a wider than academic public. Hence many are popularizers of conservationist scientific values; among these are such well-known figures as Barry Commoner. A more sociologically informed supporter of the conservationist approach is Jerome Ravetz, who follows Commoner in expounding a conservationist 'critical science', but in other respects owes much to Polanyi and the High Churchmen.

'Critical science' is also the battle cry of the revolutionists, many of whom tend to be neo-Marxists opposed to the conservationist anti-technology and anti-industry mentality. Our main attention is devoted to those of the joint international school that congregate around the journal *Sociology of the Sciences Yearbook* with which Norbert Elias, Richard Whitley and the German finalization theorists are associated. There are also similar groups at Edinburgh, at Sussex and around Pierre Bourdieu in Paris. Doctrinally more orthodox Marxist revolutionists in science, such as Brian Easlea and Steven and Hilary Rose, are associated with the journals *Science for the People* and *Radical Science Journal* in England and *Science and Nature* in the United States.

Among the radicals are some who are marked by an extreme aversion to any authority in science and who therefore might be distinguished as a third category—anarchists. Not surprisingly from a political point of view, a reactionary tendency is current among the anarchists which makes them susceptible to non-scientific departures, for example, to pre-scientific lore in medicine and to Eastern techniques and philosophies. Feyerabend is a prime example of one who holds this attitude; some conservationists, such as Capra, also share such a predisposition; and for very different reasons Foucault might be placed in the anarchist camp because of his extreme iconoclasm towards the established psychological and social sciences. Clearly the anarchists are a more heterogeneous and less unified group than any of the others.

Even from this schematic survey it may be noted that the polity of science at present is analogous in several ways to the political structure of society in general. Indeed, as we have seen throughout this book, there are always close structural analogies between sacerdotum, imperium and studio. There is a dominant scientific Establishment and against it are ranged numerous scattered groups of critics and reformers who are frequently not very self-conscious about their role and position in the polity of science. Some serve as ideological defenders of the Establishment itself, such as many among the conservatives, and some have been co-opted into it, such as most of the mechanist systemists and even some of the conservationists. Besides, the reformers are so opposed to each other that they constitute little threat to the Establishment at present. The separate isolated factions are weak and unrepresented within the scientific formal hierarchies or elites; apart from the mechanist systemists, none has any part to play in industry or technology, and apart from the conservationists none has any public standing or popular following outside science. At present such factions are no better than sectarian groupings each at odds with all the others, for they also differ bitterly on the reforms they wish to institute in science.

The conservatives are committed to an idealized backward-looking version of 'small science' which they set up as a bulwark against what they see to be the current excesses of Big Science—industrial science and high technology. The Methodists wish to continue the work of grand theory building as promulgated in the Classical pure science program, and they seek to unify the established theories into a comprehensive unity of science. The High Church conservatives are no less given to pure science on the Classical model, but they are averse to any unified theoretical systematization and are more intent on preserving the specificity of method and irreducibility of objects of each separate major science. Both kinds of conservatives are united in extolling the pursuit of science as an ideal vocation undertaken for the sake of pure knowledge alone according to the traditional established norms. This scientific individualism is matched by a laissez-faire, free-market approach to the direction and regulation of science as an enterprise and is opposed to any planning, direction or control of scientific research, especially of a political kind such as advocated by Marxists and other radicals. The conservatives are opposed to the intrusion of any values into science apart from the inherent norms of objectivity and truth; all others they deem to be corruptions of science.

Both the mechanist and organicist systemists seek to reform science by instituting novel approaches, techniques and schools. Both have responded to the growing fragmentation of the World sciences resulting from excessive specialization which had already begun in the late stages of the Classical sciences. The systemists have sought to overcome this fragmentation, which threatens to make communication between the sciences impossible, by developing systemic approaches and procedures that hold good for many fields at once: cross-disciplinary departures such as cybernetics, information theory, game theory, systems analysis and General System Theory. In line with this orientation, they have advocated the setting up of institutions based on teams of co-workers to handle multidisciplinary sciences and borderline areas between the Classical disciplines. They have, therefore, implicitly set themselves against the individualism and 'pure' science ideals of the conservatives. But at the same time they differ amongst themselves on the question of what is a system and how systems ought to be approached: the mechanists adopt a reductivist, arithmomorphic and technological approach, whereas the organicists are more inclined to a naturalistic bent favouring a hierarchy of systems and insisting on the irreducibility of life systems and eco-systems.

The radicals of both the Red and the Green variety have not developed any new sciences or scientific procedures, even though they continually stress alternatives in science and alternative sciences—in fact, few among the former are working scientists. However, they are very much aware of the political aspects of science and tend to concentrate on public activities and academic struggles to reorient the ends of scientific research. They are thus intent on the political process of bringing about a revolution in science, and like other radicals some are inclined to promise scientific 'utopia after the revolution'. The conservationists have more obvious and simpler aims in the forefront, for which they campaign vigorously through quasi-political movements. But they also project visions of a new orientation to nature which in the distant future might totally transform the sciences in ways which they cannot satisfactorily specify now. The revolutionists also work for some drastic break in the course of science, and on general grounds they predict the possibility of new revolutionary paradigms in science; but they, too, provide little specificity about these.

All these differences and conflicts among the reformers of science are perhaps not as irreconcilable as they at first appear. Individualist 'pure' science, collective multidisciplinary 'systems' science and politically directed 'critical' science appear contradictory. But considerable consensus could arise if the proponents of these approaches were to enter into a reformist dialogue with each other. Just as during the Reformation, conciliar meetings to spell out differences as well as to effect reconciliations between the movements for scientific reform would seem to be essential as a preliminary step. Perhaps partial agreements between some like-minded bodies—on analogy with the Consensus Tigurinus between the Swiss reformers—could be quickly hammered out. Perhaps even the Establishment, prodded by the conservatives, might undertake its own reformist council of Trent. One dare not push the analogy too far, of course, for the wars of religion are obviously not to be emulated in the name of science, though that is hardly a danger. And even if considerable diversity in the practices and procedures of science were to arise, and, worse still, irreconcilable differences as to what is to count as scientific, these would not be developments to avoid at all costs. Science can cope with and even thrive on much more variety than it is allowed at present, as the history of science has repeatedly demonstrated. Toleration of diversity must be one of the first aims of reform. In the meantime in the absence of such dialogue it is essential to confront the different reformist positions with each other at least in an imaginary debate. To do so it is necessary to spell out fully the views of each and to note the areas of possible convergence as well as divergence among them, in the process making the necessary corrective criticisms.

Methodists

The contemporary Methodist approach in science is perhaps the oldest and most conservative of all, harking back to the scientific method propounded at the very origins of modern science during the Scientific Revolution. However, not till much later, beginning early in the nineteenth century, when scientific method was interpreted as methodology, did Methodism in its present sense begin to be formulated. By the end of the century the expression 'scientific method' lost its older all-inclusive sense and assumed the narrower and more specialized one of methodology—as such it became synonomous with and usurped the place of philosophy of science in the minds of most scientists. They saw it as the crucial rational component of science, and some took this aspect to be even more important than science itself. Nietzsche, echoing current scientific beliefs of his time, expressed this view:

> It is not the victory of science that distinguishes our nineteenth century, but the victory of scientific method over science. History of scientific method considered by Auguste Comte as virtually philosophy itself. The great methodologists: Aristotle, Bacon, Descartes, Auguste Comte. The most valuable insights are arrived at last; but the most valuable insights are *methods* (Nietzsche 1968, 261).

Merz, the most important historian of science at the time, expresses a similar idea when he states: 'as in other instances when the old problem has been taken out of the hands of the philosophers, there still remains the philosophical task to examine the methods by which mental work is carried out in these fields and the principles upon which it rests' (Merz 1965, 3:626).

Any general approach to science which concentrates on methods, method or methodology in this sense can be considered a contemporary version of Methodism. However, with the decline of Positivism, the movement is on the wane; it has few leading exponents at present and, apart from Popper, fewer still of any great philosophical distinction—though, as we shall see in Chapter 8, there is some outstanding scientific work being done in its spirit. Hence, to deal with it at its strongest we must turn back to an earlier thinker who exemplifies an undeniably Methodist approach, though a most individual and even heretical one—the great social scientist Max Weber. Though it is of the past, it is not passé—Weber's Methodism has still much to teach us even now and will continue to be relevant in the future.

In some respects Weber's methodology of the social sciences belongs with that phase of Positivism at the turn of the century when the movement was at its strongest. Together with his friend Simmel, Weber helped define some of the basic features of a Positivist approach to the social sciences: the logical distinction between the empirical and the evaluative, the notion of value-neutrality, and the criteria of objectivity in the causal explanation of action. However, in most other respects Weber eschewed any of the reductive assumptions which later became characteristic of Positivist social science methodology and which were subsequently erroneously ascribed to him. In keeping with his neo-Kantian predispositions, he insisted on the necessity of value presuppositions for all sciences; following Dilthey, he stressed the meaningful nature of social action and the need for hermeneutic understanding; together with Rickert he distinguished nomothetic from ideographic approaches without relinquishing the role of general causal explanations, and in doing so he specified the crucial notion of objective possibility. At times Weber even writes as if he did not subscribe to any Positivist conception of methodology or any á priori fixed logical canon of science, as if he is really advocating a sociological study of the changing roles of methods, method and methodology, somewhat in the spirit of Ravetz:

> methodology can only bring us reflective understanding of the means which have demonstrated their value in practice by raising them to the level of explicit consciousness; it is no more the precondition of fruitful intellectual work than the knowledge of anatomy is the precondition for "correct" walking. . . . Only by laying bare and solving substantive problems can sciences be established and their *methods* developed (Weber 1949, 115–6).

Unfortunately, Weber does not always maintain a position on method consistent with this injunction. He does not always reflect on the actual methods involved in his own work but expounds a quasi-Positivist methodology for the social sciences.

When Weber turns away from this methodology and proceeds to examine the actual practices of scientific work he does succeed in establishing the basis for a sociologically informed approach to science. This approach is, however, premised on his unquestioned belief that Classical science as he knew it is science per se or universal science, the only possible rational approach to knowledge. In keeping with this conservative assumption, Weber first emphasises the notion of vocation in the practice of science. One might say that according to Weber Methodism in science and Methodism in religion have more than just a name in common. Science as a vocational pursuit is a secularized version of the Puritan theological injunction to labour in one's vocation; hence the spirit of science, like the spirit of capitalism, also derives from the Protestant ethic. This vocational devotion to science and the individualism that it fosters, on which science depended for so long, has now been eroded to an extent that Weber would hardly have believed possible though he already foresaw the start of the process. The professionalization of science, its organization in teams around large technological enterprises, the role of the State in determining the direction of so much scientific work—all these and more make it increasingly difficult now for any individual to practice science as a vocation. This limitation creates problems concerning the role of individual initiative in scientific work and the cultural meaning of such work which have since become critical but which Weber was perhaps the first to broach.

'Science today is a "vocation" organized in special disciplines in the service of the self-clarification of interrelated facts' (Weber 1971, 152). The scientific universe is thus broken up into sets of 'interrelated fact'. It has become subject to the same rationalization and intellectualization of which it is itself the foremost exponent—'scientific progress is a fraction, the most important fraction, of the process of intellectualization' (ibid. 138)—and the outcome of this progress for the sciences themselves is inevitably specialization:

> In our time, the internal situation, in contrast to the organization of science as a vocation, is first of all conditioned by the fact that science has entered a phase of specialization previously unknown, and this will forever remain the case. Not only externally, but inwardly, matters stand at a point where the individual can acquire the sure consciousness of achieving something truly perfect in the field of science only in case he is a strict specialist (ibid. 134).

Weber does not fully explain why this must be so. He seems to think it is simply a matter of the sheer volume of routine work necessary to develop and explore an idea, so that only the specialist can acquire sufficient knowledge to be 'in the position to control, to estimate, to exploit the idea in its bearing' (ibid. 136), which as a mere idea might also occur to the dilettante who is precluded from doing it full scientific justice. He also seems to think it is a moral matter of dedication; only the specialist has 'the capacity to put on blinders, so to speak, and to come up to the idea that the fate of his soul depends upon whether or not he makes the correct conjecture at this passage of his manuscript' (ibid. 135).

Weber's attitude and response to the problem of scientific specialization are at one with his stance on the whole problem of specialized bureaucracy and the rationalized division of labour of the technocratic world as such. He recognizes the dangers—indeed he was one of the first to do so—he warns against them, but he regards the trend as inevitable, as historical 'fate', and so he has to resign himself to it. The highest virtue is 'to bear the fate of the times like a man' (ibid. 155). His reaction to the encroaching bureaucratization of the university is along these lines. He even sees something positive in the coming multiversity, for 'as with all capitalist and at the same time bureaucratized enterprises, there are indubitable advantages in all this' (ibid. 131). The scientist or scholar must comport himself with dignity in face of all these inevitable adverse developments; the 'salvation of his soul' lies in pursuing science as a vocation, for only that will give the scientist's life inner meaning. And if this pursuit requires submitting to the yoke of a specialized discipline, then that is fate. This kind of moral bearing has many historical precedents: there is something of Stoic resignation in it as well as Puritan inner-worldly devotion to duty, and 'it is immensely moving when a mature man . . . is aware of a responsibility for the consequences of his conduct and really feels such responsibility with heart and soul' (ibid. 127). However, is this stance any longer appropriate in the changed conditions of our time over half a century later?

In Weber's own time the state of the sciences and the condition of the university allowed a thinker like him to flourish and a new science like sociology to arise. Weber himself, in his advocacy of the necessity of practicing specialized science as a vocation, has curiously forgotten to take his own position into account. He has overlooked himself and his own favourite science. In a mood of self-abnegation that amounts almost to a perverse self-denial, and is no mere modesty—a quality uncharacteristic of Weber—he even discounts the importance of his own work and subject:

> All work that overlaps neighbouring fields such as we occasionally undertake and which the sociologist must necessarily undertake again and again is burdened with the resigned realization that at best one provides the specialist with useful questions upon which he would not so easily have hit from his own specialized point of view. One's own work must inevitably remain highly imperfect. Only by a strict specialization can the scientific worker become fully conscious, for once and perhaps never again in his lifetime, that he has achieved something that will endure. A really definitive and good accomplishment is today always a specialized accomplishment (Weber 1971, 135).

One might ask Weber whether his *Economy and Society* does nothing more than at best provide the specialists with useful questions. It is true that where specialist issues are concerned 'only the specialist is entitled to a final judgement' (Weber 1967, 28). It is also true that 'dilettantism as a leading principle would be the end of science', that 'he who yearns for seeing should go to the cinema', and 'whoever wants a sermon should go to a conventicle' (ibid. 24). But it is not true that a 'good accomplishment is today always a specialized accomplishment'.

The whole account Weber offers here of sociology totally falsifies his own work. It goes against the very theoretical exposition of sociology as a comprehensive science of social action that Weber gives elsewhere. Sociology as practised by Weber is a general social science based on historical premises and is capable of theoretically explaining human action in its full social complexity and historical specificity. To say that this theoretical edifice is a mere dilettante's play of ideas which might provide useful questions and the odd hypothesis for specialists is a travesty of everything that Weber achieved. Unfortunately, Weber's work has tended to be used by specialist sociologists and others precisely in this way—to the defeat of its real achievement. Weber is only remembered as having made useful suggestions about Protestantism or bureaucracy or status groups which the specialists think they can now take up better with their latest research methods. It is as if the spite of history has been at work in vindicating Weber's own low self-estimate as expressed in his speech on science.

When the king builds, there is work for the carters: when a Weber writes, there is research for the specialists. The theorist of scope builds with the raw, poorly theorized data of countless specialists and transforms this inchoate material into the theoretic edifice of a proper science. Such a science then provides the specialists with new problems, hypotheses and issues for further research on the new scientific footing. Thus Weber's sociology gave a scientific meaning to the more or less stray assemblage of disparate materials from countless specialists working in law, economy, history, art and scholarship and in such oddities as comparative theology. He unified all this unco-ordinated information in terms of general concepts, ideal types and overarching theories and hypotheses which permitted the focussing on detailed causal explanations. The corpus of Weber's work should have led to innumerable research projects, which, had they been carried out under the guidance of his over-all theory, would have produced a comprehensive body of sociological investigations. Unfortunately, this never happened on any scale; only in exceptional cases was Weber's work taken up and pursued in the way that it demanded. This was partly the result of historical exigencies, such as the suppression of his influence in Nazi Germany but more crucially of the whole trend towards ever narrower specialization which has made it difficult for anybody to master more than a fraction of Weber's work and so has defeated its real intent. The irony of history has in this instance told against him.

Sociology as Weber conceived it was intended to play a central role in the social sciences and in the human sciences in general. Weber was critical of the aspirations to totality of the Comtean hierarchical scheme with sociology as the crowning apex, as well as of the Marxist science of historical materialism, both of which were at least partly intended as attempts to make up for the loss of metaphysics following the collapse of the Hegelian system. Nevertheless, Weber (1947, 88) did not turn his back on the need for a comprehensive science able to explain 'social action in order thereby to arrive at a causal explanation of its course and effect', and 'in action is included all of human behaviour when and in so far as the acting individual attaches a subjective meaning to it'. Weber's general concepts of sociology are intended to cover the whole extent of human social action, so in this respect they stand on par with the general concepts of any other science, though, of course, they do not function in the same way. The exact definitions Weber is able to provide for such a range of social concepts indicates the degree of theoretical exactitude that he had achieved.

Weber's interlinked definitions of the basic concepts of sociology covering all of human action are one of the outstanding accomplishments of Methodism in the social sciences. They are still of continuing relevance and will form the basis of much future work. These concepts permit an integration of the social sciences, including the whole of history, that had not been achieved before or equalled since. Weber derived them from his voluminous studies in all areas of social and historical reality. His work taken as a whole is an integrative accomplishment which is the very opposite of the narrow specialization that has beset such fields as disciplinary sociology and the other academic social sciences since Weber. This integrative scope is the reason Weber's work points to the future in a way that no other does and why any reformation of the social sciences must begin with his contribution. His accomplishment is, perhaps, nowhere more apparent than in politics, an old science that has come on hard times. Weber's speech 'Politics as a Vocation' constitutes an integrative achievement without equal in the history of this science. The speech sketches in all the functions that a science of politics would need to carry out: it defines the meaning of political action and sets out the problems inherent in acting politically by developing a general theory of power, authority and the State; it provides an historical picture of the various forms political action has taken in the past and the various types of actor involved; and, finally, it defines the ethical problematic of political action and outlines the ethical paradoxes governing it. This delineation goes quite counter to and beyond Weber's own quasi-Positivist methodological strictures or his emphasis on specialization.

Many different sciences come effortlessly together to provide his general outline of politics, as Weber draws on his knowledge of sociology, history, political science, constitutional law, the ethics of world religions, theodicy, Kantian criticism and interpretations of the great Russian novelists. Any sharp separation of sciences or narrow specialization is as little apparent in Weber as it is in Aristotle, Machiavelli or Hobbes, even though Weber displays a much more detailed and theoretically developed knowledge than any previous political philosopher could deploy. But as for any Methodist scientist, for Weber concepts, definitions and ideal types are constructed to act as 'axioms' of the systematic exposition which leads directly into a comprehensive account of the factual realities of politics, and this in turn to a critical exposition of the values and ethics governing political action. Hence the Positivist methodology to which Weber is philosophically committed is hardly in evidence; he transcends his own methodological restrictions or puts them aside as the complexity of the issues requires. Though he is formally bound to scientific value-neutrality, or the logical separation of factual and normative propositions in line with his basic Positivism, and to the distinction between formal and substantive norms in line with his Kantian presuppositions, nevertheless, these methodological restrictions do not govern the account of politics and do not make themselves felt as categorial barriers. In practice Weber proves superior to his own methodological blinders. Thus, his very definition of the State—'a human community that (successfully) claims the monopoly of the legitimate use of violence within a given territory' (Weber 1971, 78)—already contains the ethical paradox stemming from the unavoidable necessity that 'politics operates with very special means, namely power backed up by violence' (ibid. 119), and that he who operates with violence 'has to realize these ethical paradoxes, he must know that he is responsible for what may become of himself under the impact of these paradoxes . . . he lets himself in for the diabolic forces lurking in all violence'. Ethical dilemmas are thus built into the very nature of politics. In a similar way, any absolute, 'logical' opposition between fact and value or between scientific and moral choice clearly breaks down.

Perhaps Weber's most distinctive methodological accomplishment was his conception of ideal-type concepts which I utilized in Chapter 3 and elsewhere (Redner 1986, 24–5). These concepts are one of the great theoretical discoveries in science, which must be placed alongside the original Socratic search for exact definitions of concepts and Aristotle's elaboration of a metaphysics of categories, as well as with Descartes' invention of method. The ideal-type concept is crucial for the social sciences for it permits an exact and systematic definition of objects in social and cultural reality, that is, a definition of complex historical terms—'a "definition" of such synthetic historical terms according to the schema of genus proximum and differentia specifica is naturally nonsense' (Weber 1949, 93). Adorno is perhaps the first philosopher to realize that to approach cultural objects through a 'constellation' of such ideal-types is to have discovered a completely new way of describing, one that abrogates any assumptions about inner essences or natures: 'how objects can be unlocked by their constellation is to be learned not so much from philosophy, which took no interest in the matter, as from important scientific investigations. The scientific accomplishment often ran ahead of its philosophical comprehension' (Adorno 1973, 164). Even Weber's own Methodist comprehension was not up to his scientific accomplishment and its philosophical implications. Adorno believes that working with constellations of ideal types constitutes a mode of philosophical thought that goes beyond any available in modern philosophy: 'in Weber's case the constellations take the place of systematics, which one liked to tax him with lacking, and this is what proves his thinking to be a third possibility beyond the alternative of positivism and idealism' (ibid. 166).

Thus Weber's work demonstrates that Methodism is still viable as an approach in the sciences provided that it is separated from the so-called logic of Positivist methodology, which Weber had already implicitly accomplished in his science though not in his explicit philosophy. Weber's work provides a starting point for a redefinition of a Methodism suitable for the social sciences, and it could be further developed for the natural sciences as well. In Chapter 8 I shall discuss a number of approaches in the natural sciences which might become the basis for a new neo-Methodism. I hope that these will be proof against the attacks on traditional Methodism usually launched successfully by the High Church conservatives.

High Church Conservatives

The intellectual struggle between the Methodists and High Church conservatives, which became pronounced in the contemporary post-war epoch, has a long pre-history going back to the last century if not before. James Clerk Maxwell saw the conflict between John Stuart Mill and William Whewell more or less in these terms when he called the former an exponent of 'low' philosophy and the latter of 'high' philosophy (Cannon 1978, 233).

Whewell might be considered one of the earliest of the High Churchmen of science—and in fact he was a High Church Tory in religion and politics as well who in the 1850s led the opposition to Parliament's attempts to reform Cambridge. But, of course, High Churchmen in science need not necessarily also be such in religion and politics.

The Low Churchmen and High Churchmen in science, though opposed, are all conservatives who subscribe to the norms and ethos of Classical science; the two parties hold much in common, as we have seen, and this is perhaps one reason why the differences that divide them are felt so acutely. The High Churchmen are particularly intent on attacking and discrediting the Methodist's belief in methodology, especially in its formalized Logical Positivist guise. In particular, they attack the reductivist and constructivist account of scientific explanation and theory elaboration, the hypothetico-deductive method, the formalized notions of verifiability or falsification, the experimentum crucis idea associated with these, and the whole conception of one rational system of knowledge constituting a unified science. Instead they tend to advocate the view of science as an on-going practical activity with many of the characteristic features of the arts and crafts, carried out by communities of practitioners each of which might follow its own tradition of research. As in a religious or political community, in a scientific one consensus and authority play essential and mutually reinforcing roles in determining what is accepted and rejected from among the various conflicting 'discoveries', that is, contributions made by individuals. Individual scientists commit themselves to specific scientific approaches and theories as a matter of acceptation or 'faith' in the belief that these will lead to future discoveries. And finally, controversies, which are always bound to arise, are settled within each community through a reasoned debate carried out in the specific language of science acceptable to all its members—a discourse that has its own specific values, criteria of proof, norms of work and even rhetorical style. The mode of presentation and publication of completed and certified work is quite different from the process of research and of argumentation that led to the published results. And so, too, the eventual retrospective evaluation of what had been achieved is also different from the anticipation of what might be achieved entertained by the scientist committed to an idea. In all these respects the High Churchmen differ fundamentally from the Methodists who would deny these points or give them a different emphasis.

Many of these elements of a High Church approach were already contained in the work of Ludwik Fleck, first published in 1935, which, according to his own admission, exerted later a strong influence on Thomas Kuhn (1964, p. ix). Fleck's approach was specifically intended to serve as a riposte to the then reigning Methodism of the Vienna Circle, above all to Rudolf Carnap who is singled out for critical attention. Published at about the same time as Karl Popper's *The Logic of Scientific Discovery,* the work acts as a direct challenge, possibly unbeknown to either author, of the main assumptions of Falsificationism; eventually this fact became known through Kuhn's work. The very title of Fleck's book *Genesis and Development of a Scientific Fact* (1979)—underlining the idea of the historical constitution and social construction of scientific facts—is anathema to the whole Positivist approach which, in line with its progenitor, Empiricism, assumes that facts are there as data to be discovered. Fleck's ideas in this respect anticipate similar later accounts of the constitution of scientific facts found in Ravetz and other authors, who also seem unfamiliar with his work. Fleck questions the Methodist conception of observation and experimentation in science, calling it a 'naive story'; the reason researchers themselves believe it is that 'tradition, education and familiarity have produced a readiness for stylized (that is, directed and restricted) perception and action' (Fleck 1979, 85). Instead he shows how an experiment is a gradually refined and constructed technique, perfected to conform with the requirements of a specific scientific approach, its methods and the kinds of problems that can arise in terms of its discourse, or what Fleck calls its thought style. Outside such a context, the experimental results obtained would be meaningless or indicate something quite different. Hence there can be no question of constructing theories as inductive generalizations out of empirical data, verifying or falsifying hypotheses in this way, or of making observations without assumptions—'there is no "firm ground of facts"' (ibid. 92). Rather, 'all empirical discovery can therefore be construed as a supplement, development, or transformation of the thought style' (ibid.). Hence, finally, Fleck urges Carnap and his colleagues to 'renounce the concept of "unified science"' (ibid. 177).

The main problems with Fleck's account arise from the fact that he treats science as if it were like art. His key term, 'Denkstil', is modelled on an art term like 'Jugendstil'; and his other terms, such as 'Denklinien', 'kollektive Vorstellungen' and 'kollektive Gebilde', also have aesthetic origins. He continually draws analogies between style in art and in science, as when he states 'an artistic painting also exhibits its own constraining style' just as science does (ibid. 101). He even interprets truth in terms of style, stating that where there is 'only one solution to any given problem conformed to that style [then] such a stylized solution, and there is always only one, is called truth' (ibid. 100). His distinction between the esoteric and exoteric circles of science is much like that between connoisseurs and the general public of art lovers. He speaks of the 'vanguard, the group of research scientists working practically on a given problem' (ibid. 124) much as one might have spoken of an artistic avant garde in the 1930s.

Fleck's approach tends to obfuscate the fundamental divergencies in content, procedure and social form between art and science. Art is much more a matter of individual creation than is science. At least in the modern period, it can be loosely said that there are as many distinct styles of art as there are great artists, each fashioning an individual style. But this can never be said of science; each scientist is much more compelled by the apparent inexorable unfolding of the discourse, technique and procedure of a particular science as it is institutionally and socially guided. These constrictions explain why simultaneous discoveries are so common in science as to be considered the norm; thus one can usually safely surmise that if one scientist did not make the given discovery it would almost inevitably have been made by another—which is why there is usually a race for the next discovery. By contrast artistic repetition occurs rarely, and when it does it is most likely a matter of conscious imitation or plagiarism. This is not to deny the existence in art of firm and long-lasting stylistic traditions but merely to insist that the individual artist relates differently to these traditions than a scientist does to the paradigmatic procedures and methods of a science. An artist can utilize different traditional styles in different works or combine elements from them in one work. In science what Fleck calls 'the individual's belonging to several thought communities and acting as a vehicle for the inter-collective communication of thought' (ibid. 110) is very rare. The fact that, as Fleck himself admits, 'the conflict between closely allied thought styles makes their coexistence within the individual impossible' is more than just a psychological fact, and it cannot be overcome by the 'creation of a special style on the borderline of the field' (ibid.), as it could in art. Rather, this fact points to the quasi-logical exclusiveness of what Kuhn was later to call paradigms in science. Paradigms are in these respects 'incommensurable' not just for psychological reasons alone.

In his introduction to the translation of Fleck's book, Kuhn raises difficulties with Fleck's basic sociological terms the 'thought collective'. Fleck resorts to the then current psychology of crowds and of group mind to account for how a thought collective imposes its thought style on the individuals constituting it and how this imposition in turn shapes their perception of reality in a Gestalt sense and literally constitutes the objects they see: 'a collective produces the "real image" in exactly the same way as the feverish mood produces an hallucination' (ibid. 180). This account has obvious and dangerous irrationalist connotations, which are also present in Kuhn's work. It seems the wrong way to explain the social compulsion of scientific thought and the reality constitutive effect that this produces. A better way would have been to develop much more comprehensively the political metaphor to which Fleck alludes without taking it fully seriously. He avails himself of the mass-elite distinction elaborated for political parties by Michels and Pareto and seeks to apply it to science. This approach is clearly far too simple for the full complexities of the organizational 'politics' of science. Nevertheless, as the following quotation reveals, he also has a much better insight into what has to be accounted for in a proper exposition of scientific politics:

A vademecum is built up from individual contributions through selection and orderly arrangement like a mosaic from many colored stones. The plan according to which selection and arrangement are made will then provide the guidelines for future research. It governs the decision on what counts as a basic concept, what methods should be accepted, which research directions appear most promising, which scientists should be selected for promising positions and which should simply be consigned to oblivion. Such a plan originates through esoteric communication of thought—during discussion among experts, through mutual agreement and mutual misunderstanding, through mutual concessions and mutual incitement to obstinacy. When two ideas conflict with each other, all the forces of demagogy are activated. And it is almost always a third idea that emerges triumphant: one woven from exoteric, alien-collective, and controversial strands (ibid. 119–20).

Fleck momentarily senses but cannot explain how all these negotiations take place. He speaks vaguely of 'the plan' but does not show how it is arrived at, struggled for or altered. What are the specific political inter-actions that govern all the different steps in the articulation of this so-called 'plan'? Fleck cannot answer for he does not possess a theory of scientific authority.

The much better known Polanyi, the most renowned High Church conservative, develops precisely such a necessary theory of scientific au-thority. But he, in turn, cannot conceive how a struggle for authority takes place and how this determines 'the plan' according to which a science is to proceed. In a piece entitled 'The Republic of Science', Polanyi insists on the necessity for authority in science:

> The existence of this paramount authority, fostering, controlling and protecting the pursuit of free scientific inquiry, contradicts the generally accepted opinion that modern science is founded on a total rejection of authority. . . . The more widely the republic of science extends over the globe, the more numerous become its members in each country, and the greater the material resources at its command, the more there clearly emerges the need for a strong and effective scientific authority to reign over this republic (Polanyi 1969, 65).

Polanyi puts forward both a political and an economic model of science: 'the community of scientists is organised in a way which resembles certain features of a body politic and works according to economic principles similar to those by which the production of material goods is regulated' (ibid. 49).

Unfortunately, Polanyi has a thoroughgoing old-fashioned Liberal con-ception of politics and economics: his politics is that of the night-watchman State and his economics that of the laissez-faire marketplace. Thus authority in science is founded on consensus, and consensus is based on opinion or the mutual agreement of scientists concerning each other's work. Agree-ment in opinion is produced through a process of mutual supervision such that each scientist oversees the quality of the work of those scientists adjoining his or her own field of expertise; and they in turn assess and certify the scientist's work and that of others in close propinquity. In this way, according to Polanyi, through a series of overlapping neighbourhoods, a common public opinion in scientific matters is secured throughout the whole length and breadth of the field of science. Consensus is established through this agreement in opinion, and on this consensus authority can be exercised. 'Scientific opinion is an opinion not held by any single human mind, but one which, split into thousands of fragments, is held by a multitude of individuals, each of whom endorses the others' opinion at second hand, by relying on the consensual chains which link him to all others through a sequence of overlapping neighbourhoods' (ibid. 56).

Polanyi is aware of the fact that the opinion of some scientists carries much more weight than that of others, but he makes light of it, insisting that ultimately 'once the novice has reached the grade of an independent scientist, there is no longer any superior above him' (ibid.). Hence 'the authority of scientific opinion remains essentially mutual; it is established between scientists, not above them' (ibid.). This highly idealized situation is hardly ever encountered in the present-day multiversity–research institute complex. A scientist is not free of superiors once he or she has graduated to independent status. And the opinion of scientists is not mutual given the prevailing strong disagreements and the wide differentials of authority and power by which some scientists can impose their opinions on others in the practical respects that matter. This becomes patently obvious if one merely considers the function of authority in science which Polanyi himself outlines:

> how great and varied are the powers exercized by this authority. Appointments to positions in universities and elsewhere, which offer opportunity for independent research, are filled in accordance with the appreciation of candidates by scientific opinion. Referees reporting on papers submitted to journals are charged with keeping out contributions which current scientific opinion condemns as unsound, and scientific opinion is in control, once more, over the issue of textbooks, as it can make or mar their influence through reviews in scientific journals (ibid.).

The view that the opinion of all independent scientists counts equally in all these matters or that there is some kind of consensus in these respects is totally unreal. Even more unreal is Polanyi's view that 'the uniformity of scientific standards throughout science makes possible the comparison between the value of discoveries in fields as different as astronomy and medicine' thereby enabling 'the rational distribution of efforts and material resources throughout the various branches of science' (ibid. 57). If this were so then why is there a constant and continual competition and battle for funds between sciences? And do those sciences that lose out invariably deserve to do so and are their complaints really unjustified? Polanyi has clearly not taken into account the real academic politics that determines the status of competing sciences and the subsequent allocation of funds. Nor has he developed a realistic picture of the exercise of authority in appointments, journal policies and practices, the handling of competitors and the supervision of textbooks. Fleck's account is much more realistic in all these respects even though it predates Polanyi's by many decades and does not have the benefit of hindsight in the subsequent post-war developments which make these things even more obvious.

Polanyi's republic of science is an utopian vision of an idealized liberal democracy based on a free-market economy of competing individuals. It is a picture of scientific politics explicitly designed to counter creeping 'socialism' in science or any attempt to control and direct science from a centralized agency. He sets himself against all science policy measures to allocate funds and guide research whether these are Marxist-inspired attempts at science planning or merely the dirigisme arising from the need to make science more useful. All such measures to restrict the free-market competition of scientific ideas are seen by Polanyi as counterproductive for scientific advance. He insists that 'a central authority cannot effectively improve on the spontaneous emergence of growing points in science' (ibid. 62). Where science does develop and advance it will be in spite of rather than because of such attempts to direct it. He is therefore relieved that at least in Britain 'the movements for guiding science towards a more direct service of the public interest, as well as for co-ordinating the pursuit of science more effectively from a centre, have all petered out' (ibid. 63). The presumed failure of 'socialist' planning in science is at one for Polanyi with the apparent failure of socialism or state direction in general. The role of scientific authority, like that of the night-watchman State, is to prevent restrictions or obstacles to the perfect marked competition between individuals. It can rationally distribute grants for the pursuit of research by following the dictates of current scientific opinion. And so long as it does so, 'by giving preference to the most promising scientists and subjects, the distribution of grants will automatically yield the maximum advantage for the advancement of science as a whole' (ibid. 57). The market automatically adjusts itself to produce the optimal results in science as in business.

There is clearly some plausibility to this liberal free-market model of science when applied historically to Classical science in the nineteenth century German university system or in the contemporaneous British scientific associations. At that time scientists could compete as free entrepreneurs in the market-place of scientific ideas. But under contemporary conditions of Big Science and the merging of science and technology little of the model is any longer real. Indeed, the attempt to apply such an idealized model to contemporary conditions can serve as an ideological covering protecting the scientific Establishment from outside criticism. Not to interfere with science, to leave it to scientific opinion and consensus to settle all issues is tantamount to allowing the Establishment to rule and science to proceed as it has done so far to the detriment of everything else. It has some of the same consequences as not interfering with the market mechanism in economics and can lead to monopolistic and authoritarian results. Polanyi makes it clear that the current authorities of science have the right, and indeed the duty, to eliminate anything that goes against current opinion, even when such opinion is mistaken: 'for scientific opinion may, of course, sometimes be mistaken, and as a result unorthodox work of high originality and merit may be discouraged or altogether suppressed for a time. But these risks have to be taken. Only the discipline imposed by an effective scientific opinion can prevent the adulteration of science by cranks and dabblers' (ibid. 57). Thus in the name of keeping out cranks, critics are also excluded.

Liberal individualism in science, as elsewhere, pursued to its logical conclusion leads to status quo conservatism. Ultimately it leaves no room for differences of opinion, for criticism or for toleration of alternatives. It eventually goes against its own first principles of individual autonomy and the right of each scientist to follow his or her intellectual conscience and vocation. It does not allow that individual freedom has to be institutionally defended by authority in science as elsewhere; Polanyi does not provide a definition of authority which could exercise the tolerance required for individual freedom.

Polanyi bases his approach to science on the individual—on 'personal knowledge', on 'intellectual passions', on 'commitment' and vocation. But at the same time he advocates 'submission to authority' and tradition: 'when I speak of science I acknowledge both its tradition and its organised authority, and I deny that anyone who wholly rejects these can be said to be a scientist, or have any proper understanding and appreciation of science' (Polanyi 1958, 164). In principle it is not impossible to reconcile a liberal individualist and a conservative traditionalist outlook, but Polanyi cannot do so because he identifies authority with orthodoxy and tradition with traditionalism. Thus he speaks of 'the authority wielded by scientific orthodoxy' (Polanyi 1964, 55); and to submit to authority is tantamount for him to the surrender of oneself to the 'authority of a personal example as carrier of a tradition', and that means submitting to a tradition (Polanyi 1958, 53). He sees tradition in British conservative terms as a matter of precedence in the legal sense and prejudice in the political sense of Burke. But if the scientists have to submit to orthodoxy and traditionalism, what can be left of their personal freedom to pursue their intellectual passion and individual commitment to their visions of the truth?

Polanyi seeks to overcome this contradiction by invoking the paradox of the simultaneous submission to authority and rebellion against it:

> The professional standards of science must impose a framework of discipline and at the same time encourage rebellion against it. They must demand that, in order to be taken seriously, an investigation should largely conform to the currently predominant beliefs about the nature of things, while allowing that in order to be original it may to some extent go against these. Thus, the authority of scientific opinion enforces the teaching of science in general, for the very purpose of fostering their subversion in particular points (Polanyi 1969, 54–5).

Polanyi requires that the scientist be at once a conformist and dissenter. He imagines that by enforcing this paradox he can overcome the deeper problem of the rival claims of subjective belief and objective validation in science. Science is at once a matter of the subjective beliefs of the individual and the objectivity of the shared convictions of a community and its traditions which provide the 'fiduciary framework' for validating the individual beliefs. 'We must now recognise belief once more as the source of all knowledge. Tacit assent and intellectual passions, the sharing of an idiom and of a cultural heritage, affiliation to a like-minded community: such are the impulses which shape our vision of the nature of things on which we rely for our mastery of things' (Polanyi 1958, 266).

Unfortunately, this paradox puts the scientist in an impossible position. If the scientist conforms to authority and tradition then he or she cannot follow personal insights and individual intellectual beliefs. If the scientist dissents from authority and tradition then he or she must inevitably provoke the wrath of orthodoxy and traditionalism and be branded a heretic, rebel or crank. The opposed values of conformity and dissent cannot be reconciled in the context of Polanyi's view of authority and tradition. To argue, as Polanyi tries to do, for a mere partial dissent on particulars within a general conformity on principles does not provide an escape mechanism. As Polanyi himself demonstrates through numerous examples drawn from the history of science, mere partial dissent could never amount to real scientific originality. For real originality a comprehensive scientific critique is required such as the ones that Polanyi credits to Copernicus, Kepler and Einstein in physics or Lavoisier, Dalton and van't Hoff in chemistry. But as Polanyi himself shows, such a critique amounts to more than just partial dissent within a general orthodoxy. By rights, according to Polanyi's norms, each of these revolutionary innovators should have been suppressed for going against authority, and all other scientists should have sided with the orthodox opponents of these novel departures. Polanyi himself wants to be on both sides: to lead the revolutionary dissenters and to uphold the right of the orthodox authorities to suppress them. If, as Polanyi states, 'the Ptolemaic and Copernican theories opposed each other for a long time as two virtually complete systems separated by a logical gap' (ibid. 152), then what becomes of the orthodoxy of authority, of tradition, of consensus, of common opinion and of the rest of his conservative assumptions? Polanyi admits that in such a case the two schools of science 'think differently, speak a different language, live in a different world, and at least one of the two schools is excluded to this extent for the time being (whether rightly or wrongly) from the community of science' (ibid. 151). On Polanyi's assumptions of authority and consensus there is no reason why one school should not be permanently, rather than temporarily, excluded and rightly so for it goes against common opinion.

What Polanyi refuses to acknowledge is that there is always a struggle for authority within science, that different authorities are often in irreconcilable conflict and that individuals can oppose authority in the name of other values. He cannot acknowledge this authority struggle because he confuses authority with orthodoxy in the traditionalist way of conservative thinkers. He shuns the view that science is an arena of struggles for authority, preferring instead to believe that there is always a rightful authority, a just consensus and an enlightened common opinion. Thus he is forced to maintain both that 'every great scientific controversy tends therefore to turn into a dispute between the established authorities and a pretender' and that 'these pretenders do not deny the authority of scientific opinion in general, but merely appeal against its authority in a particular detail and seek to modify its teachings in respect of that detail' (ibid. 164). However, the scientific controversies that he discusses show conclusively that every major dispute in science pits one set of authorities against another and that each denies not merely a single detail in the other's general picture, but more like the whole of it. Kuhn's description of paradigm revolutions and the controversies surrounding them bears out this view. Polanyi's conservative conception of authority prevents him from acknowledging this reality and puts him in a contradictory position.

However, his account of scientific controversy did prepare the ground that Kuhn and others were later to occupy. It still constitutes one of the most comprehensive refutations of most varieties of Methodism. Polanyi counters one by one all the main Methodist tenets. The idea of an experimentum crucis, on which Falsificationism is based, is shown to be groundless since every theory has anomalies which it overrules and which do not refute it: 'contradictions to current scientific conceptions are often disposed of by calling them "anomalies"' (ibid. 293). The processes of validation and refutation of theories are shown to be the same as those for their acceptance or rejection, which are themselves continuations of the process of their original discovery. Hence, the Positivist distinction between a context of discovery and a context of justification is untenable: 'any critical verification of a scientific statement requires the same powers for recognising rationality in nature as does the process of scientific discovery, even though it exercises these at a lower level' (ibid. 13). There is no scientific method in the sense of a methodology that can act as a decision procedure in science separating the scientific from the non-scientific or the sound from the unsound. Rather, a method in science is context determined and bound to the theories of which it is a part and can be opposed by other methods derived from other theories: 'the rules of scientific procedure which we adopt, and the scientific beliefs and valuations which we hold, are mutually determined' (ibid. 161).

As opposed to Methodism, Polanyi advocates a practical view of science as pursued through the exercise of 'skills and connoisseurship', craft knowledge and the tacit intimations that such a practice requires. Science is as much a matter of knack, intuitive feel, unspoken assumptions and the lore passed on through traditional training, as it is one of intellectual formalizing and theorizing. This is why science is a matter of personal knowledge and not to be reduced to method or routine but acquired and disposed of by each individual scientist as a personal accomplishment.

However, this account of science as a practical craft is subject at a deeper level to two mutually contradictory interpretations: it can be taken at once in a Platonic Realist and in a culturally Relativist manner. This contradiction is analogous at a deeper level to the one diagnosed earlier between conformity and dissent, orthodoxy and rebellion, tradition and innovation. On the one hand, Polanyi adopts a highly traditionalist quasi-metaphysical view that scientific 'truth lies in the achievement of a contact with reality—a contact destined to reveal itself further by an indefinite range of yet unforseen consequences' (ibid. 147). On the other hand, he accounts for scientific disputes in a highly relativistic fashion, speaking of alternative 'conceptual frameworks, by which [each scientist] identifies his facts and within which he conducts his arguments' (ibid. 151). On the Realist assumption, 'the discovery of objective truth in science consists in the apprehension of a rationality which commands our respect and arouses our contemplative admiration; that such discovery, while using the experience of our senses as clues, transcends this experience by embracing the vision of a reality beyond the impressions of our senses, a vision which speaks for itself in guiding us to an ever deeper understanding of reality' (ibid. 5). But on the Relativist assumption, 'antagonists on either side of a great scientific controversy do not accept the same facts as real and significant' (ibid. 240): 'the two sides do not accept the same "facts" and still less the same evidence as evidence. These terms are ambiguous precisely to the extent to which the two opposing opinions differ. For within two different conceptual frameworks the same range of experience takes the shape of different facts and different evidence' (ibid. 167).

These two interpretations are mutually incompatible. On the Relativist view two opposed fundamental theories are 'separated by a logical gap'; that is, they are incommensurable: 'formal operations relying on one framework of interpretation cannot demonstrate a proposition to persons who rely on another framework. Its advocates may not even succeed in getting a hearing from these, since they must first teach them a *new language,* and no one can learn a new language unless he first trusts that it means something' (ibid. 151). It follows that two such frameworks are equally true to the facts and to the available evidence; in that sense they are both equally in contact with empirical reality. Advocates of one framework cannot demonstrate that their theory is true and that their opponent's theory is false. They can only seek to convert them to their point of view: 'the persuasive passion too finds itself facing a logical gap. To the extent to which a discoverer has committed himself to a new vision of reality, he has separated himself from others who still think on the old lines. His persuasive passion spurs him now to cross this gap by converting everyone to his way of seeing things' (ibid. 150). There is no strictly rational or logical way of crossing the 'logical gap'; only 'illumination is then the leap by which the logical gap is crossed' (ibid. 123). Fundamental controversies are not resolvable by purely rational or strictly scientific means:

> We can see, therefore, why scientific controversies never lie altogether within science. For when a new system of thought concerning a whole class of alleged facts is at issue, the question will be whether it should be accepted or rejected in principle, and those who reject it on such comprehensive grounds will inevitably regard it as altogether incompetent and unsound (ibid. 150).

It follows from this relativistic interpretation that one fundamental theory cannot falsify another by being shown to be more rational or more in contact with reality.

But on the Realist interpretation this is precisely what Polanyi wants to argue. He maintains that there is a deeper reality and more profound rationality, according to which one fundamental theory is true and another false. Thus the Copernican system was true and the Ptolemaic system false: 'the Copernican system did not anticipate the discoveries of Kepler and Newton accidentally: it led to them because it was true. In saying this we are using the term "true" to acknowledge the indeterminate veridical quality of Copernicanism' (ibid. 147). By the same token, the Newtonian system was also true—true, that is, for as long as it was not displaced by the Einsteinian system. Polanyi does want to insist that Einstein proved Newton false just as Copernicus proved Ptolemy false: 'Newton's conception of space was far from untestable. Einstein who realized this showed that the Newtonian conception of space was not meaningless but *false*' (ibid. 12). Once this happened, then Einstein's theory became 'inherently rational', 'in contact with reality', standing 'for those peculiar intellectual harmonies which reveal more profoundly and permanently than any sense-experience, the presence of objective truth' (ibid. 16). But presumably before Einstein this description could have been equally well applied to the theory of

Newton, and before Copernicus of Ptolemy. And after Einstein, when a new fundamental theory arises, it will no longer be possible to apply it to Einstein either. So where is inherent truth, objective reality, the rational core of science, to be found?

The only way out of this predicament for Polanyi is to argue that each new fundamental theory is a closer approximation to the final truth, the real objectivity, the ultimate rationality. But if that is so, then these absolutes are in themselves unknowable and play no part whatever in the course of science. We do not accept or reject a scientific theory because we can apply to it some absolute standard of objectivity, reality and truth. Rather, once we have accepted it, on whatever sound scientific grounds we do so or—put in Polanyi's relativistic terms—once we have been converted to it, then we can say that it is objective, real and true—at least for the time being till a better theory comes along.

Polanyi fell into all these contradictions largely because he sought to model science on religion, just as Fleck tried to model it on art. Religion is at once a matter of individual faith and subjective commitment and also of dogma, communal authority and orthodoxy. Religion is a culturally varied social form and—for the believer—a set of infallible doctrines that represent and reveal a supernatural objective reality. Cultural Relativism and Platonic Realism can both be maintained of religion by the believer. Polanyi sought to apply all these attributes to science with the contradictory consequences that we previously criticized. In his case, High Church conservatism in science assumed a literal religious expression.

Kuhn, who followed on Polanyi's ideas in some respects, simply tacitly dispensed with all these features of High Church, neo-Platonic Realism and took over the Relativism of alternative conceptual frameworks which he called 'paradigms'—a grammatical term he derived from Wittgenstein. Wittgenstein's language philosophy provided a new basis for High Church conservative approaches to science, such as were developed by the neo-Wittgensteinians Toulmin, Winch and Hanson as well as Kuhn. Alternative conceptual frameworks could be taken at a more basic level as alternative language games. The relation between such language games and reality was explicated by arguing that each constituted its own 'world' or form of life. Wittgenstein's quasi-Gestaltist approach to perception as a matter of alternating aspects or points of view was invoked to argue that those who subscribe to different language games see reality differently and inhabit a different world of experience. Hanson, in particular, invoked this idea for fundamental scientific theories, holding that the Copernican world-view amounted to seeing the world differently as compared to the Ptolemaic. Similar Gestalt-aspect conceptions of science had already been anticipated by Fleck. Kuhn acquired such ideas from all these sources; he has since been followed and bettered by Feyerabend who carries this idea to the reductio ad absurdum of cultural solipsism. Against this approach it is essential to stress the difference between perception and theoretical interpretation, which is what science is.

Thus the Wittgensteinian approach served to dissolve and eliminate the older conservative Platonic and Realist vestiges still present in thinkers like Polanyi. Wittgenstein had already countered such a Platonist assumption in the interpretation of logic and mathematics as expounded by Frege and Russell. In opposition to it he elaborated almost a sociology of mathematics, one that involved a linguistic and conceptual constructivist interpretation of inference, derivation, deduction, existence, proofs and truth, and he thereby reconceived the meaning of rationality in the strictly logical sciences. He was followed in this by Toulmin in the natural sciences and Winch in the social sciences: the former has sought to develop an evolutionary progressivist view of rationality and science; the latter espouses a cultural relativism of rationality which he links to the Weberian notion of subjective understanding. In this way the neo-Wittgensteinians reconceive the basic terms such as 'reality', 'rationality', 'objectivity' and 'truth', which Polanyi still treated as absolutes and which are purely operationally defined by the mechanist systemists.

Mechanist Systemists

The appearance of Wiener's book *Cybernetics* in 1948 marked the launching of the mechanist research program for it coincided with the appearance of Shannon and Weaver's information theory and von Neumann and Morgenstern's game theory. The mechanist movement took off with remarkable vigour and excessively high hopes and expectations. Most of the exponents of the movement have since learned to temper these with more realistic proposals and to scale down their promises. But at the dawn of the mechanist systemist revolution it seemed bliss to be alive and young and in Cambridge (Mass.). Everything seemed possible and most outstanding problems in science appeared on the verge of solution or at least solvable. Information theory in particular seemed capable of providing a new paradigm for all the sciences, as well as for engineering and planning enterprises; even the arts were not unaffected and music eagerly took up the new terminology. The revelation that the 'secret of life' was really a puzzle of information decoding of the DNA molecule seemed to confirm all these hopes. Something of this new spirit is already apparent in Wiener's book.

Wiener's programmatic pronouncement makes it quite clear that he is launching a general reform movement in the sciences to overcome the problems of excessive specialization and fragmentation of fields with which all sciences are beset:

> science has been increasingly the task of specialists, in fields which show a tendency to grow progressively narrower. . . . Today there are few scholars who can call themselves mathematicians or physicists or biologists without restriction. A man may be a topologist or an acoustician or a coleopterist. He will be filled with the jargon of his field, and know all its literature and all its ramifications, but, more frequently than not, he will regard the next subject as something belonging to his colleague three doors down the corridor, and will consider any interest in it on his own part as an unwarrantable breach of privacy (Wiener 1965, 2).

More seriously still, as a result of such self-enclosed specialization, new areas of knowledge might be opened up by several specialized disciplines each unaware of what the others are doing. The outcome is a tangle of terms, concepts, empirical fields and areas of interest overlapping in total confusion. As we have seen, this common pathology of science is still being accepted as if it were the normal course of scientific specialization.

Wiener thought he had found a way of overcoming this. He called for reforms that were at once institutional, cognitive and instrumental. The new technologies developed during the war years would act as the new instruments of a new science. New cognitive paradigms would emerge from the concepts, theories and models required by these instruments, such as cybernetic 'feedback', information theory and computer models. Finally, on the basis of these developments there would arise new institutions of science with reformed authority structures. Insofar as mechanist systemism has succeeded, it has done so in that order of decreasing importance. Extraordinary new technologies have indeed been developed. However, the new cognitive forms have proved much more limited than at first imagined even by critics. New institutions or authority relations have not arisen.

Such were some of the grand visions of the founding mechanist systemists. What has become of them after forty years? In a review article James Fleck (1982) outlines the subsequent history and politics of one wing of this movement, Artificial Intelligence (AI). The very fact that such a specialization exists indicates that a comprehensive cybernetics school as envisaged by Wiener has already broken up into numerous, frequently hostile, specialities. An Artificial Intelligence sub-discipline emerged in the early 1950s on the basis of a new machine then being rapidly improved, the digital computer. This development led to sustained organizing and lobbying at a series of conferences and summer schools to constitute a new disciplinary grouping undertaken by the quartet of McCarthy, Minsky, Simon and Newell, who have ever since remained the eminences in the field. They succeeded in hammering out a general project for research on which they could at least temporarily agree; major differences between them emerged only later. Of equal importance was their success in attracting large funding from the U.S. Department of Defense which saw obvious military potential in the work.

As James Fleck's account makes evident, what had begun as part of a general movement for reform in the sciences was gradually being transformed into just another specialty co-opted into the Establishment and eager to serve the powers that be. Far from Wiener's vision of interdisciplinary institutes of collaborators on joint enterprises, the AI network has constituted its own disciplinary establishment characterized by the typical authority structures. Patronage is its dominant form of authority. Each of the present masters was a student of one of the founders, and subsequently 'this intergenerational establishment reproduction process continued, and students of McCarthy, Minsky, Simon and Newell have dominated the field by and large' (Fleck 1982, 179). Because nearly all research in this field in the United States is concentrated at four major centres— MIT, Princeton, Stanford University and Stanford Research Institute (itself the outcome of funding policies)—talent has been concentrated, giving rise to a small collegial elite made up of the top practitioners. The relatively few formal-professional positions have tended to be monopolized by them as well. Thus an undue concentration of authority has arisen; at the same time, because the field is new and expanding, students who are well positioned can publish and make very decisive contributions, sometimes even before the Ph.D. stage, which is very unusual in science.

In Britain it seemed momentarily in the mid-1960s as if a Wiener-style project would be instituted at Edinburgh. After a late start, then largely due to the entrepreneurial skills of Michie, a surprising confluence of diverse scientific talent occurred; among the many participants were Longuet-Higgins, a theoretical chemist of international repute; Gregory, a psychologist; Salter, a technical inventor; and Meltzer, an electrical engineer. Initially they had strong institutional and funding support from the British scientific Establishment. Nevertheless, within a few years the school was torn by internal dissension; it became externally discredited and broke and dispersed as it was denied further resources. The complex denouement of this drama, as painstakingly reconstructed by James Fleck, reveals the reasons why the cybernetic project as outlined by Wiener and later the AI program failed in their reformist aspirations.

This sad story reveals that the failure was the result at once of academic-political and intellectual reasons in an indivisible and indissoluble amalgam. The failure of any scientific project, especially one which had the potential for redirecting the course of science in certain major respects, is to be explained in exactly the same way as the success of any scientific project which did in fact decisively determine the course of science. The latter kind is not necessarily more rational than the former, which need not be purely contingent or illogical either. The cybernetic project could have succeeded in the way its founders intended; that it did not tells us much about the difficulties of instituting reforms, both because of flaws in the reform movements themselves and because of the inhibiting power of the scientific Establishment in general.

The cybernetic project was flawed internally in both cognitive and academic-political ways. These flaws became quickly apparent at Edinburgh during the course of the basic conflict between Michie and Longuet-Higgins. The former pursued American-style AI research in direct imitation of the way the program was already established in the United States both cognitively and politically; 'he favoured a rather swashbuckling style of directing large team projects oriented to goals which could be linked with industrial applications' (Fleck 1982, 188). Longuet-Higgins, an already successful Oxford scientist, 'favoured a more restrained, academic style, preferred an individual basis of working with a few colleagues on research chosen purely for its intrinsic scientific interest, and was dubious about the advisability of mixing commerce and industry with research'. In other words, there arose a basic contrast between a Big Science and a 'small science' approach, because their whole cognitive orientation was opposed:

> Longuet-Higgins thought that "artificial intelligence" was not a science or technology in its own right, but a new way of tackling problems in those existing sciences which were relevant to the phenomena of intelligence. It set new standards of precision and detail in the formulation of models of cognitive

processes, those models being open to direct and immediate test. Michie's position, on the other hand, was closer to the view " . . . that success in achieving the long-term aims of Machine Intelligence should be regarded as the major goal of Computing Science. Furthermore, progress in Machine Intelligence is continually generating pressures for solutions to fundamental problems of Computing Science in an environment where they will be used" (Fleck 1982, 188).

Thus there were two fundamentally contrasting conceptions of the cybernetics project, and implicitly of science in general, which might be referred to as the American and European models. Under better conditions a synthesis between them might have been possible, but under the constraints of science in Britain it could not be achieved.

In this tense situation of internal dissension, the British scientific Establishment intervened in a characteristically crude political manner in the person of Sir James Lighthill (FRS, Lucasian Professor of Applied Mathematics at Cambridge), an eminent hydrodynamicist, appointed as temporary inspector-general of cybernetics. Such an intervention seemed called for in the British context because of stringencies in the allocation of very limited funds; in America, where there is enough money to go around for everyone, the issue would have been settled by rival schools being established under the auspices of different funding agencies, and it might have made an interesting experiment in diversity. Lighthill's forced entry and his condemnatory report on the whole field—based, as he himself confessed, on a mere two months' survey of the literature by a rank amateur—destroyed the promising Edinburgh initiative, very nearly destroyed the whole field in Britain, and 'delivered a blow to the prestige of research in the area from which it has never fully recovered' (ibid. 192). The heavy hand of the British Establishment blighted what should have been a delicate process of adjustment both political and cognitive and which might have acted as an example for far-reaching reforms in other sciences as well.

This small incident in Britain was a localized instance symptomatic of the general failure of mechanical systemism as a reform movement in science. Its failure is all the more apparent given the excessive hopes and promises held out by the founders of the movement and still reiterated by their followers. In principle it was all possible; in practice it was far from being achievable. The whole Artificial Intelligence program assumed that since in principle all intelligent activities must be reproducible through some computer program, no matter how large; hence in practice it would be an easy matter to model some of the simpler performances.

Invariably between 'in principle possible' and 'in practice achievable' falls the shadow of complexity. Even in modelling a simple and easily formalized activity like playing chess or proving simple theorems, the number of possibilities runs to such astronomic dimensions that no available computers can pursue exhaustively all the steps. The only way of proceeding is to eliminate the number of steps to be taken through programs that contain heuristic rules of procedure; 'the principle of looking for and using certain heuristics, that is, rules of thumb which might help in finding a solution but which would not guarantee a solution, became established' in AI, as James Fleck (1982, 177) points out. The need to invent such heuristic devices made programming an art requiring a practised facility and almost intuitive feel for computers and the masses of numerical material they print out. The almost universal prevalence of 'hacking' among the journeymen of the field made of the art a mere craft —which for some, called 'hackers', becomes compulsively addictive (Weizenbaum 1976, 117). The conservative High Church approach to science, which took the basic craft element to be all-important, was here unwittingly substantiated in a field which began with the opposite logico-mathematical Methodist assumptions. Minsky has pointed out that programmers can no longer keep track of really big programs, for they cannot oversee in detail all the subroutines and their myriads of possible interactions and because frequently such programs are the result of the co-operative labours of a number of programmers: 'when a program grows in power by an evolution of partially understood patches and fixes, the programmer begins to lose track of internal details, loses his ability to predict what will happen, begins to hope instead of know, and watches the results as though the program were an individual whose range of behaviour is uncertain' (Minsky 1967, 121).

Some of the early founding fathers of the field, such as Minsky, have begun to appreciate how the 'in principle' possibilities evaporate and fade into limitless numerical horizons when they begin to be distilled into more palpable 'in practice' actualities. Minsky, who had once in the early years declared that 'the brain is a meat machine', has started to have serious conceptual doubts about what is meant by 'machine' and therefore what machines can and cannot do and how they might differ from brains. After many decades' work in Artificial Intelligence with computer programs, Minsky asks rhetorically: 'Do these programs bring us any closer to understanding how our minds work, or are they too "mechanistic"—too "scientific", whatever that might mean—to give us any fundamental insights? Perhaps what they show is that the closer we get to making machine models of ourselves the less we understand the functioning of the machines' (Bernstein 1982, 121). Minsky has become aware that a mechanist approach to the brain is limited and cannot provide the full answer, for 'even if we had a diagram containing every one of the billions of neurons in the human mind [sic] and the billions of interconnections it would stare at us mutely as the grains of sand in a desert' (ibid. 122).

Minsky had already been preceded in his qualms by critics of the AI program and the early expectations held out for it. The philosopher Dreyfus (1972) has criticized the whole mechanist approach to human intelligence and its mental faculties on the general ground that such capacities are holistic and not to be mechanically broken down into atomistic data. The computer scientist, Weizenbaum (1976, 12), though disagreeing with Dreyfus' argument on the inherent limitations of what a computer can accomplish in modelling intelligence, nevertheless, insists that society must place ethical limits on the mechanist program; otherwise, it risks dehumanizing people. He also maintains that the actual results of over twenty years' work in Artificial Intelligence from any useful point of view have been largely nugatory:

> The achievements of the artificial intelligentsia are mainly triumphs of technique. They have contributed little to either cognitive psychology or to practical problem solving. . . . With few exceptions, there have been no results, from over twenty years of artificial-intelligence research, that have found their way into industry generally or into the computer industry in particular (Weizenbaum 1976, 229).

Lilienfeld (1978) offers an analogous critique of the social science applications of mechanist systemism, such as game theory, operations research, systems analysis, linear programming and information theory. It seems that such highly technified approaches, so promising in theory, have proved counterproductive or useless in practice.

Organicist Systemists

Contemporary organicist systemism is in many respects a direct response to the failures and shortcomings of mechanist systemism. Von Bertalanffy includes the new mechanist sciences as part of his all-embracing systemist movement—which he optimistically sees sweeping the world as a veritable Kuhnian revolution—but he is very critical of the mechanist shortcomings and limitations which, according to him, only organicist systemist sciences can overcome:

> Disappointment of overextended expectations has occurred. Cybernetics, e.g. proved its impact not only in technology but in basic sciences, yielding models for concrete phenomena and bringing teleological phenomena—previously tabooed—into the range of scientifically legitimate problems; but it did not yield an all-embracing explanation or grand "world view", being an extension rather than a replacement of the mechanistic view and machine theory. Information theory, highly developed mathematically, proved disappointing in psychology and sociology. Game theory was hopefully applied to war and politics; but one hardly feels that it has led to an improvement of political decisions and the state of the world; a failure not unexpected when considering how little the powers that be resemble the "rational" players of game theory. Concepts and models of equilibrium, homeostasis, adjustment, etc. are suitable for the maintenance of systems, but inadequate for phenomena of change, differentiation, evolution, negentropy, production of improbable states, creativity, building-up of tensions, self-realization, emergence, etc. (von Bertalanffy 1968, 123).

This comprehensive critique was developed and amplified in the work of the other organicist systemists. Rapoport wrote an article critical of game theory and its pretensions, for as he states, 'in some quarters game theory was hailed as one of the most outstanding scientific achievements of our century'—presumably rivaling relativity theory and other such accomplishments (Buckley 1968, 474).

The organicists treat mechanisms as a lower order of generality. In a table setting out an evolutionary hierarchy of objects and sciences, Boulding distinguishes sharply between the cybernetic level of control mechanisms, which are modelled by theories based on the principles of feedback and information theory and the next higher level of open systems covering self-maintaining structures, the level of life (Buckley 1968, 7). Thereby he affirms an irreducible boundary between mechanist and organicist systems, one that the mechanist systemists deny exists. Von Bertalanffy explains this difference separating the two types of systems in terms of the concept of 'equifinality':

> In a general way, limits of automata will appear if regulation in a system is directed not against one or a limited number of disturbances, but against "arbitrary" disturbances, i.e., an indefinite number of situations that could not possibly have been "foreseen"; this is widely the case in embryonic (e.g. experiments of Driesch) and neural (e.g. experiments of Lashley) regulations. . . . This, as von Neumann himself conceded, seems connected with the "self-restoring" tendencies of organismic as contrasted to technological systems; expressed in more modern terms, with their open-system nature which is not provided even in the abstract model of automaton such as a Turing machine (von Bertalanffy 1968, 26–7).

On this view, the crucial distinction separating the mechanist from the organicist systemists is that between the closed and the open system. This is the previously referred to separation between level (iii), that of the thermostat, and level (iv), that of the cell, in Boulding's evolutionary schema of the hierarchy of systems. It amounts to the basic distinction between machines and living organisms—even though simple open systems, like flames and rivers, are processes at a chemical level that are not organic. As he puts it: 'what is clear, however, is that by the time we have got to systems which both reproduce themselves in the midst of a throughput of material and energy, we have something to which it would be hard to deny the title of "life"' (Buckley 1968, 7). The separations between the other levels (e.g., between clockworks and thermostats, or between lower organisms and animals) do not have the same key role in the schema as that between thermostats and organic cells.

However, there are serious conceptual problems with Boulding's evolutionary systems hierarchy for it lumps together real species with technical inventions and with sciences or conceptual systems. It does not distinguish natural levels, based on tables of elements or the biological evolution of species, from others historically based on the sequence of invention of artifacts, and from those which depend on arranging the sciences in some kind of logical order. In fact, the order of sciences Boulding adopts is analogous to the one already expounded by Comte, except that Boulding places the abstract mathematical and logical sciences last among the symbolic systems rather than first as the basis for all the sciences, as Comte did. Any such arrangement is at least partly arbitrary, for it involves to some extent an evaluative ordering of the sciences. Hence, it differs fundamentally from the evolutionary or developmental stages of natural kinds and also from the historical sequence of inventions. Thus the various levels of systems do not synchronize for each is made up of heterogeneous items derived from natural history, technological history and logical schemas for arranging the sciences. For example, on the first level of the so-called static structures, atoms and molecules certainly come first in the current cosmological theory of the development of the universe, but the sciences dealing with them, say, quantum physics and astrophysics, certainly do not come first either in history or in any logical arrangement of the sciences. The second level, that of clockworks and machines, is based on neither the constitution of matter nor on evolution but rather on handicraft technology which has nothing to do with the sciences with which it is aligned in the schema, namely, physics and chemistry—except perhaps for the metaphor of the clockwork universe ascribed to Newtonian physics, but obviously inapplicable to that of Einstein. It is apparent even from this cursory critique of Boulding that the idea of a system of systems which is at once a universal evolutionary and historical sequence and a unified science system is open to serious objections in that it confuses real objects with artifacts and these with sciences as a result of an undifferentiated use of the term 'system'. This points to some further criticisms of organicist systemism and in particular of General System Theory.

General System Theory is the generalized expression of organicist systemism. It is variously conceived of and presented by different organicist theorists. Sometimes it is thought of simply as a science to be set beside the others, but one of more general scope. Thus von Bertalanffy describes it as follows:

> a logical-mathematical discipline, in itself purely formal but applicable to various empirical sciences. For sciences concerned with "organized wholes", it would be of similar significance to that which probability theory has for sciences concerned with "chance events"; the latter, too, is a formal mathematical discipline which can be applied to most diverse fields, such as thermodynamics, biological and medical experimentation, genetics, life insurance statistics, etc. (von Bertalanffy 1968, 37).

Others see it as a methodology rather than a science in its own right. Thus Mattessich states: 'the systems approach seems to be such a special methodology rather than a new science or superscience. In particular, it is a methodology which grows out of a holistic view, and thus is not bound to a single discipline or limited number of them' (Mattessich 1978, 299). For other system theorists it also figures as a quasi metaphysics which they set in opposition to Positivism. Von Bertalanffy thinks of it as a new Kuhnian paradigm; and Laszlo sees it as a general revolution in all knowledge, a new stage in a grand evolutionary development of civilization: 'the systems view is the emerging contemporary view of organized complexity, one step beyond the Newtonian view of organized simplicity, and two steps beyond the classical world views of divinely ordered imaginatively envisaged complexity' (Laszlo 1972, 15). Von Bertalanffy (1960, 202) clearly concurs with this idea. And Boulding, too, emphasizes the non-scientific directions of the approach: 'General Systems is not so much a body of doctrine as it is a point of view or even an intellectual value orientation' (Gray and Rizzo 1973, 2:951).

The organicists aim for an overall synthesis of sciences under the general direction of General System Theory, and, using this as a basis, to establish an 'integrative education' for scientific 'generalists'. This education would constitute the culmination of a systems movement in the sciences which educationally takes the form of an 'interdisciplinary movement', in Boulding's phrase. Hybrid disciplines like biophysics, biochemistry, and astrophysics and 'interdisciplines' like cybernetics and the other sciences launched by the mechanist systemists are seen as the beginnings of a general trend towards the integration of the sciences to be carried through by General System Theory. Von Bertalanffy seeks to go even further and to promote 'a unitary conception of the world . . . based on the isomorphy of laws in different fields' as the grounding of a new education:

> the educational demands of training "Scientific Generalists" and of developing interdisciplinary "basic principles" are precisely those general system theory tries to fill. They are not a mere program or a pious wish since, as we tried to show, such a theoretical structure is already in the process of development. In this sense, general system theory seems to be an important headway towards interdisciplinary synthesis and integrated education (von Bertalanffy 1968, 51).

In this way the organicist systemists sought to overcome what Boulding saw as 'the crisis of science' and which von Bertalanffy interpreted even more ominously as the decline of European civilization in Spengler's sense. To do so they did not rely on persuasive argument alone but organized themselves politically, forming a Society for General Systems Research, to campaign within scientific Establishment circles for the new movement. They saw themselves as an internal movement of reform in science and as the spearhead of a more general intellectual and cultural reformation. What has been the fate of this promising movement in the thirty years or more since it was first launched?

The organicist systemists were defeated in the academic-political arena. The scientific Establishment never bothered much with arguing out the cognitive rights or wrongs of General System Theory. There was little debate on the scientific merits of the approach; few scientists of any standing took the trouble to refute it. To this day there exist only a few isolated critical works on the issue, and most of the available texts are by non-scientists or marginal scientists. The main refutation took place by deed rather than word. The Establishment succeeded in confining the members of the organicist systems movement to the dimensions of a small scientific sect given a restricted and out-of-the-way niche in very large scientific congresses and no more. As Barry Commoner comments:

> The question of differences in approach such as atomism and holism is ludicrously [sic] important, and yet there is a total lack of concern about this kind of question among practicing biochemists and molecular biologists— it is really a peculiar sort of cultural situation: the rigidity of the establishment extends to censorship, condemnation, inhibiting grants and so on. There's a

vast cultural superstructure here and I think it's important to keep it in mind (Goodell 1977, 67).

Of even greater importance was the fact that institutional presence was denied General System Theory. No departments were established to provide a training base in the universities. The special institutes or centres of systems research first established could not maintain themselves for long. The organicist systemists have fared far worse than the mechanist systemists, who have gained research institutes and even whole departments and whose economistic and administrative extensions, such as operations research, linear programming and systems analysis, have increasingly been resorted to by policy makers at all levels. But these gains have been won at the cost of forfeiting their reformist zeal, not criticizing the Establishment and faithfully serving their military paymasters. It is possible, however, that eventually organicist systemism will have greater success through the conservationist radicals and their publicly espoused ecological programs. These carry greater academic-political weight than the mere ideas of the systems theorists. Thus indirectly some of their educational interdisciplinary proposals might be achieved in a limited way in ecology, for 'such studies require many persons with diverse skills and interests, such as aquatic chemists, experts on different groups of plants and animals and modelers, working together toward a common goal' (*Outlook for Science and Technology* 1982, 212). However, for this to happen organicist systemism might have to be adapted and possibly made less doctrinaire to suit the interests of the conservationists.

The academic-political failure of organicist systemism and the paucity of serious criticism of it must not be taken as an indication that there are no cognitive shortcomings in the approach. The organicist systemists have not shown themselves overly self-critical or willing to subject their theories to correction and modification. Thus von Bertalanffy perfunctorily lists a few standard objections without any indication of their source or what is behind them and just as summarily dismisses them. To the potentially serious objection that 'if so-called isomorphic laws of growth occur in entirely different processes, it has no more significance than the fact that elementary arithmetic is applicable to all countable objects, that 2 plus 2 make 4, irrespective of whether the counted objects are apples, atoms or galaxies', he retorts as follows:

> Not just in the example quoted by way of simple illustration, but in the development of system theory, the question is not the application of well-known mathematical expressions. Rather, problems are posed that are novel and partly far from solution. . . . Here those problems arise which are circumscribed by such notions as wholeness, organization and the like, and which demand new ways of mathematical thinking (von Bertalanffy 1968, 35).

But the reply misses the real point of the objection, which is not that the isomorphisms discovered in different realms are so simple as to be trivial but that the discovery of mere isomorphisms, no matter how complicated or counter-intuitive, is in itself not sufficient to explain anything for it might simply constitute an interesting curiosity. Laszlo, who also maintains that 'general system theory is the attempt to formulate a set of concepts, mathematical, cybernetic, information, game, decision or network-theoretical, or even philosophical in nature, through which the significantly recurring regularities of phenomena in diverse realms of investigation could be exhibited as isomorphisms at the level of basic invariance', attempts to meet this objection as follows:

> The attempt is not trivial in that quantitatively exact formulations can be shown to apply equally to phenomenally divergent entities, and it is not reductionist in that qualitative differentiation is allowed for the (non-metaphysical) emergence of qualities associated with different levels of complexity and with different transformations of a basic invariance. (E.g. homeostasis as well as religious conservatism exhibit structural uniformities due to operating by means of negative feedback controlled by a set of historically evolved norms, although the qualitatively phenomenal aspects are entirely different) (Gray and Rizzo 1973, 1:147).

But the instance he gives to illustrate his point seems to have been maladroitly chosen, for what interest can it be to either the engineer or the sociologist of religion to be told that some vague and ill-defined notion of negative feedback applies to both thermostats and religious traditions? Can an adequate concept of negative feedback applicable to such diverse realms ever be properly defined? All the difficulties in treating mechanical and meaningful phenomena as alike stand in the way of this. The point cannot be taken as an accidental slip on Laszlo's part since the systematic confusion of organisms and organizations has become a trademark of the organicist systemist approach to the social sciences extolled and practiced by von Bertalanffy and Boulding. Von Bertalanffy (1968, 47) declares that 'characteristics of organization, whether of living organism or a society, are notions like those of wholeness, growth, differentiation, hierarchical order, dominance, control, competition, etc.' But, one can ask, to take the last term first, does competition between two people mean the same as competition between two species or competition between two organs in a body or between two cells? Is a concept of 'competition' definable which holds for all of these alike, or is it rather suggestive of vague analogies and no more? It is difficult to see how organizations in which each individual can potentially play a totally unpredictable role in changing the whole are really structurally isomorphic to organisms in which each cell has its own fixed function.

When faced with the objection that notions like wholeness, growth or equifinality are really too general and abstract to afford a basis for scientific explanation, von Bertalanffy (1968, 36) can only retort that 'in complex and theoretically little-developed fields we have to be satisfied with what the economist Hayek has justly termed "explanation in principle"'. As we have seen, the mechanist systemists also resort to such explanations in principle, believing that all complex and theoretically little-developed fields can be reduced to computations which in practice prove to be nearly unending. It seems, therefore, that there are corresponding opposite and inverse difficulties in the handling of such complexities by the mechanist and the organicist systemists alike: the former wish to reduce complexities to denumerable elements which in practice cannot be computed; the latter to sublimate them into highly general notions which in practice cannot be refuted. Science must find a more heuristically useful way of dealing with complexities, one that lies between these two extremes. It must seek to discover the specific configurations of complex wholes that are neither holistic generalities nor programmes that are never complete. This is not to deny that both of these extreme approaches might prove useful as initial complementary approximations. One might begin to handle systems or complex 'objects' by first trying to build computer models of the available data elicited and simultaneously by searching for general structural isomorphisms between these and other objects which are perhaps better understood. By approaching given 'objects' from both these extreme ends one might get a better sense of their complexity and the difficulty involved in grasping their unique conformations. Ultimately an adequate scientific explanation will arise only when a theory evolves capable of accounting for the specific forms and principles required by the 'object' in question.

An example of such a convergent approach as an initial approximation is provided by geology before its so-called tectonic revolution. In geology two approaches were proceeding side by side: the more traditional geologists, geographers and oceanographers were amassing literally mountains of data and subjecting them to computer coding and information processing whereas astronomers and physicists were speculating holistically about the fundamental physico-chemical processes involved in the slow changes within the earth. Neither approach would have progressed much further on its own, though each was necessary as a lead-up to the final solution. This solution was only provided by the theory of plate tectonics which postulated a unique and specific configuration of earth processes that was neither a numerical program nor a generalized structural law. Once the plate tectonics theory was substantiated and accepted, both the numerical data and the physico-chemical models fell into place (Laudan 1983, 92). Indeed, as an authoritative source puts it, 'the plate tectonics concept, in providing a logical framework for understanding and linking other earth processes, has helped to unify the earth sciences' (*Science and Technology* 1978, 12). It is interesting to note from an academic-political point of view that this concept had been around for a long time, but to no avail. Its sudden and rapid acceptance and dissemination in the 1960s were more than just a matter of new evidence becoming available.

By analogy, the relation between a mechanist and an organicist systemist approach in other fields could take something of this general form. It is possible that neither will be fully adequate on its own: the former too calculative and entangled in large numbers, the latter too vague and only taking in large wholes. But out of the two general approaches as converging starting points, specific explanations suitable for each given field in question might emerge which will be neither simply the one nor the other but some third way. Such a tertium quid can only be arrived at through insight born of long familiarity with each field in question and the unique difficulties it presents. In Chapter 8, we shall examine a number of fields where work is at present proceeding more or less from these opposite ends and where an appropriate theory might eventually emerge which will be quite surprising and not fit into any such predetermined approaches.

Much more thought will have to be devoted to the refining and redefining of concepts before organicist systemism with its loose panoply of terms can even begin to function adequately as an overall heuristic method. For even at best it is that and no more—a way of helping to elicit substantive and substantial theories which must be more than just mere holistic models. Part of this work will require modifying General System Theory so that it will be proof against criticisms. Some of these criticisms can already be easily met; for example, the philosophically inspired attack by Phillips can be shown to be largely irrelevant. Much of it consists in demonstrating that General System Theory derives historically from Idealist and Vitalist sources which are unsavoury to anyone positivistically-minded. Phillips then goes on to try to show that the approach is still tainted by its origins and that 'all modern organicism is, in a sense, no more than the Hegelian theory of internal relations writ large' (Phillips 1976, 20). A set of five theses dubbed Holism I—including such quasi-philosophical laws as that 'the whole is more than the sum of its parts'—are then indiscriminately foisted on both the old and the new approaches and the claim is made that 'system theory is actually another form of Holism I' (ibid. 46). The fact that system theory has developed new concepts and principles of its own which are far removed from such philosophical inanities as contained in Holism I is hardly taken note of by Phillips. He contents himself with reiterating as knock-down objections what were first spelled out by Stafford Beer (1961) as problems of which system theory must be mindful, not as insurmountable obstacles. The difficulties of distinguishing system from environment, of specifying those elements that constitute a system as against those that are irrelevant, of determining the place of a given system in a hierarchy of subsystems and supersystems—all these are well-known problems to which system theorists have addressed themselves, not without some success. Phillips' final ploy is to subject systems theory to the test of Popperian falsificationism without apparently realizing what so many theorists of science, above all Polanyi, had long since demonstrated: that no scientific approach can stand up to that test, but is none the worse for it. Lilienfeld (1978, 256) makes much the same kind of criticism of system theory, asking whether 'any of its propositions can be tested and thereby verified or falsified', and going on to indict it for 'arbitrarily selected problems and areas and arbitrarily selected lines of demarcation' (ibid. 257).

The problems raised by Phillips and Lilienfeld have to be dealt with by continually redefining the methodology of the approach and its concepts. Thus it is becoming recognized that systems are not simply natural or social objects given to us ready-made for scientific investigation; rather they are in some sense theoretical constructs. Organisms or even organizations as specimens ready to hand are in themselves not what is meant by systems in a scientific sense; only theoretically demarcated and selected features of their operations or functions constitute such systems. Thus system theory, like structuralism, is not a simple empirically descriptive science, but a constructivist theorization. Laszlo grants this point when he states that such sciences 'are sophisticated theoretical frameworks which do not pretend to simply describe observable phenomena and to penetrate their essence. Rather, they build models of certain *perspectival* features of phenomena and hold up the models for investigation and comparison' (Gray and Rizzo 1973, 144).

The crucial task is to determine on what basis and by what criteria are such models of systems theoretically constructed. Mattessich, who has explicitly undertaken this task, insists that 'the peculiar feature of the systems approach . . . is the flexibility of forming more or less arbitrary systems for specific purposes without losing sight of the super-system or environment in which the system is embedded' (Mattessich 1978, 300). It is clear from this that the construction of systems in the natural sciences is not unlike that of ideal types, in Weber's sense, in the social sciences. Values inevitably enter the theoretical process because the purposes of the investigation—which determine the goals for which it is carried out and thereby what is of significance and interest to it—act as directives and guidelines for the identification of those elements whose systemic interactions are to be subjected to detailed empirical studies. This is explicitly acknowledged in a recent authoritative study on ecology:

> Because ecologists and systematists often try to understand and predict the characteristics of large systems, they confront a problem faced by all scientists who deal with complex systems having many interacting parts. These separate parts must be grouped, and to form such groups certain relationships must be emphasized while others are deemphasized. The problem is that it is difficult to know if one has made the best groupings. Moreover, the very process of setting up aggregate units channels thinking about problems in subtle but powerful ways. Thus, forming a group such as herbivores emphasizes the sources of food common to those organisms, plants, while deemphasizing such attributes as size, color, behavior, or tolerance to temperature changes. Clearly, the category of herbivore will be useful in discussing flows of energy in ecological communities, but will not be appropriate for many other problems (*Outlook for Science and Technology* 1982, 203–4).

But this is not to argue that systems are 'mental constructs', a view that Weiss seeks to rebut in the wrong way by insisting that 'systems are products of our experience with nature, and not mental constructs, and whoever without being privy to that primary practical experience would try to abrogate them, would do so only by arrogation' (Phillips 1976, 35). To recognise the cognitive constructive character and conceptual definition of systems is not to deny their reality as objects in Nature. Once a system has been theoretically specified it must be locatable in concrete objects and situations by means of experimental tests, field studies or whatever other method is used to substantiate the reality of every scientific 'object'. I shall explore this issue of the constitution of systems and the role that interests and values play in it both in the next section devoted to the conservationists, who are in a way the heirs to the organicist systemists, and in Chapter 8 where I shall examine the application of system theory to some specific ecological problems.

Conservationists

Ecology is the master science for conservationists. In their architectonic of the sciences all others are referred back to ecology, which they see as the science of the relationship between humankind and the total global environment. By now many different branches of the ecological sciences have developed, and diverse methods and approaches are utilised by them. There are differences of scale between them as well, for some study small populations of similar organisms, others communities of different organisms within a controlled environment, others still consider the possible inter-actions between organisms and the general environment or the total eco-system. Some of these studies almost amount to 'pure' science research, either completely theoretical, such as population statistics in genetics, or narrowly empirical with controlled experiments, such as are found in small-pond aquatic ecology; other studies constitute applied and useful science research concerned with achieving desirable ends in the management of natural resources. Most of these ecological studies tend to be systems sciences since they deal with complex wholes involving interactions of numerous elements. Hence they draw ideas, methods and techniques from both the organicist and the mechanist system theorists: the organicists provide general concepts of systemic flow, adjustment, crisis or systems evolution and change; the mechanists provide computer models for dealing with large quantities of field data and population statistics.

However, the popular political upsurge of the conservation movement has had the greatest impact on all the ecological sciences:

> Because ecological knowledge is a key to solving important environmental problems, ecologists found themselves thrust into the political arena. Initially, the expectations of the environmentally concerned public and the hopes of many professionals tended to be unrealistically high. Now a pattern is emerg-ing in which the modest but useful contribution of ecologically related sciences are being appropriately applied to solve environmental problems (*Outlook for Science and Technology* 1982, 204).

The conservationist radicals are continuing to make excessive claims for their master science which it is thus far incapable of meeting. As Max Nicholson noted, 'the opportunities for new discoveries of great dynamic significance both for other branches of science and for human practice' seem enormous; yet ecology has failed to capitalize on them: 'the unfolding of such a science, some believed, would bring with it wisdom, refreshment and a balanced understanding, and would correct the inhuman distortions imposed by the runaway expansion of physics and chemistry, and by the brazen materialist greed of an exploiting civilization. Unhappily, as yet, things have not worked out like that' (Nicholson 1970, 248).

The reasons why things have not worked out like that have much to do with the external and internal academic political environment in which ecology has to find a niche for itself to survive. In the academic ecosystem the status of ecologists in the hierarchy is still very lowly. The power-brokers of the Establishment tend 'to look down upon ecologists, and consequently to deny them resources, opportunities and collaboration [and this] is an attitude which has partly been responsible for the pitiably small current role and contribution of ecology in science and in public affairs' (ibid. 171). As a result of this treatment, 'ecology has bred only a handful of outstanding pathfinders and has tended to settle for a somewhat inef-fective existence dispersed in small institutions and schools each convinced that the others fall below first-rate scientific standards, in which they are often right' (ibid. 248). Thus Nicholson concludes that 'far from breeding a race of benevolent superminds modern ecology has either been content or been compelled to accept a lowly role on the sidelines of biology, which has itself undergone a sad depression of relative status since the great days of Darwin and Huxley' (ibid.). According to Nicholson, the only answer to this situation is for ecologists to initiate a revolution in academic politics; 'redoubled efforts must promptly be made to secure for them the status which the world situation demands, and to ensure that they live up to it' (ibid.). Presumably after this revolution ecology will give rise to 'men and women who are destined to restore unity and coherence to science in its quest for a key to the workings of nature . . . and inspiring and enlightening mankind to throw off the perversions of outlook which mar our relations with the natural environment' (ibid.).

But Nicholson makes clear that before ecology can revolutionize science and the world it must reform itself. Above all it must transform its authority structure to become a 'vigorously expanding science making a series of successive breakthroughs on a basis of imaginative but down-to-earth teamwork' (ibid. 249). At present there is a 'fragmentation and isolation of ecology'. Ecologists are split into small feuding clusters 'who exercise a veto wherever possible on steps leading to its advance, in order that they may comfortably play out time in the more or less cosy ecological niches which they have created for themselves and their intimates' (ibid. 251). As a result they are ill thought of by other scientists; 'their scientific standards and methods, and above all their sectarian divisions into con-flicting or standoffish groupings, have been not unjustly criticized elsewhere in the scientific community' (ibid. 249). Nicholson recommends many changes needed to bring ecology up to scratch with other better established sciences, some of which have since been instituted. There are now 'con-trolled experiments in the field'; ecologists have learned biometrics and methods of analysis and measurement; they have cultivated 'a type of consumer demand for ecology' and have made some studies 'because of the keen interest and stimulating pressure of groups who wanted the answer to some problems' (ibid.). But despite all these recent improvements, ecology still has far to go before it can challenge any of the established sciences; when 'new studies such as molecular biology have rocketed to fame and leadership within a mere decade, ecology can point only to a below average rate of expansion during now over half a century of organized effort' (ibid. 248). The reasons for this, which Nicholson does not give, are not far to seek in the academic-political milieu.

So far, then, the conservationist radicals have failed to develop an overall approach to the reformation of science, as opposed to simply mitigating the effects of science and technology on the environment, despite notable individual contributions to specific aspects such as on alternative technology or on an ecological planetary awareness. To find something approximating a comprehensive view of science within a conservationist ambit we must turn to Ravetz, a writer who is not simply a propagandist for the ecological movement but who aligns himself closely with the project for a 'critical science' as developed by Commoner and his colleagues. As he states, 'it was through reading the work of Professor Barry Commoner and his group at St. Louis that I came to the conception of "critical science", which gives this whole work what unity it has' (Ravetz 1971a, p. x). The main role of critical science is to wage 'struggles for the exposure and correction of practices damaging the environment' and to counter 'the powerful interests which derive profit or convenience from polluting and degrading the environment [which] have more political and economic power than a scattering of "conservationists"' (ibid. 425). From such small and innocuous beginnings, Ravetz sees the possibility of a new radical 'movement of critical science' developing to challenge the present Establishment and what he calls 'industrial science'. However, though the difficulties that he foresees are immense and the process of the reformation of science will be extended and complicated, nevertheless the ultimate upshot might be revolutionary:

> For if the style of critical science, imposed by the very nature of its problems, becomes incorporated into a coherent philosophy of science, it will provide the basis for a transformation of scientific inquiry as deep as that which occurred in early modern Europe. The problems, the methods, and the objects of inquiry of a matured and coherent critical science will be very different from those of academic science or technology as they have developed up to now; and together they can provide a practical foundation for a new conception of humanity in its relation with itself and the rest of nature (Ravetz 1971a, 428–9).

The 'coherent philosophy of science' that Ravetz provides oddly enough owes little to the organicist systemists from whom most other conservationist radicals derive their substantive ideas; it owes more to the High Church conservatives, above all to Polanyi. Following from Polanyi, Ravetz expounds perhaps the most thoroughgoing critique of Methodism in the literature. In opposition to it Ravetz, like Polanyi, emphasizes the craft aspect of scientific practice as well as hostility to the routine planning of science:

> But the attempt to eliminate the element of craft experience and personal wisdom in these judgements and substitute for them a bureaucratic routine would soon produce gross errors of planning from which committed scientists would need to protect their field by clandestine research. For the unknown is full of surprises; and the extent that previous experience is codified and made a rigid base for criteria of value in decision-making, the further penetration into the unknown will be blunted, and eventually reduced to the

routine and the trivial (ibid. 167).

Unlike Polanyi, however, Ravetz follows a radical persuasion in insisting on 'criteria of value in decision-making' of science. According to Ravetz, values are crucial components of scientific methods, both in the external direction of scientific work and in the internal furtherance of theory and research. Ravetz insists that he is 'clearly arguing that complex judgements of value which are in principle highly fallible, condition or even determine the selection of those facts that eventually come to be'—a view reminiscent of Fleck (ibid. 166).

Ravetz's value orientation in science and his main interest is directed towards ethics. He is intent on developing an appropriate ethics of science and maintaining a high morale among scientists. This is very much in keeping with his artisanal, craft-of-science approach. Nevertheless, he does extend this conservative ethical orientation in a more political direction, especially when dealing with his proposed critical science: 'and hence critical science is inevitably and essentially political . . . it is like the politics of the Enlightenment, where a small minority uses reasons, argument, and a mixture of political tactics to arouse a public concern on matters of human welfare' (ibid. 425). This muted political emphasis, made on behalf of a conservationist critical science, also touches on revolutionist critical science as well. It is to the latter that we turn next.

Revolutionists

The most thoroughgoing theory of the politicization of science has been propounded by the revolutionist radicals in successive phases over the last century or so. To begin with, the early Marxists accepted the usual norms of objectivity of Classical science and merely tried to show that the purposes of science and the uses to which it is put can vary depending on political and other evaluative considerations. However, subsequent revolutionist schools in science, by no means all of them Marxist, have tried to show that every aspect of science, including theory formulation, is value determined. Science, they contend, is at every point directed by values, both during the course of research and in the application of the knowledge gained. And the sources of these values they tend to see as political, especially in a contemporary context.

The most decisive recent influence on the revolutionists' cause was Kuhn's *The Structure of Scientific Revolutions* (1964), which gave the term 'revolution' a new political sense in the history of science (Cohen 1985). Kuhn was strongly influenced by Bachelard's notion of epistemological breaks, as well as by cognate ideas derived from Fleck, Polanyi and Wittgenstein. He succeeded in devising a synthesis of all these sources which proved extraordinarily influential. So well is it known that there is hardly any need to expound it in any detail. Its shortcomings, however, are not so well understood. I have already alluded to them in the previous chapters so only a brief mention will suffice. Kuhn has no sense of the problematic character of contemporary science given his own historical paradigm of continual paradigm revolutions ensuring the onward progress of science. This conception of science is derived from the past achievements of Classical science and is on the whole uncritical of present developments. This aspect is reinforced by his picture of normal science as a communal and conformist activity which allows for no disputes and on-going struggles between groups of scientists over what is to be the reigning paradigm. Only a total break-down of the paradigm followed by a revolution is allowed to punctuate the course of normal science. Thus Kuhn's work lends itself to the conservative purposes of the Establishment which is glad to enforce the requirement of conformity to the reigning paradigm for all but the occasional genius who is usually safely dead and long lost in the past.

Following Kuhn's work, but in a more radically revolutionist spirit, are the German finalization theorists. The finalization theorists are renowned for their controversial thesis which has provoked much sharp opposition and even attempts at political suppression (Schäfer 1983, 275), but they also expound a parallel constitution thesis of science. The finalization thesis applies to the further elaboration of scientific theories once these are in a fully mature stage when they are valid, comprehensive and complete, which, by and large, only happens in a post-Classical contemporary setting. By contrast, the constitution thesis applies to the formation of scientific theories and scientific concepts and objects at the origins of scientific development, that is, primarily at the inauguration of Classical science during the Scientific Revolution, though, of course, sciences founded later can also be considered in the same terms. Taken together the constitution thesis and the finalization thesis cover the beginnings and endings of the sciences, their opening and closing stages. They, therefore, are potentially a much better basis for a theory of scientific origin, development and change than that provided by either Ravetz or Kuhn, whose basic models they have considerably refined and extended.

Just as the finalization thesis permits the introduction of a social interest—and under contemporary conditions also of a political direction—within science itself at the level of theory construction, so, too, does the constitution theory at the level of concept and object definition. The objects of science are not simply given in experience, nor can they be constructed through the formal manipulation of what is given empirically, as the positivist constructivists supposed. Objects as they are apprehended pre-scientifically do not lead to science. Science is a social process of cultural reconception whereby the understanding of ordinary objects is recast in accordance with constructed concepts and theories so that they are transformed into the special 'objects' of science to which theoretic properties and quantified relations and laws can be ascribed. Such a redefinition to constitute scientific 'objects' is governed by the constitution of each of the sciences in accordance with its given value predispositions and interests. As Boehme (1979, 114) notes, 'the interest one has in an object may have consequences for its formal properties'. He illustrates this point by reference to the controversy in psychology between Titchener and Baldwin concerning their opposed conceptions of the constitution of the experimental situation, reflecting their differing interests, and 'through the formulation of the experimental rules the different interests become the determinants of the object of scientific inquiry' (ibid. 115). The same point on a vastly enlarged scale holds for the constitution of whole sciences. As van den Daele (1977) argues, the primary definition of the new physical sciences during the Scientific Revolution—which became definitive for the subsequent conception of positive science as such—was carried out under political pressures and compromises with monarchical power; this was necessary in order to separate the new sciences both from the old Aristotelian learning of the universities and from the new threatening radical currents, such as the Paracelsians and puritan Baconians. The constitution theory can be applied at both a micro and a macro level of scientific development.

The combined effect of the finalization thesis and constitution theory is to open up the possibility of radical alternatives in science. Alternatives become counterfactually admissible even retrospectively in the history of science. In accordance with the constitution theory, science could have taken an alternative course at every stage of its development if there had been other requirements placed on it, or if other pressures had asserted themselves, or if other opportunities existed. As we have seen, to some extent one can speculatively entertain such missed opportunities. It becomes more crucial when one becomes aware that the same conditions apply to sciences that are presently being constituted. But of even greater relevance in this respect is the finalization thesis for it shows that the sciences which are finalized can easily develop on alternative courses if their goals and external directives were to be altered. This thesis obviously has great potential as a theory of reformation in science.

Proceeding along these lines, Boehme attempts to define an alternative project of a so-called Good Science which will be the converse of so many of our present 'bad' sciences:

> The idea of realizing the good science . . . finds its support in studies of the epistemology and philosophy of science, such as constitution theory and the finalization in science thesis. They show that how an object is originally thematized, determines the way in which a science develops and that the intended practical applications are the determinants for the advancement of a mature science. If the goals we set ourselves determine the kind of science we have, then science will no longer be usable arbitrarily, for any kind of purpose (Boehme 1979, 121).

Boehme makes it quite clear that such alternatives must be sought within the conceptual bounds of the presently established sciences and not outside them in utopian proposals. 'Alternative science' as advocated by Capra or Feyerabend, the sciences of the counter-culture, such as primitive lore, Eastern mysticisms and even Western eccentricities such as Goethe's theory of colours—in itself a fascinating aesthetic departure—all of these are implicitly abjured by Boehme.

> Evidently, to try to give universal validity to a systematic cognitive venture, even if it is in its own right successful, is useless, if it is not linked to the advancement of modern science. . . . Even if what we hold to be science is viewed as the product of an historical and often violent process of demar-

cation the question concerning alternatives, motivated by critique of this science, must ask for alternatives within science (ibid. 112).

The lesson is clear: reactionary trends must be avoided if one wishes to be radical in science—a lesson driven home by van den Daele and Schäfer (1983, 217).

It follows from this, too, that a Good Science of the future will not be attained simply by changing the political directives of science. A changed politics will not necessarily produce a changed science—despite the suggestiveness of the finalization thesis for those who want to revolutionise science by political means alone. Simple-minded Marxism to the contrary, science in a socialist society need not be any different from science under capitalism. To effect a real reformation of science will require much more than politics, though that can help in furthering other necessary changes. Such a reformation is more like a cultural revolution, which can never be politically willed, than a political revolution. And as in any large-scale cultural transformation, intensive ferment and critical debate will be required to chart the way ahead. All the movements of reform we have discussed will need to participate.

In summary, it is necessary to stress that the exposition and critique of the various movements of reform in science which I have presented in this chapter are not intended to disparage or dismiss any of them. On the contrary, it is only designed to expose them so as to eliminate their weaknesses and biases and ensure that what remains will be stronger for having been tempered in the critical fire. It should serve as an initiating example of the kind of debate and dialectical confrontation in which these movements ought to be engaging. For each of the major reform movements sees the problems of science differently and each has different solutions to offer. These differences seem at present irreconcilable. In fact, the reformers are as much engaged in denouncing each other as in opposing the Establishment. In this respect they are not unlike the religious reformers during the Reformation who were also intent on their own battles even while fighting the Church. Yet even there, some consensus on reform between some of them was achieved, usually after lengthy disputations and conciliar compromises. Our present scientific reformers will need to engage in similar exchanges in order to arrive at some, even if only partial, agreements on reform. For such exchanges to begin, their differences must be exposed and confronted. We have made a start towards this.

As we have seen, the scientific reformers differ in both their diagnosis and their cure of what they take to be the pathologies of science. The scientific conservatives—the High Churchmen even more than the Methodists—are most opposed to the planned, directed and routinized research procedures of Big Science and its technological applications. They propose to counter this by a return to 'small science', that is, to the norms of the older Classical science with its emphasis on pure research, following its own autonomous knowledge goals and pursued by individuals with a true vocational calling. The systemists of both factions, mechanist and organicist alike, are most disturbed by the excessive specialization and narrowing of the current disciplinary regime which make it impossible for one science to relate to another or for scientists to communicate and which leads to duplication of work, confusion in what has been discovered, trivialization of findings and loss of any sense of the whole endeavour. To overcome these problems they propose to launch an 'interdisciplinary synthesis and an integrated education', in von Bertalanffy's words, echoed also by Wiener. To this end they developed general sciences spanning numerous disciplines such as cybernetics, information theory and General System Theory and laid plans for integrated scientific schools in which to educate and employ new generalists who would arise in opposition to the present specialists. The scientific radicals, both the Greens and Reds, are most disturbed by the present uses of science in exploitative industry which degrades the environment and in the military-industrial complex which threatens humankind itself with destruction. In opposition to this 'bad science' they advocate one version or another of a Good Science, a science firmly embedded in the right values—a marriage of the true and the good—directed and controlled by higher purposes and so serving the real needs of humanity and the natural environment. If these, then, are the differing approaches of the scientific reformers, are they in any way reconcilable? And how can even a partial consensus be established?

In Chapter 8 I shall show how amidst the clamour and confusion of the struggles and controversies of present science one might catch a darkling glimpse of the outlines of a possible future science. But these potentialities that we can even now discern for alternative developments of science need not necessarily win out and might not come to anything. The future course of science is never preordained. What will eventuate will depend on the outcome of present struggles, and these need not necessarily be in favour of the reform movements.

8
On the Way to Future Science

What is scientifically possible is determined by science, not by reflection on science. It appears that the only method of proving that an alternative science is possible is actually to make it.

—van den Daele (1977)

Science does not stand still. Novel developments continue even though the old view of unilinear, cumulative progress, based largely on the Classical sciences, no longer holds true for the present stage of science. Science does not develop along one course or in one progressive direction; at all times different lines of research in any one field proceed side by side. At present in most of the dominant fields few detours or alternative paths are being taken, the main way is the technology-directed, super-highway of World science, constructed and policed by the academic Establishment. But there are by-ways—frequently in the minor fields, some no better than single tracks hacked out by intrepid adventurers—which promise a more interesting journey than that along the speedway of fast-moving break-throughs heading for eventual break-down. Among these we might find new departures in science which satisfy our requirements for reform and hold out the promise of a new future science.

Thus far I have considered those movements of reform in science which set out general programs relatively remote from on-going scientific research. In general the mechanist and organicist systemists tend to be engaged in actual research work, the Methodists to be further removed from it than the High Church conservatives, and the conservationists to be much closer than the revolutionist radicals, who are perhaps furthest from it. But some kinds of research work more or less fit into each of these movements; some even constitute new departures in science. Scientists carrying out these researches often do not consciously adhere to any general reform scheme and may be averse to associating with such a program. Nevertheless, their work might still be placed within the ambits of the reform movements. And furthermore the practical examples of new scientific departures provided by this work indicate—more clearly than the pronouncements of propagandistic exponents of reform—how a consensus on reform might be reached. This suggests that the consensus so far unattainable in theory may yet be found in practice.

To relate such new departures to the main course of science we need to place them in context and to distinguish them both from the previous Classical sciences and from the contemporary normal World sciences, as well as these from each other. As shown in Chapter 1, the Classical regime in science was dedicated to the discovery of law and order in Nature. It sought the simplest and clearest regularities within the welter of natural relations and represented them in the basic languages of mathematics, tabular categorizations and regular sequences. To do so it had to abstract from all the complexities of objects those few simple parameters that could lend themselves to lawlike description. Classical science, as much as any other science, chose what features of reality to emphasize, but it took itself to be the only possible science because its philosophical interpreters regarded the features it selected as the only real constituents of things and therefore as rationally determined. All else was treated as non-rational, disorderly, subjective, accidental and thus not worthy of scientific study. The Classical scientific program was thus inherently reductive. Through a restrictive method of simplification and abstraction complex objects were reduced to simple elements or models of such elements which could be related in an orderly and law-like way. These elements would be further reduced to more basic ones as the various separately discovered laws were unified and the more general theories integrating different fields were devised.

Classical scientific method maintained that reduction or analysis would in theory be complemented by synthesis: the complex object which was broken down to its simplest elements would be reconstructed again out of these elements. Analysis and synthesis, or reduction and integration, would together function to provide the complete explanation of any object of science. However, scientists soon found that reduction, though reversible in principle, was not so in practice; it is not possible to deduce a complex object from the simple elements and laws to which it is reducible. Thus the Classical science approach is unidirectional and, therefore, incomplete: it moves down from complexity to simplicity, but it cannot reverse itself and return from simplicity to complexity. For this reversal a different kind of approach is required, which might be called the Integrative method. Integrative problems have come to the fore in many current sciences, and scientists have become aware that these cannot be tackled with the old reductive methods.

The 'normal' World sciences, those characterized by a high level of technification, formalization, abstraction, problem-solving and finalization, are also frequently incapable of dealing with issues of integration of any complexity. Thus, for example, conventional molecular biology is highly successful in genetic engineering on prokaryotes but relatively unsuccessful in dealing with problems of development in eukaryotes. For the latter, new integrative departures are called for which to a greater or lesser degree distinguish themselves from the main trends of World science and point to future science. These new scientific departures aim at integration on both the level of the object being investigated and that of the sciences doing the investigation. The two levels are in fact one, for to provide an integrative theory able to explain a complex object requires integrating a number of sciences which approach the object from complementary points of view. Prigogine makes this double character of integration evident when he asserts that to seek for the unity of time, the prime object of his scientific investigations, is at the same time to seek for the unity of the physical sciences that deal with time: 'Have we reached some unity of knowledge or is science broken into various parts based on contradictory premises? Such questions will lead us to a deeper understanding of the role of time. The problems of the unity of science and of time are so intimately connected that we cannot treat one without the other' (Prigogine 1980, 14). In what follows I shall pursue this integrative effort, beginning with Prigogine's work, which best exemplifies the organicist systemist approach, and then go on to outline a number of other researches currently being carried out, each of which fits approximately one of the scientific reform movements previously outlined.

Organicist Departures

Prigogine takes as his point of departure the tripartite division of the evolution of science postulated by the organicist systemists: the Classical sciences of organized simplicity, the thermodynamic sciences of disorganized complexity, and the systems sciences of organized complexity. However, he goes an important step further than these purely analytic distinctions; he argues that each of these sciences entails a different time order and furthermore that these time orders seem prima facie to be in contradiction with each other. The time of Classical physics, including relativity and quantum theory, is one of reversible dynamic paths; the time of thermodynamic processes is irreversible and tends towards entropy or devolution; and finally, the time of organized systems, especially biological ones, is an irreversible time of evolution. These concepts of time seem on the face of it incompatible. And yet they must be compatible since they all apply to the same phenomena.

> In the classical view, the second law expressed the increase of molecular disorder; as expressed by Boltzmann, thermodynamic equilibrium corresponds to the state of maximum "probability". However, in biology and sociology, the basic meaning of evolution was just the opposite, describing instead transformations to higher levels of complexity. How can we relate these various meanings of time—time as motion, as in dynamics; time related to irreversibility, as in thermodynamics; time as history, as in biology and sociology? (Prigogine 1980, 14).

This is the basic question Prigogine poses for future science. He sets about answering it by locating what it is in nature that makes for the various kinds of irreversibility—that is, for time. And he believes this search can be carried out at a fundamental level of nature, that 'we can go beyond the macroscopic level, and discover the microscopic meaning of irreversibility' (Prigogine and Stengers 1984, 289). This approach might be the way to locate the source of irreversibility at the higher macroscopic levels of chemistry and biology and furthermore to account for the fact that some systems at these levels tend towards spontaneous organization and evolution towards complexity, rather than thermodynamic devolution towards disorder and thermal equilibrium. Ultimately, he even aims to account for irreversibility at the highest levels, those of social systems and historical development. If these various modes of irreversibility can be related to each other and made compatible, a new system of sciences will have arisen, one based on an integration of ever higher levels of description, the very converse of the reductivist tendency of the Classical sciences towards lower levels of description. The old unity of the sciences based on reduction will give way to a new unity based on integration. As he puts it in his joint work with Stengers: 'a new unity is emerging: irreversibility is the source of order at all levels. Irreversibility is the mechanism that brings order out of chaos. How could such a radical transformation of our views of nature occur in the relatively short span of the past few decades? We believe that it shows the important role intellectual construction plays in our concept of reality' (Prigogine and Stengers 1984, 292).

In proposing a new 'intellectual construction' Prigogine and Stengers are attempting to inaugurate a revolution in science that will constitute a fundamental departure from Classical science and possibly even from the whole history of Western science since the Greeks: 'a basic aim of this book is to convey to the reader my conviction that we are in a period of scientific revolution—one in which the very position and meaning of the scientific approach are undergoing appraisal—a period not unlike the birth of the scientific approach in ancient Greece or of its renaissance in the time of Galileo' (Prigogine 1980, p. XIII). The comparisons are not apt, but some kind of transition is certainly at hand which in time might amount to a reformation. Prigogine speaks of a revolution in science, but he means a revolution less in the political sense of the revolutionist radicals and more in the sense of evolution—a term he uses interchangeably—as understood by the organicist systemists. He thus takes himself to be inaugurating a new evolutionary epoch of science, going beyond the levels of organized simplicity and unorganized complexity to that of organized complexity. In fact, the evolution of organized complexity as such is the basic problem examined in his scientific departure. He is in a sense asking the Kantian question, 'how is organized complexity possible given the thermodynamic laws of physics?' and answering it not in any a priori fashion but in a strictly empirical experimental manner: 'the scheme we have presented is not an a priori scheme—deducible from some logical structure. There is, indeed, no logical necessity for dissipative structures actually to exist in nature; the "cosmological fact" of a universe far from equilibrium is needed for the macroscopic world to be a world inhabited by "observers"—that is, to be a living world' (Prigogine and Stengers 1984, 300).

Prigogine is well aware that the full scientific solution to this problem will produce not only a new kind of science but also a new vision of nature: 'our vision of nature is undergoing a radical change toward the multiple, the temporal and the complex' (ibid. 292). He asks himself, have we lost the 'essential elements of classical science in this recent evolution?' And he answers:

> The increased limitation of deterministic laws means that we go from a universe that is closed, in which all is given, to one that is open to fluctuations, to innovations. For most of the founders of classical science—even for Einstein—science was an attempt to go beyond the world of appearances, to reach a timeless world of supreme rationality—the world of Spinoza. But perhaps there is a more subtle form of reality that involves both laws and games, time and eternity (Prigogine 1980, 215).

Prigogine sees this new conception of the universe as so far removed from Classical science that he even toys with the idea that it might have more in common with Aristotelian science:

> modern science was born when Aristotelian space, for which one source of inspiration was the organization and solidarity of biological functions, was replaced by the homogeneous and isotropic space of Euclid. However, the theory of dissipative structures moves us closer to Aristotle's conception. Whether we are dealing with a chemical clock, concentration waves, or the inhomogeneous distribution of chemical products, instability has the effect of breaking symmetry, both temporal and spatial. In a limit cycle, no two instants are equivalent; the chemical reaction acquires a phase similar to that characterizing a light wave, for example. Again, when a favoured direction results from an instability, space ceases to be isotropic. We move from Euclidian to Aristotelian space (Prigogine and Stengers 1984, 171).

But is it quite true to claim that 'we are quite close to the Aristotelian view of the cosmos, which contrasted the world of divine eternal trajectories with the world of sublunar nature, the description of which was clearly influenced by biological observation?' (Prigogine 1980, p. XIV). To a large degree one can only take this statement as hyperbole for Prigogine clearly does not intend to advocate a new teleology or to propose one unified theory of the whole cosmos in a metaphysical manner. He recognizes that 'the application of Aristotle's views to physics has had disastrous consequences' (ibid. p. XV). Nevertheless, he wants to show 'that the two concepts—the geometrical world and the organized functional world—are not incompatible' and that 'an essential characteristic of our scheme is that it does not suppose any fundamental mode of description; each level of description is implied by another and implies the other. We need a multiplicity of levels that are all connected, none of which may have a claim to prominence' (Prigogine and Stengers 1984, 300). Thus instead of the static, geometric approach adopted by Classical science, and even by relativity theory, the new science of the future will adopt 'a dynamic view in which time plays an essential role' (Prigogine 1980, p. XII). In such an approach 'the concept of evolution seems to be central to our understanding of the physical universe' (ibid).

It is precisely the concept of evolution that raises all the problems of time to which Prigogine addresses himself. The law of universal evolution in the sense of the temporal development of complexity, structure and form seems contradicted by the law of universal devolution in the sense of the second law of thermodynamics. This problem, which forms Prigogine's point of departure, had already been explicitly posed since the nineteenth century, when both the new science of thermodynamics and the numerous evolutionary sciences were propounded at the same time. It received its classic formulation from Norbert Wiener as the key unsolved problem even after the Second World War:

> We are immersed in a life in which the world as a whole obeys the second law of thermodynamics: confusion increases and order decreases. Yet, as we have seen, the second law of thermodynamics, while it may be a valid statement about the whole of a closed system, is definitely not valid concerning a non-isolated part of it. There are local and temporary islands of decreasing entropy in a world in which the entropy as a whole tends to increase, and the existence of these islands enables some of us to assert the existence of progress. What can we say of the general battle between progress and increasing entropy in the world immediately about us? (Wiener 1954, 36–7).

At stake in this problem is the scientific version of the metaphysical conundrum expressed by Leibniz when he asked, 'why is there being rather than nothing?' Or in Prigogine's terms, 'why is there order rather than chaos?' That is, 'why is there becoming rather than the non-being of undifferentiated homogeneity?' This is the same as asking how complexity is possible—which, as we have already seen, is Prigogine's problem of how integration takes place at any level.

Prigogine means to solve this basic problem by accounting for what Herbert Spencer called 'the instability of the homogeneous' in the process of revealing 'the detailed mechanism through which structure may originate in far-from-equilibrium conditions' (Prigogine 1971, 2). The structures of particular concern are those which manifest the irreversible processes of an open system which exchanges matter and energy with its environment. These are exemplified in chemistry by the so-called dissipative structures which contrast with the purely equilibrium structures of closed systems that do not exchange energy or matter with their environment. Thus snowflakes and crystals generally are equilibrium structures which are thermodynamically stable. By contrast, 'dissipative structures are maintained only far from thermodynamic equilibrium through exchange of matter and energy with the outside world' (ibid. 3). Such structures arise from instabilities resulting from fluctuations which maintain far-from-equilibrium conditions. Hydrodynamic flows that produce instabilities which become amplified rather than dampened down can lead to large-scale order, as in certain kinds of storms and weather patterns, most dramatically exemplified in the so-called Red Spot on the planet Jupiter. But of greater interest are the instabilities that lead to dissipative structures in chemical processes for these play a crucial role in biological phenomena, as, for example, in the metabolic functions of the cell. How such structures arise and maintain themselves is the most important problem in non-equilibrium thermodynamics, the problem of accounting for 'order through fluctuations'.

We now know that far from equilibrium, new types of structures may originate spontaneously. In far-from-equilibrium conditions we may have transformations from disorder, from thermal chaos, into order. New dynamic states of matter may originate, states that reflect the interaction of a given system with its surroundings. We have called these new structures dissipative structures to emphasise the constructive role of dissipative processes in their formation (Prigogine and Stengers 1984, 12).

Prigogine insists that the emergence of complex orders, such as dissipative structures, is highly improbable if one relies solely on the principles of thermodynamics. Hence, it follows that other, higher order principles and modes of description are involved, ones that also serve to organize molecular structure: 'it is interesting to note that Bolzmann's order principle would assign almost zero probability to the occurrence of Benard convection. . . . A new molecular order appears that basically corresponds to a giant fluctuation stabilized by the exchange of energy with the outside world. This is the order characterized by the occurrence of what are referred to as "dissipative structures"' (Prigogine 1980, 89–90).

In emphasizing the role of fluctuations in the constitution of order, Prigogine and Stengers revert to a view of nature that goes back to the ancient Atomists, to Lucretius in particular, rather than to Aristotle. And this brings them to the most contentious aspect of their work, that which departs furthest from Classical science and even from the very idea of science as now entertained: the reintroduction of chance. The idea of science as providing completely deterministic representations of nature, at least in principle, is abandoned in favour of permitting descriptions of occurrences that are in principle unpredictable to play a role alongside determinism. As in Lucretius, a free play of chance and determinism governs the fluctuating flow of natural phenomena, but the chance collisions of atoms are not now in question—they are accounted for statistically in Classical thermodynamics—rather it is the random path taken by complex systems in far-from-equilibrium conditions near critical bifurcation points:

It is remarkable that near-bifurcations systems present large fluctuations. Such systems seem to "hesitate" among various possible directions of evolution, and the famous law of large numbers in its usual sense breaks down. A small fluctuation may start an entirely new evolution that will drastically change the whole behaviour of the macrocosmic system. Far from opposing "chance" and "necessity", we now see both aspects as essential in the description of non-linear systems far from equilibrium (Prigogine and Stengers 1984, 14).

Even more explicitly, Prigogine and Stengers emphasize that the random element in such cases cannot be eliminated as mere macroscopic appearance, that is, as merely phenomenal and not real: 'there is an irreducible random element; the macroscopic equation cannot predict the path the system will take. Turning to a microscopic description will not help. We are faced with chance events very similar to the fall of dice' (ibid. 162).

But the usual scientific conception of the fall of dice is that the outcome is not the result of chance but of all the incalculable little forces acting on the flight path of each cube. If these could be known then the fall of the die could be predicted with certainty. And so, too, it is argued against Prigogine that bifurcations in systems are not a matter of chance but merely appear to be because of the overly great complexity involved. It is argued that not even the onset of chaos is a matter of pure chance, but the expression of deterministic processes. A new mathematical approach called chaos theory aims to generate chaotic-looking phenomena out of regular motions through strict mathematical techniques such as Feigenbaum's 'period doubling'. It is hoped that in this way the onset of turbulence and fluctuations can be described mathematically and eventually accounted for deterministically. It is too early at present to decide between Feigenbaum's chaos theory and Prigogine's chance theory; the issue is still open, but it points to some fundamental problems for future science.

An analogous contradiction seems also to have arisen between Prigogine's hypothesis of chance outcomes at the points of bifurcation and Thom's catastrophe theory which also deals mathematically with the outcomes at the points of crisis. Thom's approach (which we shall further discuss under the heading of neo-Methodism) attempts to deal with the kinds of complex physical, chemical and biological phenomena that Prigogine discusses. In fact, Prigogine believes that his approach is compatible with Thom's especially in the area of morphogenesis, so crucial to biology, which I shall examine in the next sections from such viewpoints as mechanist systemist and molecular genetics. Prigogine and Stengers state their position on this as follows:

> The concept of chreod is part of the qualitative description of embryological development Waddington proposed more than twenty years ago. It is truly a bifurcating evolution: a progressive exploration along which the embryo grows in an "epigenetic landscape" where coexist stable segments and segments where a choice among several developmental paths is possible. C. H. Waddington's chreods are also a central reference to René Thom's biological thought. They could thus become a meeting point for two approaches: the one we are presenting, starting from the local mechanisms and exploring the spectrum of collective behaviour they can generate; and Thom's starting from global mathematical entities and connecting the quantitatively distinct forms and transformations they imply with the phenomenological description of morphogenesis (Prigogine and Stengers 1984, 326-7).

However, as one might have expected from a neo-Methodist like Thom, Prigogine's offer of a belle alliance has been decisively rejected by the other side; Alvin Toffler reports that 'thinkers such as René Thom reject the idea of chance as illusory and inherently unscientific' (ibid. p. XXII). Here once again there are problems of reconciliation whose solution is already being attempted, for example, in the work of Herman Haken (1983) on synergetics or the self-organization of disequilibrium processes, following the lead of both Prigogine and Thom.

Prigogine's decision to let chance enter science might not find favour among the strict systemists or the conservatives of either variety, but it ought to appeal to some radicals in science. For to allow chance some scope in the social sciences is tantamount to giving the individual a role in the overturning or consolidation of social systems. This is precisely the consequence Prigogine and Stengers expect:

> A system far from equilibrium may be described as organized not because it realizes a plan alien to elementary activities, or transcending them, but, on the contrary, because the amplification of a microscopic fluctuation oc-curing at the "right moment" resulted in favouring one reaction path over a number of other equally possible paths. Under certain circumstances, there-fore, the role played by individual behaviour can be decisive (ibid. 176).

If the system in question is a social system, this view permits the individual once more to play a decisive part in society, a constructive or revolutionary part, but in any case, one much greater than strict historical determinism ever permitted. Prigogine's idea not only opens a way of escaping complete determinism in the social sciences; it also provides a way to account for order, meaning and rationality in society and history in a non-teleological manner. It is not some impersonal agent, such as a spirit of the times, invisible hand, cunning of reason, logic of domination, or whatever other apostrophised abstraction has been invoked to account for the evidently meaningful course of history; rather it is the actions of individuals in the buffeting fluctuations of social turmoil that steer the course of history in a given rational direction. As we shall see in the section on the revolu-tionists, the sociologist Norbert Elias puts forward just this kind of view in accounting for the apparent purposefulness of large-scale historical de-velopments and for the decisive role of key individuals at critical junctions of events.

Prigogine's ideas on chance have also been accepted by conservationists in the natural sciences, especially those dealing with environmental issues. As we shall see in the section on the conservationists, Bradbury, Hammond, Reichelt and Young in their work on Environmental Impact Assessment invoke Prigogine's view that 'there is an element of unpredictability in the behaviour of complex systems':

> systems operating inside a domain of possible states within which their buffering mechanisms operate effectively to maintain the system's integrity, are resilient to a certain range of environmental perturbations, or impacts, which do not push them beyond the edge of this domain. In instances where the edge of the domain is reached—that is, when the environmental per-turbation or impact is severe enough—the system in its existing form breaks down because the buffering mechanisms fail to maintain all the elements of it. A new configuration—a new system—emerges within a new domain. What Prigogine has shown, and what is not yet well understood, is that there are generally many possible new systems that could emerge from a severe impact, and that the identity of the system which eventually emerges is inherently unpredictable (Bradbury et al. 1983, 324).

They give the example of the sudden and totally unexpected failure of the major herring fisheries of the world which had been subject to careful scientific management to ensure that these systems did not collapse.

It so happens that the methodology and the basic biological theories underlying this disastrous fisheries management program derived from the work of von Bertalanffy. Only a few years before the unexpected collapse, a fisheries management expert, Radway Allen, had written in praise of von Bertalanffy's work in this field: 'one of the most successful examples of the application of mathematical techniques to the description of the biological processes involved in the management of a natural resource is found in the field of fisheries. . . . The growth curves formed on the principles originally suggested by Dr. Ludwig von Bertalanffy have proved to be particularly suitable for this purpose' (Gray and Rizzo 1973, 623-4). It is difficult to say to what extent the failure of the methodology behind the fisheries management program can specifically be ascribed to von Bertalanffy's overly deterministic models. Nevertheless, some very general criticisms of the older organicist systemist approach and of the methodology of General System Theory are suggested by this case.

General System Theory is a generalized approach supposedly applicable to all types of systems and supposedly capable of being articulated with full mathematical rigour. It tends to be deliberately indifferent to the specifics of different kinds of system and certainly to the vagaries of individual systems in their concrete particularity. And this is precisely the methodology and habit of mind that Bradbury et al. (1983, 324) identify as responsible for the fisheries management disaster: 'simply stated, the fault lies in the blurring of scientific goals as a result of the blurring of distinctions among types of natural systems'. As I shall show in some detail later, they argue the general case that for ecosystems scientific explanation and prediction do not coincide, as these do for thermodynamic and other lower level systems. They contend that 'the analytic techniques and scientific cast of mind that evolved to understand [these latter] systems are still pervasive today' (ibid.). To counteract these tendencies an appeal to Prigogine is almost inevitable and indispensable, nowhere better than in his work do the differences between systems at different levels and in various fields emerge with such clarity.

Mechanist Departures

Prigogine's work on the emergence of order is merely the most theoretically self-conscious instance of much new work in many different sciences on complexity and integration. As Hooker has recently pointed out, 'self-organization has appeared as a theoretically important concept recently and almost simultaneously in systems theory, neurophysiology, electrical engineering, biology and cognitive psychology. This constellation of developments is linked to network thermodynamics, control theory and artificial intelligence' (Hooker 1984, 357). In this section I shall concentrate on some new departures along these lines in biology and artificial intelligence which best fit the mechanist systemist approach. But the very same problem of order and self-organization is involved at this level, for as Prigogine and Stengers (1984, 175) see it, 'the problem of biological order involves the transition from the molecular activity to the supermolecular order of the cell. This problem is far from being solved'. This is the unsolved problem of integration now belatedly being addressed by molecular genetics.

This spectacularly successful science, which, as shown in Chapter 2, completed the reductive programme of Classical genetics and went on to develop as genetic engineering, a technified World science, has increasingly been concerned with problems of integration. Its leading exponents have tended to adopt a mechanist systemist approach to these issues. Information theory and computer modelling have provided their basic conceptions of method and procedure. But in the course of dealing with problems of integration, they have of late been coming closer to the program advocated by the organicist systemists, as well as been obliged to recognize the validity of conservative approaches in genetics which they had spurned for a long time, such as the recently rediscovered work of McClintock. Thus in pursuing the problem of how to integrate the organism they have almost unwittingly been furthering the integration of sciences as well. Let us briefly look back to see how this development ensued.

The reductive program of molecular genetics was one of the last triumphs of Classical science. It amounted to a sequence of successive reductions: the reductions of the characteristics of inheritance to genes and chromosomes; the reduction of these to DNA; the reduction of DNA to its bio-chemical constituents; the reduction of the complex chemicals to atoms in a helical arrangement to constitute a genetic code—the last step completed by Crick and Watson. Somewhere beyond this point, as a result of the further work of Monod and others, it seemed as if the science of genetics appeared to be theoretically complete. As discussed in Chapter 2, some geneticists—Gunther Stent, for instance—took it that any further work in this field was no longer of any deep theoretical interest, that it was merely a matter of applied science and genetic technology which by gene splicing would map the exact location of the different genes on the DNA molecule. The age of discovery, it seemed, had given way to detailed geographic surveying; one day that would be complete and all theoretical interest in the science would be over.

As shown in Chapter 2, Stent is at least partly right in that the Classical reductive program is indeed nearing completion and the science is now mature in the sense of the finalization theorists. But he is also partly wrong in that this achievement does not exhaust the possibilities of the complex objects the science is studying, namely, the molecular constitution of organic beings. And it seems that these complex objects are inexhaustible. As Judson (1984, 66) notes, 'any higher organism, any mammal, any human, is the product of stupefyingly complex interactions'. Geneticists are realizing that complexities of this scope cannot be treated as if they were merely a routine matter of mechanical combination, the inverse of reduction. As Judson points out, 'the founding generation of molecular biologists were triumphant reductionists, [but] their successors are more cautious and more sophisticated' (ibid.).

Even the very members of the founding generation of molecular biologists have begun to realize that the problem of integration is not a simple matter of reversing reduction. In a series of interviews with Crick and Brenner, Judson elicits this view from them. Crick recognizes that the

Classic achievements of molecular biology were made possible by abstracting and eliminating from the biological phenomena all but the most simple and orderly relations:

> the basic biological mechanisms are, nevertheless, in principle, comparatively simple, and they turn out, with minor variations, to be the same throughout nature. . . . The simplicity and universality of these mechanisms is, I think, the main reason why molecular biology has been able to advance so rapidly. . . . The other reason for the rapid progress was that at a certain stage a set of hypotheses emerged that were very simple. A well-defined theoretical framework with which we could guide experimentation and from which we could predict, to some extent, what was likely to be discovered. The framework was provided by the middle fifties. The main reason it was possible was the nature of the nucleic-acid molecule, because the functions of these are rather limited. This helps in constructing theories—because the easiest way to make the theory is to impose a restriction of some sort (Judson 1979, 204–8).

This statement could act as a methodological prescription for the Classical phase of any science. But Crick realizes that this was only an initial phase of the science and that inevitably another phase will have to be embarked on if the outstanding problems of biology are to be solved. He now knows the difficulties involved much better than does Monod for whom these were only problems of detail: 'for a simple living creature to be synthesized, in my opinion there is no further principle that needs to be discovered. . . . I would say that the genetic problem, by and large, is solved. But the embryological problem remains' (ibid. 216). Yet it is precisely this 'embryological problem' that cannot be separated from the 'genetic problem' as soon as science turns to entities more complex than the prokaryotes, that is, to the eukaryotes which constitute the vegetable and animal kingdom.

Crick realizes that 'at this point one moves beyond classical molecular biology': 'as soon as one begins working with multicellular organisms, one faces the problems of development: embryology, differentiation of the several kinds of cells, organs and tissues, the healing of wounds; regeneration, and so on. This is not one problem but lots of problems' (ibid. 205). To tackle these problems means once again picking up all those issues in biology which were put aside when Morgan and others turned to the new genetics opened up by Mendel. As Brenner puts it:

> In one way, you could say, all the genetic and molecular biological work of the last sixty years could be considered as a long interlude—sixty years of following out Morgan's deviation into the tractable genetic problems. And now that that program has been completed, we have come full circle—back to the problems that they left behind unsolved. How does a wounded organism regenerate to exactly the same structure it had before? How does the egg form the organism? (ibid. 209).

Crick makes it clear that we are still a long way from answering these questions: 'for the new areas of molecular biology, what are the unifying ideas? It must be said that we don't yet have attractive, unifying hypotheses to test' (ibid. 209). His colleague Brenner thinks that it is not a matter of unifying hypotheses and 'that it will not be enough to know the general mechanism'. He believes that what is called for is a mechanist systemist approach based on computer modelling:

> If you were to say to me, Here is a protein, what is its genetic specification?—we could answer in tremendous detail. But if you say to me, Here is a hand, here is an eye, how do you make a hand or an eye, what is its genetic specification?—we can't do it. It is necessary to know the exact number and sequence of the genes, how they interact, what they do. We have to know the program, and know it in machine language which is molecular language. We have to know it so that in principle one can generate a set of procedures for making a hand or an eye (ibid. 220).

Brenner is also aware that he is calling for a completely different approach from that of Classical science even as practised till recently by molecular biology: 'where a science like physics works in terms of laws, or a science like molecular biology, to now, is stated in terms of mechanisms, maybe now what one has to begin to think of is algorithms. Recipes. Procedures' (ibid. 221). The mechanist systemist orientation is unmistakable. Hence all the difficulties inherent in that approach are likely to follow. If, as he puts it, 'we have to know the program, and know it in machine language', then the attempt could be doomed to failure for such programs could well turn out to be too complex ever to be known in this way. As we shall see, both Stent and Minsky encounter problems of surveying and knowing in dealing with very complex programs. Analogous problems probably will be encountered in biology as well, if Brenner's way is followed much further.

The Brenner path is only one approach to the biological summit; others are available. He outlines two converging lines of attack on these problems, from above and from below: 'we are trying to approach it in two ways. Through the whole organism by doing genetic analysis of mutants and so on—the rather classical approach, which depends on the choice of the animal and how deeply you go into it. But the real way, the way one will have to employ in the long run, is actually to work with cell culture, to build organs (ibid. 220). The two ways suggested by Brenner might be taken as corresponding to the opposition between the conservatives and organicist systemists on the one hand, and the mechanist systemists on the other. Brenner believes that the new biological science of the future lies in the realm of systems of both kinds: 'I think in the next twenty-five years we are going to have to teach biologists another language still. I don't know what it's called yet; nobody knows. But what one is aiming at, I think, is the fundamental problem of elaborate systems. Especially, elaborate systems that arise under conditions of natural selection' (ibid. 220). However, as a mechanist systemist, Brenner tends, in the last resort, to be skeptical about the viability of an organicist approach that starts from above with the whole organism. He prefers to start from below with the basic genetic elements and build up complexities mechanistically:

> I believe that in biology, programmatic explanations will be algorithmic explanations. You will have to say, next switch on gene group number fifty-eight. And then one has that whole lot of molecular biology—what is gene group fifty-eight and what does it do. And one takes for granted that gene group fifty-eight performs its computation. And then the simultaneous steps, the alternative steps, the sequential steps. In great detail. So, I feel that this new molecular biology has got to go in this direction—to explore the high-level logical computations, the programs, the algorithms of development, in molecular terms. We've got to carry the analysis to that level—and to carry molecular biology with it (ibid. 221).

Despite this strongly mechanistic bias, Brenner is not altogether prepared to abandon a holistic approach that moves from the whole to its components. He acknowledges that biology is once again raising the old questions after its detour into DNA: 'the questions that people raised in the 1870s . . ., but of course we are doing it with modern tools' (ibid.). And he admits that this entails another approach which he would like to incorporate as well: 'one would like to be able to fuse the two—to be able to move between the molecular hardware and the logical software of how it is all organised, without feeling they are different sciences' (ibid.). As we shall see, this will require bringing back to a central place in biology the kind of work that had been abandoned as old-fashioned during the DNA detour. And this has already happened with the belated recognition given to the older style conservative work of Barbara McClintock, dealing precisely with 'the genetic analysis of mutants—the rather classical approach' which Brenner had relegated to second place.

Brenner is groping for an understanding of why the mechanist systemist approach that he advocates will not provide theories as understood by Classical science but rather what he calls 'algorithms, recipes, procedures'. He reaches out to von Neumann's assertion, regarding the quite different field of Artificial Intelligence, that the problem of describing pattern vision cannot be solved by formulating a theory of pattern vision: 'you can't give a theory of pattern vision—but all you can do is to give a prescription for making a device that will see patterns' (ibid. 210–11). Hence if we follow the work of those actually engaged in this problem of pattern vision we shall be approaching from another direction the kinds of issues and difficulties likely to be encountered by the mechanist systemists in biology. The work of David Marr and his associates is perhaps the most interesting in this field, and it reveals clearly what is involved in such an attempt.

Marr seeks to describe pattern vision by semantically decoding the information contained in the visual image and then modelling that information by means of computer programs and mechanistic cybernetic procedures. There is a strong analogy here with Brenner's two simultaneous approaches from opposite ends, organicist and mechanist, in the task of describing organic growth. The problems of the recognition of forms and the growth of forms have obviously much in common, and both give rise to what might be called configurational sciences, which are quite different from the causal and dynamic sciences of the past. Marr's approach to the science of visual form recognition is premised on what Stent (1981) has called a hermeneutic pre-understanding of the visual image. It begins, by making some basic holistic assumptions about the image as a whole, deriving from ordinary general knowledge of the visual world: 'an example of such general knowledge is the pre-understanding that the world is constituted mainly of solid, non-deformable objects of which only one can occupy a given place at any time' (ibid. 111). Stent identifies numerous of these apparently obvious pre-understandings which Marr requires in order to undertake his computer modelling procedure: 'the physical factors in the world that actually determine the light intensity variations present in the image', 'the general pre-understanding that the object in motion is rigid', 'some general pre-understanding that allows us to infer shape from a surface contour', and many others (ibid). Marr proceeds downwards from the whole form by analysing it into its systemic factors much in the way that perceptual psychologists had already done. He then complements this with an approach upward by mechanistically modelling in terms of computer programs each of the basic steps in the analysis of the image. He begins by modelling the process of contour separation through a mechanical technique of locating the light gradients and discontinuities, thus initiating 'a transformation of the grey level array of the image into what he calls the primal sketch' (ibid.). Many other ingenious techniques, both mathematical and cybernetic, were developed by Marr and his colleagues to model the other levels of perception, such as the description of the surfaces and shapes of three-dimensional objects.

The general approach outlined in Marr's posthumously published book *Vision* (1982) is now being followed by researchers in many institutions. A recent article by William Broad (1984) gives an overview of the present state of research and outlines the different 'hermeneutic readings' adopted by various researchers. Broad refers to the work of Binford at Stanford who is following Marr's cylindrical or cubist method for identifying three-dimensional shapes, to Kanade at Carnegie-Mellon who has adopted an 'origami' technique which 'assumes the world is made of planar surfaces and that the operations you are allowed to do are cutting, folding and glueing along straight edges' (ibid.), and to Kender at Columbia who is pursuing Marr's quest of identifying objects whose parts are missing or indistinct. Much of this work is being financed by the Pentagon for it has obvious military applications, especially in the Star Wars initiative, though industry is also very interested since it brings closer the long promised totally automated factory. The scant success achieved so far proves just how difficult it is to model mechanically even the very simplest forms of vision. This failure brings into doubt the facile comparisons that used to be made between computers and brains, as when Minsky spoke of 'meat machines'. It is also said that Minsky 'once asked a graduate student to solve the problem of machine vision as a summer project' (ibid.).

However, what little has been achieved in this field shows that it is not a matter of providing a theory of pattern vision in the old sense of some scientific law or causal regulative mechanism. Nor is it even a matter of trying to imitate the neurological process of perception, though research in this field could lead to the discovery of further features in that process by suggesting experiments to be undertaken in neurology. Stent's (1981, 221) 'tough-minded' question of 'whether there is any chance of ever proving such a theory as Marr's, or whether it is just idle speculation', does seem somewhat off the point, since no theory provable or disprovable in the old way is in question. Rather, we are dealing with the task of constructing a systemic model of what 'on first sight appears as a hopelessly complex phenomenon' (ibid. 123). Stent's own speculations as to what this implies about science in general are of considerable interest.

Stent believes that this example affords a way of distinguishing in general between the 'hard' and the 'soft' sciences, or between mechanics and psychoanalysis at either extreme:

> There is an aura of objective truth about the laws of classical mechanics because the phenomena which mechanics consider significant, such as steel balls rolling down inclines, are of low complexity. Because of that low complexity it is possible to adduce critical observations or experiments about rolling steel balls. By contrast, there is no comparable aura of truth about propositions of analytical psychology, because phenomena of the human psyche which it attends are very complex (Stent 1981, 123).

Stent applies this insight to neurobiology, arguing that this broad-ranged science covers both ends of the 'soft' and 'hard' scale. As the 'hard' end of cellular electrophysiology the simplicity of phenomena is such that they can be 'accounted for in terms of explanations that are susceptible to seemingly objective proof'.

> But at its soft end, neurobiology is represented by the study of the function of large and complicated neural networks. The output of these networks comprises phenomena whose complexity approaches that of the human psyche, in fact, include the human psyche. Hence at that soft end neurobiology takes on some of the characteristics of hermeneutics: the student of a complex neural network must bring considerable pre-understanding to the system as a whole before attempting to interpret the function of any of its parts. Accordingly, the explanations that are advanced about complex neural systems may remain beyond the reach of objective validation (ibid.).

Once again we find here a convergent approach from the 'soft' and 'hard' ends, from the 'system as a whole' downwards, and from the simple network arrangements upwards. But at neither end is it a matter of testing law-like theories, such as the Classical laws of mechanics for rolling balls. Rather, systems analysis and system reconstruction is involved; the reconstruction can be mechanistic and mathematically rigorous, but it depends on the initial interpretation of the system as a whole—Stent's hermeneutic proviso. Since numerous such alternative interpretations of any one complex system must be possible—for example, in identifying the brain processes responsible for a psychological function—it follows that there can be no such thing as a single, objectively true interpretation. But from this it does not follow that once an interpretation is offered, or once a psychological function such as pattern vision is analyzed in a given way, it cannot be mechanistically reconstructed and in that sense objectively tested and validated. Whether this specific mechanistic model is the one that actually operates in the brain itself is another matter, but that too can be experimentally tested; any such model certainly suggests possible experiments for uncovering the precise nature of the neural workings in the brain. As a number of such alternative models can be proposed and tested at once, it is possible that in some instances complementary models will be found to hold, in which case there can be no such thing as a single, correct model. Cerebral hermeneutics does open up the possibility of complementarity without necessarily denying that of objective validation, as in physics in general.

But the problems are of staggering complexity. Even Minsky, one of the original founders of Artificial Intelligence, who once held out such high hopes for what it would soon achieve, has now begun to realize the nature of what is involved and to scale down his expectations. The problems are in a sense conceptual for they revolve around an analysis of what is meant by the terms 'machine', 'program', 'complete description' and 'surveyability' or the 'understanding' of such a 'description'. Minsky now admits that the mathematical description of complex functions, whether of a brain or a machine, 'will not be like the great unifying descriptions in physics in which a single equation or a few equations can be derived from what appear to be self-evident principles, and which describe and predict vast realms of phenomena. If the artificial intelligence programmes are a clue, the more lifelike they become, the more they resist simple description in mathematical terms' (Bernstein 1982, 122). Even a description of all the component parts of the brain and their interconnections, like the wiring diagram of a computer, if it could ever be obtained, would be scientifically useless for it would be too complicated to be followed. 'Even if we had a diagram containing every one of the billions of neurons in the human mind and the billions of interconnections, it would stare at us as mutely as the grains of sand in a desert' (ibid. 122). Thus it is possible, at least in principle, that no single description of the brain will ever be available, or if available, 'not in any single form of language that would enable us to understand the entire picture in a unified sense' (ibid.). This does not rule out, however, the possibility that 'in time the functional parts of the brain will be identified and their function described in some language we can understand' (ibid.). As we have seen, this is indeed the case with Marr's model of pattern vision and the neurological experiments that are likely to follow from it in identifying and describing the visual functions of the brain.

Such functions of the brain will probably be understood by being modelled in some way without necessarily also being described in a mathematical language. As we have seen, referring to embryology Brenner has said that such an understanding cannot be 'stated in terms of mechanisms' and suggests that perhaps 'now what one has to begin to think of is algorithms. Recipes. Procedures' (Judson 1979, 221). This may also be true for Artificial Intelligence and neurology. In a sense computer programs are such recipes and procedures. Thus modelling of the mind might take the form of computer programs which are so complex that they 'resist simple description in mathematical terms'. Minsky notes that the programs utilized for this purpose are already too complex to be overseen in detail;

they can no longer be understood as single descriptions in mathematical terms:

> The programs that are now in use in the most sophisticated parts of artificial intelligence are at the limit of the ability of the human programmer to keep track of them—to keep all the details straight. . . . Moreover, because of the abilities of the machine to function conditionally and, with the new programming languages, to adjoin new pieces to their own programs and thus to make the programs iterate on themselves, what will happen in the end cannot be predicted. The route that the machine will take cannot be predicted. While it may be possible in principle to make the machine print out the steps it followed in a certain algorithm, it is reaching a point where in a practical sense, it is, in effect, impossible (Bernstein 1982, 52).

Thus, in a certain sense, the more a program approaches the intelligent functions of the brain, the less we can understand it. And in general, the more any model in science approximates the complexities of living objects, the less it can be understood as a single description.

To overcome the problems of complexity in modelling intelligence, Minsky turns to an approach that works from both ends: from the general system downwards and from the details upwards. He calls this 'an administrative theory of the mind':

> Right now I am working on the society of the mind theory. I believe that the way to realize intelligence is to have some parts of the mind that know certain things and other parts of the mind that know things about the first part. If you want to learn something, the most important thing is to know which part of your mind is good at learning that kind of thing. I am not looking so much for a unified general theory. I am looking for an administrative theory of how the mind can have enough parts and know enough about each of them to solve all the problems it confronts (ibid. 128).

Perhaps Minsky does not fully realize that this approach opens up all the difficulties of cerebral hermeneutics that Stent raised in relation to the work of Marr on pattern vision, which is an example of the kind of work Minsky has in mind. Any such science of Artificial Intelligence will have to face the issue of pre-understanding and the possibility of alternative and complementary models. It also remains to be seen whether the kind of programming involved in this approach—dividing the task between a number of interlinked computers—offers better results than the traditional unitary program.

All this has important consequences for future science. Brenner, Marr, Minsky and others who started off from a basically mechanist systemist approach have had to complement it with an approach deriving from organicist systemism—to work from above and below. Thus a consensus between the two rival systemist approaches is gradually being worked out in practice, in actual ongoing scientific research.

Neo-Methodist Departures

The issues of organized complexity and integrative structures with which the systemists were so concerned have also been tackled in another way by strict mathematical techniques. These might be called neo-Methodist approaches, for despite evident differences they have something in common with the Methodisms of the Classical sciences. Two new approaches of this kind have developed side by side, one in Europe and the other in America, apparently without much influence from each other: catastrophe theory and chaos theory. The former is concerned with problems very like the ones that Prigogine has raised: how does order emerge out of chaos? The latter is concerned with exactly the inverse problems: how does chaos emerge out of order? Chaos theory studies how simple order or law-like phenomena gradually break down into chaotic unpredictability. Catastrophe theory studies how chaotic processes of undifferentiated homogeneity organize themselves spontaneously to produce forms and configurations. Thus both of these neo-Methodist approaches seem to be complementary, and an attempt to integrate them with each other as well as with the systemist approaches ought to be made. As yet, however, this synthesis has not been attempted, so it remains one of the essential tasks of future science. At present the two appear to pass each other by without serious engagement.

Catastrophe theory was invented by René Thom and applied to biological phenomena with the collaboration of the renowned biologist C. H. Waddington. Woodcock and Davis (1978, 92) claim that 'models based on catastrophe theory permit description—and perhaps prediction—of qualitative changes far too complex for modelling by traditional methods'. By 'traditional methods' they mean classical physics and its mathematical techniques, based on the calculus, which are unable to cope with such simple complexities as the three-body problem or with such ordinary events as a stone splashing in a pool of water. 'Nowhere is the gap between mathematical theory and even the most common phenomena more striking than in Thom's area of special interest: morphogenesis, the origin of form in both life and inorganic nature' (ibid. 77).

Catastrophe theory was devised to describe mathematically the dynamic processes that give rise to stable formations and forms. It is the quantified science of qualitative features and phenomena. In biological fields it seeks to provide a mathematical treatment of what Waddington had dubbed homeorhesis or the process whereby organic developments proceed on a stable pathway or course of change without deviations. But non-organic processes are also subject to stabilities which give rise to readily perceived forms, such as the breaking of waves or water crystals of hoarfrost and snow, and these, too, cannot be fully explained in Classical science: 'we have an elegant theory of crystalization—indeed we have a number of them—but we don't really know what shapes the feathery branching of frost crystals on a cold window. Catastrophe theory opens up new ways to approach phenomena such as these' (Woodcock and Davis 1978, 92). In terms of Classical science the explanation for why a snowflake should assume a hexagonal star form is elementary physics. Yet, as shown in Chapter 1, predicting the precise shape of any one snow crystal is beyond the capacity of science at present; it is of such staggering complexity. In miniature this simple example points up once again the basic distinction between the Classical science of simplicity and the future sciences of complexity. These are not new problems; systems theorists had long set themselves to study such dynamic processes and open systemic flows but rarely with the degree of rigour or exactitude proposed by catastrophe theory. How catastrophe theory relates to systems theory in general in still a matter which future science will have to settle. But on the face of it, some kind of reconciliation is not impossible.

Catastrophe theory is not so much a scientific theory as a new kind of method. Thom calls it 'an art of models'; by this he means 'a way of generating and classifying analogies both within and across disciplines'. He states that 'the catastrophe model is at the same time much less and much more than a scientific theory; one should consider it as a language, a method, which permits classification and systemization of given data. . . . In fact, any phenomenon at all can be explained by a suitable model from catastrophe theory' (ibid. 29). The phenomena for which catastrophe theory is designed are precisely the configurational and qualitative features of reality that are too complex to be grasped by the quantitative methods of Classical science. Thom puts it as follows:

> The choice of what is considered scientifically interesting is certainly to a large extent arbitrary. Physics today uses enormous machines to investigate situations that exist for less than 10^{-23} second, and we surely are entitled to employ all possible techniques. . . . But we can at least ask one question: many phenomena of common interest, in themselves trivial (often to the point that they escape attention altogether!)—for example, the cracks in walls, the path of a falling leaf, or the froth on a pint of beer—are very difficult to formalize, but is it not possible that a mathematical theory launched for such homely phenomena might, in the end, be more profitable for science? (ibid. 9).

As these quotations reveal, the work of René Thom breathes something of the spirit of René Descartes; he too approaches the world geometrically, but through the topology of multidimensional spaces, a remote development of Cartesian geometry. The mathematics of catastrophe theory involves a revision of many of the basic assumptions behind the application of Cartesian geometry and the calculus in Classical science. The continuities in Nature premised by Classical mathematics, relying on principles of linear causality which assume that small causes only give rise to small effects, are abandoned in catastrophe theory. The latter is a theory of sudden, discontinuous movements, where small changes can generate large effects—the so-called catastrophes—that can occur within a smooth, regular flow and which account for the cyclic and systemic nature of such processes. This theory provides a new method of mathematically modelling qualitative and form phenomena which had hitherto resisted quantitative treatment. The method is general; it has even had applications in the realm of the social sciences.

Not only is Thom's approach neo-Methodist; his personal attitude to science also has many of the features we have identified as conservative. He is an individualist who has developed his topological mathematics more or less single-handed by going back to the classic work of Poincaré and Darboux. He is referred to as a 'natural philospher' in the style of Newton, not a specialist in any one discipline—one 'who has thought deeply about the order of nature, and about how it is reflected in all scientific theories' (ibid. 2). He advocates the intuition of forms and a qualitative grasp in science rather than purely quantitative, law-like methods. Imaginative leaps play a more important part in his mathematical structures than chains of rigorous proofs. Hence the aesthetic dimension is strongly emphasized in his approach.

As might be expected with any novel approach, the introduction of catastrophe theory has provoked a fierce debate and resulted in a bitter struggle for authority. Some have hailed it as a new scientific paradigm comparable to Newton's; others have denounced it as a blind alley. As yet no clear picture has emerged of the political alignment for and against it. It is not clear where those who rushed to embrace the method stand in the authority hierarchy nor from where the main opposition has come. All these points will require careful study in the field of scientific politics. On the substantive level of ideas and intellectual content, there is dispute over almost every aspect of catastrophe theory. Although the mathematics itself is not challenged, yet even in this respect complaints have been voiced concerning the lack of proof. Otherwise nearly all applications of the method are in question. In an article in *Nature* Zahler and Sussman (1977, 761) contend that 'the claims made for the theory are greatly exaggerated and its accomplishments, at least in the biological and social sciences, are insignificant'. Zeeman (1977, 381) replied in strong terms. It is impossible for an outsider either to take part in the struggle or to give a ruling on issues that have arisen in the debate. Those who support the theory are themselves not quite sure what is right or wrong with it. Commenting on Thom's belief that 'the shapes of the catastrophe surfaces may appear in biological forms just as they do in caustics [phenomena of light]' Woodcock and Davis ask the leading question: 'is there a fundamental correspondence between these forms, or is the similarity coincidental? Most biologists are suspending judgement, for it will take years of experiment to develop detailed models correlating the control dimensions of the catastrophes with the three dimensions of space and one of time in which living morphogenesis takes place' (Woodcock and Davis 1978, 90).

The move in catastrophe theory from disorder to order can be complemented by that from order to disorder undertaken by chaos theory. For this new 'method', 'the break-through was Feigenbaum's work, finding a way to study the borderline between organized behaviour and chaotic behaviour' (Gleick 1985, 58). Feigenbaum, however, was not the first to initiate work in this direction; scientists in all kinds of hitherto unrelated disciplines were moving towards a common meeting point unbeknown to each other. As one of them, Joseph Ford, the organizer of the first joint conference of chaos theorists at Como in 1977, puts it: 'in disciplines from astronomy to zoology, people were just publishing in their narrow disciplinary journals, totally unaware that the other people were around. In their own areas, they were regarded as a bit eccentric. But if you just changed the words, they were all doing the same thing' (Gleick 1985, 62). All in all, this situation is unfortunately familiar in the sciences. Thus chaos theory is another integrative venture in science which breaks through the inhibitions created by disciplinary boundaries and brings together in a common enterprise scientists from almost every field. In order to succeed it would require a different kind of authority structure from the one operative at present. But so far it does not seem to be developing any new authority forms of its own.

Chaos theory is a mathematical approach which is very highly technified for it relies almost exclusively on computers to model the onset of chaos in orderly phenomena. These apparently purely abstract studies are of practical significance; they seek to explain how turbulence arises in laminar fluid flow, namely, how 'orderly behaviour, explicable in terms of simple fluid dynamics, becomes a mathematical mess' (*The Economist*, September 8, 1984, 77), or how with an increase in food supply an insect population departs from a stable level to fluctuate more or less at random, or how the regular heartbeat breaks down into the usually fatal ventricular fibrillation, and many other such cases. The key to all this work is the discovery of orderly routes to chaos and the numerical laws governing them, such as the Feigenbaum number which governs the rate of period doubling, and of patterns in the onset of chaos, such as the so-called 'strange attractors'. The theory is applicable to complex situations far too difficult for Classical science to handle, situations where there is a sensitive dependence on initial conditions which can only be modelled mathematically by non-linear equations of cause and effect. Weather forecasting, for example, is notoriously subject to such conditions.

Like catastrophe theory, chaos theory tries to account for the small events which are too difficult for Classical science to encompass: the dripping faucet or a child swinging on a swing. It is believed that an adequate explanation of these events would represent an enormous breakthrough in accounting for whole areas of complex phenomena of great practical importance. Chaos theory is also beginning to challenge Classical science in some of its own domains. In astronomy it is accounting for the small perturbations of planets as well as the large fluctuations of irregular planetary moons such as Saturn's Hyperion. In plasma physics it tries to deal with the onset of turbulence in fusion reactors. It challenges conventional quantum mechanics in the explanation of ionization effects. High hopes are being held out all round; already some speak as if they have stumbled on a new way of looking at the whole of nature. 'Practically speaking, it means that scientists have to think differently about the problems of nature. It changes their intuitions about what the answers can look like, and that changes the questions they ask. Chaos becomes a technique for doing science—but it also becomes a conceptual framework on which theoreticians can hang some of their most treasured suspicions about the workings of the universe' (Gleick 1985, 63). Most likely such aspirations are premature at present. Chaos theory is not the royal road to future science; it may have to merge with parallel routes before there will be a new pathway.

At present chaos theory, like these other approaches, 'seems to challenge conventional science on many fronts' (*The Economist*, September 8, 1984, 79). It thus joins in the struggle for authority on the level of great scientific politics whose outcome cannot now be predicted but which contains within itself the potential of a new polity of science. Chaos theory has sought to link itself to the new geometry of fractals, as developed by Benoit Mandelbrot; this provides a mathematical description of broken and ruptured forms such as those found in clouds, landscapes, earth fissures, cracks in metals and species densities. Feigenbaum believes that 'one has to look for scaling structures—how do big details relate to little details . . . the only things that can ever be universal, in a sense, are scaling things' (Gleick 1985, 63). Such combined theories may in the future provide a way of approaching rigorously from one direction the boundary regions between order and disorder that are also being approached by catastrophe theory from the opposite direction.

All these mathematical theories are also being applied to social phenomena, with as yet uncertain results. Chaos theory has been applied to the arms race by Alvin Saperstein, although he admits that the model is very crude. Zeeman has applied catastrophe theory to numerous social and psychological situations of abrupt change and breakdown, ranging from prison riots to angry dogs. Woodcock and Davis have extended these applications to such situations as swarms of locusts, panic in crowds and armies, status and marriage, oil monopolies, inflation, reactive schizophrenia, anorexia nervosa, democracy and revolution, and even the rise and fall of the Roman empire. Clearly some of these applications, especially the last one, are trivial. That the western half of the Roman empire gradually broke down over more than a century, but the eastern half did not, is known to everyone. Historians are still debating why it should have happened in this way. No mathematical theory can contribute anything to this debate. Catastrophe theory, apart from the misleading connotations of its name, has no more to offer in explaining the catastrophe that befell the western empire than any other mathematics. Thus the main problem concerning catastrophe theory will be to determine where it is substantively applicable and where it is only trivially applicable. The necessary restrictions of the scope of the theory have not yet been determined. Much of the contention and struggle for authority in connection with the theory is over this issue. Eventually when the struggle is resolved we will have a much clearer idea of the nature and range of the theory.

Nevertheless, it is possible to judge that some applications look more plausible than others, even outside the natural sciences. In an ingenious and amusing elaboration of catastrophe theory, whimsically called 'rubbish theory', Michael Thompson (1979) has convincingly applied it to a number of anthropological phenomena. He refers the cusp catastrophe graph to the periodic cyclical exchange of pigs, the so-called moka of the New Guinea highland clans, which over a four-year cycle ends with the ritual slaughter and consumption of thousands of pigs previously carefully husbanded. The details of the practice as well as the theory are too complex to be set out in full, but its general importance is undeniable since it bears considerable resemblance to the boom and bust cycles of advanced capitalist economies. It offers a new way of understanding rational economic behaviour—the New Guinean pig breeder being as much constrained by rational maximizing considerations as a modern entrepreneur. Thompson concludes this study with the very large claim that 'catastrophe theory will allow us to write the general equation of which Keynesian theory, with its social constant, is the special case' (ibid. 214). That remains to be seen, but certainly Thompson has made a start in integrating anthropology and economics.

Despite its facetiousness, Thompson's work is profoundly serious and points to a number of novel departures in the social sciences and humanities which have so far not been pursued. Beginning with the trivia of rubbish and excrement—all that we eliminate and reject so completely that we do not even see them any longer—Thompson notes the paradox that what is dismissed as rubbish can suddenly and 'catastrophically' be elevated into a precious possession: the rubbish of yesterday becomes the antique of today. Out of such seemingly simple insights, he develops a comprehensive model of the production, circulation and consumption of goods which is based on an original valuation, subsequent devaluation and sometimes sudden revaluation. This model does not merely relate economic to artistic value; it also offers a way of understanding value in socio-cultural systems as a whole. Thus the concept of 'rubbish' ultimately becomes a cognitive category in the articulation of world views: it is that which we conspire not to see or to banish from view when it intrudes. In this sense, 'rubbish is a universal feature, not necessarily of the human mind, nor of language, nor of social interaction, but of socio-cultural systems' (ibid. 88). 'The survival of a world view can be ensured only by eliminating, rejecting, or ignoring those intrusive and dangerous elements that preclude the continued coexistence of differing world views. These elements that elicit such response constitute the cultural category "rubbish"' (ibid. 90).

Thompson goes on to elaborate a theory of the formation and transformation of world views through the mutual cyclic interaction of world view and action. In essence this amounts to 'a sociological theory of creativity (and its dark side, destructivity)' (ibid. 147). With great perspicacity he grasps the point that the formation of a world view is as much a matter of what is excluded as of what is included. What tends to be excluded is that which is anomalous, paradoxical, contradictory, or, in short, monstrous. Monster exclusion and monster conservation are seen by Thompson as two opposed strategies, and he himself favours the latter. He links this monster-conserving style with Thom's 'art of models' and tries to show how it goes against the determinism and chance of reductivist genetics as preached by Monod. He also shows how it goes against Positivist reductivism which restricts what there is to what is known. Every world view entails a cognitive loss: that which it renders invisible as well as that which it makes unseen, or as he puts it, 'a way of seeing is also, most importantly, a way of not seeing' (ibid.). This explains changes in a world view and its associated system of values: when the rejected and suppressed 'unruly elements get through into the world view domain

. . . , the arrival of such new elements is likely to mess up the ordering process, in some cases giving rise to quite serious contradictions between hitherto integrated patterns of value' (ibid.). This also gives rise to what he calls 'destructivity' or 'negative creativity', which acts for change in world views, a view also independently propounded in *In the Beginning Was the Deed* (Redner 1982). .

The approach to this important topic is, as yet, merely sketched and much more work will have to be done. This development will depend not merely on intellectual considerations alone: any further elaboration of Thompson's ideas, and, therefore, the extent to which they will be allowed to alter the course of social science, depends also on how they are taken up and absorbed into the orthodox disciplinary structure of academia. But academic politics is clearly against him. It is unlikely that anyone less eccentrically placed than Thompson within the academic polity could have produced anomalous ideas of this kind. By the same token, ideas developed outside any disciplinary framework are not going to be taken seriously. They are themselves an academic 'monster' which will tend to be excluded rather than conserved: rubbish theory will itself be dismissed as rubbish. As we shall see, this is the probable fate of a number of other original thinkers whose work arose outside an academic setting. Indeed, as the next case reveals, this can likewise be so for those who become too individual even after they have proved themselves by the orthodox standards.

High Church Departures

To the foregoing instances of neo-Methodist approaches to the problems of form and formation can also be added examples of promising scientific work on these issues which stem more from a High Church conservative source. Above all there is the belatedly recognized work on genetic formation and development by Barbara McClintock, to which we have already alluded. It has now been accepted even by the very founders of molecular biology who dismissed it when she first put it forward; some others are hailing it as a second 'revolution' in biology. The long detour in molecular biology via the decoding of DNA in the simplest organisms has finally caught up with the problems of form and complexity in higher organisms. Monod's confident assertion that 'what is true for the E Coli will be true for the elephant as well' is not true—McClintock has shown that it is not true for maize either. Only when the orthodox molecular biologists began to suspect that even the *E. Coli* is more complex than they at first supposed and that lowly bacteria can rearrange their genetic make-up, did they condescend to take note of McClintock's much earlier work on maize. The reductivist program in molecular biology from the elephant down to the *E. Coli* can now be complemented by an integrative program from the *E. Coli* up to the elephant. And as McClintock has shown, different levels of the organic hierarchy display different genetic functions and laws of mutation and variation.

On the level of academic politics, however, the recognition of her work signals final victory in a battle for authority which was being lost for over thirty years. When McClintock first presented her ideas in 1951 and again in 1953 and 1956 she was met with stunned incomprehension. By then the reductivist program, first put forward by Schrödinger and taken up by Delbruck and Luria and the other phage-group physicists who colonized biology, had already assumed a dominant position. The decoding of DNA by Crick and Watson and the continuing success of their pupils and protégés at the Gordon Research Conferences confirmed the authority of this new collegial elite. Although McClintock had an established reputation in genetics and considerable formal-professional authority standing in that discipline—she was president of the Genetics Society and a member of the National Academy of Sciences—not even she could command a hearing. She was dismissed in the usual way as incomprehensible and mad—'they thought I was crazy, absolutely mad'—and some may have added 'just an eccentric old maid'. The upshot was that work, such as that of Jacob and Monod, produced within the molecular biology establishment, which paralleled hers, and eventually relied on her for support, did not at first acknowledge her contribution. As Judson reports: 'in their great synthesis for *The Journal of Molecular Biology* . . . Jacob and Monod did not cite McClintock's work—an unhappy oversight, Monod told me. ("They did not understand the technical aspects of maize genetics", McClintock said.)' (Judson 1979, 461). Eventually she gave up publishing her results, saying 'nobody was reading me, so what was the use?'

The complex interaction of ideas and politics in any major scientific dispute is well illustrated by this case, even though it is complicated by sexual discrimination. Her work was dismissed because it ran counter to the dominant idea maintained by the molecular biology establishment: Crick's central dogma. Indeed, this openly espoused dogma had something of the role of canonic doctrine in more ways than Crick perhaps intended. It became the shibboleth and rallying standard of a group of largely physics-trained molecular biologists who, as Yoxen claims,

> presented themselves as occupying a central role, as being an avant garde, and as possessing a style and rigour eminently worthy of imitation by those who were able to do so. . . . One can explain for example the tenacity and dogmatism with which certain apparently general principles, such as the universality of the genetic code or the double helical model of DNA structure, have been defended, in terms of the insecurity of an initially marginal group attempting to re-organize the conceptual map of biology, and thereby claim superior status in the life sciences (Yoxen 1982, 137).

Thus there was a strong elective affinity between the central dogma and the new authority structure arising in molecular biology. The central dogma affirmed genetic determinism and the reductive procedures of research in biology which the ex-physicist collegial elite favoured. The authority structure which had proved so successful in physics was imposed on biology. The splitting of the atomic nucleus seemed to augur the splitting of the cell nucleus by the same methods. The central dogma was formulated to affirm that program and to prevent anyone from departing from it. McClintock was among the very few whose work required that they depart from it; as a result she was punished by exclusion, intellectually, professionally and personally. As she herself comments:

> They had no feel for what these cells had to undergo in development.
> . . . Trying to make everything fit into set dogma won't work. . . . There
> is no such thing as a central dogma into which everything will fit. It turns
> out that any mechanism you can think of, you will find—even if it's the
> most bizarre kind of thinking. Anything . . . even if it doesn't make much
> sense, it'll be there. . . . So if the material tells you, "It may be this", allow
> that. Don't turn aside and call it an exception, an aberration, a contaminant
> (Fox Keller 1983, 179).

Now that she has won her battle—and the academic politics of that fact still have to be unravelled—her work can act as an instigation of a High Church reform movement not only in genetics but in science in general. Based on older-style procedures in the language of maize genetics, which had become nearly incomprehensible in the meantime to the laboratory-trained generation of molecular biologists, her approach to science is by virtue of this very fact more forward looking than the later DNA revolution. As her biographer Evelyn Fox Keller puts it:

> The "molecular" revolution in biology was a triumph of the kind of science
> represented by Classical physics. Now, the necessary next step seems to be
> the reincorporation of the naturalist's approach—an approach that does not
> press nature with leading questions but dwells patiently in the variety and
> complexity of organisms. The discovery of genetic lability and flexibility
> forces us to recognize the magnificent integration of cellular processes—the
> kinds of integration that are "simply incredible to our old-style thinking"
> (Fox Keller 1984, 72).

The last quoted phrase from McClintock herself indicates that she sees her work as pointing to a future science of integration processes, the converse of reductive science. She states, perhaps in the somewhat overoptimistic spirit of final vindication, that 'we are in the midst of a major revolution that will reorganize the way we look at things, the way we do research' (ibid.).

If, as a result of McClintock's work, 'a revolution that will reorganize the way we look at things' is to ensue then it will be what Gould (1984, 3) calls 'a second revolution [that] transmutes our view of inheritance and development', the view that had resulted from the first revolution of Watson and Crick. The first revolution concluded the quest for the reduction of the gene and by means of its central dogma reaffirmed genetic determinism of the strict Mendelian variety. The second revolution, by contrast, shows that 'the genome is fluid and mobile, changing constantly in quality and quantity, and replete with hierarchical systems of regulation and control' (ibid.). According to Gould, 'the implications for embryology and evolution are profound, and largely unexplored' (ibid.). The implications for embryology, one of the key outstanding problems in molecular biology, are likely to put in doubt many features of Brenner's previously outlined mechanist systemist project. The picture of groups of genes switching themselves on or off on command in strict sequence ('next switch on gene group number fifty-eight') like a computer code working by means of 'high-level logical computations, programs, [and] algorithms of development' (Judson 1979, 221)—all this and more is called in question by McClintock's jumping genes. These lead to the alternative picture of what Gould calls 'a more mobile genome subject to rapid and profound rearrangement'. If the implications for embryology and biological development are likely to be profound, the implications for evolution are likely to be even more so. Fox Keller speaks of McClintock's work as implying a third way of understanding evolution, one that goes beyond both Lamarck and Darwin:

> Without question, the genetic apparatus is the guarantor of the basic stability of genetic information. But equally without question, it is a more complex system, with more complex forms of feedback, than had been previously thought. Perhaps the future will show that its internal complexity is such as to enable it not only to program the life cycle of the organism, with fidelity to past and future generations, but also to reprogram itself when exposed to sufficient environmental stress—thereby effecting a kind of "learning" from the organisms experience. Such a picture would be radical indeed, and would be one that would do justice to McClintock's vision: it would imply a concept of genetic variation that is neither random nor purposive—and an understanding of evolution transcending that of both Lamarck and Darwin (Fox Keller 1983, 195).

Finally, we might consider McClintock's claim that her work will lead also to a revolution in 'the way we do research'. If so, this is likely to be the paradoxical revolution of the conservatives, namely a counter-revolution, for it will bring a return to a High Church approach. The elements of High Church science are all there in McClintock's procedure and attitudes: all the vocational, personal, art and craft or 'tacit' knowledge features which we previously explored in Chapter 7. She has persevered in 'small science', shunning the Big Science high-technology instrumentation on which all molecular biologists now rely; she preferred direct perception of the object with no more than a microscope to aid the naked eye. She has worked with utmost dedication, frequently in total solitude, devoting herself to one piece of nature, the plant maize, which she has come to understand with personal intimacy. She has thereby brought back into the natural sciences the need for understanding, something that had been driven out completely from the World sciences:

> The word "understanding", and the particular meaning she attributed to it, is the cornerstone of Barbara McClintock's entire approach to science. For her, the smallest details provided the key to the larger whole. It was her conviction that the closer her focus, the greater her attention to individual detail, to the unique characteristics of a single plant, of a single kernel, of a single chromosome, the more she would learn about the general principles by which the maize plant as a whole was organized, the better her "feeling for the organism" (ibid. 101).

Few biologists now are 'able to sustain the kind of feeling for the organism that was so productive—both scientifically and personally—for McClintock, and to some of them the difficulties of doing so seem to grow exponentially' (Fox Keller 1984, 72). Under the present scientific regime there is little time allowed for looking and feeling, especially when these must be done slowly with an organism such as maize, which only yields at most two crops per year, rather than (say) countless generations of bacteria in hours or even fruit flies in months. McClintock exhorts students to 'take time and look', but they know that if they do they will be left behind in the race for authority and standing and soon eliminated from science. Institutions and authority structures are lacking that could make it possible to practise science in this conservative way. McClintock is critical of 'conventional science [which] fails to illuminate not only "how" you know, but also, and equally, "what" you know' (ibid.). Yet 'she is confident that nature is on the side of scientists like herself' (ibid.). Unfortunately, Nature cannot change the institutions of science, and as long as these remain unreformed there is little hope for work of such quality being produced in that way again.

The solitary individual toiling away in the vineyard of a grand theory, driven by a pure passion, is still a recognizable figure outside the institutionalized fields of science. An unusual case is the now acclaimed novelist Elias Canetti, whose social science work has not as yet received any recognition. Lack of academic authority standing has obviously been a great handicap even for a Nobel prize winner in literature. Some sense of the reception of his major work *Crowds and Power* when it first appeared in 1962 can be gathered from the references to it in the novel *Herzog* by Saul Bellow, himself a literary laureate, but also an established academic who was probably voicing a negative academic opinion on the value of Canetti's work which was widespread in the social science disciplines: 'a curious, creepy mind, that one, convinced that madness always rules the world. . . . A gruesome and crazy book . . . fairly inhuman and filled with vile paranoid hypotheses' (Bellow 1965, 83, 323).

Canetti's work is in many respects arch-conservative; its style and approach are almost anachronistic, antedating by nearly a century the established approaches in sociology, history, anthropology and social psychology, the fields to which his ideas approximate. It harks back to the looser modes of literary speculation on history and social reality which are to be found in Tolstoy's *War and Peace*, to which Canetti obviously owes much, as well as to Broch, Kraus, Ernst Fisher and Brecht. The more scientific works to which his study relates belong largely to the last century: Tarde and Le Bon on crowds, Macdougal on groups, Darwinian social evolution and Frazer on myths. The largest influence is clearly Freud, whom Canetti seeks to counter at all points without ever naming him, for some obscure reason of his own. Nevertheless, he implicitly offers a critique of many of Freud's theories: the relation between leaders and led, what brings and holds people together in crowds, archetypal symbols and totem and taboo or the role of religion. In general, he seeks to displace the Freudian psychology based on sex and libido with one based on eating and incorporation which he then applies to give an anti-Freudian reading of the celebrated Schreber case. Much of this, whether in Freud or Canetti, must now be considered extremely dubious, together with the other nine-teenth-century sources of Canetti's ideas. Nevertheless, Canetti affords us unusual insights; time and again he observes and illuminates odd aspects of human conduct usually passed over as too irrational, perverse, mad or trifling to deserve attention—the rubbish and offal of history. Regardless of whether he succeeds in unifying all this into one grand theory of individual and social behaviour, which is his ambition, at every point the concrete details he notes stand out like jewels in a cabinet of curiosities. The rich and varied tapestry of human life glows from his pages. Not all of the cases he studies will always bear the interpretation he gives them, and sometimes he is plainly mistaken, but nearly always there is a point to his speculations. It is not possible here to undertake extensive exposition of his work or to provide the necessary corrective criticisms, for it cannot be simple accepted wholly as it stands. Nevertheless, it can be treasured and appreciated like a magnificent collection of human social phenomena arranged by a connoisseur of the perverser side of human nature.

Further acceptance of his work will depend on studies to show how it relates to the classic approaches in the fields with which it deals, the scientific work in history, sociology and psychology such as that of Marx, Simmel, Durkheim, Weber, Levi-Strauss, Piaget, Lacan and many contemporary social scientists. Is it an alternative to their approaches or a supplement to them? This is really a specific instance of the general question of how the truths of literature relate to those of science, for Canetti's ideas are often more like literary visions and metaphors than like scientific theories. A provisional answer can certainly be given, since Canetti's studies add to and enlarge many obscure aspects of well known and by now undisputed theories. Thus, for example, Weber's theory of charismatic authority and its routinization is complemented and supplemented by Canetti's treatment of the transformation from open to closed crowds, of the role of crowd crystals and of the leader as survivor. The current theories of mass society and mass behaviour can also gain much from his understanding of crowds and packs. Work in psychiatry on survivors, so necessary in an age of mass exterminations—work such as that of Robert Lifton, who barely acknowledges Canetti's influence—has also much to profit from Canetti's pioneering efforts.

High Church conservative reformers themselves tend to be unusual survivors such as McClintock, Chargaff and Canetti, who seem to have remained from another age of science. Far from being out of date, however, their work points to future developments and is ahead of the present routines of World science. Although they look back to the past, they head for the future and are thus the opposite of many progressively-minded scientists who look to the future but are drifting back to the past. The revolutionists, whom I shall discuss next, also look to the future, but they have a different future in view than do the others.

Revolutionist Departures

'Future science will not be politically immune'—Churchman's (1961, 209) statement may well be taken as the credo of the radical revolutionist approach to the future of science. As it comes from a systems theorist, it also shows that a consensus on the role of politics in science is being approached. As we have seen, Prigogine, an organicist systemist, also stresses the importance of the social, cultural and political dimensions of science. The idea of a revolution in science to be fought for politically is no longer unique to the revolutionists; even McClintock, a conservative, expresses herself in similar terms.

However, the revolutionist radicals in science specify with the greatest self-awareness the steps to be taken towards this end, both in the external politics of directing the goals of scientific research and through the internal academic political struggles that decide which scientific approaches and even which sciences will come out on top in the hierarchy of scientific authority. The revolutionists aim to overthrow the hierarchy of authority imposed by the scientific Establishment which favours arithmomorphic science, reductive science, Big Science and technological applied science serving military and industrial ends. They seek instead to give a much greater value to the critical sciences that aim to alter the existing conditions of society and science itself, the useful sciences of individual, social and environmental health and in general the configurational sciences that arise out of the complex interaction of the human and natural environments. However, it must be noted that such an altered valuation is not in itself sufficient to initiate a new scientific development; it can easily be accommodated within the old dispensation. Among the revolutionists, despite their bold talk of scientific revolutions and paradigm changes, it is difficult to find specific stipulations for new scientific approaches or examples of these which have been followed in practice. Nevertheless, some new developments fall roughly within a revolutionist orientation and might provide a basis for future science.

Such an approach to future science, both in theory and in practice, is most interestingly exemplified in the work of Elias which has only recently begun to receive general attention. His main opus, *The Civilizing Process*, was first published in 1939 in Switzerland but disappeared from view in the turmoil of war and was then scarcely noticed for nearly forty years in England where Elias, a refugee, taught in provincial universities, and remained throughout in a lowly academic position. This work initiates promising future developments in history, sociology and the social sciences in general. But before discussing this and later works in detail, it is essential to outline the basically radical revolutionist outlook on science which Elias has only explicitly developed in more recent writings on the sociology of science.

Elias' studies of history as well as his conception of science are informed by his political perspective. Taken all together, his work constitutes a general theory of power relations or what he calls 'an established-outsiders theory'. This he distinguishes from the narrower class theory of the Marxists:

> Not all forms of social oppression of one group by another have the form of class relations. At present one often tries to use the conceptual apparatus developed in connection with class relations for all forms of group oppression

or, alternatively, group emancipation. However, the class model is too narrow; one needs a broader overall conception to deal with the varieties of group oppression and group rise. I have found it helpful to use the term established-outsiders relationships as a more comprehensive concept in that sense (Elias 1982b, 315).

Elias applies this established-outsiders theory both to the sociology of politics and to the sociology of science, thereby seeing the rise of the State and the development of science in the same theoretical terms. Elias thinks of this theory as itself constituting a new future science, a new social science as well as a new science of science. He thinks of it in the stock revolutionist terms of a 'paradigm change': 'what is needed, therefore, is a sociological type of enquiry, capable of working out process models of the development of knowledge, fitting into, but not reducible to, models of the long-term development of human societies. In this case the paradigm change does not concern one particular discipline. It concerns the whole tree of knowledge with all its branches' (Elias 1982a, 37).

Elias does not distinguish between revolution and reformation, but he really means the latter for he explicitly uses that term when he tries to specify the nature of the 'paradigm change': 'if I were asked to say briefly and superficially what I regard as the linchpin of the reformation to which I have alluded, I would say it is the rethinking of our theory of knowledge in terms of evolving figurations of people, of developing groups of inter-dependent individuals as the subject of knowledge rather than of an isolated individual of the homo clausus type' (ibid. 62). This reformation is, how-ever, to be carried out politically, above all, by means of academic politics, for Elias envisages a wholesale struggle within and between academic establishments to win acceptance for and to institutionalize the new par-adigm:

> Inevitably, it will get entangled in interdisciplinary tensions and disputes. It cannot fail to be affected by power and status differentials between different disciplines. Thus, one cannot hope to bring about such a shift without including in one's theory of knowledge and of science the role played by interdisciplinary relationships in scientific developments and especially by the relationships between different scientific establishments (ibid.).

Elias' academic-political, established-outsiders theory of science embraces all aspects of scientific work. As he puts it: 'needless to say, the striving for absolute autonomy of scientific establishments, their status rivalry and the differentials of their power resources are not without influence on the construction of theories, the framing of problems and the character of the techniques used for solving them' (ibid. 44–5). The very content of knowl-edge is thus to a considerable extent—though never totally—determined by the struggles of scientific establishments for a monopoly of scientific knowledge. Scientific establishments, 'by virtue of their monopolistic control of an existing fund of knowledge, and of the skills needed for developing it, for producing new knowledge, can exclude others from access to these resources or admit them to their use selectively' (ibid. 40). The physicists in particular have exercised a 'hegemonic claim based on the idea that their method of research is the only scientific method and ought to be imitated by all other scientists' (ibid. 63). As against this hegemony of reductive methods and procedures, Elias strives to institute a new integrative approach based on the sciences of configuration and form and to show that 'the actual terms used in different sciences concerned with the exploration of composite units whose properties depend—more or less—on the configuration of the component parts are often very different: conformation, shape, form, organization, integration, figuration are some of them' (Elias 1974, 26). Such an approach requires thinking in terms of numerous levels of integration, rather than attempting to reduce all complex phenomena to the one basic level of atomic properties with which the physicists are concerned. Like Prigogine, Elias stresses the importance of those levels where irreversible processes occur, the temporal levels at which biological phenomena like the cell are to be found. 'The difficulty for many people is to think in terms of not only three or four but, perhaps 20 or 30 levels of integration superimposed upon each other like the part-units of a Chinese box. Such units require, in fact, different forms of thinking. Here there are, at every higher level of integration, regularities which cannot be explained alone in terms of the properties of the lower constituent parts' (Elias 1982a, 66). This holds for the social sciences as well as for the biological sciences: 'in their case, too, the figuration of constituent units, of human beings, has an explanatory function of its own in conjunction with the explanatory function to be derived from the properties of the constituent parts' (ibid.).

A prime example of the kind of configurational science advocated by Elias is his own sociological science of historical figurations as developed in *The Civilizing Process*. This work is a direct continuation of that of Max Weber and his now neglected younger brother Alfred Weber. Elias' concept of the 'civilizing process' comes from Alfred Weber's (1920) trio of three basic concepts: 'civilization process', 'cultural movement' and 'social process'. Elias' principle of monopoly formation, especially the monopoly of the means of violence which governs the civilizing process, derives from Max Weber's definition of the state as 'a human community that (successfully) claims the monopoly of the legitimate use of physical force within a given territory' (Weber 1971, 74). In a later work Elias asserts that 'the sociology of power has found its most fruitful treatment so far in the work of Max Weber' (Elias 1983, 21).

Elias approaches these weighty matters from the same starting point, concentrating on the same stuff as Michael Thompson in his 'rubbish theory': on snot and spit. The history of nose-blowing, spitting, drinking, eating at table, as well as the more serious activities of love-making and war-making, is the initial subject of Elias' account of the historical development of civilization. From these unpromising and seemingly trifling beginnings Elias develops a theory of the historical formation of the ego through self-restraint, social constraint, the habituation to a sense of privacy, the recourse to rational calculation and other such socializing devices. 'The learning of self-controls, call them "reason" or "conscience", "ego" or "super-ego", and the consequent curbing of more animalic impulses and affects, in short the civilizing of the human young, is never a process entirely without pain; it always leaves scars' (1982b, 141). Elias is perhaps too greatly influenced by Freud's theory of instincts and their repression as expounded in *Civilization and Its Discontents*. He has not considered that so-called natural impulses are themselves socially constituted through upbringing and that consequently no society, no matter how primitive and uncivilized, is without its social controls and repressions. What distinguishes the growth of civility in Western Europe from the middle ages onwards is merely the nature of these controls, the fact that they are exercised through manners and morals rather than in other ways and that they are directed at some bodily functions rather than others.

Notwithstanding such criticisms, however, there is great theoretical potential for future social science in the model Elias provides of how to mediate between the single person level of social psychology and the group level of social structure. This model permits an integration between individual and social systems sciences. For that purpose Elias deploys the concept of a 'figuration', which is both a system and a group of individuals who are mutually interdependent. In a later work the key example of such a figuration is a court society: 'a princely court, a court society, is a formation consisting of many individual people. Such a formation can certainly be called a "system". But it is not very easy to bring the use of this word into close touch with the phenomenon it refers to in sociological research. It does not sound very convincing to speak of a "system of people". For this reason the concept of the figuration is used here instead' (Elias 1983, 141). Behind this change in nomenclature is an important conceptual revision, one which 'somewhat reduces the difficulty that has led with a certain regularity, in the history of sociology up to now, to inconclusive contests between theoreticians who focus on individuals as such and others who concentrate on society as such' (ibid).

Thus by this move Elias seeks to establish a consensus between systems theories in the social sciences, such as the functionalist approach of Talcott Parsons, and individualizing approaches, such as are favoured by the Methodist and High Church conservatives, each of which on its own is one-sided and inadequate. The latter Elias calls 'nominalist theories of sociology whose exponents, while paying lip service to the study of human societies, finally postulate only isolated, closed individuals as really existing, so that everything they have to say about societies appears as features abstracted from isolated individuals' (ibid. 209). He puts his own position as follows:

> Unlike these nominalist tendencies, a study of social formations as figurations of interdependent individuals opens the way to a realistic sociology. For the fact that people do not exist as isolated, hermetically closed individuals, but as mutually interdependent individuals who form figurations of the most diverse kinds with each other, can be observed and demonstrated by particular studies. In such studies the genesis and evolution of specific figurations, in this case a royal court and a court society, can be determined with a high degree of certainty even though they are, of course, only a step on the way (Elias 1983, 209).

At this point Elias' work links up with that of Prigogine, for this key problem of the interaction between systems and individuals, and, therefore, also the even more difficult problem of the relation between determinism and choice, has already been broached on the level of the natural sciences by Prigogine and Stengers:

> The ideas to which we have devoted much space in this book—the ideas of instability, of fluctuation—diffuse into the social sciences. We know now that societies are immensely complex systems involving a potentially enormous number of bifurcations exemplified by the variety of cultures that have evolved in the relatively short span of human history. We know that such systems are highly sensitive to fluctuations. This leads both to hope and a threat: hope, since even a small fluctuation may grow and change the overall structure. As a result, individual activity is not doomed to insignificance. On the other hand, this is also a threat, since in our universe the security of stable, permanent rules seems gone forever. We are living in a dangerous and uncertain world that inspires no blind confidence (Prigogine and Stengers 1984, 313).

Elias' main study of figuration, that of a court society, is a continuation of his earlier work on state formation; it covers the epoch of the absolutist monarchies of the ancient regime. The earlier work deals with the preceding period of the feudal consolidation of the national monarchies. Elias postulates the growing monopolization of taxation and the means of violence by a central monarch as the sociological mechanism for the consolidation and unification of even larger territorial units, until finally the present state boundaries were attained.

> We see the following movement: first one castle stands against another, then territory against territory, then state against state and appearing on the historical horizon today are the first signs of struggles for an integration of regions and masses of people on a still larger scale. We may surmize that with continuing integration even larger units will gradually be assembled under a stable government and internally pacified (Elias 1982b, 88).

Thus Elias foresees a continuing struggle for power monopolies over increasingly larger areas, 'and if at present it is supremacy over continents that is at issue, there are clear signs, concomitant with the inter-dependence of larger and larger areas, of struggles for supremacy over a system embracing the entire inhabited earth' (ibid. 320).

Present developments towards integration—the formation of communities of nations such as the EEC (European Economic Community) and even towards looser associations such as ASEAN, (Association of Southeast Asian Nations)—seem to bear out this trend towards even larger territorial units. However, there are crucial differences between these developments and those which brought about the European state system. Now area unification does not seem to be taking place through an 'encompassing monopoly of force' (ibid. 321) as formerly in Europe. Neither U.S. hegemony through NATO (North Atlantic Treaty Organization) nor even Soviet domination through the Warsaw Pact, which are attempts at new monopolies of force, has succeeded in bringing the allied or satellite states under the complete control of either of the superpowers. A different process, one leading more to the formation of looser or tighter federations, and not that through domination by force, seems to be at work in the world. Elias in this case falls into the error of extrapolating tendencies of European history onto a world stage. His whole account of the civilizing process in terms of the history of European manners suffers from similar shortcomings. Now that the dominance of Europe over the world is over, it is doubtful that the previous process of civilizing the world through the inculcation of European customs and culture can continue. No longer are these synonomous with civilization itself. Native traditions are reasserting themselves everywhere. Elias' notion of civilization seems in retrospect far too Eurocentric.

The details and emphases may need correction, but thanks to the general issues it raises and its overall approach, Elias' work can be taken up and developed further. The major problem addressed is that of historical change itself and the role within it of freedom and determinism, and to this old question he suggests a new answer:

> What poses itself here with regard to the civilizing process is nothing other than the general problem of historical change. Taken as a whole this change is not "rationally" planned; but neither is it a random coming and going of orderless patterns. How is this possible? How does it happen at all that formations arise in the human world that no single human being has intended, and which yet are anything but cloud formations without stability or structure? (Elias 1982b, 230).

Cloud formations may not be as unstable as Elias' metaphor suggests; Prigogine has set himself to explore precisely the cohesion of such natural formations. In fact, these questions posed by Elias about the human world are closely analogous to those Prigogine asks about the natural world. How does social order emerge from the chaos of personal passions? How does the tendency to social structure overcome that towards disintegration and social entropy? Sometimes Elias makes out that these problems, which he likens to a kind of social chemistry, can be solved with the same rigour and precision as those of natural chemistry: 'the structure of a given system of rule, as a figuration of interdependent people, can be determined with almost the same rigour as that of a specific molecule by a scientist' (Elias 1983, 119). But he hastens to add that 'this is not to assert any ontological identity between the objects of the physical sciences and of sociology' (ibid). And elsewhere he asserts that 'the imminent regularities of social figurations are identical neither with the regularities of the "mind", of individual reasoning, nor with regularities of what we call "nature", even though functionally all these different dimensions of reality are indissolubly linked to each other' (Elias 1982b, 231). Such different dimensions of reality call for levels of integration in science 'superimposed upon each other like the part units of a Chinese box' (Elias 1982a, 66).

A reality stratified in levels does not need to be totally determined throughout in the way required in order to reduce reality to the one level. Each of the higher levels has its own degree of freedom. At the highest levels, those of humankind and society, freedom and determinism coexist as people act freely and yet are bound to act in certain predictable ways because they are bound together in social figurations. 'How and why people are bound together to form specific dynamic figurations is one of the central questions, perhaps even *the* central question of sociology. We can only begin to answer this question if we define the interdependence of people' (Elias 1983, 208). To answer this question Elias deploys his basic concepts of 'figuration', 'inter-dependence', 'balance of tensions' and the 'evolution of a figuration' (ibid. 210). This is for him the 'linchpin of the reformation' of the social sciences and of knowledge in general, as already indicated (Elias 1982a, 62). Thus, according to Elias (1983, 209), 'a study of social formations as figurations of interdependent individuals opens the way to a realistic sociology'.

Notwithstanding this conscious and careful attempt both to relate and to differentiate the social sciences from the natural sciences, however, Elias does seek to model his 'realistic sociology' on the natural sciences. He foresees a coming revolution in the historical sciences which will parallel the Scientific Revolution in the natural sciences.

> The deeper we penetrate the wealth of particular facts to discover the structure and regularities of the past, the more clearly emerges a firm framework of processes within which the scattered facts are taken up. Just as in past times people observing nature, after following many blind alleys in thought, gradually saw a more coherent vision of nature take shape before them, in our time the fragments of the human past gathered in our minds and books by the work of many generations, are beginning slowly to fall into place in a cohesive picture of history and of the human universe in general (Elias 1982b, 319).

The natural science emphases are unmistakable: structures and regularities, systems of balances, territorial imperatives, divisions of function, power accumulation and monopoly formations. A neo-Darwinian struggle for survival between groups and territorial entities is the pervading theme of Elias' work. The emphasis on formation of systems monopolizing force and money is highly reminiscent of Boulding's later conception of eco-systems of threat and exchange. Elias, too, readily succumbs to a kind of economic ecology, if not social chemistry.

One of the restrictive consequences of this emphasis is that ideas play little part in his general account. Unlike the Weber brothers, from whom his work derives, he seems less concerned with understanding and meaning in sociology. In his early work he pays little attention to cultural and intellectual institutions; churches, heresies, schools, movements of thought and art are rarely mentioned. Politics is considered in terms of force and finance, rarely in terms of legitimation and law. Dialectical processes of controversy and debate are subsumed under quasi-economic processes of competition for monopoly and domination.

In his later work Elias unsuccessfully attempts to correct this imbalance. In his study of court society he tries to interpret the meaningful self-understanding of the actors involved, especially of the passions and rivalries motivating them, but intellectual ideas rarely form part of this self-understanding. The intellectual struggles between the Jesuits and Jansenists, which other historians of the age of Louis XIV have found so significant, are not even mentioned. Religion seems to enter the lives of these courtiers only as ceremonial. Elias makes some attempt to account for courtly art, especially pastoral, but only succeeds in rendering it as ideology or the outward symptoms of inner affects. This is not too great an exaggeration when dealing with the *roman sentimental* mode exemplified by D'Urfé's *L'Astrée* but becomes a travesty when he attempts to account in the same way for the subject-object opposition of the new epistemology and specifically of Descartes' philosophy: 'the uncertainty over the nature of "reality", which led Descartes to the conclusion that the only certainty was thought itself, is a good example of the reification of an emotive idea corresponding to a structural peculiarity of people at a certain stage of social development, and therefore of human self-consciousness' (Elias 1983, 253). It is true that Descartes' personal motto was *larvatus prodeo*; this does not mean that the mask of social self-control produced the 'existing wall between himself and the object of his thought'. To discuss Descartes' philosophy and the new epistemology in the context of court society, leaving out of account the intellectual history of philosophy, science and religion, not to mention other background social forces, such as capitalism, which were of greater influence, is certainly farfetched and one-sided.

Elias goes even further, attempting to attribute almost all the intellectual and cultural currents of the baroque period to the affect control of court society:

> Descartes' doubt concerning the "reality" of everything that takes place outside thought, the transition to illusionistic types of painting, the stress on the outward-looking facade in church and domestic architecture, these and many related innovations are manifestations of the same change in the structure of society and of the people forming it. They are symptoms of the fact that people, through the greater emotional restraint imposed on them, no longer experience themselves in the world simply as creatures among others, but more and more as isolated individuals, each of whom is opposed, within his shell, to all other beings and things, including all other people as something existing outside his shell and separated by it from his "inner" self (Elias 1983, 254–5).

Thus what amounts to the wholesale transformation of modes of representation in all spheres of culture and politics during the Reformation and counter-Reformation period is ascribed to nothing more decisive than the lives of a few kings and their courtiers. These momentous changes in representation in fact had their main roots in theology, were implicated in religious wars for over a century, and thus require to be explained in a much more substantive fashion. Subjectivity, which originates more from Luther's and Calvin's theologies than from Descartes' philosophy, cannot simply be seen as a by-product of the courtly ethos. Elias' notion of court rationality, by which 'people and prestige are made calculable as instruments of power' (ibid. 111), and which he places alongside the bourgeois-industrial rationality discussed by Max Weber, is surely a far weaker and more limited source of the rationalism of the modern West than the characteristically Western religious and intellectual movements. Many other monarchies outside the West have also had a form of court rationality, but in none of these cases was this decisive for a general rationalization of the whole of their societies.

However, despite these serious shortcomings, Elias has made a significant contribution 'to a science that does not yet exist, historical psychology' (Elias 1982b, 282). Indeed, he has contributed to future social science by reconceiving the whole relation between history and sociology on a psychological basis. Thus the long sought-for integration of the classic work of Marx, Weber and Freud seems closer as a result of his efforts.

Conservationist Departures

Conservationists tend to draw their examples of novel departures in science solely from the ecological sciences, but this view is a little short-sighted. The conservationists' contribution to future science transcends ecology in the narrow sense and touches on many other problem-directed sciences. Ultimately it might even be said that the whole future relation of humankind and Nature, insofar as the one interacts with and transforms the other, is both subject to finalized research and falls under the conservationists' aegis. This confluence points to an integration of conservationist and revolutionist concerns, for as Schäfer (1983, 215) puts it: 'our concept of a normative finalized science has been shaped by ecology'.

Most novel developments in the ecological sciences tend to be instances of finalized science. This is so almost by definition in those researches which Ravetz (1971a, 424), following Commoner, calls critical science; these are 'practical problems involving the discovery, analysis and criticism of different sorts of damage inflicted on man and nature by run-away technology, followed by their public exposure and campaigns for their abolition'. Clearly what are to be considered 'problems' and hence what is to be researched and even the manner and extent of the research are all the outcomes of values which are frequently politically invoked, struggled over and maintained. Such problem-oriented science has received specific treatment by the finalization theorists, as shown in Chapter 3. Groups practising critical science also form task communities which point to novel institutional developments for future science, as the finalizationists have noted:

> The emergence and functioning of task communities in the transition area between the traditional disciplines of the nature sciences and technological fields have scarcely been investigated. It is clear, however, that they point to a new social organization of science in which research is tied neither to the regulatives of a disciplinary matrix nor to specific political or industrial projects, but is able to investigate the implications of a pre-given problem in relative independence (Schäfer 1983, 166).

Finalization theory also reveals that dealing with complex ecological objects and systems produces a situation in the natural sciences closer to that obtaining in the social sciences—one which even the finalizationists in their more Kuhnian moments condescendingly condemn as merely the passing effect of immaturity or of a pre-paradigm stage which eventually will be overcome when the social sciences come of age. Instead, the very opposite process seems to be taking place, for as the natural sciences mature they develop features long associated with the social sciences and other supposedly undeveloped sciences—among these are functional modes of explanation. Since the causal mechanisms underlying complex objects and systems often cannot be exhaustively specified, recourse must be had to overall global explanations and these might be functional, as the finalizationists themselves note:

> Functionalism, therefore, is a tendency enhanced by the complexity of the object. Without recourse to functionalism complex objects cannot be structured scientifically nor are they always sufficiently relevant to causal theory formation. . . . The greater the complexity of the areas to which natural science research is extended, the more science will be compelled to work with macro-variables in order to organize the multiple and complex interrelationships (Boehme, van den Daele and Krohn 1976, 321).

But two of the very authors of this statement, van den Daele and Krohn, assert in a later article the more conventional view that functional research—'an orientation which cannot draw on causal theories, and which provides no explanation of the problem'—characterizes only the 'early phase of disciplinary development' (van den Daele, Krohn and Weingart 1977, 232). There they explicitly limit functionalism to the pre-paradigmatic, exploratory stage of scientific development: a view reiterated later by Boehme, van den Daele and Hohlfeld in 'Finalization Revisited' (Schäfer 1983).

However, in their earlier article they correctly recognize that 'functional thinking can better satisfy the scientific regulatives of any discipline the more complex its subject matter' (Boehme, van den Daele and Krohn 1976, 320). This statement means that functionality is itself a function of complexity and not of the state of maturity of a discipline. It suggests that the conception of the maturity of a discipline on which finalization theory is based is ambiguous, if not inherently flawed. Functionality is inevitable once any science reverses the Classical programmatic goal of reductive simplification and moves in the obverse direction to integrative complexity. External influences might indeed act as a stimulus for such a reversal, as has been happening in contemporary World science. There has been a 'technical interest operative in the management of complex subject matters':

> This interest is no longer directed towards reconstruction—the reproduction of automata—but is directed toward control and regulation—the modification of behaviour, crisis management, etc. Functional theories characterize the type of science which is appropriate for a strategic age. A complex system cannot be reconstructed unless its mechanisms are understood but it can be handled strategically, provided, whatever mechanism may be operative, its most important functional structures are known (Boehme, van den Daele

and Krohn 1976, 320).

Many useful contemporary sciences can afford to by-pass the construction of mechanistic causal theories 'because the lack of explanatory power of a science does not preclude the utilization of its findings for specific purposes [of control]' (ibid.).

Indeed, the disjunction between explanation and control or prediction has begun to emerge in many of the World sciences which deal with complex systems. This is likely to become even more pronounced in future science. One of the inherent assumptions of Classical science, namely, that explanation affords prediction and that sound prediction must be based on a knowledge of the explanatory mechanism, has begun to break down. It has long been recognized that this assumption does not hold for the social sciences, but this was ascribed to a deficiency of these supposedly immature sciences which would in time be rectified. But now the very same so-called deficiency has begun to emerge in the natural sciences as well.

Recent research in ecology has reached that point at the threshhold of complex systems where the divergence between explanation and prediction is becoming more pronounced. Bradbury, Hammond, Reichelt and Young (1984, 221) recommend accepting such a disjunction as an explicit heuristic strategy, 'as an adaptive way of coping with the problems of complex systems'. In their earlier work they specifically address themselves to ecosystems which 'are generally of an order of complexity such that the distinction between explanation and prediction is very real', but they extrapolate their conclusion to all complex systems and objects in general: 'it may be shown that for sufficiently complex systems, robust models are either explanatory or predictive but not both' (Bradbury et al. 1983, 324). This is the obverse condition to that of the Classical reductive sciences where 'for many simple systems these goals overlap: prediction yields explanation and explanation yields prediction': 'one thinks here of such simple physical systems as pure gases generating the gas laws and classical thermodynamics. These models provide at once prediction and explanation' (ibid.).

Bradbury et al. apply their insight to resolve problems that have arisen in Environmental Impact Assessment studies with which they are professionally concerned. Environmental Impact Assessment is one of the key instances of the critical science advocated by the conservationist reformers; it deals with the interaction between humankind and Nature, or specifically between human industry and the environment, which is so critically important to the whole ecological movement. Similar theoretical problems are bound to arise in other finalized critical sciences and will require similar treatment. The problems of Environmental Impact Assessment have been revealed in a startling way in such minor catastrophies as the sudden collapse of the major herring fisheries of the world. These fisheries had hitherto been subject to scientific management on the basis of theories that attempted to be both explanatory and predictive: 'the fisheries scientists attempted to provide methods for predicting yields under different conditions and hence predicting optimal fishing regimes' (ibid.). For a time this approach proved successful, but then failure was sudden and unexpected: 'the scientists could not generate the one prediction that is the precondition of all others—the answer to the question, will the system survive? In fact, they may have done worse, giving clients a false sense of security by providing predictions which, though accurate, were trivial compared to the basic one of system survival' (ibid.).

What explains the possibility of such a startling catastrophic collapse of the whole system is the theoretical feature 'that there is an inherent element of unpredictability in the behaviour of complex systems', as indeed argued by Prigogine (ibid.). A system can maintain its stability so long as the disturbances or perturbations that buffet it can be contained so that it returns to a domain of possible states which are still within its systemic range:

> when the environmental perturbation or impact is severe enough—the system in its existing form breaks down because the buffering mechanisms fail to maintain all the elements of it. A new configuration—a new system—emerges within a new domain. What Prigogine has shown, and what is not yet well understood, is that there are generally many possible new systems that could emerge from a severe impact, and that the identity of the system which eventually emerges is inherently unpredictable (ibid.).

At this point catastrophe theory may have a part to play in accounting for such systemic breakdowns and reconstitutions, though it may be that the element of unpredictability is too large to be accommodated within strict mathematics.

Bradbury et al. argue that such features of complex systems call for a functional differentiation and separation of quite different scientific strategies, leading to the tactical separation of explanatory scientific methods from predictive ones. Bradbury et al. point to studies of ecological community structures and the techniques associated with them, such as classification, ordination, canonical variate analysis or seriation, as being essentially explanatory, or really descriptive, without much predictive potential. On the other hand, there are predictive theories which do not seek to describe the detailed causal mechanisms involved in the behaviour of a system, but are merely concerned with its functional workings. Then the 'task is to construct a model having the optimal degree of complexity, based only on empirical data, without any preconceived ideas of the system's structure; that is, using only simple input-output relationships of the system' (ibid. 325). These, of course, are basically functionalist theories. Among these they further differentiate those which deal only with a system in its steady state, when it is operating within its domain and subject only to minor perturbations, from those which apply when the system is severely disturbed and near the edge of breakdown, but short of collapse, since it is not possible to predict exactly what will happen when it does collapse. Numerous instances of both kinds of theories are given; 'each type of prediction needs a specific suit of analyses, optimising for that particular purpose' (ibid.).

Such conclusions go counter to the reductivist approach of Classical science where it is unquestioningly assumed that explanation and prediction depend on each other. The Positivist Methodists have enshrined this connection in their conception of the hypothetico-deductive explanatory method and its testability through the falsification of predictions. The work of Bradbury et al. is not only challenged for these philosophic reasons but also on the more substantive grounds that it constitutes a mistaken approach to ecology and complex systems in general. In a strongly worded rejoinder Ivan Kennedy (1984, 219) argues that 'it could have a negative impact in discouraging the study of basic mechanisms in ecosystems, the most obvious nexus of explanation and prediction'. He maintains the general principle that 'the difference between simple systems and complex systems is a combinatorial one of degree and not one of kind' (ibid.). 'The thesis advanced here is that the complexity of natural systems, no matter how great, does not involve new principles not recognisable in simpler systems such as chemicals reacting, particularly if open as in the chemostat. The difficulty in dealing with ecosystems lies in their complex non-equilibrium behaviour and the fact that the systems are continuous or with poorly defined boundaries' (ibid. 220). Kennedy proposes to deal with these systems by means of models of energy flow which in theory would be both explanatory and predictive. In their reply to this rejoinder Bradbury, et al. (1984) argue that such thermodynamic models are inappropriate to systems that are the products of evolution. Thermodynamics, they maintain, is too basic a mode of explanation for the higher levels of ecological systems. Hence the reductionist approach breaks down, and the separation of prediction from explanation has to be maintained at least as a heuristic strategy in science.

Obviously, the debate will go on, since what is at stake is crucial for the shape of future science. If Bradbury et al. are right then not only is the choice of system to be investigated a matter of values, but so too is the nature of the investigation itself—that is, whether it is to be predictive or explanatory. On this view science is subject to numerous value choices determining the nature, scope, extent and depth of any research. In other words, the conditions of research long familiar and theorized about in the social sciences would begin to invade the natural sciences as well.

The finalization theorists Boehme, van den Daele and Krohn (1976) identify other respects in which this is taking place. They note that the 'concern with complex and, in a sense, unique objects of inquiry', especially in ecology and the sciences of evolution, has led to a 'process of the historization of natural science' (ibid. 321). This means a tendency away from law-like generalizable theories. In some of these sciences there is a further consequence: repeatable controlled experiments are no longer possible since each experiment transforms the experimental situation itself and renders it non-repeatable. Thus, for example, continued 'experimentation' with DDT in killing insects leads to the selection of resistant insect strains which no longer produce the same experimental results. Such a 'de-generalization of scientific knowledge is something that seems to be connected with the increase in complexity and concreteness of the object area' (ibid. 323). The more science experiments with objects in the full complexity of their natural state, the more likely it is that the experimental operation itself will transform the object of inquiry. Thus science does not just objectively observe Nature without interfering with it; science also transforms Nature in the very process of coming to know it. This paradox is long familiar in the social sciences, where, for instance, the continued presence of anthropologists inevitably alters the mentality of the tribe they are studying. And obviously, economists, sociologists and historians also know that any prediction they make concerning the future of the subjects they are investigating could be acted on by these very subjects themselves and invalidated. This kind of interaction of humankind and Nature has led Boehme and Schäfer to foresee 'the merging of the natural and the social sciences into a Social Science of Nature' (Schäfer 1983, 266).

Human beings' capacity to alter Nature in a radical way through the action of science takes on another dimension where nuclear war is concerned. Conservationists and others are now engaged on the ultimate Environmental Impact Assessment Study: that of modelling the likely ecological effects of a nuclear disaster. The recently discovered and now strongly corroborated nuclear-winter thesis shows that the whole ecology of the planet could be catastrophically altered forever and perhaps even the normal course of evolution could be put into reverse. This is, of course, the study of a unique and unrepeatable event. The only parallel to it is the study of the ecological catastrophe that was most probably responsible for the extinction of the dinosaurs. It is amusing to note that some very Velikovsky-like hypotheses are now being canvassed by eminently respectable scientists as to the likelihood of an asteroid having crashed into the earth and thrown up enough dust to blanket out the surface. The study of catastrophies and their role in evolutionary development has taken on a new significance since Gould and Eldredge have challenged the accepted neo-Darwinian view of gradual and continuous evolutionary selection. The failure to find enough missing links between species has led them to propose an alternative view of evolution which requires the rather sudden appearance of new species, through a process they designate as 'punctuated equilibrium'.

Thus catastrophies and the sudden break down of systems will assume even greater importance in future science. Such discontinuous events can range from the sudden disappearance of a species in a carefully managed fisheries program through to the also relatively sudden appearance of new species in the evolutionary sequence. Catastrophies caused by humans are of particular importance in such studies, especially the ultimate human catastrophe of nuclear war. It is possible that the so-called catastrophe theory of Thom will be of use in some of these instances of discontinuous breakdown, though it is unlikely that a rigidly geometric technique will be able to do more than provide generalized models. And the same might be said of Feigenbaum's chaos theory. Prigogine's work on the sudden emergence of dissipative structures might also serve to provide parallels on the chemical and biological levels of nature. All this is not without its impact on the social sciences, as the work of economists such as Murray Wolfson (1986) demonstrates, for these theories of sudden breakdowns are also providing parallels for the modelling of disruptive historical processes, such as depressions, and mediate a move away from the classical economics of equilibrium or near-equilibrium systems towards a more historically realistic economics of non-equilibrium.[1] All in all, the conservationist preoccupation with the breakdown and emergence of complex systems links up with many of the trends in science previously discussed and shows how a working consensus about future science is being attained.

Integrative Science

Inherent in all the examples of potential developments in future science is an emphasis on form and configuration which entails an implicit weakening of the sharp separation of the natural sciences from the social sciences and humanities enshrined in Rickert's distinction between the nomothetic and ideographic principles which Weber upheld and the Classical scientific regime enforced in a disciplinary fashion. Stent makes this point quite explicit in his interpretation of Marr's work in Artificial Intelligence on form and shape recognition when he grants the need for pre-understanding and refers to it as a cerebral hermeneutics. So, too, does Minsky when he speaks of an 'administrative' approach to the brain. And even more significantly, Fox Keller refers to the work of McClintock as calling for understanding and 'a feel for the organism', a qualitative, almost intuitive grasp of the complexities inherent in a simple plant. Even Brenner, whose work derives from the successful reductive project of molecular biology, advocates a new integrative program for the study of developing organic forms and configurations. The same problems of morphogenesis are approached by Thom in a topological manner by means of catastrophe theory, which, as Zeeman and Thompson have shown, is equally applicable to the form-creating discontinuities of the natural and the social sciences. The emphasis on configurations is made in another way by Elias whose work traces the large-scale social figurations subtending the almost lawlike stabilities and changes of history. In all these scientific endeavours involving complex objects, valuations and strategically determined heuristic choices become crucial; this is brought out by the finalization theorists for the natural sciences in their contemporary phase, and it has always been known to be the case in the social and cultural sciences. In ecology the heuristic choice between the methods of explanation and those of prediction, as expounded by Bradbury, Hammond, Reichelt and Young, obviously depends on value assumptions and directions. All of these issues are summed up in the work of Prigogine where the concept of time serves as a guiding thread through the labyrinth of the sciences, tracing the passages from one to another and establishing the connections called for in a new 'alliance with Nature'.

This integration of the sciences is as yet in its beginnings, but already alliances are being forged which would have been unthinkable in World science with its separations and specialisations. These alliances are forming between sciences which focus in common on the large and complex objects of scientific investigation. A number of such objects can be identified and roughly ordered in a hierarchy of mutual dependence. The most basic object of all is energy and matter, both in its smallest and largest dimensions ranging from the nucleus of the atom, the microcosm, to the whole universe, the macrocosm. Placed between these two extremes is the middle object of most concern to us, the human body and in particular that part of it that is the most complex object known to us: the brain. The natural milieu in which such a body and brain evolved, the planetary ecosystem, is another global object of fundamental scientific concern. Linking all these basic objects is time, itself the object of greatest potential integrative scope for it ranges over the irreversible processes of physics and chemistry, the evolutionary processes of biology and ecology and the cultural processes of anthropology and sociology. Finally, within the time of history are to be found the large-scale cultural objects of human creation: social systems, systems of production, civilizations and the present global world-system. At each of these levels and between them one can find an integration of sciences taking place.

The physical sciences of the microcosm and the macrocosm, the smallest particle and the universe, have almost become integrated. Panofsky (1984) has said, 'I am exaggerating a bit, but cosmology and particle physics has almost become one field'. What permits this integration is the technological project of building ever larger accelerators whereby processes that take place at the farthest reaches of the universe in space and time can be tested in the laboratory. As there are clear limits to the size of these machines, economic limits if not others, it follows that there will also be limits to the integration achievable in this way. It is possible, of course, that a total integration of physics will be attained before such limits are reached. Already many researchers are looking forward to a Grand Unified Theory of all the basic forces and fundamental particles and thereby a completion of the whole project of physics. At the same time such a unified theory will describe how the universe was formed from the primeval ball of exploding energy, the so-called Big Bang, and how, as the temperature cooled and the simple symmetries were broken, the various forces and particles were formed. The accelerators required to confirm the features of such theories might not be feasible on earth, but confirmation might be achieved by further observation of star formation, black holes and other mysterious objects of cosmology. Once again the smallest and the largest might coincide.

At present wild and fantastic integrative surmises abound at all levels, as to how both particles and the universe were formed. Perhaps the most plausible of these unified theories is the so-called superstring theory, proposed by such accomplished and established physicists as C. N. Yang, Michael Green and John Schwartz. As with all such theories, this one depends on multiple dimensions, at first twenty-six, but by now reduced to ten. There seems little physical reason why one number is more plausible than any other, apart from mathematical convenience. And, as Yang insists, 'there is as yet not a single experimental hint' of the validity of the theory (Sullivan 1985). Green is even more cautious: 'I've seen many bandwagons come and go' (ibid.).

Apart from these orthodox attempts, physics also abounds with unconventional theories attempting a total integration. The two leading contenders are Bohm and Hiley's implicate order theory and Chew's S-matrix theory, the so-called boot-straps approach. Both depart in significant ways from accepted physical theory and reject the on-going search for ultimate particles and forces, preferring instead a holistic approach where physical systems are to be taken as unities. Capra believes that the future of physics lies in the integration of these two theories:

> Bohm's theory is still tentative, but there seems to be an intriguing kinship, even at this preliminary stage, between his theory of the implicate order and Chew's S-matrix theory. Both approaches are based on a view of the world as a dynamic web of relations; both attribute a central role to the notion of order; both use matrices to represent change and transformation, and topology to classify categories of order. Finally, both theories recognize that consciousness may well be an essential aspect of the universe that will have to be included in a future theory of physical phenomena (Capra 1983, 96).

Such a holistic systemic approach to basic reality, one even incorporating consciousness, has opened up room for all kinds of unconventional theories in other sciences as well. Briggs and Peat (1984) seek to establish links between such maverick scientists as Bohm, Prigogine, Sheldrake, Jantsch and Pribram in the fields of physics, chemistry, biology, ecology and neurophysiology, embracing all the key objects of science from the universe through the ecosystem to the brain. They believe that such an integrative effort will produce a complete 'science of wholeness', an alternative science to the conventional World sciences. This approach is somewhat along the same lines as Capra's 'turning point', and although it is free of his quasi-religious and quasi-political pretentions, it suffers from many of the same weaknesses. Plausible scientific theories are placed side by side with unsubstantiated speculations merely on the basis of formal resemblances, so the illusory impression is created that these correlate with each other and that all can be brought together in one comprehensive approach. Thus they speak of 'joining paradigms' in such a way that Prigogine's 'dissipative-structure' and Jantsch's 'co-evolution paradigm seem parallel or actually convergent with Bohm's implicate order' (ibid. 221). They themselves admit that these are mere speculations, but they persevere with them without stressing the difficulties and implausibilities involved. Clearly these theories are not on the same level; Prigogine's hypotheses, subject to controlled chemical experiments, are not to be equated with the more fanciful theorizations of the others. They are even further removed from Sheldrake's biological and morphogenic fields, which are pure speculation. Integration in the sciences can not be so easily obtained.

Viable integration means forging alliances between sciences in actual research work in the way that Prigogine has done in his multiple theory of time. Time itself is a multiple notion of very great generality involving a series of temporalities. There is, to begin with, universal time, as determined by the direction of expansion from the Big Bang onwards through the whole evolution of the universe. Next, there is the time of entropy or thermodynamic time. Finally, in the physical sciences there is the time of disentropic processes, those that generate structure and order, such as the chemistry of dissipative systems. Beyond this basic 'chemical time' there develops the 'biological time' of genetic evolution. And that in turn leads to the time of evolution proper which culminates in the time of anthropology and ultimately, of history. An exploration of all these time orders calls for an integration of their sciences, such as Prigogine undertakes.

The sciences of evolution bring into focus at least three global objects of special interest and importance to us: the ecosystem, the human species and human society. The ecosystem as an integrative object of scientific research has already been extensively explored by numerous sciences, each from its own disciplinary point of view. The primary aim must be to bring together all their disparate findings. The innumerable partial systems that constitute the planetary ecology which have so far been explored singly need to be related by being integrated into larger, more global systems. And this needs to be done both for the past of the ecosystem as well as for its likely future. The study of the evolutionary past, of how the ecosystem arose and how it functions, needs to be complemented by a study of how it will continue to evolve. In this respect one of the most interesting areas of research is Environmental Impact Assessment for it studies the interaction of humankind and Nature, namely, the effects of human activity on the rest of the ecosystem. Economic activity—which comprises industry, agriculture, the use of natural resources, the release of energy and pollutants, urbanization, and so on—is foremost among the effects to be studied. What is called for in this area of science is an integration of ecology and economics. The work of Boulding is an important theoretical start in this direction. On a more practical level there are specific empirical projects, such as the world systems models of Forrester and others of that type. Unfortunately, much of this work has proved poor in terms of usable predictions, both because too few parameters were taken into account and also because of the tendency to isolate the use of resources as if it were a self-contained system, rather than treating it as a variable aspect of economic activity (Lilienfeld 1978). Other social sciences will need to be brought in to qualify and complement such over simple systemic models.

The study of human evolution must ultimately focus on the brain, the final frontier which is likely to bring together just about every science. As we have already seen, it involves the convergence of molecular biology and genetics with Artificial Intelligence and neurology; almost all the medical sciences, including psychiatry, are being drawn in for obvious reasons; psychology, especially of the experimental kind, is also an essential participant; social psychology, linguistics and other social sciences and humanities play a part; and finally, cybernetics and branches of engineering come in at the side of Artificial Intelligence as well. Numerous theories about the brain and its functions are current in all these sciences. Few have the capacity to be comprehensive and to link up with others. Perhaps Karl Pribram's 'hologram' theory has greater potential in this respect than others, but it is still far from being confirmed, so it must be treated more as an interesting speculation. Although in time the basic secrets of the brain undoubtedly will be unlocked, there are obvious dangers in the knowledge that will be won in the future. Genetic engineering opens up

the possibilities of superior forms of eugenics that may be ethically un-
acceptable. A greater knowledge of brain neurology makes possible forms
of mind control which might be of use to repressive political authorities.
Though no-one can specify now how such future developments might be
guarded against, almost certainly safeguards will have to be active at the
level of the social application of scientific knowledge and not at the level
of the discovery of that knowledge itself. But the process of discovery will
probably reveal all kinds of limits to knowledge, for knowledge of the
brain is self-knowledge for the human species and thus has limiting paradoxes of self-reflection built in.

Self-knowledge for the human species also involves knowledge of human
society, another of the basic objects of scientific inquiry. This inquiry
begins with evolution, especially the evolution of language and culture,
and it culminates in history. A start in this direction has recently been
made in socio-biology. It is likely that this new science will eventually
contribute to the anthropological search for human universals. Structural
anthropology has already postulated a number of these, for example, the
universal taboo on incest which some theoretical anthropologists, above
all Lévi-Strauss, have linked to psycho-analysis and Freud's rather amateur
anthropological theorizing. Lévi-Strauss has explored the separation and
nexus of anthropology and history in his characterization of primitive
'cold' societies and historical 'hot' societies. He has also defined anew the
basic distinction between primitive and advanced thought, that is, between
magic and science. Lévi-Strauss and others are fully aware that what is
at issue in developing such connections is the attempt to establish a unified
science of developmental time spanning at least human evolution, social
development and historical change. As Lumsden and Wilson (1982, 1)
declare, 'we regard the linkage between biological and cultural evolution
to be one of the great unsolved but tractable problems of contemporary
science'. Whether this problem is tractable will depend on how it is
formulated and how cultural evolution is understood in relation to its two
opposed poles of biology and history.

A study of historical time involves the integrative efforts of the social
and cultural sciences as well as the humanities. Many of these are now
coming together in diverse ways around the large-scale objects of world
history and world society. There are two distinguishable trends at present
in this scientific endeavour, each of which brings together different constellations of sciences. There is the older departure which focuses on the
comparative history of world civilizations, such as was initiated by Spengler
and subsequently developed further by Toynbee, which had the sympathy
of von Bertalanffy (1968). The other more recent trend, which has the
support of Boulding, focuses on world-systems. One interesting example
of this is the recently proposed world-system theory now being worked
on by Wallerstein and his colleagues. The civilizational approach tends to
proceed from the past to the present, from dead or moribund civilizations
to the present world. It mainly brings together the more traditional historical, cultural and political sciences. The world-system approach tends
to proceed in the opposite direction, from the present world to its origins
in the past. It mainly brings together the current economic, historical and

political sciences, sometimes, as with Wallerstein, on a Marxist basis. Both kinds of theories have serious shortcomings, which suggests that a third approach might be necessary, one capable of embracing and unifying the others.

The Spengler-Toynbee civilizational perspective relies too exclusively on its conception of the basic unit of study as a civilization that is a self-enclosed and self-contained entity, even to the extent of seeing a civilization as a hermetically sealed unity or cultural soul, as Spengler maintained. But rarely if ever in history are such units to be found. Perhaps the closest approximations are the early river-valley civilizations; but that impression might only arise from our relative ignorance of their origins and inter-actions, which archeology will in time dispel. The attempt by both Spengler and Toynbee to foist this kind of model on diverse later social formations and their complicated histories leads to the arbitrary concoction of civi-lizational constructs, such as Spengler's so-called Magian civilization. The further attempt to impose on all civilizations a homologous time grid of rhythmic sequences of phases has led to all the absurdities of a procrustean treatment of history, justly mocked by empirical historians. What has received less criticism, because it is more rarely noticed, is the fact that this civilizational approach cannot come to terms with the modern world. Spengler treats the present world simply as the West or Europe in its post-cultural phase of static civilizational expansion all over the globe. Toynbee (1964, 536–45) also sees the West as continuing unbroken and opposes it to the East whose main representative he takes to be the Soviet Union, which he treats as traditional Russia, an offshoot of Byzantium, to whose civilization sphere it supposedly still belongs despite its altered character. Both fail to come to terms with the unique and unprecedented phenomenon of a new kind of World civilization.

The world-system theorists tend to the opposite error. They implicitly note the unprecedented nature of the new world-system but anachronist-ically read this back into past historical stages, especially those of the recent European past. Thus Wallerstein sees the present world economy as already there in the sixteenth century: 'specifically, this arena of modern social action has been and continues to be the modern world-system, which emerges in the sixteenth century as a European-centred world-economy' (Wallerstein and Hopkins 1977, 112). He uses the terms 'world-system' and 'world-economy' in such a broad fashion that the present global economy as well as the nascent colonialism of the sixteenth century are both referred to as world-economies, but so also is the Russian economy of the sixteenth century which he explicitly calls 'a separate Russian world-economy' (Wallerstein 1974, 306). It is difficult to see what the term can mean if used to refer to such totally diverse economic formations. Fur-thermore, one of the unfortunate effects of this ambiguity is that concepts and theories which refer to the present global system are continually projected back on to the past. Thus the neo-colonialist discourse of 'core-periphery' and 'unequal exchange' is referred back to sixteenth century Europe and the origins of capitalism. This approach makes capitalism appear to have been totally dependent on colonialism and hence to seem as if it were not a new mode of production but merely a world-wide mode of exploitation, not unlike the political capitalism of the Roman empire, which Wallerstein would very likely refuse to recognize as such, following Marx in regarding capitalism as uniquely a modern European phenomenon. On the political plane, Wallerstein makes an analogous error in seeing the old European state system as basically the same as that of world politics at present and not allowing for the unprecedented nature of the East-West nuclear confrontation and of the two rival power blocs spanning the world. He regards the Cold War as no different from all the other European conflicts, beginning with the Reformation wars of religion—a view contradicted by Morse (1976) and many others.

Apart from these relatively minor indiscretions of historical interpretation there are deeper problems with this world-system perspective which derive from its basic character as an attempted synthesis of Marxism with a world-systems approach. 'If there is one thing which distinguishes a world-system perspective from any other, it is its insistence that the unit of analysis is a world-system defined in terms of economic processes and links, and not any units defined in terms of juridical, political, cultural, geological, etc. criteria' (Wallerstein and Hopkins 1977, 137). By relying solely on the economic criterion to specify a world-system and determine its boundaries, Wallerstein by definition excludes all other dimensions, the political-military as well as the cultural-religious, as merely superstructural. Hence when it comes to actually specifying the sixteenth century European world-system Wallerstein (1974) runs into great difficulties in having to include on purely economic grounds Poland and the Americas but exclude Russia, the Levant and the East Indies whose trade with Europe was just as significant. To do so he has to resort to ad hoc provisions as well as what amount to covert moral judgements: 'it is not a question of the simple volume of trade or its composition' (1974, 301); 'now luxuries take second place to food . . . also to bullion' (ibid. 333). In fact, of course, Poland and the Americas have to be included for extra-economic reasons, being part of Latin Christian Europe. Such religious and cultural criteria as well as ideas in general hardly count for Wallerstein, who is, for example, contemptuous of Weber's Protestant ethic thesis (ibid. 152) as well as Webernian conceptions of legitimation (ibid. 143), both of which he has misunderstood. Thus world-systems theory sits somewhat uneasily with what is at bottom a rather doctrinaire Marxism—elsewhere Wallerstein (1984) even revives the proletarianization and withering-away-of-the-state theses which most other Western Marxists have given up.

An alternative approach to world studies as a focus for integrating the social and cultural sciences needs to be developed, one whose basic unit is neither the self-enclosed civilization nor the totalizing world-system. Such an approach might be founded by taking the city as the fundamental unit of history and using Max Weber's (1958) classic study *The City* as a starting point. A comparative study of cities in their changing roles in history calls for all the available social and cultural sciences at once and thus constitutes the object of greatest historical integration. Weber's major work *Economy and Society*—to which *The City* belongs as a chapter—is so far the best single instance we possess of such an integrative effort. There is hardly a social science he did not touch on and somewhere incorporate into this complex opus. Unfortunately, he did not focus all these separate, partial studies on the central chapter, *The City*, but in doing so for him we can link his sociological approach with a study of civilizations, as well as with more contemporary studies of the world-system. His younger brother Alfred had already moved in the direction of civilizational studies, following his lead as well as that of Spengler.

Throughout recorded history the city has been the primary locus of civilized life. This fact is brought out by the etymological link between 'cive' or 'civilitas' and 'civil' or 'civilization', as well as between 'polis' and 'politics'. Civilized life has invariably been based on two fundamental contrasts deriving from the city: the internal opposition between city and country and the external opposition of the civilized to the barbarian. The external opposition has invariably been that between nomads and city dwellers, that is, between steppe horsemen or bedouin camel riders and the peoples who built walled towns in the midst of cultivated land. The internal contrast of cultivated to rude has been that between the dwellers in the urban area within the walls and those of the hinterland or contado outside—the basic contrast of city to country around which so much of the internal dynamic of the history of any society turns. History in all its aspects—political, military, cultural, economic and religious—involves a continual interplay between barbarian nomads and civilized city dwellers, and between the latter and country folk. From its inception and throughout its historical development, the city is the social body containing all the basic organs of civilization: it is the citadel, burg or borough; it is the marketplace, forum, souk or bourse; it has an acropolis, temple or cathedral; it is ruled from a medina or palais, or whatever seat of power and justice; it holds a theatre, stadium or pleasure gardens; and it is the centre of consumption and production of human goods. For most of history it has been true to say, as Dr. Johnson said of London, that he who tires of the city tires of life. And yet those in it have always periodically sought to escape from it as much as have those outside to enter it. The city is not only the dwelling of civilization; it is also its prison.

Taking the city as the basic unit, one can go on to define a civilization as a regional conglomeration of cities connected to each other in different ways. These differences, more than anything else, give rise to the sense of the uniqueness or cultural specificity of each separate civilization. Thus civilizations can be viewed as loose or tight constellations of cities held together by some unique combination of cultural, religious, linguistic, economic and political bonds, frequently in a changing relation to each other. Rarely is such a complex of cities rigidly bounded in time or space, and even more rarely is it completely cut off from other adjacent complexes forming rival civilizations. Thus there are always borderline cities between civilizations that frequently have as much in common with each other as with their own centres. Such border outposts are themselves frequently the foci of new alignments of cities, and thereby they eventually become loci of new civilizations. In marked contrast to such liminal cities are the core cities, most frequently metropolises at the centres of civilizations. Sometimes one such central city predominates over all others in a civilizational area, as Rome did in the Mediterranean area of the ancient world and as Paris has almost done in European civilization. Such a city can even persist from civilization to civilization to become a veritable eternal city, as Rome has continued to do.

Even the now on-going transformation from the localized civilizations of the past to a global world civilization, the very first of its kind, can be seen in terms of the development of cities. This process began within the European civilization that had already succeeded in colonizing or conquering much of the rest of the world without unifying it. This latest phase of the history of Europe and its offshoots and possessions was marked by a new kind of city: the industrial metropolis as the centre of a world-wide empire. Already the European capitals of the nineteenth century had become larger and more complicated urban structures than anything in previous history. Then also a process of general urbanization started whereby the bulk of the rural population was eventually crowded into the newly burgeoning cities of capitalist production. This process extended outside Europe to America, Russia and parts of Asia such as Japan, China and India, and now it has become world-wide.

In the present post-European phase of world civilization fundamental changes have taken place in the nature and role of cities. These changes have led to the disappearance of the age-old oppositions of city to country and civilized to barbarian on which all previous civilizations were based. The old opposition between civilized and barbarian has disappeared as the nomads and primitive peoples have been absorbed finally into the civilized spheres. And the equally marked contrast between city and country has become attenuated as most people everywhere have been drawn into the ambit of the city. Already in the nineteenth century, as its population swelled, the city burst its containing walls and spilled out into the country-side in an ever widening ring of suburbs that eventually expanded into a regional conurbation when adjacent cities finally met. Like a giant sponge, these growing cities sucked the rural population from the country, leaving it no more than the site for mechanized agricultural production and holiday resorts. At the same time, communication, exchange, intercourse and other links between cities were continually increasing in a network of inter-connected cities which now spans the globe.

What we can now see, following both the civilizational and systems approaches, as a world civilization and world-system is constituted by all the links that join cities all over the world. These links form a network of strands, no one of which runs like a red thread throughout the whole fabric, for what joins one group of cities does not always extend to all. The nodes where most of the threads meet and mesh, the centres of largest linkage, are such relatively few cosmopolises as New York, London, Paris, Moscow, and Tokyo. These are the economic, political, cultural and in-tellectual centres of the world. Most other cities take their lead from the patterns set by these in all areas of life. In this way human life on earth is dominated by them, in their rivalries as well as in their spheres of cooperation.

The explanation of the rise of a world civilization out of the ruins of the previous European civilization provides the single most immediate and basic problem for the integrative effort of the social and historical sciences.

A distant parallel to this kind of issue for historians was the age-long fascination with the fall of the Roman empire and the rise of European civilization. But obviously the decline of Europe and the rise of a new world civilization in its stead concern us much more because we are still in the midst of this transformation. Some of the key questions that arise are the following: How and why did Europe succeed in expanding all over the world? Why did the other surviving civilizations fall so easily before it? Having more or less conquered the world, why did Europe not manage to unify it? Why did it not unify itself or even keep itself stable, rather then tear itself apart and destroy itself in two cataclysmic world wars and numerous revolutions, depressions and other crises? What accounts for the rise of the two daughter cultures of Europe, the United States and the Soviet Union, America and Russia, and what is their role as dominant powers in the new world-system? What part have the earlier pre-European civilizational remnants—especially in the Soviet Union and in such Asian countries as Japan, China, and India and in the Arab world—still to play in the context of a near universal world civilization? How universal in fact are the dominant features of world civilization and how important are these earlier traditional survivals, including the traditions of the now fast disappearing European civilization itself?

This last question brings into immediate focus the role of science and technology, for these civilizational forms have perhaps greater universality than any others and are, therefore, closest to being defining characteristics of world civilization. As I have demonstrated throughout this book, science and technology are alike throughout the world, despite some local variations; this is why we have referred to the new scientific epoch as one of World science. We examined in Chapter 1 some of the historical reasons that World science arose out of the matrix of European Classical science. Most of the book has been concerned with specifying the differences between these two fundamental scientific modes which reflect a basic change in civilization.

Thus the question of the transition from a European to a World science is one aspect of the still broader question of the transition from a European to a world civilization. This work might serve as an example of one attempt to integrate the numerous sciences dealing with science around this key problem. The problem is not merely a historical one since the kind and quality of scientists' response to it will determine the future of science. I began this book with precisely such responses by a number of renowned scientists. I may, therefore, now conclude it by returning to and recapitulating their reflections on this issue, starting once again with Heisenberg:

As Heisenberg reflected over the climax of physical science in his lifetime, he agreed with his colleague, Weizsäcker, that the great age of natural science was nearing its end. In finishing his own Unified Field theory, he felt that an era was over. When he was a young musician Heisenberg had felt that the great era of European music had reached its consummation and that the mind of Europe could be better raised to new heights in physics. His intuition had always been good, and now he intuitively felt our culture was reaching its limit. . . . There was no sadness in Heisenberg's sense of the passing of the great age of natural science. . . . He saw the limit and accepted it with humility. . . . Heisenberg felt that human culture could now reorient itself by making the limit part of its new bearing (Thompson 1973, 89).

Notes

Chapter 1: The Great Transformation

1. The sense in which ideas have ceased to be free is the same sense in which minds are not free—the academic is no longer a 'free-thinker'. The strenuous selection process designed to ensure that those chosen should be free to think tends to achieve the opposite effect by eliminating those most capable of it. Lewis Coser remarks on this paradox:

> Sixty years ago William James could proudly say at a Harvard Commencement Dinner "Our undisciplinables are our proudest products". It is no longer so—not because modern administrators possess vices from which earlier administrators were exempt but rather because the older pattern in a few elite universities could permit "undisciplinables" a freedom that has been much more difficult to grant in a highly bureaucratized organization. In the modern, intricately organized university, men not fitted into tables of organization might create long-range administrative havoc far beyond their immediate and direct impact (Coser 1965, 290).

2. In Marxist terms one might say that the forces of production and the relations of production have been transformed but that ideology has not shifted, which in Marxist theory is rather odd. But it is doubtful whether one can apply such a Marxist schema of the mode of production to the production of scientific knowledge, except as a metaphor. Only Althusser has attempted to apply to scientific knowledge the Marxian theory of the mode of production with strict literalness, and consequently his view of scientific work is questionable in most respects. But there is in this context no need to account for what might look like an anomaly only in strictly Marxist terms. A very different mode of explanation will be required to account for the backward role of culture in advanced societies and analogously for the recessive place of theory in the sciences.

3. The distinction between the 'restricted' and 'unrestricted' sciences was elaborated by C.F.A. Pantin (1968, ch. 1). The restricted sciences, above all physics and chemistry, epitomize the Classical epoch of science during which they were methodologically the dominant sciences, providing the approved models for all others. In the contemporary epoch of World science the unrestricted sciences have tended to come into their own, above all such environmental sciences as ecology, oceanography, and atmospheric physics.

Chapter 3: The Characteristics of World Science

1. The purely problem-solving character of the discovery has not escaped notice. The mathematician Hodges points out the close analogies between the decipherment of DNA and cryptanalysis:

The point was that X-ray crystallography, which was now [in 1949] being applied to the problem of determining the structure of proteins, was remarkably similar in nature to cryptanalysis. The X-rays would leave a diffraction pattern, which could be regarded as the encipherment of the molecular structure. Performing the decipherment process was closely analogous to the problem of finding both plain-text and key, given the cipher-text alone. . . . The analogy with cryptanalysis is even closer in that the crystallographer attacks the problem, at first sight too enormous for contemplation, by making a hypothesis about the structure of the crystal. Thus Watson and Crick pursued the DNA analysis, as did Pauling, by making good guesses about the helix structure, and thus getting closer and closer to the solution (Hodges 1985, 410).

In a review of *The Double Helix,* Ziman states that 'by the time they [Watson and Crick] had ventured into battle, victory was certain; it was largely chance that put the symbol of it into their hands' (Zuckermann 1977, 54). See also Judson (1979), but he is, unfortunately, unwilling to make the requisite scientific judgements in order to evaluate the various contributions to genetics. These judgements are the ones that Zuckermann (1977, 54) quotes anonymously when she refers to the fact that 'qualified observers who emphasise the immense value of the Crick-Watson discovery also go on to to note that it involved neither the profound foresight required for exploration into largely unknown territory nor the deep skepticism needed to recast old ideas in fundamentally new ways'. Zuckermann's book shows in general how the procedure of awarding Nobel prizes for the culminating solutions of problems—to the neglect of so much else in science, especially conceptual innovation—and the practice of valuing scientific work by its Nobel rewards, has had the unforeseen effect of pushing science even further in the direction of problem-solving.

2. As van den Daele, Krohn and Weingart maintain:

These examples suggest that the separation of nomologically-oriented fundamental disciplines from artefact-oriented technologies has become obsolete. In present-day science, research fields subject to the control of science policy are complex aggregates of concerns dealing with the structure of matter, technological construction (e.g. acceleration to extreme velocities, realization of extreme pressures) and social normative expectations (e.g. profitability, security, health). Thus the political direction of science implies the initiation of special developments both in basic research and in technology. Or, to put it another way, the strategic direction of science may assume such complexity that problem-solving can no longer depend on the application of advances made in basic research but instead implies the production of new forms of fundamental knowledge (van den Daele, Krohn and Weingart 1977, 220).

Chapter 4: Knowledge and Authority: An Introduction

1. Bourdieu's major work *Homo Academicus* (1984) has only come into my hands in far-off Australia (thanks to Richard Teese) as this book goes to press, too late to make effective use of this most comprehensive and incisive study of French academia. Chapter 3 entitled 'Espéce de capital et formes des pouvoir' is particularly relevant to this book. However, it is not apparent that Bourdieu has basically altered his conception of the field; this is demonstrated by his attempt to account for the opposition in literary criticism between the 'orthodox' work of Raymond Picard and the 'heretical' work of Roland Barthes largely in terms of

the function of the '*champ universitaire*' (ibid. 151), not taking much account of the intellectual content of these opposed literary theories.

2. As Olby comments: 'it is notorious that Mendel failed to arouse any interest in the local Society or in any of the institutions to which the journal was sent', that is the journal of the *Naturforschenden Vereins* in Brno. Olby goes on to imply that his work might have been received better if it had been published in a more prestigious journal: 'Mendel published his work locally because he lectured on it locally, but this does not mean that he would have refused to publish it in the *Berichte der deutschen botanischen Gesellschaft* if he had been requested to do so. But he did not dare to ask' (Olby 1966, 118, 192).

3. Lewis Coser seconds this view:

The modern academy is divided into a number of departments corresponding to scholarly disciplines and professional training centres. As the fields represented in these departments develop and as the departments grow, departmental boundaries tend to become rigid and to discourage intellectual curiosity beyond the administratively defined departmental settings. Lip service may be paid to "cross-fertilization", but in actual fact young scholars are generally advised to stay within the general boundaries of the "field". In addition, as a particular academic field becomes professionalized, those active within it are expected to take their colleagues in the profession, as well as their professional clients as their main reference groups (Coser 1965, 282).

Chapter 5: The Forms of Scientific Authority

1. This is not to deny that patronal authority has been a serious handicap, especially in the development of the natural sciences in France. This fact was already apparent in the nineteenth century, for after a brilliant start during the Napoleonic era, the sciences began to falter. Crosland, who gives an account of the Napoleonic period in his book, *The Society of Arcueil,* nevertheless states in his concluding paragraph: 'Arcueil has a connotation of patronage extending to the support of one's own candidate to the exclusion of all outsiders. . . . However great French science was at the beginning of the nineteenth century, this attitude has persisted and has been a weakening factor ever since' (Crosland 1967, 474).

2. As an anonymous lecturer in French literature, quoted by Fyvel (1968, 141), remarks: 'the paradoxical advantage is that the [French] system excludes the imaginative and the brilliant, who wouldn't accept this dull grind and after their Agrégation go straight into (a) journalism (b) administration, and (c) nowadays, the international civil service—today three very central professions'.

3. One of the key ways in which authority makes for authorship is the procurement of funding required for the production of most scientific work. Without the requisite authoritative backing such funding is rarely forthcoming. The quality or interest of the work itself counts for little on its own. Such a distinguished scientist as von Bertalanffy, already with major achievements to his name when he migrated to North America in the post-war years, was advised as follows by his friend Aldous Huxley as to how to go about securing a Ford Foundation grant in a letter of 18 January 1954: 'the project has to go to the heads of several departments, all of whom are academic personages of much importance, upon whom nothing but academic backing will make any impression. So if you want them to sit up and take notice, prepare your way with a barrage of heavy guns from respectable institutions' (Gray and Rizzo 1973).

4. Bennis describes this state very vividly:

The Development project was threatened by the yearly scrutiny of the Foundation and consequently, an annual bout with uncertainty. For the past two years the Foundation has not announced the grant till the end of May . . . the Development personnel see the Foundation as a towering, overshadowing Moloch. Each year, during the past two years, with growing intensity from January to May, the payoff question raised by the Development personnel has been, "will the funds come through?" (Coser 1965, 288).

5. Dr. Scott Henderson, director of the National Health and Medical Research Council's social psychiatry research unit at the Australian National University, has stated that 'while research had been done on student mental disorders, nothing at all was known about the mental health of staff at tertiary education institutions' (*The Age* [Melbourne], 20 February 1984). Nevertheless, indirect epidemiological evidence suggests that the risk of mental health problems is higher in the humanities than the science faculty. This already shows up at the student level; 'the students enrolling in the arts faculty had a significantly higher average neuroticism score (EPI) at enrollment than students enrolling in other faculties [and] there was greater help-seeking among arts-and-humanities students than among science students; arts and behavioural science students were over-represented in the psychiatric clinic user population' (McMichael and Hetzel 1974, 204). Another study has shown that among school teachers '17% had symptoms of severe psychological distress compared with an expected figure of 9% for the community generally' (Finlay-Jones 1986, 304). If any group of university teachers approaches this level for school teachers, it is more likely to be found in the humanities since the level of frustrated expectation—as determined by rates of publication and promotion—is higher than in the sciences, and that is a strong predisposing factor for mental stress.

6. See the statement by Q. D. Leavis:

Another relevant point is that intellectual matters are hopelessly overlaid by social life, e.g. the reasons for professorial and other appointments would often repay investigation, as in general the extent to which intellectual standards have in different places been stultified by social factors and academic politics. Outside the sciences, careers founded solely on log-rolling and social contacts are not unknown, and keeping the right company is in many fields the best, if not the indispensable, means of advancement. There is a pretty general recognition that the further the subject is from being a science the less have real qualifications to do with appointments or influential positions in the academic world of the humanities (Leavis 1968, 4).

Though this was written in 1943, it probably still applies today, given the persistence of the established ways of doing things at Oxbridge.

7. A curious case is precisely that of the outstanding English literary critic of the twentieth century, F. R. Leavis, who despite extensive publications and almost single-handedly running the journal *Scrutiny,* remained in a junior position at a Cambridge college—a fact which he very much resented all his life. His wife, Queenie Leavis, never attained any official position even though she published widely and virtually founded the sociology of literature in England, as well as, in passing, the sociology of the university—work which, unfortunately, nobody else took up after her, perhaps having learned the lesson from her experience.

Chapter 6: Pathologies of Science

1. Much attention has been devoted to crime in science and its eradication. Frauds and even hoaxes have been a permanent feature of science; some have been

extremely long lasting, such as the notorious Piltdown Man. They have invariably
been discovered and have rarely been very damaging. But now there is reason to
believe that the incidence of hidden fraud is rising in proportion to the volume
of work produced. There are very many books on this popular subject, among the
latest that by Broad and Wade. As an example of the 'crime rate' they claim that
of the 12,000 clinical investigators in the United States 'perhaps as many as 10
per cent do something less than (honest research)', according to Food and Drug
Administration Officials in 1980 (Broad and Wade 1982, 83).

2. It cannot be accepted as altogether fortuitious that Derek Freeman (1983)
published his devastating critique only after Margaret Mead died in 1978. His
work was begun as early as 1940, and it refutes the inadequate field work Mead
carried out in 1925 on adolescent sexuality in Samoa. According to his own
admission, Freeman revealed the gist of his criticisms privately to Mead in 1964.
Her reaction, according to Freeman, was that 'she was puzzled and incredulous,
her jaw dropped'. (See report by Ken Hayley in *The Age* [Melbourne], 25 February,
1983.) But neither of them made any of this public, and another generation of
students in anthropology and other allied disciplines was inculcated with falsehoods.
Mead refused to revise the book. 'To revise it would be impossible', Mead wrote
in the preface to the 1973 edition, as Boyce Rensberger reports (*Dialogue*, no. 63,
1/1984). He also adds that 'nobody liked to cross Margaret Mead', which perhaps
explains a lot. The attempts by her followers to drum Freeman out of the profession
also repay close study.

3. This is exactly what A.J.R. Prentice, a mathematical astronomer, complains
of in the press. He states that his theory of the solar system, which he claims was
recently confirmed by the NASA spacecraft *Voyager 2*, was for over ten years held
back from publication by the vagaries of the refereeing system in the person of
A.G.W. Cameron of the Harvard College Observatory, who holds the more conventional, authoritative theory which is contradicted by Prentice's. *Science* and
Nature both rejected his papers because, Prentice claims, they sent them to Cameron
for refereeing: 'for 10 years I have had to put up with this absurd situation where
I knew I had a reasonable model for the solar system, yet I couldn't find a market
for it because of this fellow Cameron. To put it bluntly, he made sure there was
no competition' (*The Age* [Melbourne], 30 January 1982).

4. Note also Sayre's comment about Franklin: 'had she read *The Double Helix*,
and realized what she never did realize in her lifetime, that her work was appro-
priated and used without proper credit, I doubt very much if she would have
laughed, and considered it a clever joke on the part of "honest Jim"' (Sayre 1975,
194). Note, too, Sayre's comment on the consequences of this:

> A generation of graduate students in science read *The Double Helix* and
> learned a lesson: the old morality was dead, and they had just been told
> about its demise by a respected highly successful Nobel Laureate, an up-to-
> date hero who clearly knew more about how science was acceptably "done"
> than the old-fashioned types who prattled about ethics (ibid. 195).

5. See, for example, a report by Jane Ford in *The Australian* (21 February
1983), where medical researchers Ian Clark, Bill Cowden and Peter Hunt of the
John Curtin School of Medical Research at the ANU (Canberra) made the following
charge:

> Last Christmas, their latest research findings and deductions appeared in the
> British medical journal, *The Lancet*, under the name of Dr. Anthony Allison,
> a scientist with a worldwide reputation from Syntex research, a major drug

company at Palo Alto in California. This paper appeared to have been written when Dr. Allison knew a similar article by the ANU group would appear in the January issue of the American Journal, *Infection and Immunity.* The ANU article had been made available to Dr. Allison last August, but luckily for its authors, to other international colleagues some months before. New anti-malarial drugs are constantly being sought by international drug companies who see a potential multi-million dollar market for any new commercial product in the field because of the growing resistance of the malaria parasite to conventional drugs.

6. Project Camelot was a mammoth study project of potential insurgency in Latin America conceived, designed and funded by the U.S. Army's Office of Research and Development in 1963. It was enthusiastically taken up by a team of social scientists who wanted to use Chile as their testing ground. Not surprisingly, the Chileans objected, and the whole project was aborted in 1965 (Nisbet 1969).

7. Sometimes the status differentials in some disciplines seem incomprehensible to an outsider and sound very silly, such as the well-known fact that land archeologists (those excavating sites) tend to look down on sea archeologists (those searching for wrecks). It also used to be the case that land geologists looked down on oceanographers, before plate tectonics reversed this status differential.

8. In an appendix entitled 'Professor Friedman and Statistics', Lord Balogh (1982) questions the cavalier attitude to facts and figures adopted by Friedman to bolster his basically historical case that the quantity of money is closely correlated with other economic indices such as inflation. This challenge seems to have been borne out by an econometric study entitled 'Assertion Without Empirical Basis' (published by the Bank of England late in 1983) by David Hendry and Neil Ericsson. Hendry is reported by *The Guardian* (December 15, 1983) as stating that Friedman 'resorts to simply incredible manipulation of official data and almost every assertion in (his) book is false'. If this criticism is correct, then it would seem that Monetarism is more than just an anachronism: it is something of an academic confidence trick as well.

9. The view that not only present science but the whole of modern science since the Scientific Revolution is a pathological development on the level of civilization was expressed by Needham in favour of the traditional sciences of China, so well suited to its civilizational stability:

China's slow and steady progress was overtaken by the exponential growth of modern science, with its consequences, after the Renaissance. . . . The inventions and discoveries of the Chinese were mostly put to great and widespread use, but under the control of a society which had relatively very stable standards. There can be no doubt that there was a certain spontaneous homeostasis about Chinese society and that Europe had a built-in quality of instability. When Tennyson wrote his famous lines about "the ringing groves of change" and "better fifty years of Europe than a cycle of Cathay", he felt impelled to believe that violent technical innovation must always be advantageous; today we might not be quite so sure (Dawson 1964, 304–5).

This view contrasts sharply with Weber's previously quoted phrase 'Chinese ossification' which is not all that removed from Tennyson, for Weber held that the great danger facing Europe was the 'iron cage' of bureaucracy to which China had succumbed. Weber ultimately sided with the Rationalism of the West and with its science against the stability of traditional civilizations. The contrast with Weber is less pronounced in Needham's major work on Chinese science which clearly points out its shortcomings as compared to Western science (Redner 1987).

Chapter 8: On the Way to Future Science

1. Wolfson's attempt takes off from the work of Georgescu-Roegen in economics and of Haken in synergetics, as well as the other developments in disequilibrium theory such as those of Prigogine, Thom and chaos theory. It is the start of a comprehensive onslaught on classical marginalist economics, one which goes back to Marx for its inspiration. In discussing the instability of systems subject to feedback mechanisms Wolfson states:

> In characterizing such systems, Prigogine differentiates between the stable "thermodynamic branch" and the unstable branch of solutions. The former which is characteristic of closed systems, leads to equilibrium state variables in the sense we have discussed. As subject as human relations are to random shocks and as sensitive as these systems are to variations in initial conditions, the acceptance of the view that economic behaviour can be explained as the "thermodynamic branch" is not warranted by theory and certainly not by the facts of continued economic evolution, not to speak of catastrophe and discontinuity. The addition of stochastic elements means that which branch will be followed by the system cannot always be determined in advance. The point that the synergistic school of thought suggests is that qualitatively different structures can arise from those branched processes, exhibiting orderliness and stability at various levels of aggregation. . . . No social scientist who has read Hegel or Marx can help but react to this development with the feeling that this is a computer driven dialectics (Wolfson 1986, 28–9).

Bibliography

Adorno, T. W., *Negative Dialectics,* trans. E. B. Ashton (Routledge and Kegan Paul, London, 1973).

Ambio: A Journal of the Human Environment (The Royal Swedish Academy of Sciences, Pergamon Press), Vol. XCI, No. 2–3, 1982.

Atlas, James, 'Intellectuals on the Right', *Dialogue,* Vol. 73, No. 3, 1986.

Auger, Pierre, *Current Trends in Scientific Research* (UNESCO, Paris, 1961).

Bachelard, Gaston, *Le Rationalisme Appliqué* (Presses Universitaires de France, Paris 1949).

Balogh, Thomas, *The Irrelevance of Conventional Economics* (Weidenfeld and Nicolson, London, 1982).

Barnes, B., and D. Edge, *Science in Context* (M.I.T. Press, Cambridge/Mass., 1982).

Becker, T., and M. Kogan *Process and Structure in Higher Education* (Heinemann, London, 1980).

Beer, S., 'Below the Twilight Arch—A Mythology of System', in D. E. Eckman (ed.), *Systems: Research and Design* (Wiley, New York, 1961).

Bellow, Saul, *Herzog* (Penguin Books, 1965).

Ben-David, J., 'Scientific Growth: A Sociological View', *Minerva,* Vol. II, 1964.

Ben-David, J., *The Scientists Role in Society* (Prentice-Hall, Englewood Cliffs, New Jersey, 1971).

Bernstein, Jeremy, *Science Observed* (Basic Books, New York, 1982).

Bloor, D., *Knowledge and Social Imagery* (Routledge and Kegan Paul, London, 1978).

Blume, S. S., *Toward a Political Sociology of Science* (Free Press, New York, 1974).

Blume, S. S. (ed.), *Perspectives in the Sociology of Science* (John Wiley, Chichester, 1977).

Boehme, Gernot, 'The Scientification of Technology', in W. Krohn, E. Layton and P. Weingart (eds.), *The Dynamics of Science and Technology,* Sociology of the Sciences Yearbook 1978 (Reidel, Dordrecht, 1978).

Boehme, Gernot, 'Alternatives in Science—Alternatives to Science?' in H. Novotny and H. Rose (eds.), Sociology of the Sciences Yearbook 1979 (Reidel, Dordrecht, 1979).

Boehme, G., W. van den Daele, and W. Krohn, 'Finalization in Science', *Social Science Information,* Vol. 15, No. 2–3, 1976.

Bohr, Niels, *Atomic Physics and Human Knowledge* (Interscience-Wiley, New York, 1963).

Bourdieu, Pierre, 'La Defence du Corps', *Social Science Information,* Vol. 10, 1971, p. 456.

Bourdieu, Pierre, 'The Specificity of the Scientific Field and the Social Conditions of the Progress of Reason', *Social Science Information,* Vol. 14, No. 6, 1975.

Bourdieu, Pierre, 'The Production of Belief: Contribution to an Economy of Symbolic Goods', trans. R. Nice, *Actes de la Recherche en Sciences Sociales (1977),* Vol. 13, pp. 3–43.

Bourdieu, Pierre, *Homo Academicus* (les Editions de Minuit, Paris, 1984).
Bradbury, R. H., L. S. Hammond, R. E. Reichelt and P. C. Young, 'Prediction versus Explanation in Environmental Impact Assessment', *Search,* Vol. 14, No. 11–12, December 1983.
Bradbury, R. H., L. S. Hammond, R. E. Reichelt and P. C. Young, 'Prediction and Explanation as a Dialectical Pair in Ecology', *Search,* Vol. 15, No. 7–8, August/September 1984, p. 221.
Briggs, J. P., and F. D. Peat, *Looking Glass Universe: The Emerging Science of Wholeness* (Collins/Fontana, Glasgow, 1984).
Broad, W. J., and N. Wade, *Betrayers of the Truth* (Simon and Schuster, New York, 1982).
Broad, W. J., 'Seeing Machines Are Not in Sight—yet', *The Age* (Melbourne), October 15, 1984 (Reprinted from *The New York Times*).
Broad, W. J., 'Today's Best Science Stems From More Than One Brain', *The Age* (Melbourne), January 14, 1985 (Reprinted from *The New York Times*).
Brooks, Harvey, 'The Future Growth of Academic Research', in Harold Orlans (ed.), *Science Policy and the University* (The Brookings Institution, Washington, D.C., 1968).
Brown, W. R., *Academic Politics* (University of Alabama Press, Alabama, 1982).
Browne, Malcolm W., *The New York Times,* February 26, 1980.
Brzezinski, Zbigniew, 'America in the Technotronic Age', *Encounter,* Vol. XXX, January 1958.
Buckley, W. (ed.), *Modern Systems Research for the Behavioural Scientists* (Aladin, Chicago, 1968).
Cannon, S. F., *Science in Culture: The Early Victorian Period* (Dawson and Science History Publications, New York, 1978).
Capra, Fritjof, *The Turning Point* (Bantam Books, New York, 1983).
Carlson, E. A., *The Gene: A Critical History* (W. B. Saunders, Philadelphia, 1966).
Cavalieri, L. F., *The Double-Edged Helix* (Columbia University Press, New York, 1981).
Chargaff, Erwin, *Heraclitean Fire* (Rockefeller University Press, New York, 1978).
Chomsky, Noam, *Language and Responsibility: Based on Conversations with Mitsu Ronat* (Pantheon Books, New York, 1977).
Chubin, D., and T. Connolly, 'Research Trials and Science Policies', in N. Elias, H. Martins and R. Whitley (eds.), *Scientific Establishments and Hierarchies,* Sociology of the Sciences Yearbook 1982 (Reidel, Dordrecht, 1982).
Churchman, C. West, *Prediction and Optimal Decision: Philosophical Issues of a Science of Values* (Prentice-Hall, Englewood Cliffs, 1961).
Clark, Burton R., *Academic Power in Italy* (University of Chicago Press, Chicago, 1977).
Clark, Terry N., *Prophets and Patrons: The French University and the Emergence of the Social Sciences* (Harvard University Press, Cambridge/Mass., 1973).
Cohen, Habiba S., *Elusive Reform: The French Universities, 1968–1978* (Westview, Boulder, 1978).
Cohen, I. B., *Revolution in Science* (Harvard University Press, Cambridge/Mass., 1985).
Coser, Lewis, *Men of Ideas: A Sociologist's View* (The Free Press, New York, 1965).
Crane, Diana, *Invisible Colleges* (University of Chicago Press, Chicago, 1972).
Crosland, Maurice, *The Society of Arcueil: A View of French Science at the Time of Napoleon I* (Heinemann, London, 1967).
Curie, Eve, *Madame Curie,* trans. V. Sheean (Heinemann, London, 1939).
Dawson, R. (ed.), *The Legacy of China* (Clarendon Press, Oxford, 1964).
Dolby, R. G. A., 'On The Autonomy of Pure Science: The Construction and Maintenance of Barriers Between Scientific Establishments and Popular Culture',

in N. Elias, H. Martins and R. Whitley (eds.), *Scientific Establishments and Hierarchies,* Sociology of the Sciences Yearbook 1982 (Reidel, Dordrecht, 1982).

Dreyfus, H. L., *What Computers Can't Do—A Critique of Artificial Intelligence* (Harper and Row, New York, 1972).

Driver, C. P., *The Exploding University* (Hodder and Stoughton, London, 1971).

Dyson, F. J., 'The Future of Physics', *Physics Today,* September 1970.

Dyson, F. J., *Disturbing the Universe* (Pan Books, London, 1979).

Easlea, Brian, *Liberation and the Aims of Science* (Chatto and Windus, London, 1973).

Ehrlich, Paul, et al., 'Long Term Biological Consequences of Nuclear War', *Science,* Vol. 222, No. 4630, December 23, 1983, pp. 1243–1300.

Einstein, Albert, *Ideas and Opinions* (Crown, New York, 1954).

Eisenhower, Dwight D., *Public Papers of the President of the United States: Dwight D. Eisenhower 1960–61* (Office of the Federal Register, Washington, 1961).

Elias, Norbert, 'The Sciences: Towards a Theory', in Richard Whitley (ed.), *Social Processes of Scientific Development* (Routledge and Kegan Paul, London, 1974).

Elias, Norbert, 'Scientific Establishments', in N. Elias, H. Martins and R. Whitley (eds.), *Scientific Establishments and Hierarchies,* Sociology of the Sciences Yearbook 1982 (Reidel, Dordrecht, 1982a).

Elias, N., *Power and Civility: The Civilization Process,* Vol. II (Pantheon Books, New York, 1982b).

Elias, N., *Court Society,* trans. E. Jephcott (Blackwell, Oxford, 1983).

Ellul, Jacques, *The Technological Society,* trans. John Wilkinson (Alfred A. Knopf, New York, 1973).

Eysenck, Hans, *The Listener,* April 29, 1982.

Finlay-Jones, Robert, 'Factors in the Teaching Environment Associated with Severe Psychological Distress Among School Teachers', *Australian and New Zealand Journal of Psychiatry,* Vol. 20, September 1986, pp. 304–313.

Fisher, R. A., 'Has Mendel's Work Been Rediscovered?', *Annals of Science,* Vol. I, 1937, pp. 115–37.

Fleck, James, 'Development and Establishment in Artificial Intelligence', in N. Elias, H. Martins and R. Whitley (eds.), *Scientific Establishments and Hierarchies,* Sociology of the Sciences Yearbook 1982 (Reidel, Dordrecht, 1982).

Fleck, Ludwik, *Genesis and Development of a Scientific Fact,* with foreword by T. S. Kuhn (University of Chicago Press, Chicago, 1979).

Fleming, D., and B. Bailyn, *The Intellectual Migration: Europe and America, 1930–1960* (Harvard University Press, Cambridge/Mass., 1969).

Foucault, Michel, *The Order of Things* (Tavistock Publications, London, 1970).

Foucault, Michel, 'Orders of Discourse', *Social Science Information,* Vol. 10, No. 2, 1971.

Foucault, Michel, *The History of Sexuality,* Vol. 1, trans. Robert Hurley (Vintage Books, New York, 1978).

Foucault, Michel, *Power/Knowledge: Selected Interviews and Other Writings, 1972–1977,* Colin Gordon (ed.) (Pantheon Books, New York, 1980).

Fox Keller, Evelyn, *A Feeling for the Organism* (W. H. Freeman, San Francisco, 1983).

Fox Keller, Evelyn, 'Barbara McClintock, Nobel Scientist', *Dialogue,* Vol. 65, No. 3, 1984.

Freeman, Derek, *The Making and the Unmaking of an Anthropological Myth* (Harvard University Press, Cambridge/Mass., 1983).

Fyvel, T. R., *Intellectuals Today: Problems in a Changing Society* (Chatto and Windus, London, 1968).

Gamow, G., *Thirty Years that Shook Physics: The Story of Quantum Theory* (Heinemann, London, 1972).

Gaston, J., *Originality and Competition in Science* (University of Chicago Press, Chicago, 1973).

Gellner, Ernest, and J. Waterbury (eds.), *Patrons and Clients in Mediterranean Societies* (Duckworth, London, 1977).

Georgescu-Roegen, N., *The Quantification and Entropy Law and the Economic Process* (Harvard University Press, Cambridge/Mass., 1971).

Gieryn, Thomas F., and Anne E. Figert, 'Scientists Protect their Cognitive Authority', in G. Boehme and N. Stehr (eds.), *The Knowledge Society,* Sociology of the Sciences Yearbook 1986 (Reidel, Dordrecht, 1986).

Gleick, James, 'The Riddle of Chaos', *Dialogue,* Vol. 66, No. 2, 1985 (Reprinted from *The New York Times*).

Goodell, R., *The Visible Scientists* (Little Brown, Boston, 1977).

Gould, S. J., 'Triumph of a Naturalist', *New York Review of Books,* March 29, 1984.

Gouldner A. W., *The Coming Crisis of Western Sociology* (Heinemann, London, 1970).

Grabner, I., and W. Reiter, 'Meddling with "Politics"—Some Conjectures about the Relationship between Science and Utopia', in E. Mendelsohn and H. Nowotony (eds.), *Nineteen Eighty-four: Science Between Utopia and Dystopia,* Sociology of the Sciences Yearbook 1984 (Reidel, Dordrecht, 1984).

Gray, W., and N. D. Rizzo (eds.), *Unity Through Diversity* (Gordon and Breach, New York, 1973).

Green, Philip, and Sanford Levinson (eds.), *Power and Community: Dissenting Essays in Political Science* (Vintage Books, New York, 1970).

Greenberg, D., *Politics in American Science* (Penguin, Harmondsworth, 1969).

Haberer, Joseph, *Politics and the Community of Science* (Van Nostrand Reinhold, New York, 1969).

Habermas, Jurgen, *Theory and Practice,* trans. J. Viertel (Heinemann, London, 1974).

Hagstrom, O. W., *The Scientific Community* (Basic Books, New York, 1965).

Haken, Herman, *Synergetics: An Introduction* (Springer, New York, 1983).

Heilbroner, R. L., 'Modern Economics as a Chapter in the History of Economic Thought', *History of Political Economy,* Vol. II, No. 2, Summer 1979.

Hodges, Andrew, *Alan Turing: The Enigma of Intelligence* (Unwin Paperbacks, London, 1985).

Hooker, C., book review of *From Being to Becoming,* in *Philosophy of Science,* Vol. 51, June 1984, pp. 355–57.

Hudson, Liam, *The Cult of the Fact* (Cape, London, 1972).

Janke, H. J., and M. Otte (eds.), *Epistemological and Social Problems of the Sciences in the Early Nineteenth Century* (Reidel, Dordrecht, 1981).

Johnston, Ron, and Tom Jagtenberg, 'Goal Direction of Scientific Research', in W. Krohne, E. Layton and P. Weingart (eds.), *The Dynamics of Science and Technology,* Sociology of the Sciences Yearbook 1978 (Reidel, Dordrecht, 1978).

Joravsky, D., *Soviet Marxism and Natural Science* (Routledge and Kegan Paul, London, 1961).

Judson, H. F., *The Eighth Day of Creation* (Simon and Schuster, New York, 1979).

Judson, H. F., *The Search for Solutions* (Hutchinson, London, 1980).

Judson, H. F., 'Genetic Engineering: Current Concerns', *Dialogue,* Vol. 63, No. 3, 1984.

Kennedy, Ivan R., 'Prediction with Explanation and Description of Ecosystems', *Search,* Vol. 15, No. 7–8, August/September 1984.

Kevles, D. J., *The Physicists* (Vintage Books, New York, 1979).

Kimball-Smith, Alice, 'Los Alamos: Focus for an Age', in R. S. Lewis and I. Wilson (eds.), *Alamagordo Plus Twenty-five Years* (Viking, New York, 1970).

Kline, Morris, *Mathematics: The Loss of Certainty* (Oxford University Press, Oxford, 1980).

Koestler, Arthur, *The Sleepwalkers* (Hutchinson, London, 1959).

Kostelanetz, Richard, *The End of Intelligent Writing: Literary Politics in America* (Sheed and Ward, New York, 1974).

Kuhn, T. S., *The Structure of Scientific Revolutions* (University of Chicago Press, Chicago, 1964).

Kusch, Polykarp, 'A Personal View of Science and the Future' in T. C. Robinson (ed.), *The Future of Science: 1975 Nobel Conference* (John Wiley, New York, 1977).

Kuttner, Robert, 'On the State of Economics', *Dialogue,* Vol. 73, No. 3, 1986.

Ladd, C. E., and S. M. Lipset, 'Politics of Academic Natural Scientists and Engineers', *Science,* Vol. 176, 1972, pp. 1091–1100.

Lask, Thomas, in *The New York Times,* December 30, 1979, p. 23.

Laszlo, E., *The Systems View of the World* (Braziller, New York, 1972).

Laudan, Larry, *Progress and its Problems: Towards a Theory of Scientific Growth* (University of California Press, Berkeley, 1978), p. 111.

Laudan, Rachel, 'Redefinition of a Discipline', in L. Graham, W. Lepenies and P. Weingart (eds.), *Functions and Uses of Disciplinary Histories,* Sociology of the Sciences Yearbook 1983 (Reidel, Dordrecht, 1983).

Leavis, F. R. (ed.), *A Selection from Scrutiny* (Cambridge University Press, Cambridge, 1968).

Leitenberg, Milton, 'The Classical Scientific Ethic and Strategic-Weapons Development', *Impact of Science on Society,* Vol. XXI, No. 2, April–June 1971.

Lentricchia, F., *After the New Criticism* (University of Chicago Press, Chicago, 1980).

Lepenies, Wolf, 'Anthropological Perspectives in the Sociology of Science', in E. Mendelsohn and Y. Elkana (eds.), *Sciences and Cultures,* Sociology of the Sciences Yearbook 1981 (Reidel, Dordrecht, 1981).

Lerner, A. B., *Einstein and Newton* (Lerner Publications, Minneapolis, 1973).

Lettvin, Jerome Y., paper given at UNESCO symposium on 'Culture and Science', Paris, September 6–10, 1971, in Robin Clarke (ed.), *Notes for the Future* (Thomas and Hudson, London, 1975).

Lilienfeld, Robert, *The Rise of Systems Theory: An Ideological Analysis* (Wiley, New York, 1978).

Lindblom, Charles E., and David K. Cohen, *Usable Knowledge: Social Science and Social Problem Solving* (Yale University Press, New Haven, 1979).

Lumsden, Charles J., and Edward O. Wilson, 'Précis of Genes, Mind, and Culture', *The Behavioural and Brain Sciences,* Vol. 5, No. 1, March 1982, pp. 1–37.

McEltey, V. K., 'Kapitsa's visit to England', *Science,* Vol. 153, 1966.

McKeon, Richard (ed.), *The Basic Works of Aristotle* (Random House, New York, 1968).

Maddox, John, 'Snowflakes Are far from Simple', *Nature,* Vol. 303, November 3, 1983.

Manwell, C., 'Peer Review: A Case History from the Australian Research Grants Committee', *Search,* Vol. 10, No. 3, March 13, 1979.

Manwell, C., and C. M. A. Baker, 'Honesty in Science: A Partial Test of a Sociobiological Model of the Social Structure of Science', *Search,* Vol. 12, No. 6, June 1981, pp. 151–60.

Manwell, C., and C. M. A. Baker, 'Evaluation of Performance in Academic and Scientific Institutions', in B. Martin, C. M. A. Baker, C. Manwell and C. Pugh, *Intellectual Suppression* (Angus and Robertson, Sydney, 1986).

Marias, Julian, *Philosophy as Dramatic Theory* (Pennsylvania State University Press, University Park, 1971).

Marr, D., *Vision* (W. H. Freeman, San Francisco, 1982).

Mattessich, Richard, *Instrumental Reasoning and Systems Methodology* (Reidel, Dordrecht, 1978), p. 283.

McMichael, A. J., and B. S. Hetzel, 'Patterns of Help-Seeking for Mental Illness Among Australian University Students', *Social Science and Medicine,* Vol. 8, No. 4, April 1974, pp. 197–206.

Merton, Robert K., *The Sociology of Science* (University of Chicago Press, Chicago, 1973).

Merz, J., *A History of European Thought in the Nineteenth Century,* Vol. III (Dover, New York, 1965).

Michie, D., 'Peer Review and the Bureaucracy', *Times Higher Education Supplement,* August 4, 1978, p. 11.

Mitroff, I., *The Subjective Side of Science* (Elsevier, Amsterdam, 1974).

Minsky, Marvin, 'Why Programming Is a Good Medium for Expressing Poorly Understood and Sloppily Formulated Ideas', in M. Krampen and P. Seeitz (eds.), *Design and Planning II* (Hastings House, New York, 1967).

Morse, E. L., *Modernization and the Transformation of International Relations* (The Free Press, New York, 1976).

Mullins, Nicholas C., 'A Sociological Theory of Scientific Revolutions', in K. D. Knorr, H. Strasser and H. G. Zilian (eds.), *Determinants and Controls of Scientific Development* (Reidel, Dordrecht, 1975).

Nicholson, Max, *The Environmental Revolution* (Hodder and Stoughton, London, 1970).

Nietzsche, Friedrich, *Will to Power,* ed. W. Kaufmann (Vintage, New York, 1967).

Nisbet, Robert, *History of the Idea of Progress* (Basic Books, New York, 1980).

Nisbet, Robert, 'Project Camelot: An Autopsy', in Philip Rieff (ed.), *On Intellectuals* (Doubleday, New York, 1969).

Ohmann, Richard, *English in America: A Radical View of the Profession* (Oxford University Press, New York, 1976).

Olby, R. C., *Origins of Mendelism* (Constable, London, 1966).

Outlook for Science and Technology 1982, A Report of the National Research Council (W. H. Freeman, San Francisco, 1982).

Panofsky, W., quoted by Ian Anderson in *The Age* (Melbourne), October 10, 1984.

Pantin, C. F. A., *On the Relations Between the Sciences* (Cambridge University Press, Cambridge, 1968).

Peierls, Rudolf E., 'Britain in the Atomic Age', in R. S. Lewis and I. Wilson (eds.), *Alamagordo Plus Twenty-five Years* (Viking, New York, 1970).

Peters, Douglas P., and Stephen J. Ceci, 'Peer-Review Practices of Psychological Journals: The Fate of Published Articles, Submitted Again', *The Behavioural and Brain Sciences,* Vol. 5, No. 2, June 1982, pp. 187–255.

Phillips, D. C., *Holistic Thought in Social Science* (Stanford University Press, Stanford, 1976) p. 20.

Pinch, T. J., 'What Does a Proof Do If It Does Not Prove', in E. Mendelsohn, P. Weingart and R. Whitley (eds.), *The Social Production of Scientific Knowledge,* Sociology of the Sciences Yearbook 1977 (Reidel, Dordrecht, 1977).

Polanyi, Michael, *Personal Knowledge* (Routledge and Kegan Paul, London, 1958).

Polanyi, Michael, *Knowing and Being: Essays by Michael Polanyi* (Routledge and Kegan Paul, London, 1969).

Price, Derek J. de Solla, *Science Since Babylon* (Yale University Press, New Haven, 1961).

Prigogine, I., 'Unity of Physical Laws and Levels of Description', in M. Grene (ed.), *Interpretations of Life and Mind* (Routledge and Kegan Paul, London, 1971).

Prigogine, I., *From Being to Becoming: Time and Complexity in the Physical Sciences* (W. H. Freeman, San Francisco, 1980).

Prigogine, I., and F. Stengers, *Order out of Chaos* (Heinemann, London, 1984).

Ravetz, Jerome, *Scientific Knowledge and its Social Problems* (Clarendon Press, Oxford, 1971a).

Ravetz, Jerome, 'Ideological Crisis in Science', *New Scientist and Science Journal,* Vol. 51, No. 738, July 1, 1971b, pp. 35–6.

Redner, H., *In the Beginning Was the Deed* (University of California Press, Berkeley, 1982).

Redner, H., *The Ends of Philosophy: An Essay in the Sociology of Philosophy and Rationality* (Croom Helm, Beckenham, 1986).

Redner, H., 'The institutionalization of science', *Social Epistemology,* January 1987, pp. 37–61.

Rescher, Nicholas, *Scientific Progress* (Blackwell, Oxford, 1978).

Roberts, Peter, 'Future Age', *The Age* (Melbourne), December, 1983.

Rorty, Richard, *Philosophy and the Mirror of Nature* (Princeton University Press, Princeton, 1979).

Rorty, Richard, *Consequences of Pragmatism* (Essays: 1972–1980) (University of Minnesota Press, Minneapolis, 1982).

Rose, H., and S. Rose, *Science and Society* (Penguin, Harmondsworth, 1969).

Rose, H., and S. Rose, *Ideology of/in the Natural Sciences* (Schenkman, Cambridge/ Mass., 1976).

Rosen, Sumner M., 'Keynes without Gadflies', in T. Roszak (ed.), *The Dissenting Academy* (Pantheon Books, New York, 1968).

Ross, Chuck, 'Rejecting published work: Similar fate for fiction', *The Behaviour and Brain Sciences,* Vol. 5, No. 2, June 1982, p. 236.

Ryle, Martin, *Towards the Nuclear Holocaust* (Menard Press, London, 1981).

Saller, Richard P., *Personal Patronage Under the Early Empire* (Cambridge University Press, Cambridge, 1982).

Sayre, Anne, *Rosalind Franklin and D.N.A.* (Norton, New York, 1975).

Schäfer, Wolf, *Finalization in Science* (Reidel, Dordrecht, 1983).

Schilpp, P. H. (ed.), *Einstein: Philosopher-Scientist* (Harper, New York, 1959).

Schrödinger, Erwin, 'Are There Quantum Jumps?', *The British Journal for the Philosophy of Science,* Vol. III, 1952, pp. 109–10.

Science and Technology: A Five-Year Outlook, 'Planet Earth', a National Academy of Sciences publication (W. H. Freeman, San Francisco, 1978).

Science in the Twentieth Century: New York Times, April 1974 (Arno Press, New York, 1976).

Sibatani, Atuhiro, 'An Exile's View of the Contemporary Scene', *Nature,* Vol. 240, November 24, 1972.

Sibatani, Atuhiro, 'You Carry Out Eukaryote Experiments on Shellfish Selfish DNA: An Essay on the Vulgarization of Molecular Biology', in M. Kageyama (ed.), *Science and Scientists: Essays by Biochemists, Biologists and Chemists* (Japan Scientific Societies, Tokyo, Reidel, Dordrecht, 1981a).

Sibatani, Atuhiro, 'Molecular Biology: A Paradox, Illusion and Myth', *Trends in Biochemical Sciences,* June 1981 (Elsevier/North Holland Biomedical Press, 1981b).

Sibatani, Atuhiro, 'Two Faces of Molecular Biology: Revolution and Normal Science', *Rivista di Biologia,* Vol. 73, No. 3, 1981c.

Sontag, Susan, *Against Interpretation and Other Essays* (Farrar, Straus and Giroux, New York, 1966).

Steele, E., *Somatic Selection and Adaptive Evolution* (Croom Helm, Kent, 1980).

Stent, Gunther, *Paradoxes of Progress* (W. H. Freeman, San Francisco, 1978).

Stent, Gunther, 'Origin, Limits and Future of Science' (unpublished paper 1979).

Stent, Gunther, 'Cerebral Hermeneutics', *Journal of Social Biological Structure,* Vol. 4, (Academic Press, London), 1981.
Stent, Gunther, 'Max Delbruck, 1906–1981', obituary paper, 1982.
Stockton, William, *The New York Times Magazine,* February 17, 1980.
Stretton, Hugh, *The Political Sciences* (Routledge and Kegan Paul, London, 1969).
Sullivan, Walter, *The Age* (Melbourne), July 22, 1985 (Reprinted from *The New York Times*).
Suppe, Frederick, *The Structure of Scientific Theories* (University of Illinois Press, Urbana, 1979).
Symes, John D., 'Policy and Maturity in Science', *Social Science Information,* Vol. 15, No. 2–3, 1976.
Tame, A., and F. P. J. Robotham, *Maralinga: British A-bomb: Australian Legacy* (Collins, Melbourne, 1982).
Thiemann H. (ed.), *CIBA Foundation Symposium* (Elsevier, Amsterdam, 1972).
Thompson, Michael, *Rubbish Theory* (Oxford University Press, Oxford, 1979).
Thompson, W. F., *Passages About Earth* (Harper and Row, New York, 1973).
Toulmin, Stephen, *Human Understanding* (Clarendon Press, Oxford, 1972).
Turco, R. P., O. B. Toon, T. P. Ackerman, J. B. Pollack, and Carl Sagan, 'Nuclear Winter: Global Consequences of Multiple Nuclear Explosions', *Science,* Vol. 222, No. 4630, December 23, 1983, pp. 1283–92.
Toynbee, A., *A Study of History, Reconsiderations,* Vol. 12 (Oxford University Press, New York, 1964).
Turkel, Sherry, *Psychoanalytic Politics: Freud's French Revolution* (Basic Books, New York, 1978).
van den Daele, Wolfgang, 'The Social Construction of Science: Institutionalization and Definition of Positive Science in the Latter Half of the Seventeenth Century', in E. Mendelsohn, P. Weingart and R. Whitley (eds.), *The Social Production of Scientific Knowledge,* Sociology of the Sciences Yearbook 1977 (Reidel, Dordrecht, 1977).
van den Daele, Wolfgang, Wolfgang Krohn and Peter Weingart, 'The Political Direction of Scientific Development', in E. Mendelsohn, P. Weingart and R. Whitley (eds.), *The Social Production of Scientific Knowledge,* Sociology of the Sciences Yearbook 1977 (Reidel, Dordrecht, 1977).
von Bertalanffy, Ludwig, *Problems of Life* (Harper, New York, 1960).
von Bertalanffy, Ludwig, *General System Theory* (Braziller, New York, 1968).
von Weizsäcker, C. F., *The Unity of Nature,* trans. F. J. Zucker (Farrar, Straus and Giroux, New York, 1980).
Wallerstein, I., *The Modern World-System,* Vol. 1 (Academic Press, New York, 1974).
Wallerstein, I., *The Politics of the World Economy* (Cambridge University Press, Cambridge, 1984).
Wallerstein, I., and T. K. Hopkins, 'Pattern of Development of the Modern World-System', *Review,* Vol. 1, No. 2, Fall 1977.
Ward, Benjamin, *What Is Wrong With Economics?* (Basic Books, New York, 1972).
Watson, James D., *The Double Helix,* ed. Gunther S. Stent (Norton, New York, 1980).
Weber, Alfred, 'Fundamentals of Culture Sociology: Social Process, Civilizational Process and Culture-Movement', *Archiv fur Sozialwissenschaft und Sozialpolitik,* Vol. 47, 1920–21, pp. 1–49.
Weber, Max, *The Theory of Social and Economic Organization,* ed. Talcott Parsons, (The Free Press, New York, 1947).
Weber, Max, 'Objectivity in the Social Sciences', in E. A. Shils and H. A. Finch (eds.), *The Methodology of the Social Sciences* (The Free Press, New York, 1949).

Weber, M., *The City,* trans. D. Martindale and G. Neuwirth (The Free Press, New York, 1958).

Weber, M., *The Protestant Ethic and the Spirit of Capitalism,* trans. Talcott Parsons (Unwin, London, 1967).

Weber, Max, 'Politics as a Vocation' and 'Science as a Vocation', in H. H. Geth and C. Wright Mills (eds.), *From Max Weber* (Galaxy, Oxford, 1971).

Weinberg, Alvin M., 'Scientific Institutes and the Future of Team Research', in P. C. Ritterbusch (ed.), *Scientific Institutions of the Future* (Acropolis Books, Washington, 1972).

Weingart, Peter, 'The Relation Between Science and Technology', in W. Krohn, E. Layton and P. Weingart (eds.), *Dynamics of Science and Technology,* Sociology of the Sciences Yearbook 1978 (Reidel, Dordrecht, 1978).

Weingart, Peter, 'The Scientific Power Elite—A Chimera', in N. Elias, H. Martins and R. Whitley (eds.), *Scientific Establishments and Hierarchies,* Sociology of the Sciences Yearbook 1982 (Reidel, Dordrecht, 1982).

Weizenbaum, Joseph, *Computer Power and Human Reason* (Freeman, San Francisco, 1976).

Whitley, Richard, 'Cognitive and Social Institutionalization', in R. Whitley (ed.), *Social Process of Scientific Development* (Routledge and Kegan Paul, London 1974).

Whitley, Richard, 'Components of Scientific Activities, Their Characteristics and Institutionalization in Specialties and Research Areas', in K. D. Knorr, H. Strasser and H. G. Zillian (eds.), *Determinants and Controls of Scientific Development* (Reidel, Dordrecht, Holland, 1975).

Whitley, Richard, 'Changes in the Social and Intellectual Organisation of the Sciences', in E. Mendelsohn, P. Weingart and R. Whitley (eds.), *The Social Production of Scientific Knowledge,* Sociology of the Sciences Yearbook 1977 (Reidel, Dordrecht, 1977a).

Whitley, Richard, 'The Sociology of Scientific Work and the History of Scientific Developments', in S. Blume (ed.), *Perspectives in the Sociology of Science* (John Wiley, Chichester, 1977b).

Whitley, Richard, 'The Establishment and Structure of the Sciences as Reputational Organizations', in N. Elias, H. Martins and R. Whitley (eds.), *Scientific Establishments and Hierarchies,* Sociology of the Sciences Yearbook 1982 (Reidel, Dordrecht, 1982).

Whitley, Richard, *The Intellectual and Social Organization of the Sciences* (Clarendon Press, Oxford, 1984).

Wiener, Norbert, *The Human Use of Human Beings* (Houghton Mifflin, Boston, 1954).

Wiener, Norbert, *Cybernetics* (MIT Press, Cambridge/Mass., 1965).

Wilson, Mitchell, *Passion to Know* (Weidenfeld and Nicholson, London, 1972).

Wittgenstein, Ludwig, *Philosophical Investigations,* trans. E. Anscombe (Blackwell, Oxford, 1956).

Wolfson, Murray, 'The Labour Process: First Steps Toward A Nonequilibrium View' (unpublished paper, 1986).

Wolin, Sheldon, 'Political Theory as a Vocation', *American Political Science Review,* Vol. 63, 1969, pp. 134–44.

Woodcock, A., and M. Davis, *Catastrophe Theory* (Dutton, New York, 1978).

Woollett, E. L., Physics and Modern Warfare: The Awkward Silence', *American Journal of Physics,* Vol. 48, No. 2, February 1980.

Wright Mills, C., *The Sociological Imagination* (Penguin, Harmondsworth, 1970).

Yaes, Robert, 'Physics, Fads and Finances', *New Scientist,* Vol. 71, August 22, 1974.

Yoxen, E., 'Giving Life a New Meaning,' in N. Elias, H. Martins and R. Whitley
(eds.), *Scientific Establishments and Hierarchies,* Sociology of the Sciences Year-
book 1982 (Reidel, Dordrecht, 1982).
Zahler, R. S., and J. H. Sussman, *Nature,* Vol. 269, 1977, pp. 759–63.
Zeeman, E. C., *Nature,* Vol. 270, 1977, p. 381.
Zeldin, Theodore, 'The Problem with History: A Plea for a Fresh Start', *The Age
Monthly Review* (Melbourne), Vol. 2, No. 6, October 6, 1982.
Ziman, J. M., *The Force of Knowledge* (C.U.P., Cambridge, 1976).
Zuckermann, Harriet, *Scientific Elite: Nobel Laureates in the United States* (The
Free Press, New York, 1977).

Index

3 5282 00146 7839